Keeper of Public Records

# Local Government Board for Ireland : fourth report with appendices

Keeper of Public Records

**Local Government Board for Ireland : fourth report with appendices**

ISBN/EAN: 9783741105203

Manufactured in Europe, USA, Canada, Australia, Japa

Cover: Foto ©ninafisch / pixelio.de

Manufactured and distributed by brebook publishing software
(www.brebook.com)

Keeper of Public Records

# Local Government Board for Ireland : fourth report with appendices

# ANNUAL REPORT

OF

# THE LOCAL GOVERNMENT BOARD

## FOR IRELAND,

BEING

THE FOURTH REPORT UNDER "THE LOCAL GOVERNMENT BOARD (IRELAND) ACT," 35 & 36 VIC., c. 69;

WITH

## APPENDICES.

---

Presented to both Houses of Parliament by Command of Her Majesty.

---

DUBLIN:
PRINTED BY ALEXANDER THOM, 87 & 88, ABBEY-STREET,
PRINTER TO THE QUEEN'S MOST EXCELLENT MAJESTY.
FOR HER MAJESTY'S STATIONERY OFFICE.

1876.

[C.—1493.] *Price 2s.*

Printed

# TABLE OF CONTENTS.


Page

REPORT, . . . . . . . . . . . . . . . 9

Summary of Weekly Returns of Persons relieved in Unions in Ireland, from the week ended 20th February, 1875, to the week ended 12th February, 1876, both inclusive, . . . . . . . . . . . . . 10

Tables showing the maximum, minimum, and average daily numbers receiving Relief in and out of the Workhouse, in each of the last 7 years, . . . . 12

Return of the number of persons in receipt of Out-door Relief, under the 1st sec. of 10 Vic., c. 31, on the last Saturday of February in each year, from 1857 to 1876, 13

Return of Night Lodgers or Casuals relieved in the Workhouses in the first week of each month of the year, . . . . . . . . . 13

Classification of causes of death in Workhouses, from 30th January, 1875, to 29th January, 1876, . . . . . . . . . . . 14

Number of persons assisted by Boards of Guardians to emigrate, and amount authorized to be expended for that purpose in each of the last 26 years, . . 15

Tabulated account of admissions to the Workhouse during the year, in comparison with the 16 preceding years, . . . . . . . . . 16

Statement of the average daily number in receipt of Indoor Relief during each of the 24 years ended 29th September, 1875, average number of deaths per week, and rate of mortality, . . . . . . . . . 16

Classified return of the number of Workhouse Inmates on the first Saturday of January in each year from 1851, showing the per-centage of the several classes on the total number of Inmates, . . . . . . . . . 17

Statistics relating to the collection and expenditure of the Poor-rate, and the number of persons relieved in the year ended 29th September, 1875, in comparison with similar statistics for the previous year, . . . . . . . 17

Statement of the Parliamentary Grant for Medical and Educational purposes, and of its distribution in the year ended 25th March, 1875, . . . . 18

Statement of the collection and expenditure of the Poor-rate, and of the net annual value of the property rated in each of the 22 years ended 29th September, 1875, 19

*Medical Charities Act and Vaccination Acts:—*

Number of cases in which Relief has been afforded under the Medical Charities Act, during each of the last 12 years, distinguishing Dispensary Relief from Relief at the Patient's own Home, . . . . . . . . . . 21

Table showing the progress of Vaccination at the Dispensaries and Vaccination Stations since the passing of the Medical Charities Act, . . . . 22

Total number of Vaccinations performed at Dispensaries and Vaccination Stations in each year since 1864, distinguishing the cases of children born since 1st January, 1864, . . . . . . . . . . . 23

Table showing the number of children, born since the 1st January, 1864, who were vaccinated in the years 1872, 1873, 1874, and 1875, respectively, distinguishing those who were under one year old from those who were above one year old when vaccinated, . . . . . . . . . . . 23

Classified Summary of the total number of cases of Vaccination during the year ending 30th September, 1875, in each of the four provinces compared with similar particulars for the previous year, . . . . . . . 24

| | Page |
|---|---|
| Table showing the number of Deaths in Workhouses from Smallpox, and number of cases of Smallpox treated by Dispensary Medical Officers during each of the last 12 years, | 26 |
| Summary of Smallpox cases attended by Dispensary Medical Officers in each province during each quarter of the year ended 30th September, 1875, | 26 |
| Return of the number of Deaths from Smallpox registered in Ireland during each quarter of the year ended 31st December, 1875, | 26 |
| Outbreak of Smallpox in Connaught, | 27 |
| Account of outbreak of Smallpox at Athenry, in Loughrea Union, | 28 |
| Prosecution for exposure of persons suffering from Smallpox, | 29 |
| Prosecution for inoculating with Smallpox, and conviction of manslaughter, | 30 |
| Decline of Smallpox in Belfast, | 30 |
| Expenditure under the Medical Charities Act and Vaccination Acts in each Province, and for all Ireland, in each of the last 11 years, | 31 |
| Total Expenditure under the Medical Charities Act and Vaccination Acts, arranged under various heads, for each of the last 2 years, | 31 |
| *Local Government Act:—* | |
| Provisional Orders, | 31 |
| Adoption of provisions of Towns Improvement Act, | 33 |
| By-Laws approved, | 33 |
| Orders for closing old Burial-Grounds against further interments, | 34 |
| Licences under the 10th section of the Burial Grounds Act authorizing interments in special individual cases in Burial Grounds which have been ordered to be closed, | 34 |
| *Public Health Act:—* | |
| Correspondence with the Board of Guardians of Waterford Union relating to the payment of Sanitary Salaries, | 34 |
| Payment of Salaries of Sanitary Officers, | 34 |
| Sanitary Authorities discharge their duties satisfactorily, | 34 |
| Area of charge for Sanitary Improvements in Rural Sanitary Districts, | 35 |
| Activity shown by Urban Sanitary Authorities, | 35 |
| Loans for Sanitary Improvements, | 35 |
| Filth Diseases and their prevention, | 36 |
| *Departmental Arrangements:—* | |
| Resignation of Dr. M'Donnell, Medical Commissioner, and appointment of Dr. Croker-King (Inspector) as his successor, | 36 |
| Resignation of Mr. Robinson on being appointed Assistant Under Secretary to the Lord Lieutenant, | 36 |
| Appointment of Mr. Armstrong and Dr. M'Cabe to the vacancies thus created in the Office of Inspector, | 36 |
| Changes in Inspectors' Districts, | 36 |
| Diagrams, showing the fluctuations from week to week in the number of Workhouse Inmates, and in the number of persons receiving Outdoor Relief in the 52 weeks ended the 12th February, 1876, and in the corresponding weeks of each of the 6 previous years, . *facing* | 36 |

# APPENDIX.

## APPENDIX A.—Circulars of Instructions under the Poor Law Acts.


| No. | | Page |
|---|---|---|
| 1. | Exercise and recreation of children in the Workhouse:—Circular to Boards of Guardians, . . . . . . . 9 April, 1875, | 37 |
| 2. | Form of Rate Book:—Circular to Boards of Guardians, . 21 April, 1875, | 38 |
| 3. | Notices of making Rate:—Circular to Boards of Guardians, 24 July, 1875, | 38 |
| | *Enclosures in foregoing Circular:—* | |
| | Notice when Rate is prepared, . . . . . . | 40 |
| | Notice when Rates have been made, . . . . . . | 40 |
| | Revised Form of Rate Receipt, . . . . . . | 41 |
| 4. | Payments to National School Teachers:—Circular to Boards of Guardians, 30 August, 1875, | 42 |
| 5. | National School Teachers (Ireland) Act:—Circular to Treasurers of Contributory Unions, . . . . . . . 18 November, 1875, | 46 |
| 6. | National School Teachers (Ireland) Act:—Circular to Boards of Guardians of Contributory Unions, . . . . . . 18 November, 1875, | 46 |
| 7. | Results Fees in Workhouse National Schools:—Circular to Boards of Guardians, . . . . . . . . 2 December, 1875, | 47 |
| 8. | Lunatic Asylums (Ireland) Act, 1875:—Circular to Boards of Guardians, 18 September, 1875, | 48 |


## APPENDIX B.—Circulars of Instruction under the Medical Charities Acts, and the Vaccination Acts.


| No. | | Page |
|---|---|---|
| 1. | Annual Appointment of Dispensary Committees and Wardens:—Circular to Boards of Guardians, . . . . . . . 4 April, 1876, | 49 |
| 2. | Return of Officers of Dispensary Committees:—Circular to Boards of Guardians, . . . . . . . . . 7 April, 1876, | 50 |
| 3. | Examination of Dangerous Lunatics:—Circular to Dispensary Medical Officers, 18 September, 1875, | 50 |


## APPENDIX C.—Orders, Instructional Circulars, and Correspondence under the Local Government Acts and the Public Health Act.

### I. Orders.


| No. | | Page |
|---|---|---|
| 1. | Order Amending the General Sanitary Order of 9th September, 1874, in reference to the Town of Youghal, . . . . . . . | 51 |
| 2. | Order Amending the General Sanitary Order of 9th September, 1874, in reference to the Town of Bandon, . . . . . . . | 52 |


### II. Circulars.


| No. | | Page |
|---|---|---|
| 1. | Prevention of Filth Diseases:—Circular to Sanitary Authorities, 9 August, 1875, | 53 |
| 2. | Sale of Food and Drugs Act:—Circular to Sanitary Authorities, 8 November, 1875, | 56 |
| 3. | Common Lodging Houses:—Circular to Sanitary Authorities, 6 September, 1875, | 57 |

No. Page

4. Regulation and Inspection of Common Lodging Houses:—Circular to Sanitary Authorities, . . . . . . . . 9 February, 1876, 60

5. Loans from Public Works Loan Commissioners:—Circular to Sanitary Authorities, . . . . . . . . 8 November, 1875, 61

III. Correspondence with the Board of Guardians of the Waterford Union on the subject of the Salaries of Sanitary Officers under the Public Health Act (in continuation of correspondence in Annual Report for 1875), . 62

IV. Statement of Orders issued under the 18th Section of the Public Health Act, 1874, determining the area of charge on which the Special Expenses mentioned in such orders shall be chargeable, . . . . . . . 67

V. Letter addressed by the Chief Secretary, by direction of His Grace the Lord Lieutenant, to Dr. M'Donnell, on his retirement from the office of Medical Commissioner, . . . . . . . . . . . 78

---

APPENDIX D.—Tables connected with Poor Relief and Expenditure.

1. Return (in pursuance of the 29th sec. of the Act 10 Vic., c. 31) of the Expenditure on the Relief of the Poor, and of the total numbers relieved in and out of the Workhouse, together with the receipts in each Union in Ireland, for the year ended 29th September, 1875; also showing the expenses under Medical Charities, Registration, Sanitary, Burial Grounds, Superannuation, and Cattle Plague Acts, and total expenditure during the year, . . 80

Part 1. Showing the receipts and expenditure during the year, . . 80

Part 2. Return of the number of persons who received Poor Relief during the year ended 29th September, 1875, together with the expenditure for provisions, necessaries, and clothing of workhouse inmates during the year, and the average weekly cost per head in Workhouse, . . 88

2. Classification of persons relieved in the Union Workhouses during the year ended 29th September, 1875, . . . . . . . . . 96

3. Classification of persons relieved out of the Workhouses during the year ended 29th September, 1875, including persons removed to Blind and Deaf and Dumb Asylums, . . . . . . . . . . . 97

4. Summary of Returns from Clerks of Unions, showing for each province and for all Ireland the number of persons admitted to the Workhouses during the year ended 29th September, 1875; distinguishing the number admitted in sickness; also, the number of births and deaths in the Workhouses during the year, . . . . . . . . . . . . . 98

5. Summary of Returns showing for each province and for all Ireland, the number of Sick Persons who received medical treatment in the Workhouse Hospitals and Fever Hospitals during the year ended 29th September, 1875, . . 98

6. Statement (in pursuance of sec. 20 of 12 and 13 Vic., c. 104), relative to the Audit of Union Accounts:—(in continuation of Statement in Annual Report for 1875, Appendix D, No. 6), . . . . . . . . 99

i.—Date up to which Accounts of Unions have been audited, . . . 99

ii.—Sums disallowed or found due on Audit of the Accounts of Unions up to 29th September, 1875, and whether recovered or in course of recovery from the parties debited, . . . . . . . 99

7. Union Officers' Superannuation—Statement of allowances under the Superannuation Acts in force during any portion of the year ended 29th September, 1875; showing also the cases in which the allowances had terminated during the year:—(in continuation of Statement in Annual Report for 1875, Appendix D, No. 7), . . . . . . . . . . 102

## APPENDIX E.—Tabular Returns in connexion with Relief under the Medical Charities Act.


| No. | | Page |
|---|---|---|
| 1. | Statement of alterations in Dispensary Districts in Unions in Ireland (arranged in Provinces and Counties), according to the Orders issued in pursuance of sec. 6 of 14 & 15 Vic., cap. 68 (since the completion of Table No. 1, Appendix E, in 2nd Annual Report of the Local Government Board), . . . | 112 |
| | Summary of Dispensary Districts according to Table No. 1, Appendix E, of previous Report, as altered by the foregoing Table, made up to the 25th March, 1876, . . . . . . . . . . | 113 |
| 2. | Financial and Relief Returns:—List, in pursuance of section 20 of the Medical Charities Act (14 & 15 Vic., c. 68), of all Dispensary Districts in the several Unions in Ireland (arranged in Provinces and Counties): showing the Number of Dispensaries in each, and the Expenses of each Dispensary District, for the year ended 29th September, 1875; with a Return—for the year ended 30th September, 1875—of the Number of Cases of Medical Relief afforded to Patients at the Dispensary and at their own Homes, respectively; the Number of Tickets for Medical Relief cancelled by the Committee of Management, under section 9 of the Act; Number of Cases of Vaccination; Number of Dangerous Lunatics certified; of Patients attended in Bridewells, &c., . . . . | 114 |
| | Summary of foregoing Table, No. 2, . . . . . . . . | 149 |
| 3. | General Summary of previous Tables, in Provinces:—containing, 1. Statistical Statement; showing the number of Unions, Electoral Divisions, and Dispensary Districts formed under section 6 of the Medical Charities Act, 14 & 15 Vic., c. 68; the total and average Population, Area, and Valuation; Number of Dispensaries, Officers, &c.:—2. Financial Statement; showing the Expenditure under the Medical Charities Act for the year, from 29th September, 1874, to 29th September, 1875:—and 3. Relief Return; showing the Number of Cases of Medical Relief afforded at the Dispensary and at the Patient's Home, respectively; the Number of Cases in which Tickets for Medical Relief have been cancelled by the Dispensary Committee; the Number of Cases of Vaccination performed; Number of Cases of Dangerous Lunatics certified; Number of Patients attended at Bridewells or Houses of Correction, &c.; during the year ended the 30th September, 1875, . . . | 150 |
| 4. | Vaccination:—Summary of the Number of Persons Vaccinated in the Workhouses and Auxiliary Establishments of the several Unions in Ireland, by the Medical Officers of those Institutions; and of the Number Vaccinated in the several Dispensary Districts, by the Medical Officers of Dispensaries under the Medical Charities Act; in the year ended 30th September, 1875:—abstracted from Returns made by the respective Medical Officers, . . . | 152 |
| 5. | Number of Cases of Scarlatina, Smallpox, and Fever, reported by the Medical Officers of Dispensaries in Ireland, as having been attended in the quarters ended 31st December, 1874, and 31st March, 30th June, and 30th September, 1875, . . . . . . . . . . | 152 |


## Index.


| | | |
|---|---|---|
| 6. | Index List of Dispensary Districts; with Names of Unions in which they are situate, and References to Pages in which the Districts are to be found in the Appendix, . . . . . . . . | 153 |

# ANNUAL REPORT

OF THE

# LOCAL GOVERNMENT BOARD FOR IRELAND,

BEING

## THE FOURTH REPORT UNDER "THE LOCAL GOVERNMENT BOARD (IRELAND) ACT," 35 & 36 VIC., CAP. 69.

---

TO HIS GRACE JAMES DUKE OF ABERCORN, K.G.,

&c., &c., &c.,

*Lord Lieutenant-General and General Governor of Ireland.*

*Local Government Board,*
*Dublin*, 31*st March*, 1876.

MAY IT PLEASE YOUR GRACE,

WE, the Local Government Board for Ireland, submit to your Grace this our Fourth Annual Report under the statute 35 & 36 Vic., cap. 69, entitled "The Local Government Board (Ireland) Act," 1872.

1. We submit, in the first place, in continuation of similar returns in previous Annual Reports, a summary of weekly returns of persons relieved in the workhouse and out of the workhouse for fifty-two weeks from the week ended 20th February, 1875, to the week ended 12th February, 1876, both inclusive; and we give, in illustration of these and previous returns, the two indoor and outdoor relief diagrams,* so as to afford a comparison of the fluctuations which have occurred in each year for the last seven years.

* See diagrams facing page 36.

SUMMARY of Weekly Returns of Persons relieved in Unions in Ireland, from the week

| Week ended Saturday. | RELIEF IN THE WORKHOUSE. Able-bodied. Males. | Females. | Total. | Healthy Children under 15 years of age. | Sick in Workhouse Hospitals. Fever Patients. | Other Cases. | Total. | All other Classes. Males aged 15 and upwards. | Females aged 15 and upwards. | Total. | Total Number in Workhouse. | Average Weekly Cost per head for Maintenance (exclusive of clothing). | Deaths. No. in the Week. | Weekly rate of Mortality per 1,000. |
|---|---|---|---|---|---|---|---|---|---|---|---|---|---|---|
| 1875. | | | | | | | | | | | | s. d. | | |
| Feb. 20, | 2,213 | 5,380 | 7,593 | 12,261 | 903 | 17,298 | 18,201 | 6,085 | 7,082 | 13,167 | 51,158 | 2 11½ | 274 | 5·4 |
| 27, | 2,260 | 5,320 | 7,580 | 12,314 | 855 | 17,610 | 18,465 | 6,114 | 7,117 | 13,231 | 51,590 | 2 11½ | 343 | 6·6 |
| Mar. 6, | 2,231 | 5,327 | 7,558 | 12,324 | 825 | 17,664 | 18,489 | 6,062 | 7,105 | 13,167 | 51,558 | 2 11½ | 404 | 7·8 |
| 13, | 2,161 | 5,234 | 7,395 | 12,161 | 856 | 17,610 | 18,466 | 5,988 | 7,089 | 13,077 | 51,090 | 2 11 | 335 | 6·6 |
| 20, | 2,067 | 5,136 | 7,203 | 12,811 | 873 | 17,368 | 18,241 | 5,854 | 6,979 | 12,833 | 50,288 | 2 11 | 322 | 6·4 |
| 27, | 2,062 | 5,137 | 7,199 | 11,909 | 867 | 16,991 | 17,858 | 5,768 | 6,893 | 12,661 | 49,683 | 2 11 | 278 | 5·6 |
| April 3, | 1,948 | 5,016 | 6,964 | 11,742 | 893 | 16,872 | 17,765 | 5,581 | 6,762 | 12,343 | 48,814 | 2 2½ | 285 | 5·8 |
| 10, | 1,886 | 4,952 | 6,838 | 11,737 | 871 | 16,876 | 17,747 | 5,577 | 6,707 | 12,284 | 48,606 | 2 11 | 293 | 6·0 |
| 17, | 1,769 | 4,744 | 6,513 | 11,485 | 940 | 16,735 | 17,675 | 5,512 | 6,668 | 12,180 | 47,893 | 2 10½ | 287 | 6·0 |
| 24, | 1,714 | 4,631 | 6,345 | 11,305 | 920 | 16,513 | 17,433 | 5,186 | 6,881 | 12,067 | 47,154 | 2 10½ | 262 | 5·6 |
| May 1, | 1,711 | 4,569 | 6,280 | 11,179 | 953 | 16,368 | 17,321 | 5,382 | 6,579 | 11,961 | 46,738 | 2 10½ | 248 | 5·3 |
| 8, | 1,600 | 4,522 | 6,122 | 11,116 | 942 | 16,027 | 16,969 | 5,449 | 6,510 | 11,959 | 46,174 | 2 10½ | 247 | 5·3 |
| 15, | 1,560 | 4,452 | 6,012 | 10,983 | 936 | 15,914 | 16,850 | 5,407 | 6,471 | 11,878 | 45,739 | 2 10 | 212 | 4·6 |
| 22, | 1,529 | 4,369 | 5,898 | 10,975 | 879 | 15,711 | 16,590 | 5,381 | 6,450 | 11,831 | 45,294 | 2 9¾ | 203 | 4·5 |
| 29, | 1,519 | 4,297 | 5,816 | 10,964 | 843 | 15,665 | 16,508 | 5,399 | 6,407 | 11,806 | 44,988 | 2 9½ | 198 | 4·6 |
| June 5, | 1,489 | 4,224 | 5,713 | 10,704 | 880 | 15,471 | 16,351 | 5,324 | 6,382 | 11,706 | 44,470 | 2 9½ | 177 | 4·0 |
| 12, | 1,493 | 4,183 | 5,676 | 10,675 | 849 | 15,338 | 16,187 | 5,377 | 6,334 | 11,711 | 44,247 | 2 9½ | 184 | 4·2 |
| 19, | 1,451 | 4,137 | 5,588 | 10,861 | 846 | 15,336 | 16,182 | 5,377 | 6,342 | 11,719 | 44,055 | 2 9½ | 171 | 3·9 |
| 26, | 1,440 | 4,058 | 5,498 | 10,436 | 938 | 15,133 | 16,071 | 5,258 | 6,246 | 11,504 | 43,489 | 2 9½ | 199 | 4·6 |
| July 3, | 1,437 | 3,908 | 5,345 | 10,368 | 771 | 14,986 | 15,757 | 5,248 | 6,208 | 11,456 | 43,023 | 2 9½ | 184 | 4·3 |
| 10, | 1,396 | 3,958 | 5,354 | 10,272 | 739 | 14,794 | 15,533 | 5,193 | 6,150 | 11,343 | 42,402 | 2 9½ | 161 | 3·8 |
| 17, | 1,366 | 3,881 | 5,247 | 10,187 | 784 | 14,718 | 15,502 | 5,161 | 6,115 | 11,276 | 42,212 | 2 9½ | 173 | 4·1 |
| 24, | 1,361 | 3,810 | 5,171 | 9,944 | 766 | 14,746 | 15,512 | 5,049 | 6,078 | 11,127 | 41,754 | 2 9½ | 175 | 4·2 |
| 31, | 1,309 | 3,739 | 5,048 | 9,862 | 739 | 14,534 | 15,273 | 4,959 | 6,015 | 10,974 | 41,158 | 2 9½ | 182 | 4·4 |
| Aug. 7, | 1,308 | 3,674 | 4,982 | 9,849 | 742 | 14,272 | 15,014 | 4,867 | 5,920 | 10,787 | 40,632 | 2 9½ | 177 | 4·4 |
| 14, | 1,314 | 3,576 | 4,890 | 9,758 | 664 | 14,296 | 14,960 | 4,887 | 5,894 | 10,781 | 40,455 | 2 9½ | 138 | 3·4 |
| 21, | 1,383 | 3,633 | 5,016 | 9,001 | 628 | 14,249 | 14,877 | 4,804 | 5,867 | 10,671 | 40,008 | 2 9½ | 150 | 3·7 |
| 28, | 1,312 | 3,589 | 4,901 | 9,575 | 623 | 14,183 | 14,806 | 4,806 | 5,820 | 10,626 | 39,908 | 2 9½ | 128 | 3·2 |
| Sept. 4, | 1,301 | 3,592 | 4,893 | 9,591 | 682 | 14,220 | 14,902 | 4,849 | 5,832 | 10,681 | 39,763 | 2 9½ | 124 | 3·1 |
| 11, | 1,318 | 3,631 | 4,949 | 9,480 | 574 | 14,308 | 14,882 | 4,828 | 5,776 | 10,604 | 39,974 | 2 10 | 134 | 3·4 |
| 18, | 1,306 | 3,702 | 5,008 | 9,506 | 574 | 14,369 | 14,943 | 4,843 | 5,760 | 10,603 | 40,059 | 2 10 | 149 | 3·7 |
| 25, | 1,360 | 3,733 | 5,093 | 9,862 | 538 | 14,400 | 14,938 | 4,914 | 5,841 | 10,755 | 40,438 | 2 10 | 148 | 3·7 |
| Oct. 2, | 1,355 | 3,848 | 5,203 | 9,694 | 543 | 14,265 | 14,808 | 4,961 | 5,903 | 10,864 | 40,669 | 2 10 | 150 | 3·7 |
| 9, | 1,375 | 3,887 | 5,262 | 9,742 | 541 | 14,349 | 14,890 | 5,001 | 5,898 | 10,899 | 40,793 | 2 10½ | 139 | 3·4 |
| 16, | 1,414 | 3,864 | 5,278 | 9,807 | 538 | 14,491 | 15,029 | 5,034 | 5,984 | 11,018 | 41,132 | 2 10½ | 149 | 3·6 |
| 23, | 1,427 | 3,900 | 5,327 | 9,814 | 511 | 14,795 | 15,306 | 5,112 | 6,031 | 11,143 | 41,590 | 2 10½ | 167 | 3·8 |
| 30, | 1,494 | 3,963 | 5,457 | 9,902 | 536 | 14,815 | 15,351 | 5,156 | 6,048 | 11,204 | 41,916 | 2 11 | 160 | 3·8 |
| Nov. 6, | 1,543 | 4,043 | 5,586 | 10,030 | 553 | 14,962 | 15,515 | 5,274 | 6,112 | 11,386 | 42,517 | 2 11¼ | 141 | 3·3 |
| 13, | 1,549 | 4,154 | 5,703 | 10,147 | 529 | 15,248 | 15,777 | 5,358 | 6,199 | 11,557 | 43,214 | 2 11¼ | 190 | 4·4 |
| 20, | 1,570 | 4,310 | 5,880 | 10,247 | 543 | 15,511 | 16,054 | 5,445 | 6,252 | 11,697 | 43,878 | 2 11¼ | 204 | 4·6 |
| 27, | 1,762 | 4,309 | 6,071 | 10,360 | 619 | 15,633 | 16,252 | 5,529 | 6,273 | 11,802 | 44,491 | 2 11½ | 220 | 5·0 |
| Dec. 4, | 1,808 | 4,382 | 6,190 | 10,862 | 689 | 15,911 | 16,600 | 5,683 | 6,345 | 12,028 | 45,277 | 2 11½ | 263 | 5·8 |
| 11, | 1,911 | 4,473 | 6,384 | 10,810 | 741 | 16,060 | 16,801 | 5,697 | 6,357 | 12,054 | 46,049 | 2 11½ | 280 | 6·1 |
| 18, | 1,973 | 4,467 | 6,440 | 10,836 | 740 | 16,022 | 16,762 | 5,669 | 6,289 | 11,958 | 45,996 | 2 11½ | 286 | 6·2 |
| 25, | 2,018 | 4,592 | 6,610 | 10,867 | 652 | 15,831 | 16,483 | 5,532 | 6,348 | 11,880 | 45,840 | 3 5¾ | 221 | 4·8 |
| 1876. | | | | | | | | | | | | | | |
| Jan. 1, | 2,083 | 4,580 | 6,663 | 10,974 | 633 | 15,874 | 16,507 | 5,724 | 6,236 | 11,960 | 46,214 | 3 1½ | 226 | 4·9 |
| 8, | 2,138 | 4,570 | 6,708 | 10,975 | 634 | 16,247 | 16,881 | 5,683 | 6,391 | 12,074 | 46,640 | 2 11 | 219 | 4·7 |
| 15, | 2,060 | 4,719 | 6,779 | 11,140 | 676 | 16,512 | 17,188 | 5,806 | 6,428 | 12,234 | 47,337 | 2 11 | 256 | 5·4 |
| 22, | 2,041 | 4,741 | 6,782 | 11,111 | 701 | 16,656 | 17,357 | 5,831 | 6,440 | 12,271 | 47,521 | 2 11 | 256 | 5·4 |
| 29, | 2,157 | 4,746 | 6,903 | 11,139 | 678 | 16,749 | 17,427 | 5,834 | 6,476 | 12,310 | 47,677 | 2 11 | 251 | 5·3 |
| Feb. 5, | 2,095 | 4,767 | 6,862 | 11,151 | 702 | 16,817 | 17,519 | 5,787 | 6,451 | 12,238 | 47,770 | 2 11 | 211 | 4·4 |
| 12, | 2,068 | 4,783 | 6,851 | 11,308 | 702 | 16,977 | 17,679 | 5,885 | 6,416 | 12,301 | 48,036 | 2 11 | 251 | 5·2 |

**ended 20th February, 1875, to the week ended 12th February, 1876, both inclusive.**

| No. of Persons included in the foregoing Cols., who were admitted to the Workhouse under the 3rd and 4th secs. of 25 & 26 Vic., c. 83. No. of Patients, under the 3rd sec. of 25 & 26 Vic., c. 83. Fever Cases. | Other Cases. | Total. | No. of Constabulary Patients, under the 4th sec. of 25 & 26 Vic., c. 83. Fever Cases. | Other Cases. | Total. | No. of Persons under treatment in Hospitals not connected with Workhouse, who have been sent there by the Guardians, under sec. 14 of 6 & 7 Vic., c. 92, or sec. 7 of 25 & 26 Vic., c. 83. In Fever Hospitals. | In other Hospitals. | No. of Blind and Deaf and Dumb persons maintained in Asylums at the expense of the Poor Rates under sec. 14 of 6 & 7 Vic., c. 92. Blind. | Deaf and Dumb. | Out-door Relief. Relievable under section 1. No. of Cases. | No. of Persons. | Not relievable under section 1. No. of Cases. | No. of Persons. | Under 25 & 26 Vic., c. 83, & 32 & 33 Vic., c. 25. Number of Orphans and Deserted Children out at Nurse. Males. | Females. | Total. | Total Number of Persons in receipt of Out-door Relief. | Total Number of Persons in receipt of Relief. |
|---|---|---|---|---|---|---|---|---|---|---|---|---|---|---|---|---|---|---|
| 73 | 209 | 272 | 4 | 17 | 21 | 16 | 7 | 192 | 336 | 17,309 | 30,739 | 138 | 198 | 707 | 817 | 1,524 | 32,461 | 84,171 |
| 78 | 297 | 375 | 4 | 17 | 21 | 11 | 7 | 192 | 340 | 17,385 | 30,928 | 163 | 223 | 707 | 818 | 1,525 | 32,676 | 84,826 |
| 67 | 290 | 357 | 4 | 18 | 22 | 18 | 4 | 192 | 330 | 17,497 | 31,331 | 148 | 223 | 705 | 919 | 1,624 | 33,078 | 85,108 |
| 70 | 281 | 351 | 6 | 17 | 23 | 18 | 5 | 189 | 341 | 17,435 | 31,362 | 139 | 200 | 708 | 818 | 1,526 | 33,114 | 84,762 |
| 66 | 262 | 328 | 4 | 18 | 22 | 22 | 16 | 192 | 342 | 17,567 | 31,393 | 154 | 225 | 705 | 812 | 1,517 | 33,161 | 84,077 |
| 54 | 258 | 312 | 4 | 16 | 20 | 28 | 14 | 193 | 340 | 17,412 | 31,152 | 140 | 197 | 698 | 798 | 1,496 | 32,845 | 84,101 |
| 55 | 256 | 311 | 9 | 17 | 26 | 22 | 11 | 192 | 334 | 16,996 | 30,040 | 150 | 204 | 692 | 794 | 1,486 | 31,732 | 81,107 |
| 39 | 255 | 294 | 6 | 18 | 24 | 22 | 12 | 191 | 339 | 16,946 | 30,101 | 145 | 209 | 701 | 792 | 1,493 | 31,803 | 80,974 |
| 41 | 241 | 282 | 10 | 19 | 29 | 19 | 12 | 191 | 339 | 16,079 | 30,118 | 142 | 219 | 716 | 801 | 1,517 | 31,854 | 80,297 |
| 64 | 268 | 302 | 9 | 20 | 29 | 12 | 12 | 192 | 338 | 16,937 | 29,922 | 149 | 203 | 712 | 807 | 1,519 | 31,645 | 79,859 |
| 48 | 235 | 283 | 10 | 15 | 25 | 16 | 11 | 192 | 342 | 16,832 | 29,712 | 161 | 220 | 713 | 797 | 1,510 | 31,442 | 78,746 |
| 54 | 240 | 294 | 9 | 13 | 22 | 17 | 13 | 197 | 342 | 16,737 | 29,558 | 148 | 202 | 711 | 795 | 1,506 | 31,327 | 78,011 |
| 79 | 217 | 296 | 9 | 14 | 23 | 21 | 15 | 190 | 343 | 16,733 | 29,509 | 138 | 198 | 708 | 797 | 1,505 | 31,203 | 77,531 |
| 67 | 219 | 286 | 7 | 15 | 19 | 14 | 12 | 191 | 343 | 16,737 | 29,401 | 134 | 191 | 704 | 790 | 1,494 | 31,[illegible] | 76,046 |
| 60 | 202 | 262 | 10 | 14 | 24 | 12 | 14 | 191 | 349 | 16,732 | 29,442 | 133 | 197 | 710 | 789 | 1,499 | 31,188 | 76,700 |
| 58 | 194 | 252 | 5 | 15 | 20 | 16 | 14 | 192 | 351 | 16,782 | 29,438 | 130 | 186 | 708 | 785 | 1,493 | 31,117 | 76,108 |
| 40 | 202 | 242 | 7 | 10 | 17 | 28 | 13 | 192 | 350 | 16,691 | 29,362 | 128 | 186 | 704 | 786 | 1,490 | 30,988 | 73,701 |
| 45 | 206 | 251 | 4 | 11 | 15 | 27 | 14 | 192 | 352 | 16,758 | 29,311 | 130 | 193 | 702 | 786 | 1,488 | 30,[illegible] | 73,630 |
| 47 | 198 | 245 | 3 | 10 | 13 | 28 | 13 | 193 | 356 | 16,785 | 29,425 | 132 | 204 | 694 | 778 | 1,472 | 31,[illegible] | 73,176 |
| 39 | 201 | 210 | 2 | 10 | 12 | 28 | 10 | 192 | 350 | 16,747 | 29,307 | 125 | 167 | 691 | 771 | 1,462 | 30,936 | 74,463 |
| 40 | 198 | 238 | 2 | 9 | 11 | 32 | 11 | 192 | 350 | 16,687 | 28,979 | 142 | 247 | 689 | 772 | 1,461 | 30,497 | 73,679 |
| 38 | 196 | 234 | 3 | 12 | 15 | 38 | 15 | 192 | 347 | 16,638 | 28,904 | 156 | 251 | 701 | 774 | 1,475 | 30,430 | 73,448 |
| 47 | 199 | 246 | 7 | 11 | 18 | 61 | 14 | 193 | 340 | 16,596 | 28,722 | 141 | 221 | 701 | 761 | 1,462 | 30,406 | 72,763 |
| 40 | 192 | 232 | 1 | 13 | 14 | 58 | 16 | 192 | 546 | 16,446 | 28,347 | 122 | 191 | 708 | 766 | 1,474 | 29,909 | 71,672 |
| 37 | 192 | 229 | 1 | 11 | 12 | 56 | 16 | 197 | 345 | 16,265 | 27,796 | 119 | 177 | 715 | 778 | 1,493 | 29,458 | 70,699 |
| 34 | 183 | 217 | 1 | 10 | 11 | 56 | 17 | 191 | 338 | 15,687 | 26,764 | 114 | 165 | 709 | 756 | 1,465 | 28,387 | 69,448 |
| 28 | 186 | 214 | 2 | 9 | 11 | 53 | 18 | 190 | 349 | 15,536 | 26,343 | 118 | 162 | 712 | 761 | 1,473 | 27,985 | 66,668 |
| 22 | 190 | 213 | 2 | 11 | 13 | 55 | 16 | 187 | 344 | 15,807 | 25,763 | 111 | 148 | 707 | 759 | 1,466 | 27,396 | 67,906 |
| 19 | 181 | 200 | 2 | 7 | 9 | 37 | 24 | 189 | 342 | 15,007 | 25,467 | 106 | 137 | 706 | 763 | 1,469 | 27,097 | 67,647 |
| 21 | 180 | 201 | 1 | 5 | 6 | 39 | 24 | 190 | 337 | 14,998 | 25,394 | 105 | 129 | 704 | 763 | 1,468 | 26,983 | 67,347 |
| 27 | 183 | 210 | 6 | 6 | 12 | 29 | 20 | 191 | 341 | 15,097 | 25,376 | 98 | 134 | 701 | 756 | 1,457 | 26,957 | 67,606 |
| 24 | 185 | 209 | 6 | 7 | 13 | 32 | 17 | 188 | 348 | 15,116 | 25,396 | 100 | 141 | 702 | 758 | 1,460 | 27,121 | 66,145 |
| 19 | 176 | 195 | 7 | 7 | 14 | 35 | 19 | 187 | 348 | 14,916 | 25,471 | 103 | 142 | 700 | 756 | 1,456 | 27,070 | 68,318 |
| 16 | 188 | 204 | 6 | 7 | 13 | 36 | 19 | 188 | 349 | 15,107 | 25,694 | 101 | 155 | 700 | 757 | 1,457 | 27,303 | 68,978 |
| 20 | 196 | 216 | 3 | 11 | 14 | 34 | 13 | 187 | 350 | 15,251 | 25,962 | 106 | 188 | 701 | 763 | 1,464 | 27,448 | 69,133 |
| 28 | 193 | 221 | 3 | 12 | 15 | 30 | 13 | 188 | 350 | 15,396 | 26,090 | 109 | 142 | 701 | 758 | 1,459 | 27,594 | 69,765 |
| 27 | 199 | 226 | 2 | 6 | 8 | 45 | 12 | 189 | 350 | 15,381 | 26,073 | 114 | 161 | 698 | 756 | 1,454 | 27,687 | 70,198 |
| 29 | 212 | 241 | — | 12 | 12 | 39 | 14 | 188 | 353 | 15,611 | 26,318 | 118 | 165 | 701 | 757 | 1,458 | 27,948 | 71,048 |
| 27 | 220 | 247 | 2 | 9 | 11 | 23 | 14 | 190 | 350 | 15,681 | 26,693 | 118 | 164 | 698 | 757 | 1,455 | 28,331 | 72,182 |
| 29 | 221 | 250 | 3 | 10 | 13 | 36 | 14 | 191 | 354 | 15,762 | 26,859 | 126 | 174 | 690 | 754 | 1,444 | 28,5[illegible]0 | 72,931 |
| 30 | 232 | 262 | 2 | 14 | 16 | 32 | 16 | 191 | 358 | 15,890 | 27,269 | 126 | 192 | 697 | 748 | 1,445 | 28,899 | 73,843 |
| 28 | 231 | 259 | 1 | 16 | 17 | 32 | 19 | 194 | 352 | 16,112 | 27,761 | 118 | 182 | 700 | 748 | 1,448 | 29,399 | 75,369 |
| 31 | 257 | 288 | 3 | 16 | 19 | 37 | 20 | 193 | 351 | 16,347 | 28,235 | 132 | 197 | 697 | 751 | 1,448 | 29,876 | 76,426 |
| 36 | 230 | 266 | 2 | 14 | 16 | 40 | 20 | 193 | 357 | 16,631 | 28,758 | 130 | 190 | 701 | 758 | 1,459 | 30,459 | 77,038 |
| 41 | 224 | 265 | 1 | 13 | 14 | 41 | 15 | 194 | 364 | 16,835 | 29,284 | 147 | 212 | 699 | 752 | 1,451 | 30,897 | 77,251 |
| 32 | 232 | 283 | 3 | 12 | 15 | 45 | 14 | 196 | 366 | 16,872 | 29,438 | 137 | 209 | 700 | 747 | 1,447 | 31,078 | 77,913 |
| 49 | 242 | 291 | 4 | 8 | 12 | 46 | 18 | 195 | 368 | 16,904 | 29,821 | 129 | 188 | 700 | 746 | 1,446 | 31,155 | 78,491 |
| 42 | 243 | 285 | 5 | 9 | 14 | 67 | 14 | 196 | 371 | 16,981 | 29,857 | 137 | 205 | 699 | 745 | 1,444 | 31,456 | 79,450 |
| 29 | 251 | 280 | 5 | 13 | 18 | 41 | 12 | 195 | 396 | 17,114 | 30,196 | 141 | 201 | 707 | 744 | 1,451 | 31,850 | 80,048 |
| 25 | 254 | 279 | 4 | 19 | 23 | 46 | 11 | 196 | 390 | 17,334 | 30,480 | 127 | 198 | 708 | 746 | 1,454 | 32,133 | 80,451 |
| 22 | 255 | 276 | 5 | 22 | 27 | 45 | 13 | 195 | 389 | 17,308 | 30,767 | 147 | 208 | 708 | 748 | 1,456 | 32,451 | 80,832 |
| 30 | 255 | 285 | 6 | 22 | 28 | 42 | 12 | 195 | 400 | 17,488 | 31,004 | 153 | 227 | 706 | 747 | 1,453 | 32,656 | 81,383 |

2. The following tables represent in figures the maximum, minimum, and average daily numbers shown in each diagram for the whole series of seven years:—

### Relief in Workhouse.

| — | Maximum Numbers. | Date. | Minimum Numbers. | Date. | Average Daily Number. |
|---|---|---|---|---|---|
| 1869–70, . | 59,024 | 6 March, 1869 | 43,657 | 4 September, 1869 | 50,964 |
| 1870–71, . | 55,963 | 26 February, 1870 | 41,701 | 20 August, 1870 | 47,910 |
| 1871–72, . | 51,927 | 25 February, 1871 | 39,606 | 26 August, 1871 | 45,338 |
| 1872–73, . | 54,125 | 8 February, 1873 | 39,464 | 31 August, 1872 | 45,753 |
| 1873–74, . | 52,934 | 1 March, 1873 | 40,924 | 6 September, 1873 | 46,573 |
| 1874–75, . | 52,110 | 28 February, 1874 | 42,383 | 29 August, 1874 | 47,118 |
| 1875–76, . | 51,599 | 27 February, 1875 | 39,908 | 28 August, 1875 | 44,800 |

### Out-door Relief.

| — | Maximum Numbers. | Date. | Minimum Numbers. | Date. | Average Daily Number. |
|---|---|---|---|---|---|
| 1869–70, . | 22,520 | 19 February, 1870 | 15,899 | 2 October, 1869 | 18,296 |
| 1870–71, . | 25,368 | 18 February, 1871 | 18,047 | 1 October, 1870 | 21,474 |
| 1871–72, . | 28,490 | 17 February, 1872 | 22,665 | 7 October, 1871 | 22,552 |
| 1872–73, . | 32,936 | 15 February, 1873 | 24,527 | 5 October, 1872 | 27,509 |
| 1873–74, . | 33,710 | 1 March, 1873 | 26,733 | 4 October, 1873 | 30,176 |
| 1874–75, . | 32,935 | 21 March, 1874 | 26,739 | 10 October, 1874 | 30,319 |
| 1875–76, . | 33,151 | 20 March, 1875 | 26,957 | 18 September, 1875 | 30,246 |

3. The above figures are satisfactory, showing that during the latter part of the period there has been a material decrease in the number of workhouse inmates in comparison with the number at the corresponding period of last year, accompanied by a small increase only in the number receiving out-door relief.

4. The next table exhibits the fluctuation for twenty years past of the number on out-door relief.

**Return** showing the Number of Persons in receipt of Out-door Relief under the 1st Section of 10th Vic., cap. 31, on the last Saturday of February in each year from 1857 to 1876 inclusive.

| Year. | Persons permanently disabled from labour by reason of old age, infirmity, or bodily or mental defect. | | Widows having two or more legitimate children dependent on them. | | Persons being disabled from labour by reason of severe sickness or serious accident. | | Total. | |
|---|---|---|---|---|---|---|---|---|
| | Cases. | Persons. | Cases. | Persons. | Cases. | Persons. | Cases. | Persons. |
| 1857, | 396 | 541 | 34 | 120 | 181 | 435 | 611 | 1,096 |
| 1858, | 424 | 566 | 79 | 253 | 320 | 823 | 823 | 1,612 |
| 1859, | 413 | 569 | 53 | 197 | 281 | 682 | 777 | 1,448 |
| 1860, | 592 | 728 | 87 | 361 | 454 | 1,004 | 1,133 | 2,093 |
| 1861, | 1,197 | 1,517 | 175 | 688 | 961 | 2,508 | 2,333 | 4,713 |
| 1862, | 1,691 | 2,180 | 283 | 1,035 | 1,360 | 3,287 | 3,334 | 6,502 |
| 1863, | 2,650 | 3,541 | 414 | 1,584 | 1,559 | 3,924 | 4,623 | 9,049 |
| 1864, | 2,990 | 3,895 | 486 | 1,939 | 1,808 | 4,482 | 5,284 | 10,316 |
| 1865, | 3,357 | 4,338 | 606 | 2,353 | 2,095 | 5,322 | 6,058 | 12,018 |
| 1866, | 3,545 | 4,369 | 696 | 2,771 | 1,915 | 4,670 | 6,156 | 11,810 |
| 1867, | 4,608 | 6,024 | 920 | 3,684 | 2,821 | 6,758 | 8,349 | 16,466 |
| 1868, | 5,471 | 7,026 | 1,075 | 4,398 | 2,802 | 6,899 | 9,348 | 18,823 |
| 1869, | 5,816 | 7,472 | 1,157 | 4,808 | 2,632 | 6,503 | 9,605 | 1[illegible],863 |
| 1870, | 6,992 | 8,913 | 1,183 | 5,045 | 3,045 | 7,368 | 11,220 | 21,326 |
| 1871, | 7,969 | 9,746 | 1,360 | 5,829 | 3,369 | 7,989 | 12,698 | 23,544 |
| 1872, | 9,226 | 11,231 | 1,463 | 6,347 | 3,914 | 9,432 | 14,603 | 27,010 |
| 1873, | 10,835 | 13,462 | 1,684 | 7,297 | 4,295 | 10,383 | 16,814 | 31,142 |
| 1874, | 11,377 | 14,042 | 1,626 | 7,105 | 4,081 | 9,502 | 17,084 | 30,649 |
| 1875, | 11,675 | 14,115 | 1,563 | 6,937 | 4,147 | 9,876 | 17,385 | 30,928 |
| 1876, | 11,829 | 14,470 | 1,640 | 7,213 | 4,186 | 9,813 | 17,655 | 31,496 |

Thus on the last Saturday of February the total number of persons receiving relief out of the workhouse under the 1st section has increased from 30,928 to 31,496, a difference of 568; there is an increase of 355 in the class of "permanently disabled," and of 276 in class of "widows with two or more legitimate children;" but a decrease of 63 in the class of "persons disabled by severe sickness or serious accident."

5. We here subjoin a tabular statement showing the number of "night-lodgers," a term corresponding to "casuals" in England, for the past twelve months, in continuation of a similar table in last Report.

**Return of Night-Lodgers or Casuals relieved.**

| Week ended | Number relieved during the week. | | | | Number in Workhouse at close of the week. | | | |
|---|---|---|---|---|---|---|---|---|
| | Males. | Females. | Children under 15. | Total. | Males. | Females. | Children under 15. | Total. |
| 6th March, 1875, . | 818 | 264 | 295 | 1,377 | 121 | 48 | 55 | 224 |
| 3rd April, " . | 954 | 345 | 300 | 1,599 | 103 | 55 | 55 | 213 |
| 1st May, " . | 707 | 325 | 319 | 1,351 | 81 | 31 | 27 | 139 |
| 5th June, " . | 443 | 248 | 190 | 880 | 61 | 33 | 15 | 109 |
| 3rd July, " . | 533 | 251 | 217 | 1,001 | 89 | 32 | 33 | 153 |
| 7th August, " . | 387 | 201 | 189 | 777 | 62 | 28 | 16 | 106 |
| 4th September, " . | 325 | 172 | 182 | 679 | 46 | 14 | 12 | 72 |
| 2nd October, " . | 425 | 197 | 181 | 803 | 64 | 22 | 26 | 112 |
| 6th November, " . | 446 | 162 | 157 | 765 | 56 | 20 | 21 | 97 |
| 4th December, " . | 400 | 144 | 115 | 659 | 71 | 24 | 20 | 115 |
| 1st January, 1876, . | 418 | 144 | 145 | 707 | 68 | 15 | 20 | 103 |
| 5th February, " . | 558 | 194 | 176 | 928 | 101 | 33 | 41 | 175 |
| 4th March, " . | 538 | 184 | 170 | 892 | 107 | 32 | 24 | 163 |

The reduction in the number of night-lodgers or casuals is remarkable, and was occasioned, no doubt, in some degree by the practice recently introduced of a member of the Constabulary Force attending at the workhouse on the daily discharge of this class of inmates, which practice arose out of a correspondence which terminated in the issue of a circular to Boards of Guardians on the subject, which will be found in our last annual Report.*

6. As part of the statistics which are brought up very nearly to the date of this Report, the following table exhibits in the accustomed form:

CLASSIFICATION of Causes of Death in Workhouses, from 30th January, 1875, to 29th January, 1876.

| Causes of Death. | In the four Weeks ended | | | | | | | | | | | | | | Previous Year. |
|---|---|---|---|---|---|---|---|---|---|---|---|---|---|---|---|
| | 27th Feb. | 27th March | 24th April. | 22nd May. | 19th June. | 17th July. | 14th Aug. | 11th Sept. | 9th Oct. | 6th Nov. | 4th Dec. | 1st Jan. | 29th Jan. | Total. | |
| Age, | 263 | 208 | 230 | 150 | 140 | 118 | 126 | 96 | 101 | 118 | 212 | 240 | 238 | 2,347 | 2,287 |
| Apoplexy, | 5 | 12 | 11 | 6 | 5 | 7 | 6 | 4 | 4 | 6 | 6 | 11 | 8 | 89 | 105 |
| Asthma, | 16 | 30 | 13 | 15 | 6 | 4 | 10 | 1 | 4 | 13 | 6 | 18 | 8 | 134 | 107 |
| Atrophy, | 88 | 101 | 86 | 77 | 70 | 64 | 58 | 55 | 88 | 45 | 52 | 86 | 81 | 921 | 874 |
| Brain Disease, | 29 | 88 | 30 | 32 | 38 | 25 | 29 | 16 | 20 | 32 | 22 | 41 | 38 | 394 | 403 |
| Cancer, | 18 | 20 | 18 | 21 | 19 | 14 | 18 | 7 | 22 | 12 | 29 | 17 | 12 | 228 | 232 |
| Childbirth, | 2 | 1 | 1 | – | 1 | 1 | – | 1 | 1 | – | 1 | 1 | 3 | 13 | 11 |
| Cholera, | – | – | – | – | – | – | – | – | – | – | – | – | – | – | – |
| Consumption, | 85 | 90 | 75 | 83 | 59 | 89 | 87 | 46 | 40 | 80 | 62 | 71 | 58 | 841 | 830 |
| Convulsions, | 12 | 16 | 17 | 15 | 13 | 10 | 10 | 8 | 11 | 6 | 19 | 19 | 8 | 158 | 162 |
| Croup, | 3 | 3 | 3 | 2 | 3 | 2 | 1 | 1 | 2 | 3 | 3 | – | 4 | 30 | 20 |
| Diarrhœa, | 38 | 45 | 46 | 32 | 26 | 18 | 30 | 24 | 43 | 27 | 28 | 28 | 26 | 420 | 402 |
| Dropsy, | 33 | 23 | 30 | 27 | 27 | 27 | 26 | 20 | 27 | 21 | 33 | 22 | 37 | 363 | 355 |
| Dysentery, | 7 | 8 | 12 | 5 | 8 | 4 | 4 | 3 | 4 | 4 | 8 | 11 | 5 | 82 | 78 |
| Dyspepsia, | 5 | – | 1 | 3 | 3 | 2 | 1 | 3 | 1 | 2 | – | 1 | 2 | 23 | 41 |
| Epilepsy, | 10 | 13 | 10 | 10 | 7 | 7 | 4 | 6 | 8 | 7 | 7 | 9 | 11 | 107 | 111 |
| Fever, | 79 | 58 | 77 | 67 | 83 | 76 | 56 | 85 | 28 | 85 | 47 | 46 | 36 | 703 | 763 |
| Gangrene, | 5 | 3 | 5 | 1 | 4 | 3 | 3 | 4 | 4 | 1 | 5 | 5 | 4 | 47 | 44 |
| Heart Disease, | 58 | 64 | 33 | 45 | 26 | 39 | 30 | 30 | 26 | 26 | 41 | 36 | 39 | 499 | 478 |
| Hooping Cough, | 7 | 10 | 8 | 6 | 1 | 1 | 4 | 1 | 2 | 5 | 3 | 3 | 3 | 54 | 81 |
| Inflammation or other diseases of | | | | | | | | | | | | | | | |
| Bowels, | 11 | 18 | 12 | 12 | 6 | 7 | 10 | 3 | 6 | 2 | 10 | 8 | 12 | 117 | 180 |
| Kidneys, | 20 | 20 | 10 | 11 | 11 | 13 | 14 | 12 | 13 | 14 | 14 | 25 | 12 | 189 | 172 |
| Liver, | 10 | 7 | 13 | 13 | 5 | 16 | 8 | 18 | 13 | 10 | 8 | 5 | 8 | 119 | 131 |
| Lungs, | 265 | 289 | 235 | 185 | 105 | 106 | 76 | 64 | 64 | 92 | 106 | 231 | 202 | 2,045 | 1,736 |
| Measles, | 9 | 3 | 5 | 2 | – | 5 | 8 | 3 | 2 | – | 10 | 6 | 3 | 48 | 48 |
| Paralysis, | 46 | 44 | 56 | 37 | 23 | 28 | 24 | 24 | 20 | 28 | 27 | 30 | 32 | 417 | 402 |
| Pleurisy, | 1 | 1 | 3 | 4 | 2 | 2 | 1 | 2 | – | – | 2 | – | 3 | 21 | 18 |
| Rheumatism, | 8 | 9 | 10 | 6 | 12 | 6 | 5 | 2 | 9 | 3 | 12 | 14 | 13 | 107 | 69 |
| Scarlatina, | 8 | 11 | 0 | 5 | 4 | 17 | 8 | 2 | 6 | 1 | 6 | 5 | 7 | 89 | 96 |
| Scrofula, | 16 | 13 | 20 | 19 | 8 | 12 | 12 | 9 | 9 | 14 | 18 | 14 | 16 | 180 | 184 |
| Small-Pox, | 9 | 8 | 7 | 7 | 3 | 1 | 4 | – | – | – | 1 | – | – | 41 | 142 |
| Ulcer, | 11 | 10 | 14 | 9 | 11 | 8 | 11 | 10 | 10 | 11 | 14 | 7 | 17 | 143 | 153 |
| Other Diseases, | 32 | 32 | 21 | 23 | 23 | 33 | 28 | 31 | 31 | 33 | 29 | 23 | 36 | 364 | 329 |
| Total, | 1,206 | 1,328 | 1,127 | 910 | 790 | 717 | 672 | 536 | 586 | 607 | 835 | 1,042 | 989 | 11,333 | – |
| Previous year, | 1,020 | 1,051 | 1,027 | 905 | 829 | 736 | 648 | 638 | 592 | 650 | 796 | 1,170 | 1,061 | – | 11,119 |

The total number of deaths in the workhouses in the fifty-two weeks comprised in the table has been 11,333. In the corresponding table in the last Annual Report the total number of deaths was 11,119, showing that there has been an increase of 214 deaths, as compared with the number last year, and a decrease of 468 as compared with the number in the preceding year.

* Report for 1875, page 48.

The number of deaths by fever is 703 in comparison with 762 in the previous year, and with 663 in the year preceding.

The deaths from small-pox in the workhouse hospitals were 41 in comparison with 142 in 1874–5, and with 110 in the preceding year. The subject of small-pox in 1875 will be more fully dealt with in the Medical Charities branch of this Report.

7. We now continue the series of recent statistics by repeating with one additional year the table showing the number of persons assisted by Boards of Guardians to emigrate, and the cost incurred for that purpose in each year, that is to say, for now twenty-six years past ended on the 25th of March.

EMIGRATION under the Act 12 & 13 Vic., c. 104, sec. 26, dated 1st August, 1849.

| Period. | | Amount authorised to be expended by Sealed Consents. | | | Number of Persons assisted to Emigrate. | | | |
|---|---|---|---|---|---|---|---|---|
| | | £ | s. | d. | Men. | Women. | Children under 15 years of age. | Total. |
| Aug., 1849, to 25 Mar., | 1851, | 11,151 | 14 | 11 | 561 | 1,244 | 787 | 2,592 |
| Year ended 25 March, | 1852, | 21,010 | 5 | 4½ | 790 | 2,644 | 952 | 4,386 |
| " " | 1853, | 14,517 | 0 | 11½ | 492 | 2,218 | 1,115 | 3,825 |
| " " | 1854, | 12,446 | 17 | 6 | 403 | 1,202 | 996 | 2,601 |
| " " | 1855, | 24,868 | 5 | 2½ | 159 | 2,747 | 798 | 3,704 |
| " " | 1856, | 3,618 | 6 | 9 | 64 | 363 | 403 | 830 |
| " " | 1857, | 2,719 | 15 | 1 | 76 | 363 | 363 | 802 |
| " " | 1858, | 4,177 | 10 | 1½ | 58 | 469 | 302 | 829 |
| " " | 1859, | 2,555 | 16 | 6 | 37 | 270 | 130 | 437 |
| " " | 1860, | 1,729 | 19 | 2 | 45 | 178 | 141 | 364 |
| " " | 1861, | 1,465 | 19 | 11 | 44 | 178 | 125 | 347 |
| " " | 1862, | 528 | 17 | 4 | 12 | 72 | 38 | 122 |
| " " | 1863, | 2,489 | 10 | 3 | 41 | 317 | 139 | 497 |
| " " | 1864, | 4,770 | 4 | 5 | 123 | 501 | 345 | 969 |
| " " | 1865, | 2,518 | 17 | 11 | 93 | 315 | 438 | 846 |
| " " | 1866, | 3,425 | 9 | 11 | 100 | 360 | 660 | 1,120 |
| " " | 1867, | 2,028 | 10 | 0 | 66 | 238 | 459 | 763 |
| " " | 1868, | 1,983 | 9 | 6 | 71 | 263 | 485 | 819 |
| " " | 1869, | 1,838 | 18 | 9 | 71 | 205 | 439 | 715 |
| " " | 1870, | 1,959 | 12 | 5 | 49 | 219 | 449 | 717 |
| " " | 1871, | 2,268 | 9 | 11 | 53 | 226 | 422 | 701 |
| " " | 1872, | 2,092 | 3 | 10 | 34 | 223 | 339 | 596 |
| " " | 1873, | 1,564 | 14 | 8 | 44 | 173 | 364 | 581 |
| " " | 1874, | 2,246 | 3 | 8 | 67 | 323 | 474 | 864 |
| " " | 1875, | 1,247 | 15 | 1 | 36 | 192 | 380 | 608 |
| " " | 1876, | 991 | 0 | 6 | 38 | 97 | 223 | 358 |
| Total, . . | £ | 131,660 | 4 | 8 | 3,627 | 15,700 | 11,806 | 31,133 |

*Year ended 29th September,* 1875.

8. The following is a tabulated account of admissions to the workhouse during the last year, ending 29th September, in comparison with those of the sixteen preceding years:—

[TABLE.

TABLE.

| Year ended 29th September. | Number of Paupers in Workhouses at the commencement of the Year. | Number of Persons admitted during the Year. | | | | | | Number of Births in the Workhouse during the Year. | Total number of Persons relieved in the Workhouse during the Year. | Number of Deaths in the Workhouse during the Year. |
|---|---|---|---|---|---|---|---|---|---|---|
| | | Number admitted in Sickness. | | | | Number admitted who were not Sick. | Total number admitted during the Year. | | | |
| | | Suffering from Fever or other contagious Disease. | Suffering under other Diseases. | Suffering from accidental Injury. | Total number admitted in Sickness. | | | | | |
| 1859, | 38,836 | 9,553 | 32,000 | 2,107 | 44,200 | 78,394 | 114,594 | 2,276 | 153,706 | 8,022 |
| 1860, | 35,204 | 9,107 | 36,450 | 2,025 | 47,568 | 85,312 | 132,068 | 2,443 | 170,540 | 9,877 |
| 1861, | 34,294 | 9,208 | 38,378 | 2,217 | 40,853 | 114,830 | 104,803 | 2,435 | 203,422 | 10,580 |
| 1862, | 41,295 | 11,183 | 44,855 | 2,226 | 58,264 | 165,438 | 223,607 | 2,815 | 267,897 | 12,740 |
| 1863, | 45,161 | 14,469 | 44,957 | 2,431 | 61,857 | 178,270 | 240,127 | 2,077 | 288,285 | 13,306 |
| 1864, | 49,087 | 15,757 | 43,027 | 2,280 | 61,064 | 151,157 | 212,221 | 2,869 | 261,147 | 12,785 |
| 1865, | 46,032 | 16,416 | 41,493 | 2,382 | 62,291 | 139,095 | 201,386 | 2,751 | 262,170 | 12,358 |
| 1866, | 44,567 | 13,563 | 38,527 | 2,363 | 54,443 | 130,144 | 184,587 | 2,600 | 232,104 | 11,641 |
| 1867, | 44,273 | 11,703 | 43,176 | 2,433 | 57,312 | 163,895 | 211,207 | 2,654 | 253,138 | 13,162 |
| 1868, | 45,518 | 11,200 | 41,684 | 2,664 | 56,007 | 185,286 | 240,843 | 2,597 | 288,253 | 11,570 |
| 1869, | 47,775 | 9,970 | 41,609 | 2,441 | 54,019 | 131,358 | 185,377 | 2,410 | 235,063 | 11,247 |
| 1870, | 45,012 | 8,153 | 30,088 | 2,510 | 49,749 | 133,386 | 183,135 | 2,282 | 230,429 | 10,697 |
| 1871, | 42,375 | 8,718 | 38,212 | 2,010 | 49,346 | 131,492 | 181,032 | 2,103 | 223,510 | 10,058 |
| 1872, | 40,891 | 10,249 | 39,929 | 2,340 | 52,509 | 137,239 | 189,748 | 1,953 | 232,236 | 11,848 |
| 1873, | 40,884 | 8,236 | 43,747 | 2,422 | 54,404 | 162,078 | 200,483 | 1,089 | 240,293 | 12,354 |
| 1874, | 41,440 | 8,469 | 39,388 | 2,575 | 60,405 | 159,506 | 209,906 | 1,814 | 253,193 | 10,795 |
| 1875, | 42,866 | 8,015 | 37,004 | 2,888 | 47,907 | 131,162 | 180,149 | 1,759 | 213,791 | 11,470 |

It will be observed from the above that a decrease of 2,438 has taken place in the total number admitted in sickness during the year, and a decrease of 454 in the number suffering from fever and other dangerous contagious diseases.

9. The following is a statement of the result of the Weekly Summaries of In-door Relief, showing the average daily number of recipients of relief for each of the twenty-four years ended 29th September, 1875:—

Average Daily Number in receipt of Relief during the year, Average Number of Deaths per Week, and Rate of Mortality.

| Year ended 29th Sept. | Estimated Population. | Able-bodied. | | | Healthy Children under 15. | Sick in Workhouse Hospitals. | | | All other Classes. | | | Total No. in Workhouses. | Deaths in Week. | | Per-centage of In-door Paupers on Population. |
|---|---|---|---|---|---|---|---|---|---|---|---|---|---|---|---|
| | | Male. | Female. | Total. | | Fever. | Other Cases. | Total. | Male. | Female. | Total. | | Average Number during week. | Average weekly Rate of Mortality per 1,000 Inmates. | |
| 1852, | 6,422,997 | 14,818 | 37,333 | 52,251 | 75,061 | 3,918 | 22,588 | 26,506 | 4,488 | 7,618 | 12,103 | 166,821 | 451 | 2·7 | 2·80 |
| 1853, | 6,295,328 | 10,569 | 26,951 | 37,520 | 57,754 | 2,926 | 20,410 | 23,336 | 3,904 | 6,887 | 10,791 | 129,401 | 385 | 3·0 | 2·06 |
| 1854, | 6,184,369 | 7,114 | 18,335 | 25,489 | 39,894 | 2,157 | 18,869 | 21,026 | 3,182 | 5,649 | 8,831 | 95,190 | 304 | 3·2 | 1·54 |
| 1855, | 6,107,809 | 5,048 | 14,086 | 19,134 | 31,843 | 2,063 | 18,214 | 20,277 | 2,863 | 5,094 | 7,957 | 79,211 | 287 | 3·5 | 1·30 |
| 1856, | 6,077,283 | 3,578 | 10,688 | 14,264 | 23,869 | 1,518 | 16,479 | 17,997 | 2,460 | 4,645 | 7,105 | 63,234 | 206 | 3·2 | 1·04 |
| 1857, | 6,047,492 | 2,807 | 7,705 | 10,572 | 17,293 | 1,284 | 15,176 | 16,440 | 2,224 | 4,137 | 6,361 | 50,668 | 178 | 3·5 | 0·84 |
| 1858, | 6,013,102 | 2,312 | 7,121 | 9,433 | 14,206 | 1,108 | 14,839 | 15,947 | 2,129 | 4,015 | 6,144 | 45,790 | 180 | 3·9 | 0·70 |
| 1859, | 6,008,118 | 1,865 | 5,899 | 7,764 | 11,511 | 974 | 13,802 | 14,776 | 2,241 | 4,088 | 6,329 | 40,380 | 154 | 3·8 | 0·67 |
| 1860, | 5,988,820 | 1,867 | 6,060 | 7,927 | 11,316 | 994 | 13,604 | 14,598 | 2,775 | 4,755 | 7,530 | 41,271 | 184 | 4·5 | 0·69 |
| 1861, | 5,798,564 | 2,202 | 6,890 | 9,092 | 12,307 | 1,032 | 14,345 | 15,377 | 3,130 | 5,221 | 8,360 | 45,136 | 202 | 4·5 | 0·78 |
| 1862, | 5,794,674 | 3,039 | 8,310 | 11,342 | 14,917 | 1,262 | 16,138 | 17,305 | 3,956 | 6,031 | 10,007 | 53,068 | 244 | 4·5 | 0·83 |
| 1863, | 5,782,711 | 3,237 | 8,589 | 11,826 | 16,366 | 1,575 | 16,901 | 18,478 | 4,849 | 6,601 | 11,250 | 57,916 | 257 | 4·4 | 1·01 |
| 1864, | 5,728,316 | 2,849 | 7,670 | 10,519 | 16,178 | 1,634 | 16,746 | 18,400 | 4,700 | 6,722 | 11,428 | 56,525 | 244 | 4·8 | 0 99 |
| 1865, | 5,673,808 | 2,540 | 6,557 | 9,197 | 15,299 | 1,824 | 16,382 | 18,206 | 4,529 | 6,686 | 11,215 | 53,917 | 237 | 4·3 | 0·95 |
| 1866, | 5,582,635 | 2,212 | 5,873 | 8,085 | 14,278 | 1,357 | 15,672 | 17,029 | 4,411 | 6,477 | 10,888 | 50,280 | 221 | 4 4 | 0 90 |
| 1867, | 5,557,196 | 2,307 | 6,133 | 8,440 | 15,308 | 1,237 | 15,504 | 16,741 | 4,819 | 6,954 | 11,773 | 52,154 | 252 | 4·8 | 0·94 |
| 1868, | 5,543,286 | 2,406 | 6,133 | 8,539 | 18,024 | 1,196 | 15,503 | 16,699 | 5,334 | 7,094 | 12,428 | 53,590 | 221 | 4·1 | 0·97 |
| 1869, | 5,536,217 | 2,172 | 5,892 | 8,064 | 15,244 | 1,020 | 15,566 | 16,586 | 5,382 | 6,969 | 12,351 | 52,247 | 216 | 4·1 | 0·94 |
| 1870, | 5,516,674 | 2,037 | 5,270 | 7,307 | 13,637 | 946 | 15,344 | 16,290 | 5,254 | 6,698 | 11,952 | 49,186 | 205 | 4·1 | 0·89 |
| 1871, | 5,402,759 | 1,852 | 4,591 | 8,443 | 12,089 | 923 | 15,061 | 15,984 | 5,061 | 6,428 | 11,489 | 48,005 | 193 | 4 2 | 0·85 |
| 1872, | 5,368,186 | 1,760 | 4,618 | 6,397 | 11,482 | 1,039 | 15,107 | 16,146 | 5,140 | 6,606 | 11,745 | 45,752 | 229 | 5·0 | 0·85 |
| 1873, | 5,341,161 | 1,831 | 4,827 | 6,658 | 11,661 | 930 | 15,448 | 16,378 | 5,360 | 6,734 | 11,094 | 45,711 | 237 | 5·1 | 0·87 |
| 1874, | 5,314,844 | 1,875 | 4,700 | 6,575 | 11,672 | 893 | 15,610 | 16,503 | 5,454 | 6,777 | 12,231 | 46,981 | 207 | 4·4 | 0·88 |
| 1875, | 5,307,494 | 1,773 | 4,505 | 6,278 | 11,167 | 881 | 15,721 | 16,522 | 5,534 | 6,834 | 12,056 | 45,945 | 221 | 4·8 | 0·87 |

10. We here continue from last Report a form of table exhibiting for the last twenty-six years—the whole period, in fact, subsequent to the famine—the per-centage in each successive year of the several classes of workhouse inmates as compared with the whole number—

CLASSIFIED RETURN of the Number of Inmates of Workhouses in Ireland, on the first Saturday of January; and the per-centage of the several classes on the total Number of Inmates.

| First Saturday of January. | Inmates not in Hospital. | | | | Number in Hospital. | Total Number in Workhouse. | Per-centage on Total Number. | | | | |
|---|---|---|---|---|---|---|---|---|---|---|---|
| | Able-bodied Males. | Able-bodied Females. | Children under 15 years of age. | Other classes. | | | Able-bodied Males. | Able-bodied Females. | Children under 15 years of age not in Hospital. | Other classes not in Hospital. | In Hospital. |
| 4 Jan., 1851 | 22,178 | 49,738 | 91,889 | 14,867 | 28,932 | 206,504 | 10·7 | 24·1 | 44·4 | 6·8 | 14·0 |
| 3 " 1852 | 16,194 | 37,613 | 78,809 | 11,854 | 26,078 | 168,348 | 9·6 | 22·4 | 45·5 | 7·0 | 15·5 |
| 1 " 1853 | 13,281 | 30,658 | 62,044 | 10,875 | 21,900 | 138,784 | 9·6 | 22·0 | 44·7 | 7·8 | 15·8 |
| 7 " 1854 | 9,239 | 21,234 | 42,792 | 8,780 | 22,599 | 104,004 | 8·8 | 20·3 | 40·9 | 8·4 | 21·8 |
| 6 " 1855 | 6,107 | 16,207 | 34,394 | 8,398 | 20,100 | 85,296 | 7·3 | 19·1 | 40·2 | 9·8 | 23·6 |
| 5 " 1856 | 4,640 | 13,702 | 27,253 | 7,717 | 18,938 | 72,247 | 6·4 | 19·0 | 37·7 | 10·7 | 26·2 |
| 3 " 1857 | 3,512 | 9,262 | 19,177 | 8,611 | 16,571 | 56,183 | 6·4 | 16·8 | 34·8 | 12·0 | 30·0 |
| 2 " 1858 | 2,801 | 8,337 | 15,548 | 6,387 | 16,095 | 49,208 | 5·5 | 16·9 | 31·7 | 13·0 | 32·6 |
| 1 " 1859 | 2,247 | 6,780 | 12,732 | 6,447 | 15,253 | 45,899 | 5·1 | 15·9 | 29·3 | 14·8 | 35·0 |
| 7 " 1860 | 2,184 | 6,701 | 11,707 | 7,577 | 15,009 | 43,218 | 5·1 | 15·7 | 27·1 | 17·4 | 34·7 |
| 5 " 1861 | 2,823 | 7,799 | 12,705 | 8,475 | 15,750 | 47,352 | 5·5 | 16·5 | 26·8 | 17·9 | 33·3 |
| 4 " 1862 | 3,486 | 9,194 | 16,282 | 9,811 | 17,465 | 55,168 | 6·3 | 16·7 | 27·6 | 17·8 | 31·6 |
| 3 " 1863 | 4,030 | 9,644 | 16,750 | 11,193 | 18,421 | 60,038 | 6·7 | 16·1 | 27·9 | 18·6 | 30·7 |
| 2 " 1864 | 3,638 | 8,981 | 17,170 | 11,885 | 18,253 | 59,857 | 6·1 | 14·9 | 28·7 | 19·8 | 30·5 |
| 7 " 1865 | 3,363 | 8,024 | 16,681 | 12,104 | 19,346 | 59,498 | 5·7 | 13·5 | 28·0 | 20·5 | 32·6 |
| 6 " 1866 | 2,901 | 6,894 | 15,494 | 11,501 | 17,645 | 54,435 | 5·3 | 12·7 | 28·5 | 21·1 | 32·4 |
| 5 " 1867 | 3,015 | 7,228 | 15,791 | 11,891 | 17,205 | 54,930 | 5·5 | 13·2 | 28·7 | 21·8 | 31·3 |
| 4 " 1868 | 2,908 | 7,060 | 16,988 | 12,961 | 16,739 | 56,683 | 5·1 | 12·5 | 30·0 | 22·9 | 28·5 |
| 2 " 1869 | 2,831 | 7,062 | 16,944 | 13,126 | 16,870 | 56,934 | 5·1 | 12·4 | 29·8 | 23·1 | 29·6 |
| 1 " 1870 | 2,068 | 6,338 | 15,066 | 12,725 | 18,890 | 53,687 | 5·0 | 11·8 | 28·1 | 23·7 | 31·4 |
| 7 " 1871 | 2,503 | 6,870 | 13,524 | 12,368 | 16,852 | 50,815 | 4·9 | 11·9 | 26·6 | 24·3 | 33·2 |
| 6 " 1872 | 2,268 | 5,197 | 12,421 | 12,803 | 16,852 | 48,738 | 4·6 | 10·7 | 25·6 | 26·2 | 34·0 |
| 4 " 1873 | 2,331 | 5,447 | 12,860 | 12,696 | 17,023 | 48,858 | 4·7 | 10·9 | 24·8 | 25·5 | 34·1 |
| 3 " 1874 | 2,285 | 5,280 | 12,165 | 12,777 | 16,646 | 49,183 | 4·8 | 10·7 | 24·7 | 26·0 | 33·9 |
| 2 " 1875 | 2,333 | 5,190 | 12,187 | 12,883 | 17,212 | 49,805 | 4·7 | 10·4 | 24·5 | 25·9 | 34·6 |
| 1 " 1876 | 2,063 | 4,580 | 10,974 | 11,980 | 16,597 | 46,214 | 4·5 | 9·9 | 23·7 | 25·9 | 35·9 |

11. We now proceed to the statistics arising out of the accounts of the unions for the year ended 29th September, 1875.

We deal in the first place with that part of the Union expenditure which relates exclusively to the relief of the poor, of which the following table affords an abstract for all Ireland, for the year ended 29th September, 1875, in comparison with that for the year which ended on the same date in 1874.

| Year ended 29th September. | Net Annual Value. | Poor Rate lodged. | Poor Relief Expenditure during the Year. | | | | | | Numbers relieved. | | | |
|---|---|---|---|---|---|---|---|---|---|---|---|---|
| | | | In-Maintenance and Clothing. | Out-Relief. | Cost of Relief in Blind and Deaf and Dumb Asylums and Extern Hospitals. | Salaries and Rations of Officers. | All other Expenses. | Total. | In Workhouse. | Out-door. | In Blind and Deaf and Dumb Asylums. | Total. |
| | £ | £ | £ | £ | £ | £ | £ | £ | | | | |
| 1875, | 12,485,600 | 960,877 | 416,172 | 84,775 | 8,390 | 125,675 | 126,541 | 771,553 | 214,029 | 66,714 | 613 | 281,356 |
| 1874, | 12,449,553 | 941,292 | 457,914 | 93,586 | 8,401 | 126,769 | 130,581 | 817,281 | 253,195 | 66,332 | 633 | 320,160 |
| Increase, | 36,047 | – | – | 1,189 | – | – | – | – | – | 382 | – | – |
| Decrease, | – | 10,415 | 41,772 | – | 11 | 1,094 | 4,040 | 45,728 | 39,166 | – | 20 | 38,804 |

From the above table it will be seen that there has been a decrease of £41,772 in "in-maintenance and clothing," £11 in cost of "deaf and dumb and blind," £1,094 in "salaries and rations of officers," and of £4,040 in "all other expenses," but an increase of £1,189 in "out-door relief."

12. The following is a statement of the Parliamentary Grant for Medical and Educational purposes, and of its distribution for the year ended 25th March, 1875 :—

| | Amount Claimed and Granted for the Year. | | |
|---|---|---|---|
| | £ | s. | d. |
| Medical purposes, . . . | 69,962 | 10 | 8 |
| Educational purposes, . . . | 8,745 | 19 | 4 |
| Total, . . . | 78,708 | 10 | 0 |

The total amount claimed and allowed under the Parliamentary Grant for the year ended March, 1875, namely, £78,708 10s., is £2,396 5s. 5d. in excess of the claim for the previous year, and arises chiefly from increases of salary.

13. Statement of the Annual Collection and Expenditure of Poor Rates for twenty-two years, ended on the 29th September, 1875, showing the Net Annual Value of Property rated, the Amount of Poor Rate collected, and the Expenditure under the Poor Relief and Medical Charities Acts, &c., for each year ended 29th September, from 1854 to 1875, inclusive.

| Year ended 29th September, | Net Annual Value of Property rated. | Amount of Poor Rate collected. | Expenditure for Relief of the Poor: In-Maintenance | Out-door Relief | [illegible] | Salaries and Rations of Officers | Other Expenses | Total Poor Relief Expenditure | Expenditure under Medical Charities and Vaccination Acts | Repayments under Annuities Acts | Expenses under the Burial Grounds Acts, paid out of the Poor Rates | Expenses under Registration Acts | Expenses under the Sanitary Acts | Payments under Cattle Plague Act | Expenses under the [illegible] Acts | Total Expenditure | Poundage of the Expenditure on Valuation: Poor Relief | Total |
|---|---|---|---|---|---|---|---|---|---|---|---|---|---|---|---|---|---|---|
| | £ | £ | £ | £ | £ | £ | £ | £ | £ | £ | £ | £ | £ | £ | £ | £ | s. d. | s. d. |
| 1854, . | 11,4[illegible] | 926,184 | 673,[illegible] | 8,713 | - | 137,417 | 146,[illegible] | 760,[illegible] | 88,782 | 73,936 | - | - | - | - | - | 921,[illegible] | 1 4 | 1 7½ |
| 1855, . | 11,565,[illegible] | 838,[illegible] | 452,[illegible] | 4,763 | - | 119,[illegible] | 127,[illegible] | [illegible] | 86,[illegible] | 14,238 | - | - | - | - | - | 763,[illegible] | 1 [illegible] | 1 4½ |
| 1856, | 11,[illegible] | 728,[illegible] | 350,[illegible] | 2,[illegible] | - | 118,[illegible] | 102,[illegible] | 474,[illegible] | 80,[illegible] | 4,440 | - | - | - | - | - | [illegible] | 0 11[illegible] | 1 1½ |
| 1857, . | 11,877,[illegible] | [illegible] | [illegible] | 2,412 | - | 104,745 | 101,947 | [illegible] | 90,160 | 1,418 | - | - | - | - | - | [illegible] | [illegible] | 1 0 |
| 1858, | 12,[illegible] | [illegible] | [illegible] | 2,130 | - | 97,[illegible] | [illegible] | 437,173 | 92,[illegible] | 349 | - | - | - | - | - | [illegible] | 0 9 | 0 11 |
| 1859, | 12,[illegible] | [illegible] | [illegible] | 2,[illegible] | - | [illegible] | [illegible] | 413,712 | [illegible] | [illegible] | - | - | - | - | - | [illegible] | 0 [illegible] | 0 10 |
| 1860, . | 12,[illegible] | [illegible] | 272,[illegible] | 4,346 | - | [illegible] | [illegible] | 454,[illegible] | 104,347 | 87 | - | - | - | - | - | [illegible] | 0 9 | 0 11 |
| 1861, | [illegible] | [illegible] | [illegible] | [illegible] | - | [illegible] | [illegible] | [illegible] | [illegible] | [illegible] | - | - | - | - | - | [illegible] | 0 10 | 1 0 |
| 1862, . | 12,[illegible] | [illegible] | [illegible] | 14,780 | - | [illegible] | [illegible] | 51[illegible] | 109,[illegible] | [illegible] | 117 | - | - | - | - | [illegible] | 0 11[illegible] | 1 1 |
| 1863, . | 12,[illegible] | 722,[illegible] | [illegible] | 18,[illegible] | 4,[illegible] | [illegible] | [illegible] | [illegible] | [illegible] | [illegible] | 2,[illegible] | - | - | - | - | 716,[illegible] | 0 11[illegible] | 1 1[illegible] |
| 1864, | 12,764,[illegible] | 764,[illegible] | [illegible] | [illegible] | 4,[illegible] | 87,[illegible] | 104,[illegible] | [illegible] | 114,[illegible] | - | 653 | 23,[illegible] | - | - | - | 734,[illegible] | 0 11[illegible] | 1 1[illegible] |
| 1865, | 12,[illegible] | 747,[illegible] | [illegible] | [illegible] | [illegible] | [illegible] | [illegible] | [illegible] | 117,[illegible] | - | 716 | 13,[illegible] | - | - | - | 782,[illegible] | 0 11[illegible] | 1 [illegible] |
| 1866, . | 12,[illegible] | 749,747 | 271,[illegible] | [illegible] | [illegible] | [illegible] | 102,[illegible] | 611,[illegible] | 116,[illegible] | - | [illegible] | 12,[illegible] | - | 13,[illegible] | - | 784,[illegible] | 0 11[illegible] | 1 [illegible] |
| 1867, . | 12,[illegible] | [illegible] | [illegible] | [illegible] | 6,144 | [illegible] | [illegible] | [illegible] | 116,[illegible] | - | 1,[illegible] | 12,[illegible] | 16,[illegible] | [illegible] | - | [illegible] | 1 [illegible] | 1 [illegible] |
| 1868, . | 12,117,[illegible] | [illegible] | [illegible] | 44,785 | 6,[illegible] | [illegible] | 110,[illegible] | 702,[illegible] | [illegible] | - | [illegible] | 12,[illegible] | [illegible] | - | - | [illegible] | 1 1 | 1 [illegible] |
| 1869, . | 12,[illegible] | [illegible] | [illegible] | [illegible] | [illegible] | [illegible] | [illegible] | [illegible] | [illegible] | - | 2,400 | 12,[illegible] | [illegible] | - | - | [illegible] | 1 [illegible] | 1 [illegible] |
| 1870, | 12,[illegible] | [illegible] | [illegible] | [illegible] | 7,[illegible] | [illegible] | [illegible] | [illegible] | [illegible] | - | 1,[illegible] | [illegible] | [illegible] | - | - | [illegible] | 1 [illegible] | 1 [illegible] |
| 1871, . | 13,[illegible] | [illegible] | [illegible] | [illegible] | 7,[illegible] | 127,[illegible] | [illegible] | [illegible] | [illegible] | - | 1,[illegible] | 12,[illegible] | 4,[illegible] | - | - | [illegible] | 1 [illegible] | 1 [illegible] |
| 1872, . | 13,[illegible] | [illegible] | [illegible] | [illegible] | [illegible] | [illegible] | 114,[illegible] | [illegible] | [illegible] | - | [illegible] | [illegible] | 6,[illegible] | - | - | [illegible] | 1 [illegible] | 1 4 |
| 1873, | 13,[illegible] | [illegible] | [illegible] | 81,[illegible] | 7,[illegible] | [illegible] | [illegible] | [illegible] | [illegible] | - | [illegible] | 10,[illegible] | [illegible] | - | [illegible] | [illegible] | 1 [illegible] | 1 [illegible] |
| 1874, . | 13,[illegible] | 941,[illegible] | [illegible] | [illegible] | [illegible] | [illegible] | [illegible] | [illegible] | [illegible] | - | 4,[illegible] | [illegible] | 7,[illegible] | [illegible] | [illegible] | 1,[illegible] | 1 [illegible] | 1 6 |
| 1875, . | 13,[illegible] | [illegible] | 414,[illegible] | [illegible] | [illegible] | [illegible] | [illegible] | [illegible] | 141,[illegible] | - | 4,[illegible] | 13,[illegible] | [illegible] | 2,[illegible] | [illegible] | [illegible] | 1 [illegible] | 1 [illegible] |

*Collection and Expenditure.* 19

Hence it will be seen that the total expenditure of poor-rates for all purposes, viz., relief, medical relief, burial grounds, registration of births, deaths, and marriages, sanitary measures, and expenses under Superannuation Acts was in 1874 £1,001,989, making a poundage of 1s. 6*d.* on the valuation. In 1875 the expenditure for all purposes was £975,044, or 1*s.* 5¾*d.* in the pound, showing a decrease of £26,945, notwithstanding that the sanitary expenditure was £25,016 more than in 1874.

## Medical Charities Act, and Vaccination Acts.

14. We next submit to your Grace the report of our proceedings under these Acts of Parliament for the year ended 30th September, 1875.

The subjoined table exhibits in the usual form the progress and fluctuations of the medical relief afforded under the Medical Charities Act for each year of the twelve years ended 30th September, 1875, in each province, and for the whole of Ireland.

The cases are distinguished, as usual, into those prescribed for at the Dispensaries, and those attended at the patients' houses, each class of cases occupying a separate column.

SUMMARY of the NUMBER of CASES of MEDICAL RELIEF afforded under the Medical Charities Act

| Period. | Province of Ulster. | | | Province of Munster. | | | Province of Leinster. | | | Province of Connaught. | | | Total for Ireland. | | |
|---|---|---|---|---|---|---|---|---|---|---|---|---|---|---|---|
| | Dispensary Tickets. | Visiting Tickets. | Total. | Dispensary Tickets. | Visiting Tickets. | Total. | Dispensary Tickets. | Visiting Tickets. | Total. | Dispensary Tickets. | Visiting Tickets. | Total. | Dispensary Tickets. | Visiting Tickets. | Total. |
| | (1.) | (2.) | (3.) | (4.) | (5.) | (6.) | (7.) | (8.) | (9.) | (10.) | (11.) | (12.) | (13.) | (14.) | (15.) |
| Year ended 29th Sept., 1864, | [illegible] | [illegible] | 287,944 | [illegible] | [illegible] | [illegible] | [illegible] | [illegible] | [illegible] | 87,141 | 17,251 | [illegible] | [illegible] | 187,297 | [illegible] |
| " 1865, | [illegible] | [illegible] | [illegible] | [illegible] | [illegible] | 273,411 | [illegible] | 63,139 | [illegible] | [illegible] | 19,915 | [illegible] | [illegible] | [illegible] | [illegible] |
| " 1866, | [illegible] | [illegible] | [illegible] | 194,730 | [illegible] | [illegible] | 187,385 | [illegible] | [illegible] | [illegible] | [illegible] | [illegible] | [illegible] | [illegible] | [illegible] |
| " 1867, | [illegible] | [illegible] | 173,712 | [illegible] | [illegible] | [illegible] | [illegible] | 63,448 | [illegible] | 72,747 | [illegible] | [illegible] | [illegible] | [illegible] | [illegible] |
| " 1868, | [illegible] | [illegible] | 178,700 | [illegible] | 54,476 | [illegible] | [illegible] | [illegible] | 204,494 | [illegible] | 17,220 | [illegible] | [illegible] | [illegible] | [illegible] |
| " 1869, | [illegible] | [illegible] | [illegible] | 169,443 | [illegible] | [illegible] | 199,274 | [illegible] | [illegible] | [illegible] | [illegible] | [illegible] | [illegible] | [illegible] | [illegible] |
| " 1870, | [illegible] | [illegible] | [illegible] | [illegible] | 67,815 | [illegible] | [illegible] | 64,884 | [illegible] | [illegible] | [illegible] | [illegible] | [illegible] | [illegible] | 714,424 |
| " 1871, | 119,792 | [illegible] | 174,781 | [illegible] | [illegible] | [illegible] | 180,091 | [illegible] | [illegible] | [illegible] | [illegible] | [illegible] | [illegible] | [illegible] | 742,878 |
| " 1872, | [illegible] | [illegible] | [illegible] | 133,291 | [illegible] | [illegible] | [illegible] | [illegible] | [illegible] | [illegible] | [illegible] | [illegible] | [illegible] | [illegible] | [illegible] |
| " 1873, | [illegible] | [illegible] | [illegible] | [illegible] | [illegible] | [illegible] | [illegible] | [illegible] | [illegible] | [illegible] | 18,871 | 81,747 | [illegible] | [illegible] | [illegible] |
| " 1874, | [illegible] | [illegible] | [illegible] | [illegible] | [illegible] | [illegible] | [illegible] | [illegible] | [illegible] | [illegible] | [illegible] | [illegible] | [illegible] | [illegible] | [illegible] |
| " 1875, | [illegible] | [illegible] | [illegible] | [illegible] | 44,794 | [illegible] | 169,484 | [illegible] | [illegible] | [illegible] | [illegible] | [illegible] | [illegible] | [illegible] | [illegible] |

The difference in the years 1873–4 and 1874–5 is thus made up in the four provinces—

In Ulster there has been an increase of 1,479 cases at the Dispensaries, and an increase of 7,699 of those attended at the patients' houses.

In Munster there has been a decrease of 2,565 cases at the Dispensaries, and an increase of 2,875 of those attended at the patients' houses.

In Leinster there has been a decrease of 1,406 cases at the Dispensaries, and an increase of domiciliary cases of 967.

And in Connaught there has been a decrease of 3,005 cases at the Dispensaries, and an increase in the number of cases attended at the patients' homes of 983.

The three last columns in the tables show for the totals of all Ireland a decrease for 1874–5 of 5,497 Dispensary cases, and an increase of 12,524 of the more serious cases attended at the homes of the patients, giving a total increase, including both classes of cases of patients, of 7,027 cases for 1874–5, compared with the previous year.

## VACCINATION.

15. In the following table are shown the number of cases of vaccination in each year from 1853 to 1875; the compulsory Act having been passed in 1864:—

TABLE.

| | Number of Cases of Vaccination. | | Number of Cases of Vaccination. |
|---|---|---|---|
| Year ended Sept. 30th, 1853, . | 43,332 | Year ended Sept. 30th, 1865, . | 169,142 |
| " " 1854, . | 52,844 | " " 1866, . | 137,124 |
| " " 1855, . | 46,711 | " " 1867, . | 125,741 |
| " " 1856, . | 84,131 | " " 1868, . | 131,426 |
| " " 1857, . | 47,855 | " " 1869, . | 125,672 |
| " " 1858, . | 54,984 | " " 1870, . | 140,220 |
| " " 1859, . | 140,411 | " " 1871, . | 179,889 |
| " " 1860, . | 107,305 | " " 1872, . | 282,484 |
| " " 1861, . | 90,255 | " " 1873, . | 138,873 |
| " " 1862, . | 89,863 | " " 1874, . | 139,567 |
| " " 1863, . | 106,510 | " " 1875, . | 137,340 |
| " " 1864, . | 191,810 | | |

The next table presents the record of the vaccinations performed at the Dispensaries and Vaccination Stations since 1864, distinguishing the cases of children born since January, 1864, from those of persons born before that time, the former being liable to, the latter exempt from, compulsory vaccination.

[TABLE.

TOTALS for Ireland of Number of Cases of Vaccination performed during the Years ended September 30th.

| Years. | Cases of Children born since January 1st, 1864. | Other Cases. | Totals. |
|---|---|---|---|
| 1865, | 97,160 | 71,982 | 169,142 |
| 1866, | 104,730 | 82,394 | 187,124 |
| 1867, | 107,473 | 18,268 | 125,741 |
| 1868, | 118,613 | 12,813 | 131,426 |
| 1869, | 117,912 | 7,760 | 125,672 |
| 1870, | 135,057 | 5,163 | 140,220 |
| 1871, | 139,053 | 40,836 | 179,889 |
| 1872, | 142,662 | 139,822 | 282,484 |
| 1873, | 119,319 | 19,554 | 138,873 |
| 1874, | 119,337 | 20,250 | 139,587 |
| 1875, | 119,675 | 17,665 | 137,340 |

For the last four years returns have been made by the Dispensary Medical Officers of the vaccinations under the Compulsory Vaccination Act, distinguishing the cases of infants under one year old from those of children of more advanced age.

These returns are given in the next table.

TABLE.

| 1872. | | |
|---|---|---|
| Children born since 1st January, 1864. | | |
| — | Under one year old when vaccinated. | Above one year old when vaccinated. |
| Ulster, | 38,304 | 4,948 |
| Munster, | 29,908 | 15,442 |
| Leinster, | 24,461 | 7,140 |
| Connaught, | 16,549 | 5,910 |
| Total, | 109,222 | 33,440 |

| 1873. | | |
|---|---|---|
| Children born since 1st January, 1864. | | |
| — | Under one year old when vaccinated. | Above one year old when vaccinated. |
| Ulster, | 35,836 | 3,737 |
| Munster, | 26,718 | 6,776 |
| Leinster, | 22,369 | 3,201 |
| Connaught, | 15,143 | 5,544 |
| Total, | 100,061 | 19,258 |

| 1874. | | |
|---|---|---|
| Children born since 1st January, 1864. | | |
| — | Under one year old when vaccinated. | Above one year old when vaccinated. |
| Ulster, | 34,953 | 6,315 |
| Munster, | 25,450 | 6,177 |
| Leinster, | 22,042 | 3,383 |
| Connaught, | 14,405 | 6,612 |
| Total, | 96,850 | 22,487 |

TABLE—*continued.*

| 1875. | | |
|---|---|---|
| Children born since 1st January, 1864. | | |
| — | Under one year old when vaccinated. | Above one year old when vaccinated. |
| Ulster, . . . . . . . . | 33,353 | 3,585 |
| Munster, . . . . . . . . | 25,925 | 6,651 |
| Leinster, . . . . . . . . | 21,693 | 3,480 |
| Connaught, . . . . . . . | 13,399 | 11,639 |
| Total, . . . . . . | 94,370 | 25,305 |

16. The following table contains a summary of the total number of cases of vaccination during the year ending 30th September, 1875, in each of the four provinces, the cases being classified under the headings, "under one year old when vaccinated," "above one year old," and "other persons."

| Provinces. | Children Born since 1st January, 1864. | | Other Persons. | Total. |
|---|---|---|---|---|
| | Under one year old when Vaccinated. | Above one year old when Vaccinated. | | |
| Ulster, . . . . | 33,353 | 3,585 | 1,155 | 38,043 |
| Munster, . . . . | 25,925 | 6,651 | 1,281 | 33,857 |
| Leinster, . . . . | 21,693 | 3,480 | 391 | 25,564 |
| Connaught, . . . . | 13,399 | 11,639 | 14,838 | 39,876 |
| Total Ireland, . | 94,370 | 25,305 | 17,665 | 137,340 |

The following are the totals under each of the above headings for the previous year ended 30th September, 1874:—

96,830 22,487 20,250 139,587

It will be observed that there is a decrease in the total number of cases vaccinated and revaccinated in all Ireland of 2,247 cases.

There was a decrease in cases "under one year" of age in each of the four Provinces; but there was an increase in Connaught both in cases "above one year old," and "other persons." This increase was attributable to an outbreak of small-pox in that Province.

The increase is exhibited in the following table:—

| — | Children Born since 1st January, 1864. | | Other Persons. | Total. |
|---|---|---|---|---|
| | Under one year old when Vaccinated. | Above one year old when Vaccinated. | | |
| Connaught, 1874, . | 14,405 | 6,612 | 1,365 | 22,382 |
| Connaught, 1875, . | 13,399 | 11,639 | 14,838 | 39,876 |
| Net Increase, . . | — | 5,027 | 13,473 | — |
| Decrease, . . . | 1,006 | — | — | — |

17. The impulse given to vaccination in this year in Connaught was owing to the terror occasioned by the cases of small-pox which occurred, and the opportunity thereby afforded to the Medical Officers to extend the practice; the people of all classes willingly submitting to the operation under the influence of the temporary apprehension of contagion and death.

Similar results followed the widespread occurrence of small-pox in other districts heretofore; notably so in the Province of Ulster in 1874, when 57,861 cases of vaccination took place in that Province alone out of the 189,587 cases in all Ireland in that year.

But, however satisfactory it is to know that a certain number of persons have been themselves protected by vaccination from the disease of small-pox, and, so far from being a means of conveying the disease to other persons, it is not to such exceptional and spasmodic efforts that the public should be indebted for protection.

The complete vaccination of the population should be secured by sustained and continuous attention on the part of the Registrars of Births, Medical Officers of Dispensary Districts, and the several Committees of Management, and by Boards of Guardians, who are responsible for directing proceedings to enforce the provisions of the Vaccination Acts, and lastly, and mainly, by a firm administration of the law by the Magistracy, who are apt to show excessive leniency in dealing with these particular cases.

A provision is made by the 58th section of the Public Health Act, Ireland, 1874, to enable any Justice of the Peace to make an order for the vaccination of any child under the age of fourteen who has not been successfully vaccinated, nor has had the small-pox, upon information of the facts being given to him by any Registrar, or Officer appointed by the Guardians to enforce the provisions of the Vaccination Acts; but it does not appear that this power has been exercised hitherto, or, at all events, not to any extent.

## SMALL-POX.

18. The number of deaths in Workhouses from small-pox, and the number of cases of the disease treated by Dispensary Medical Officers for each of the last twelve years are given in the following table:—

[TABLE.

C

DEATHS in WORKHOUSES from SMALL-POX, and NUMBER of CASES of SMALL-POX treated by DISPENSARY MEDICAL OFFICERS.

| Deaths in Workhouses from Small-pox. | | Number of Cases of Small-pox treated by Medical Officers of Dispensary Districts. | |
|---|---|---|---|
| PERIOD. 52 Weeks ended | Number of Deaths. | PERIOD. 52 Weeks ended | Number of Cases. |
| 11th February, 1865, . . | 145 | 30th September, 1864, . . | 1,005 |
| 10th February, 1866, . . | 59 | 30th September, 1865, . . | 2,000 |
| 9th February, 1867, . . | 9 | 30th September, 1866, . . | 579 |
| 8th February, 1868, . . | 5 | 30th September, 1867, . . | 105 |
| 6th February, 1869, . . | 3 | 30th September, 1868, . . | 155 |
| 5th February, 1870, . . | 1 | 30th September, 1869, . . | 27 |
| 4th February, 1871, . . | 18 | 30th September, 1870, . . | 51 |
| 3rd February, 1872, . . | 463 | 30th September, 1871, . . | 773 |
| 1st February, 1873, . . | 677 | 30th September, 1872, . . | 10,317 |
| 31st January, 1874, . . | 110 | 30th September, 1873, . . | 936 |
| 30th January, 1875, . . | 142 | 30th September, 1874, . . | 961 |
| 30th January, 1876, . . | 41 | 30th September, 1875, . . | 881 |

The following table shows in each Province where the disease prevailed to the greatest extent, and the quarters of the year when it most prevailed:—

SUMMARY of SMALL-POX cases attended by Dispensary Medical Officers during the year ended 30th September, 1875,—taken from their Quarterly Returns.

| PROVINCES. | Quarter, 31st Dec., 1874. | Quarter, 31st Mar., 1875. | Quarter, 30th June, 1875. | Quarter, 30th Sept., 1875. | Total. |
|---|---|---|---|---|---|
| Ulster, . . . . | 41 | 27 | 41 | 37 | 146 |
| Munster, . . . . | 8 | – | – | – | 8 |
| Leinster, . . . . | – | 5 | 47 | 1 | 53 |
| Connaught, . . . | 160 | 218 | 251 | 45 | 674 |
| Total Ireland, . | 209 | 250 | 339 | 83 | 881 |

REGISTRAR-GENERAL'S RETURNS.

Number of DEATHS from SMALL-POX during the year ended 31st December, 1875, abstracted from the Quarterly Returns of the Registrar-General.

| PROVINCES. | 1st Quarter, 31st Mar., 1875. | 2nd Quarter, 30th June, 1875. | 3rd Quarter, 30th Sept., 1875. | 4th Quarter, 31st Dec., 1875. | Total. |
|---|---|---|---|---|---|
| Ulster, . . . . | 7 | 13 | 5 | 5 | 30 |
| Munster, . . . . | 8 | – | – | 1 | 9 |
| Leinster, . . . . | 2 | 8 | – | – | 10 |
| Connaught, . . . | 222 | 204 | 63 | 5 | 494 |
| Total Ireland, . | 239 | 225 | 68 | 11 | 543 |

The returns of the Registrar-General exhibit an increase in the deaths by small-pox from 540 in 1874 to 543 in 1875.

19. The most serious outbreak of the disease during the twelve months was in the province of Connaught, where 674 persons out of the whole 881 treated by the Dispensary Officers in Ireland were attacked; the disease prevailing in the most virulent form in the Unions of Claremorris, Loughrea, Swineford, Tobercurry, and Tuam. CONNAUGHT.

The disease had existed in the Swineford and Castlebar Unions more or less in the year 1874, but the first case which was reported in the Tuam Union in the year 1875 was on January the 10th, when the Medical Officer of the Workhouse furnished the particulars of the case of "a traveller" from Mullingar, who stated that— Tuam Union.

"On his way towards Athlone he went into a cabin about six miles off, where he remained for two hours, and that there was a child there who had an eruption similar to what he laboured under."

He remained two nights in Dunmore, and from thence came the next report of a case, namely, on the 16th January.

The disease soon extended its ravages to Tuam, where 88 persons were attacked.

In the Ballinrobe Union, where there were 22 cases, the infection was reported to have been brought by the family of "an itinerant pedlar and tinker," from the Ballina Union. Ballinrobe Union

In Castlerea Union, where there were 20 cases, it was stated that the disease was brought "by a tramp." Castlerea Union.

In the Claremorris Union, where there were 103 cases, the disease being more or less prevalent during the whole of the twelve months, the Medical Officer of the Ballyhaunis Dispensary District stated that he had no doubt that "inoculation" for small-pox had been practised in the District, and that he had no doubt but to that practice the importation of the disease might be entirely attributed there. Claremorris Union.

The Medical Officer had taken active steps, so far as he could, to prevent the spread of the disease, having—

"Supplied disinfectants, reported the matter to the Guardians, had the houses limewashed, and the yards cleaned up, and having on all available occasions cautioned the people against frequenting or attending 'wakes' in infected localities, and caused the speedy interment of the bodies of persons who died of the disease."

He also "re-vaccinated over 600 persons with manifest advantage; those neglecting this precaution being in many instances struck down with the disease in the midst of, and to the exclusion of other members of the same family who had lately undergone the operation."

Dr. Roughan, the Inspector in charge of Unions in the county of Sligo, in reporting in April, 1875, on the question whether it was advisable that the Sligo Militia should be assembled for training, having regard to the prevalence of small-pox in certain parts of the county during some months previous, stated that—

"Small-pox of a very malignant type still prevailed to a serious extent in Tobercurry Union, and in the neighbouring Unions of Swineford, Tobercurry Union.

Swineford Union. Castlebar Union. Castlebar, and Claremorris;" that "much alarm prevailed amongst the intelligent inhabitants; that the Magistrates had postponed holding Petty Sessions; and that the public schools were closed."

Loughrea Union. 20. The alarm and apprehension felt elsewhere when small-pox broke out were exemplified, however, in even a more remarkable degree in the Loughrea Union, where the disease assumed its largest proportions during the two last quarters of the year ending 30th September, 1875.

On the 1st of March, 1875, the Medical Officer of the Athenry Dispensary District, Dr. Leonard, reported that a very bad case of small-pox had come into the District from Tuam the day before, and that the following was the history of the case:—

"William Burke, aged about 22 years, a native of Newcastle, in this Dispensary District, took ill on Saturday, the 27th of February, in Tuam, where he was employed as a baker's assistant. He was visited by Dr. Turner on Monday, who ordered his immediate removal to hospital; as also that his bed and blanket should be either disinfected or destroyed; but instead of complying with the Medical Officer's instructions, he was conveyed by midday train to Athenry, where he arrived at about 12 o'clock, being exceedingly weak, and suffering from dreadful gastric irritation since he left Tuam. He had to remain in a house in Athenry for some hours, when a car was procured, and the poor sufferer conveyed to his father's residence, a distance of about six miles. I visited him at about 9 o'clock, P.M., and gave full instructions to his friends."

To the introduction of this case into the Athenry District may be attributed the attack of 171 persons (five of them being private patients), and the death of 49 out of this number.

His removal into the Athenry District from Tuam was *primâ facie* a wilful infraction of the 38th section of the Sanitary Act, 1866, which provides for the infliction of a penalty not exceeding five pounds on any—

"Person with infectious disorder exposing himself, or on any person in charge of such sufferer causing such exposure;"

and the Board at once directed their Inspector, Dr. Brodie, to make inquiry as to the parties responsible for the act.

It appeared on inquiry that Mr. P. Corcoran, the baker in Tuam, in whose house he had resided, recommended him to return home, assisted in getting him ready for the journey, took a railway ticket for him, and put him into a railway carriage; and then fearing, as it was stated, detection by the Constabulary, immediately left the station and went away.

The particulars having been reported to the Government the Board were informed that the Attorney-General had advised that Mr. Corcoran should be proceeded against as had been suggested by the Board; and this, after some unavoidable postponement, was done, and Mr. Corcoran was fined £2 10*s*., or in default sentenced to one month's imprisonment.

William Burke died at his father's house shortly after arriving there; and the next four cases reported in this District were those of the father of William Burke, the Rev. Mr. Walsh, R.C. Curate, who had attended his dying bed, a member of the family of Dr. Leonard, and the Parish Clerk.

The Rev. Mr. Walsh was taken ill in "Kineen's Hotel," Athenry, and died there on the 29th March, the hotel having in the meantime been compulsorily closed in pursuance of the 39th section of the Sanitary Act.

Several fresh cases were then reported, and the Board of Guardians were requested to provide hospital accommodation for the treatment of persons labouring under the disease.

The Board of Guardians, on the 17th April, ordered an iron hospital, capable of accommodating 12 patients, from a firm in London, but very great difficulty was experienced in obtaining a site whereon to place the hospital, partly from the unsuitability of some of the sites proposed, and partly to the determined and violent opposition exhibited by persons in the neighbourhood to the establishment of an hospital at all.

However, eventually a house was rented near Athenry and fitted up and used for the purpose, two skilled nurses having been obtained from the Cork-street Hospital, Dublin, to attend the patients; and an Assistant, Relieving, and Sub-Sanitary Officer was appointed.

21. During the excitement and alarm which arose in the neighbourhood of Athenry when the disease broke out, the Workhouse van which was being sent to convey a patient to the Hospital at the Workhouse was attacked by a mob, the horse and driver sent back, and the van itself burned, having been maliciously set on fire.

The town or village of Athenry had been described at the commencement of the outbreak as in a very filthy and discreditable condition, but steps were taken to improve the sewerage and improve the sanitary condition of the place. It had been ascertained that those portions of it that were drained some few years since had escaped the disease, while the streets that were undrained had suffered severely from it.

On the 13th June, Dr. Brodie, Local Government Inspector, reported to the Board that—

"The small-pox was on the decline," and that "it was to be hoped that with close attention to whitewashing, cleansing, and disinfecting the houses, together with the supply of clothes, bed-ticks, and fresh straw given to the patients leaving Hospital, through the benevolence of a few charitable ladies who had raised a fund for the purpose, the disease would soon be got under;"

and on the 1st of August Dr. Brodie reported that no one had been attacked in the town during the twenty-two days previous to that date.

The correspondence relating to the outbreak of small-pox in the Loughrea Union has already been printed, in obedience to an order of the House of Commons, dated 13th July, 1875, and is not therefore included in the Appendix.

22. The successful prosecution of Mr. P. Corcoran, of Tuam, for causing William Burke to be conveyed by railway to Athenry, Exposure.

has been already referred to, and there was another case of prosecution for exposure without proper precaution.

Mr. John J. Dillon, of Athenry, a shopkeeper, was proceeded against for wilfully exposing himself whilst suffering from small-pox, in the street and at the Railway Station, and by travelling on the railway from Athenry to Galway, contrary to the 38th section of the Sanitary Act, 1866; and on the 31st August he was fined £3, with costs of court, or in default of payment, to be imprisoned for two calendar months in the gaol of Galway, with hard labour.

Inoculation. The Board learned, from reports of the Constabulary and other sources, that the practice of inoculation with variolous matter to produce the disease of small-pox had prevailed to a great extent in the Tobercurry Union, as it had done elsewhere, and with fatal results in many cases, as it was apprehended; and the efforts to bring a quack inoculator, named "Charles Stenson," to justice were finally successful, he having been tried at the Sligo Assizes on the 22nd July, 1875, "found guilty of the manslaughter of Roger Gethins, by inoculating him with small-pox virus, and sentenced to five years' penal servitude."

Ulster. — Belfast Union.

23. With respect to the small-pox in Belfast Union, the Inspector, Mr. O'Brien, reports as follows in his periodical accounts of the condition of the Union:—

"14*th December*, 1874.—I am happy to say that the small-pox epidemic which, after having almost entirely subsided, re-appeared at the commencement of the present year, and continued from that time up to August last to extend its ravages, has since then steadily declined, and can now, I trust, be pronounced to be again extinct, there being at present no cases of the disease under treatment in any of the Districts visited by me on this occasion."

"22*nd June*, 1875.—There are four cases of small-pox in the Hospital, but they are all of a light form and are all convalescent."

"3*rd December*, 1875.—Small-pox, which so long and so extensively prevailed in this Union, may be now said to have almost entirely disappeared, not a single case being under treatment between the 13th and 27th ultimo; and when I inspected the wards appropriated to the treatment of the disease, they contained only one patient, a young man of eighteen, just admitted from the town, and whose attack appeared to be of a mild type."

With the exception of the cases in the Belfast Union, the Board are happy to be able to record that but two cases have been reported by the Dispensary Medical officers, in the quarter ended 31st December, 1875, in the whole of Ireland.

### Expenditure.

24. The next table gives the expenditure under the Medical Charities and Vaccination Acts for the last eleven years ended 29th September, 1875—

[Table.

MEDICAL CHARITIES EXPENDITURE, Years ended 29th September.

| Year. | Ulster. | Munster. | Leinster. | Connaught. | Total. |
|---|---|---|---|---|---|
| | £ | £ | £ | £ | £ |
| 1865, | 31,492 | 34,923 | 34,782 | 15,841 | 117,038 |
| 1866, | 31,149 | 34,464 | 34,459 | 16,243 | 116,315 |
| 1867, | 32,020 | 35,341 | 34,885 | 15,872 | 118,118 |
| 1868, | 34,017 | 35,431 | 36,401 | 16,135 | 121,965 |
| 1869, | 34,623 | 35,646 | 36,624 | 16,825 | 123,718 |
| 1870, | 36,464 | 37,686 | 38,130 | 17,656 | 129,936 |
| 1871, | 36,881 | 38,862 | 41,151 | 18,111 | 135,005 |
| 1872, | 38,906 | 41,378 | 42,480 | 18,884 | 141,648 |
| 1873, | 38,893 | 40,061 | 42,081 | 18,135 | 139,170 |
| 1874, | 40,334 | 39,622 | 41,953 | 19,018 | 140,922 |
| 1875, | 39,832 | 40,029 | 41,743 | 19,848 | 141,452 |

And the following shows in more detail, and under the usual heads, a comparative statement of the expenditure for the two years ended September 29th, 1874, and 1875, respectively :—

MEDICAL CHARITIES EXPENDITURE.

| | 1874. | 1875. |
|---|---|---|
| 1. Medicines and medical appliances, | £24,606 | £23,736 |
| 2. Rent of Dispensary buildings, | 8,313 | 8,811 |
| 3. Books, forms, stationery, printing, and advertising, | 1,105 | 1,252 |
| 4. Salaries of Medical Officers, | 86,070 | 87,174 |
| 4. Salaries of Apothecaries, | 2,650 | 2,713 |
| 5. Fuel, porters, and incidental expenses, | 10,322 | 10,157 |
| EXPENSES UNDER VACCINATION ACTS: | | |
| 6. Vaccination fees and other expenses:— | | |
| Fees to Medical Officers, | 7,016 | 6,748 |
| Other expenses, | 832 | 861 |
| Total, | £140,922 | £141,452 |

---

## LOCAL GOVERNMENT (IRELAND) ACTS.

### *Provisional Orders, &c.*

25. Since the date of our last Report we have issued the following provisional orders:—

A provisional order, dated 4th June, 1875, authorizing the Town Commissioners of Coleraine, acting as the Burial Board for the borough of Coleraine, under the Burial Grounds (Ireland) Act, 1856, to put in force the provisions of the Lands Clauses Act, 1845, in relation to the purchase and taking of land otherwise than by agreement, in respect to certain land therein mentioned, and to use the land so to be acquired for the purpose of providing a new Burial Ground for the borough of Coleraine. This order has been confirmed by Act of Parliament (38 and 39 Vic., ch. cxx.)

A provisional order, authorizing the Corporation of Londonderry to put in force the provisions of the Lands Clauses Act, 1845, with respect to the purchase and taking of land otherwise than by agreement, in respect of certain land therein mentioned (already in the occupation of the Corporation), and to use and continue to use such lands for the purpose of the Waterworks constructed by the Corporation thereon; authorizing the Corporation to borrow on the credit of the Improvement Rate a further sum of £15,000 in addition to the sums authorized to be borrowed under the Londonderry Improvement Acts.

A provisional order, dated 2nd December, 1875, authorizing the Corporation of the borough of Wexford to put in force with reference to certain Lands, Water, and Water-rights, therein mentioned, the powers of the Lands Clauses Acts, with respect to the purchase and taking of land otherwise than by agreement, and to use such Lands, Water, and Water-rights, in order to afford a supply of water to the District, and for the construction of Water-works; also to make rates to be called "the Domestic Water Rate," and the "Public Water Rate," to borrow money for defraying expenses incurred under the order, and to make regulations to prevent waste or contamination of the water.

A provisional order, dated 31st January, 1876, authorizing the Commissioners of the township of Dalkey to put in force the provisions of the Lands Clauses Acts with respect to the purchase and taking, otherwise than by agreement, of certain lands therein mentioned, and to use such land for the purpose of certain works for the more effectual drainage and sewerage of the township; also to make a rate to defray the expenses of preparing the plans and estimate for the works and procuring the order.

26. In the following cases we have received petitions for Provisional Orders, but the proceedings have not yet terminated:—

From the Board of Guardians of Armagh Union, for power to put in force the provisions of the Lands Clauses Acts with respect to the purchase and taking of land otherwise than by agreement, with a view to proposed Waterworks for supplying the town and district of Keady.

From the Board of Guardians of Coleraine Union for similar powers, for the purpose of supplying Water to the town of Portrush.

From the Town Commissioners of Coleraine for similar powers, with a view to proposed Waterworks for supplying the town of Coleraine.

From the Board of Guardians of Dungannon Union for similar powers, with a view of providing a supply of Water for the town of Dungannon.

From the Board of Guardians of Galway Union for similar powers, with a view to providing a new Cemetery for the town of Galway.

From the Kingstown Township Commissioners for similar powers with a view to the improvement of the drainage of the township, and for various amendments of the Local Act for the government of the township.

From the Board of Guardians of Omagh Union for similar powers, with a view to proposed Waterworks for supplying the town of Omagh and adjoining places.

From the Board of Guardians of Rathdown Union for similar powers, with reference to a scheme for the better drainage of the Workhouse. (In this case the Board have been advised by

Counsel, that the order cannot be made under the Law as it now stands).

From the Town Council of Waterford for the amendment of "The Waterford Water Act, 1871" (a local Act), by exempting a district called Ferrybank from the operation of the Act.

Applications have also been received under the 19th section of the Public Health Act from the Board of Guardians of Newtownards Union, as the Rural Sanitary Authority, and from the Town Commissioners of Newtownards as the Urban Sanitary Authority for the formation of a united district, consisting of the Electoral Divisions of Newtownards and Newtownards South, which include the town of Newtownards for the purposes of the Burial Grounds Acts.

27. We have received applications from the towns of Tipperary and Arklow, with a view to the adoption of the provisions of the Towns Improvement Act in those towns. In the case of Tipperary the provisions of the 9th George IV., c. 82, were formerly in force, but no Commissioners had been elected under the Act for several years. The requisite preliminary proceedings having been all gone through, the provisions of the Towns Improvement Act were adopted, and Commissioners have been elected. In Arklow the requisite meeting of the Rate-payers under the statute has not yet been held, but the Board have issued orders and directions as required by the Act for convening such meeting.

28. By-laws have been submitted to, and approved by us for the regulation of markets and fairs in the towns of Newtownards, Maryborough, and Roscommon; for the regulation of bathing places in the townships of Killiney and Ballybrack; for the regulation of hackney carriages, and the appointment of porters in the township of Queenstown; for the regulation of common lodging-houses, other than those under the Common Lodging-Houses Acts, in the city of Limerick; and for the regulation of common lodging-houses under the Common Lodging-Houses Acts in the following Unions and towns or townships, namely, the Unions of Loughrea, Carlow, Kilkenny, Limavady, Gorey, Carrick-on-Shannon, Celbridge, Mitchelstown, Bawnboy, Cashel, Kells, Ballymahon, Strabane, Tobercurry, Lisnaskea, Mohill, Newcastle, Trim, Bailieboro', Letterkenny, Carrickmacross, Navan, Oldcastle, Callan, Omagh, Granard, Dunmanway, Belfast, Naas, Bandon, Monaghan, Athy, Antrim, Skibbereen, North Dublin, Banbridge, Edenderry, Larne, Donegal, Rathdown, and Nenagh; the towns of Belfast, Ennis, Galway, and Enniskillen; and the township of Rathmines and Rathgar.

29. Supplementary by-laws providing for the inspection of common lodging-houses by the Constabulary in accordance with the recommendation of the Board,* have also been adopted in the following places, namely, the Unions of Loughrea, Carlow,

* See Circular of 9th February, 1876—Appendix, C. II., No. 4, p. 60.

Limavady, Gorey, Carrick-on-Shannon, Celbridge, Mitchelstown, Bawnboy, Cashel, Kells, Ballymahon, Strabane, Mohill, Newcastle, Trim, Letterkenny, Oldcastle, Callan, Omagh, Granard, Dunmanway, Naas, Bandon, Monaghan, Banbridge, Castlecomer, Castlerea, Rathkeale, Larne, Donegal, Rathdown, Nenagh, Abbeyleix, and South Dublin; and the towns of Ennis and Enniskillen.

30. Orders have been made and gazetted, prohibiting further interments in the burial ground of Artane, in the parish of Artane, in the county of Dublin, and subject to certain exception in the burial ground of Abbotstown, in the parish of Castleknock, in the county of Dublin, and in the burial ground of Monkstown, in the parish of Monkstown, in the county of Dublin. We have also issued licences under the 10th section of the Burial Grounds Act, in certain individual cases, authorizing, where the circumstances seemed to warrant it, interments in burial grounds which had been ordered to be closed. These exceptional cases applied to the burial grounds of Cruagh, Whitechurch, and Monkstown, in the county of Dublin, the burial ground attached to the Church of St. Mark's, in the city of Dublin, the burial ground attached to the Chapel of Ease, in the city of Londonderry, the burial ground of Killaconenagh, in the county of Cork, and the northern burial ground attached to the Parish Church of St. Anne, Shandon, in the city of Cork.

---

## Public Health Act.

31. In paragraphs 32 to 40 of our last Annual Report the progress of the sanitary arrangements under the Public Health (Ireland) Act, 1874, was referred to. We place in the Appendix to this Report the conclusion of the correspondence with the Board of Guardians of Waterford Union, in which resistance to the Sanitary Orders was protracted to so late a period as 1st December, in the year 1875, when the Guardians submitted to the law rather than incur the risk of the legal proceedings about to be taken against them to enforce it.*

The payment of the sanitary salaries is nowhere now resisted, and the expenditure on this head in the year ended 29th September, 1875, in both classes of Sanitary Districts, viz., the Urban and Rural, was £24,758, in aid of which £12,172 has already been recouped by the Treasury in accordance with the provisions of the 10th section of the Act.

During the same period the Sanitary Authorities have, for the most part, been discharging their duties satisfactorily, and with great benefit to the population situate within their respective districts, the Rural Authorities alone having expended on Sanitary purposes, apart from salaries, in the course of the year, £10.490 for supply of water, improvement of the sewerage, and for the removal of nuisances.

32. The cost of the latter operations when not recovered from the parties proceeded against, has been charged in accordance with the statute as General expenses; but in Rural Sanitary

* Appendix, C. III., p. 62.

Districts the supply of water and the making or improvement of sewerage has usually been provided for by a charge upon some limited area consisting of one or more Townlands, or one or more Electoral Divisions, the area being fixed, always after ascertaining the views of the Board of Guardians acting as Sanitary Authority, by a sealed order of the Local Government Board.

No less than 79 of these Orders fixing the area of charge for water supply, or sewerage, or both, have been issued in the course of the year, involving upwards of 1,200 Townlands, situate in 62 different Unions.

A detailed statement of these Orders and the several localities to which they respectively relate will be found in the Appendix.*

33. A corresponding degree of activity has been shown by the Urban Authorities, more especially in the larger class of towns, which most readily avail themselves of such assistance as it is in the power of the Local Government Board to afford them; but in Urban Districts there is no occasion for Orders fixing the area of charge, all sanitary expenditure being chargeable by law on the Town fund or rate raised for general purposes by the Urban Sanitary Authority over its entire District. The smaller class of Urban Districts ranging from 6,000 in population upwards, to 10,000 or more, are those in which least activity in Sanitary operations has been shown by the Sanitary Authority.

In both the urban and rural class, in addition to current expenditure on water supply or sewerage, loans for these purposes have been applied for and recommended by us to the Board of Works to a considerable extent within the year ended on the 25th March, 1876.

The following is a statement of the several cases, and of the amount applied for in each case, with the date of our recommendation to the Commissioners of Public Works to grant the loan applied for.

At least an equal number of applications are now before us which have not yet reached the above stage in the process.

LIST of LOANS recommended to BOARD of WORKS since the 31st March, 1875.

| Name of Sanitary Authority applying. | Amount. | Purpose. | Date of Recommendation. |
|---|---|---|---|
| | £ | | |
| Ballina Rural, . . . | 9,200 | Sewerage. | 3rd March, 1876. |
| Cookstown do. . . . | 4,000 | Do. | 21st October, 1875. |
| Downpatrick do. . . . | 605 | Do. | 28th January, 1876. |
| Kingstown Urban, . . . | 10,000 | Do. | 9th July, 1875. |
| Do. do. . . . | 1,800 | Water. | 31st July, 1875. |
| Letterkenny Rural, . . . | 600 | Do. | 20th January, 1873. |
| Limerick Urban, . . . | 2,600 | Sewerage. | 3rd June, 1875. |
| Do. do. . . . | 2,658 | Do. | 11th January, 1876. |
| Macroom Rural, . . . | 4,000 | Water. | 9th April, 1875. |
| Pembroke Urban, . . . | 1,200 | Sewerage. | 21st October, 1875. |
| Queenstown do. . . . | 1,121 | Do. | 9th August, 1875. |
| Rathdown Rural, . . . | 1,200 | Water. | 13th August, 1875. |
| Do. do. . . . | 700 | Do. | 24th August, 1875. |
| Do. do. . . . | 3,000 | Do. | 3rd January, 1876. |
| Rathmines and Rathgar Urban, . | 2,000 | Do. | 15th July, 1875. |
| Skibbereen Rural, . . . . | 400 | Sewerage. | 15th March, 1876 |

* Appendix, C. IV., p. 67.

34. In concluding this branch of our report we beg to draw attention to a circular letter, dated 9th August, 1875, which we issued to all sanitary authorities in Ireland,* accompanying a copy of the recent report of the Medical Officer of the English Local Government Board, detailing the experiences of the medical branch of that Board for a period of five years past, in regard to the causes of filth diseases, and to their prevention. We have in this country no corresponding means of inquiry, our Medical Inspectors being devoted, like the other Inspectors, to administrative functions altogether; and we therefore thought it desirable to distribute as many copies of that most valuable report as we could prevail upon the Lords Commissioners of Her Majesty's Treasury to permit the Stationery Office to supply us with, and upon the whole we obtained for this purpose 220 copies, which enabled us to supply one copy to each of the 203 sanitary authorities, and to reserve for our own use a supply of 17 copies, hoping by such means to promote a knowledge and consideration of the important results obtained from the researches of the English Medical Inspectors. We are enabled to say that the report so distributed has been received with satisfaction, and is likely to be of much practical benefit. We should have been glad to have sent a separate copy to each of the Sanitary Officers in Ireland, that is, to each Medical Officer of a Dispensary District.

## Departmental Arrangements.

35. Dr. MacDonnell, Medical Commissioner of the Local Government Board, retired from office on the 5th of January, 1876, receiving from the Chief Secretary's Office on that occasion, a letter which will be found in the appendix.†

A short time previously a Local Government Board Inspector, Mr. Henry Robinson, was appointed Assistant Under-Secretary of the Lord Lieutenant; and Dr. Croker-King, a Medical Inspector of the Local Government Board, succeeded to the office of Medical Commissioner, vacated by the retirement of Dr. MacDonnell.

Thus two Inspectorships were made vacant, to one of which Mr. William Armstrong, of the Chief Secretary's Office, was appointed; and shortly afterwards the vacant Medical Inspectorship was assigned to Dr. Frederick MacCabe, Resident Medical Superintendent of the Criminal Lunatic Asylum, at Dundrum.

Consequent upon these changes, Inspector W. P. O'Brien leaves the Belfast District for Mr. Robinson's late District, including the two Dublin Unions. Dr. Roughan is moved from Sligo to Belfast, to be succeeded by Mr. Armstrong; and Dr. MacCabe succeeds Dr. Croker-King at Cork; the Districts of the other seven Inspectors remaining as before.

We have the honour to be

Your Grace's obedient faithful servants,

M. E. Hicks Beach.
A. Power.
T. H. Burke.
R. M. Bellew.
Charles Croker-King, M.D.

* Appendix, C. II., No. 1, p. 53. † Appendix, C. V., p. 78.

# APPENDIX.

## APPENDIX A.

## CIRCULARS OF INSTRUCTIONS UNDER THE POOR LAW ACTS.

### No. 1.—Exercise and Recreation of the Children in Workhouses.

Local Government Board, Dublin,
9th April, 1875.

Sir,

The Local Government Board for Ireland are desirous of calling the attention of the Board of Guardians to the 27th Article of the General Workhouse Regulations, relating to the exercise and recreation of the children of either sex in the Workhouse.

The following is the Regulation referred to, namely:—

> Article 27.—The Master of the Workhouse may allow the paupers of each sex under the age of fifteen, subject to such restrictions as the Board of Guardians may impose, to quit the Workhouse under the care and guidance of himself, or the Matron, Schoolmaster, Schoolmistress, Porter, or some other paid officer of the Workhouse, for the purpose of exercise.

It is hardly necessary for the Board to dwell upon the importance, as regards the health of the children, which attaches to a regular observance of this Rule, under which the children may be taken out daily, or on alternate days, for exercise and for recreation beyond the Workhouse premises and grounds, for such periods as may be found convenient during the play hours or otherwise.

In a sanitary point of view, the change of air and change of scene for the children will be very conducive to their health, and a better means of freely exercising their limbs will be afforded outside the premises than exists within them.

Independently of the salutary effects in this way which a free compliance with the Regulation will secure, its systematic observance will render it necessary for the Schoolmaster and Schoolmistress, or other Officer of the Workhouse, to see that the children, when taken out to walk in the public roads and thoroughfares, are clean and neat, and tidy in their clothes and persons, and orderly in their general behaviour, and much benefit will result from the frequent recurrence of the inspection of the children.

The children will likewise be brought in contact with and be seen by persons who would not otherwise have an opportunity of observing their creditable appearance, good conduct, and suitability for self-maintaining employment hereafter.

In many Unions the Board believe that the children are regularly taken out, but there is reason to think that this is not so in all cases as it should be; and now that the season of the year is more favourable to out-door exercise, the Board are desirous of inviting the special attention of the Guardians to the subject, which is of much interest to the community as well as importance to the health of the children.

The Porter of the Workhouse should enter in his Book the hour at which the children leave and return to the Workhouse, and the number taken out, of boys and girls, respectively.

By order of the Board,

B. Banks, Secretary.

To the Clerk of each Union.

---

## No 2.—Form of Rate Book.

Local Government Board, Dublin,
21st April, 1875.

Sir,

It being required by the General Sanitary Accounts Order of the 22nd March, 1875,* that the amounts chargeable for "General

FORM OF RATE BOOK ENCLOSED

No. 1. —— UNION. —— ELECTORAL DIVISION.

A RATE for the RELIEF of the POOR of the —— UNION, made this —— day of ——, on a POUNDAGE of —— in the

| No. | Name or Situation of Property Rated. | Description of Property Rated, namely, whether Lands, Buildings, open Mines, Commons, and Rights of Common, profits issuing out of Lands, rights of Fishery, Canals, Navigations, and rights of Navigation, rights of Way, and other rights or easements over Lands and Tolls. | Where Immediate Lessor is Rated, Name of Occupier for whom he is primarily liable for the payment of the Rate. | Estimated Extent of Land, Statute Measure. | Net Annual Value. |
|---|---|---|---|---|---|
| | | | | A. R. P. | £ s. d. |

## No. 3.—Notices of making Rate.

Local Government Board, Dublin,
24th July, 1875.

Sir,

Adverting to that part of the General Order dated the 22nd March last,* which relates to the raising of a common fund for the payment of "general expenses" under the Sanitary Acts, and to making provision for payment of "special expenses" charged to contributory places, the Local Government Board for Ireland desire to state that they think that the notices which are required to be issued—first, that the rate books

* See Report for 1875, Appx. C. 1, p. 74.

Expenses," and also for "Special Expenses," under the provisions of the Public Health Act, 1874, shall be entered in the Rate Book, in a column to be provided for that purpose, and added to the ordinary Poor Rate and collected therewith, the Local Government Board for Ireland have caused the form of Rate Book now in use to be revised by the introduction of the requisite additional columns.

A specimen sheet of the revised form, which has been printed by Mr. Thom, of Abbey-street, Dublin, is enclosed, and you will take care, when ordering the books for new Rates in future, to obtain the amended form.

By order of the Board,

B. Banks, Secretary.

To the Clerk of each Union.

in Foregoing Circular.

—— Townland, in the —— of ——.

in the Year of Our Lord One Thousand Eight Hundred and Seventy- ——, Pound for Ordinary Expenditure.

| Persons on whom the Rate is made. | | | | Amount of Rate for the Relief of the Poor. | Amount of Rate for Expenses incurred under the Sanitary Acts. | Total Amount of Rate. | Arrear of former Rates (if any). | Total. |
|---|---|---|---|---|---|---|---|---|
| Occupier. | Immediate Lessor of Heredita-ments not exceeding £4. | Immediate Lessor of Heredita-ments under agreement with Guardians. | Persons receiving Rent in respect of Hereditaments exempt from Rating under 1 & 2 Vic., c. 56. | | | | | |
| | | | | £ s. d. | £ s. d. | £ s. d. | £ s. d. | £ s. d. |

are open for inspection, and secondly, that the rates have been made—should contain an intimation of the provision that has been made in the rates for expenses under the Sanitary Acts, and they have accordingly caused the forms of notice now in use to be revised with that view.

Copies of the revised forms of notice are enclosed, and should be used by you in reference to all future rates.

A slight alteration has also been made in the form of receipt for rate, in order to show the poundage of the sanitary expenses, and a specimen of the revised form is enclosed for your information and guidance when obtaining a supply of rate receipts in future.

By order of the Board,

B. Banks, Secretary.

To the Clerk of each Union.

ENCLOSURES in foregoing CIRCULAR.

FORM I.

NOTICE to be given when a RATE is prepared, and before it is signed.

Union.

NOTICE that RATE BOOKS are open for inspection of RATEPAYERS.

Notice is hereby given, that rates, as hereunder mentioned, are about to be made on the property situated in the under-mentioned Electoral Divisions of the above-named Union, rateable under the provisions of the Acts for the Relief of the Destitute Poor in Ireland.

The rates for the ordinary expenditure of the several Electoral Divisions are as follow:—

Electoral Division of a rate of in the pound.
Electoral Division of a rate of in the pound.

The said rates include in the pound for general expenses under the Sanitary Acts on all the Electoral Divisions of the Union [except such portions of the Electoral Divisions of as comprise the Urban Sanitary Authority of ]*

[And Whereas certain special expenses have been incurred by the Board of Guardians, as the Rural Sanitary Authority, which are chargeable, according to a sealed Order of the Local Government Board, on the contributory places hereunder mentioned, the following special poundage rates have been added to the rates above mentioned for the payment of such special expenses, and the same will be collected with the above-mentioned rates:—

| Name of Contributory Place. | Special Poundage Rate on Contributory Place. |
|---|---|
| | |

]†

The rate books are deposited for the inspection of any ratepayer at and will be there open for such inspection, between the hours of ten o'clock in the forenoon and four o'clock in the afternoon, during the fourteen days next ensuing the date thereof, exclusive of Sundays.

Signed this day of 18

Clerk of the Union.

---

FORM II.

NOTICE to be given when RATES have been made.

Union.

NOTICE of RATES having been made.

Notice is hereby given, that rates have been duly made on the property situated in the under-mentioned Electoral Divisions of the above-named Union, rateable under the provisions of the Acts for the Relief of the Destitute Poor in Ireland.

The rates for the ordinary expenditure of the several Electoral Divisions are as follow:—

Electoral Division of a rate of in the pound.
Electoral Division of a rate of in the pound.

* These words to be omitted in Unions which do not comprise any Urban Sanitary Authority.

† This portion of the form to be used only when provision is made for special expenses which are chargeable on any contributory district according to Order of the Local Government Board, under section 13 of the Public Health Act, 1874.

The said rates include in the pound for general expenses under the Sanitary Acts on all the Electoral Divisions of the Union [except such portions of the Electoral Divisions of as comprise the Urban Sanitary Authority of ]*

[And Whereas certain special expenses have been incurred by the Board of Guardians, as the Rural Sanitary Authority, which are chargeable, according to a sealed Order of the Local Government Board, on the contributory places hereunder mentioned, the following special poundage rates have been added to the rates above mentioned for the payment of such special expenses, and the same will be collected with the above-mentioned rates:—

| Name of Contributory Place. | Special Poundage Rate for Contributory Place. |
|---|---|
| | |

]†

The rate books are now in my custody, and may be inspected by any person affected thereby, at on any day, except Sunday, between the hours of ten o'clock in the forenoon and four o'clock in the afternoon; and the said rates will be payable from and after the publication of this notice.

Signed this day of 18

Clerk of the Union.

---

*Revised Form of Rate Receipt.*

---

No. UNION.

---

Net Annual Value, £ : s. d.

No. in Rate Book, House, &c.,

RECEIVED the day of 18 , from Mr. Pound Shilling and Pence, of the Poor's Rate for the Electoral Division, made the day of 18 , as stated on the back of this Receipt.

£ : : Rate.
£ : : Arrears.

Collector.

---

DUPLICATE FOR LANDLORD.

---

No. UNION.

---

Net Annual Value, £ : s. d.

No. in Rate Book, House, &c.,

RECEIVED the day of 18 , from Mr. Pound Shilling and Pence, of the Poor's Rate for the Electoral Division, made the day of 18 , as stated on the back of this Receipt.

£ : : Rate.
£ : : Arrears.

Collector.

---

INDORSEMENT.

———d. in the Pound for Ordinary Expenditure.
———d. in the Pound for General Expenses under the Sanitary Acts.
———d. in the Pound (in the Contributory District), for Special Expenses under the Sanitary Acts.

* These words to be omitted in Unions which do not comprise any Urban Sanitary District.

† This portion of the form to be used only when provision is made for special expenses which are chargeable on any contributory district according to Order of the Local Government Board, under section 18 of the Public Health Act, 1874.

D

## No. 4.—Payments to National School Teachers.

Local Government Board, Dublin,
30th August, 1875.

Sir,

The Local Government Board for Ireland forward to you herewith, to be laid before the Board of Guardians, a copy of "The National School Teachers (Ireland) Act, 1875," which received the Royal Assent on the 13th August, and in pursuance of the 4th sec. of the Act, the Local Government Board transmit a notice to the Board of Guardians, requiring them within forty days after the receipt thereof to inform the Local Government Board whether, for the purpose of increasing the remuneration of the teachers of National schools within the Union, they are willing to make their Union a contributory Union within the meaning of the Act.

The proceedings in this matter are to be taken in the manner prescribed by the 5th and 6th sections of the Act, namely—a resolution may be passed by the votes of a majority of the Guardians assembled after fourteen days' notice has been given in the manner required by the General Regulations, that the Union shall in each financial year contribute out of the rates a sum equal to one-third of the amount, which, on the passing of the resolution, will become payable in the year by way of results fees in respect of pupils attending the National schools in the Union;—a copy of the resolution, signed by the Chairman and the Clerk of the Union, is then to be sent to the Commissioners of National Education, and to the Local Government Board.

In forwarding this notice the Local Government Board have it in command from His Grace the Lord Lieutenant to lay before the Guardians certain documents, from which they will learn the views of Her Majesty's Government on the subject, and will likewise see clearly the extent of the liability which, according to an estimate framed by the Commissioners of National Education, they will incur by making their Union a contributory one.

The Board of Guardians will observe that the contributions above referred to will not be applicable to the payment of the teachers of the Workhouse schools, but that provision is made by the 12th section of the Act under which the Guardians may, if they see fit, pay results fees, on the certificate of the Commissioners of National Education, to the teachers of Poor Law Union National schools.

By order of the Board,

B. Banks, Secretary.

To the Clerk of each Union.

---

Enclosures in foregoing Circular.

Notice in pursuance of Section 4 of the Act 38 and 39 Vic., c. 96.

The Guardians of          Union are hereby required, within forty days after the receipt hereof, to inform the Local Government Board for Ireland whether, for the purpose of increasing the remuneration of the Teachers of National Schools within the Union, they are willing to become a contributory Union within the meaning of the Act 38 and 39 Vic., c. 96.

By order of the Board,

B. Banks, Secretary.

30th August, 1875.

---

Dublin Castle,
28th August, 1875.

Sir,

I am directed by His Grace the Lord Lieutenant to transmit herewith, for the information of the Local Government Board, the accompanying copy of "The National School Teachers (Ireland) Act, 1875," and to call your special attention to Clause 4, which directs the Local Government Board, on or before the 1st day of September, 1875, to transmit to the Guardians of each Union in Ireland a Notice requiring them within forty days after the receipt thereof to inform the Board whether, for the purpose of increasing the remuneration of the Teachers of National Schools within such Union, they are willing to become a contributory Union under the provisions of the Act.

His Grace considers it expedient that the Notice of the Local Government Board should be accompanied by an explanatory Memorandum, copies of which are enclosed, which will elucidate the general scope of the Act and its practical application to each Union.

With a view of affording the Guardians in each Union full information as to their liability in the event of their being willing to become a contributory Union, His Grace has obtained from the Commissioners of National Education Returns showing for each Union—

1. The number of Pupils examined for passes in results, and the amount earned in results fees in the year 1874-75 in each National School within the Union.
2. The total approximate amount payable by the Guardians in results fees to Teachers of National Schools within the Union for the year 1875-76, under the provisions of "The National School Teachers (Ireland) Act, 1875."

His Grace desires me to transmit herewith the aforesaid Returns, and to request you will forward a proper copy of same to each Union, together with a copy of the explanatory Memorandum and of this Letter.

I am, sir, your obedient servant,

T. H. Burke.

The Secretary to the
Local Government Board.

---

## National School Teachers Act, 1875.

### Explanatory Memorandum.

1. In the financial year 1874-75 (ended 31st March, 1875), the Teachers of National Schools were paid Results Fees for passes obtained by their pupils in the different branches of instruction as ascertained upon examination by the Inspectors of National Schools, on the scale and conditions set forth in the document appended, marked Appendix A.

2. Her Majesty's Government has decided that for the year 1875-6 (to end 31st of March, 1876), there shall be paid from the Imperial Exchequer in lieu of the above payments:—

(*a*) An addition to the class salaries of the Teachers, and,
(*b*) One half of the Results Fees that could be earned on the scale set forth in the Appendix A.

3. But, in addition to the above, the Government has engaged to provide from the Imperial Exchequer *the other moiety* of the amount that might be earned on the scale of Results Fees set forth in Appendix A, in every Union in which the Poor Law Guardians undertake to contribute, under the powers of the National School Teachers Act of the present year, an amount *equal to such moiety*, *i.e.*, a third of the whole amount payable in Results Fees to the Teachers.

4. If, therefore, a Poor Law Union become "contributory," under the powers of the Act, the Teachers of the National Schools within it will obtain in Results Fees *as much and a half* as provided by the scale of last year.

5. But if a Poor Law Union decline to become contributory, the Teachers of the National Schools within it will obtain in Results Fees only *one-half* of the scale of last year.

*e.g.* If the passes upon examination on the full scale of Results Fees given in Appendix A represented, say, £20, this would have been the amount paid by the Imperial Exchequer to the Teacher last year.

But for 1875–6 he would receive on the same passes:—

(*c*) If the Union were contributory, £30 (*i.e.*, £10 the secured amount and £10 the contingent amount from the Imperial Exchequer, and £10 from the Union).

(*d*) If the Union were *not* contributory, £10 (*i.e.* only the secured amount from the Imperial Exchequer).

6. The annexed Returns (Appendix B) give separately for each Union:—

(*e.*) The number of Pupils examined for passes in Results and the amount earned in Results Fees in the year 1874–75 in each National School within the Union.

(*f*) The total approximate amount payable by the Guardians in Results Fees to Teachers of National Schools within each Union for the year 1875–76, under the provisions of "The National School Teachers (Ireland) Act, 1875."

These Returns have been prepared under the directions of His Grace the Lord Lieutenant by the Commissioners of National Education with the view of affording the Guardians of each Union full information as to their liability for the year 1875-76, in the event of their being willing to become a contributory Union.

The total approximate amount payable by the Guardians, as stated in Part II., Appendix B, is half the amount that might be earned on the Scale of Results Fees as published in the Rules of the Board, *i.e.*, a third of the total amount of Results Fees payable to the teachers.

7. It is right, however, in reference to the earnings in Results Fees, to observe that as the amount earned in Results Fees depends on the number of schools and children examined, *and the passes obtained*, the amount earned in one year is only an indication of that which may be earned in a succeeding year.

T. H. Burke.

Dublin Castle, 28th August, 1875.

## Appendix A.—Scale of Results Fees.

| Subjects. | Classes. | | | | | | | | |
|---|---|---|---|---|---|---|---|---|---|
| | Infants. | First Class. | Second Class. | Third Class. | Fourth Class. | Fifth Class, First Stage. | Fifth Class, Second Stage. | Sixth Class, First Stage. | Sixth Class, Second Stage. |
| | *s. d.* | *s. d.* | *s. d.* | *s. d.* | *s. d.* | *s. d.* | *s. d.* | *s. d.* | *s. d.* |
| Reading, | – | 2 0 | 2 0 | 2 6 | 2 6 | 2 6 | 2 6 | 2 6 | 2 0 |
| Spelling, | – | 1 0 | 1 0 | 1 0 | 1 0 | 1 0 | 1 0 | 1 0 | 1 0 |
| Writing, | – | 1 0 | 1 0 | 1 6 | 1 6 | 1 6 | 1 6 | 2 0 | 2 0 |
| Arithmetic, | – | 1 0 | 2 0 | 2 6 | 2 6 | 2 6 | 2 6 | 3 0 | 3 0 |
| Grammar, | – | – | – | 0 6 | 1 0 | 1 6 | 1 6 | 1 6 | 1 6 |
| Geography, | – | – | – | 1 0 | 1 0 | 1 6 | 1 6 | 1 6 | 1 6 |
| Agriculture or Book-keeping, Males, | – | – | – | – | 2 0 | 2 6 | 2 6 | 3 0 | 3 0 |
| Needlework, Females, | – | – | 0 6 | 1 0 | 2 0 | 2 6 | 2 6 | 3 0 | 3 0 |
| Maximum value, Male National Schools, | 3 0 | 5 0 | 6 6 | 0 0 | 11 6 | 13 0 | 13 0 | 14 6 | 14 6 |
| Maximum value in Female National Schools, | 3 0 | 5 0 | 6 6 | 10 0 | 11 6 | 13 0 | 13 0 | 14 6 | 14 6 |
| Extras (inside or outside School hours):— | | | | | | | | | |
| Singing, | – | – | 1 6 | 2 6 | 2 6 | 2 6 | 2 6 | 3 0 | 3 0 |
| Drawing, | – | – | – | 2 6 | 2 6 | 2 6 | 2 6 | 3 0 | 3 0 |
| Other approved extra subjects (each), | – | – | – | – | – | 5 0 | 5 0 | 5 0 | 5 0 |
| Classics (outside School hours):— | | | | | | | | | |
| Greek, | – | – | – | – | – | 10 0 | 10 0 | 10 0 | 10 0 |
| Latin, | – | – | – | – | – | 10 0 | 10 0 | 10 0 | 10 0 |
| French, | – | – | – | – | – | 5 0 | 5 0 | 5 0 | 5 0 |

### Notes.

(*a*) No results fee can be paid in respect of any pupil whose attendance at the school during the year ended on the last day of the month preceding the annual examination shall be less than ninety days.

(*b*) No pupil may be presented for examination in a higher class than that in which he is enrolled. (This rule applies equally to pupils under seven years of age, and to those above that age.)

(*c*) The same results fees as in day schools are obtainable in an evening school for every branch taught in the latter; but an attendance on FORTY-FIVE evenings will be accepted as qualifying an evening school pupil for admission to examination for results. *Under no circumstances should a day school pupil be presented for examination in an evening school.*

(*d*) A written exercise signed and dated by the pupil, must be presented for every attendance for which credit is claimed in an evening school.

(*e*) Pupils *above* four and *under* seven years of age, who make the necessary minimum number of attendances in the year, may be presented for inspection as infants. *Individual* examination of such pupils may be dispensed with in those schools ONLY in which there is *bona fide* provision made for the systematic training of infants.

(*f*) In a thoroughly organized infants' school, with a separate staff, and in a separate room, a fee of 4*s.* per pupil may be paid.

(*g*) (After the results examinations of the current financial year 1874–5 no fee shall be paid in an infant school for any pupil presented in a class higher than second.)

(*h*) Only *one fee for each subject* can be paid for a pupil in any class, no matter how long the pupil may remain in the class, except in the case of *infants*, and of the fifth class (in which a pupil may be paid for twice, viz., once in each stage), and of *sixth* class pupils. Any pupil in first, second, third, or fourth class who earns for the teacher fees for reading, writing, *and* arithmetic, cannot again earn a fee for any subject in the same class. But if the pupil fails in any of these three subjects, he may be presented a second time in the same class, and earn fees in the subjects in which he failed previously, subject to conditions specified in notes (*i*) and (*l*).

(*i*) *Under no circumstances* can a pupil be presented for examination for results fees more than twice in the same class, except in the case of the *fifth* and *sixth* classes, and in that of *infants*.

(*j*) Should a pupil be presented for examination for results oftener than once in the sixth class, such pupil, to entitle the teacher to *any* results fees, must—(*a*) *If a boy*, exhibit proficiency in *three* books of Euclid; *or* in algebra, up to and including quadratic equations; *or* in plane trigonometry; *or* in navigation; *or* in one of the physical sciences; *or* in some other approved extra branch: (*b*) *If a girl*, exhibit proficiency in "cutting out" as taught in the Board's Manual of Needlework; *or* in the use of the sewing machine; *or* in the cooking of plain food; *or* in the management of poultry and other domestic animals; *or* in physical geography; *or* in some other approved extra branch. (N.B.—Payment can be made only once for the same pupil for proficiency in the use of the sewing machine.)

(*k*) In cases, however, where it is found necessary by the Inspector, to hold a results examination at a date less than eleven months after the date of the termination of the last results year, teachers will be allowed to present pupils again in the same class in which they passed at the previous examination, subject to conditions specified in notes (*i*) and (*l*). This privilege will not, however, extend to the presentation of pupils again in the *same stage* of fifth or sixth class.

(*l*) No pupil of seven years of age or above who has been enrolled for a year in any class can be presented in a lower class than that in which he is enrolled; and under no circumstances can a pupil be presented in a lower class than that next below the class in which he is enrolled.

(*m*) Results fees cannot be paid for needlework in a *female* school in which there is a workmistress paid by the Board.

(*n*) The attendance of paid monitors shall be marked on a separate roll, and included in the average daily attendance in all schools; but they are not to be reckoned as pupils for capitation payments, or (except in the case of third class monitors,) to be presented for examination as pupils at the results examination in subjects that form part of their prescribed school course.

(*o*) First and second class monitors may, however, be presented for results examination in Classics or French, or in a science branch not included in any part of their prescribed course of instruction. Only two such subjects will be allowed to be taken in any one year.

(*p*) Third class monitors presented for results examinations are subject to the same rules as ordinary pupils.

*Extra subjects*:—

(*q*) No fee will be paid for any pupil for whose proficiency in the same subject grants are made by the Department of Science and Art.

(*r*) A fee of five shillings will be paid for every pupil in the fifth or sixth class, who, *having passed in reading, spelling, writing,* AND *arithmetic,* shall exhibit satisfactory proficiency in geometry (*First Book of Euclid* on *Mensuration of Surfaces* for fifth class, *and First and Second Books of Euclid* AND *Mensuration of Surfaces* for sixth class), algebra (*Elementary Rules* for fifth class, *Elementary Rules and Simple Equations* for sixth class), one of the physical sciences, navigation, or other *approved* extra branch.

---

## No. 5.—National School Teachers (Ireland) Act.

Local Government Board, Dublin,
18th November, 1875.

Sir,

The Local Government Board for Ireland transmit to you herewith, as Treasurer of the Union, a copy of an Order under their seal which has been issued in pursuance of the provisions of "The National School Teachers (Ireland) Act, 1875," assessing the sum payable by each contributory Union, the sum so assessed upon Union being £

The Board desire at the same time to draw your attention to the 9th sec. of the Act, a copy of which is annexed, by which you will see that it is your duty forthwith, on receipt of the Order, out of the funds lying in your hands to the credit of the Guardians, or if there shall be then no sufficient assets, out of the moneys next received by you and placed to the credit of the Guardians, to pay over the amount assessed on the Union to the Bank of Ireland to the credit of the Commissioners of National Education.

By order of the Board,

B. Banks, Secretary.

To the Treasurer of the Union.

---

*Copy of Sec. 9 of* "The National School Teachers (Ireland) Act, 1875," (38 & 39 Vic., c. 96).

"Forthwith on the receipt of such order by the Treasurer of any contributory Union he shall, out of the funds then lying in his hands to the credit of the Guardians of such Union, or if there shall be then no sufficient assets, out of the moneys next received by him and placed to the credit of such Guardians, pay over the amount so assessed on such contributory Union to the Bank of Ireland, to be there placed to the credit of the Commissioners of Education to a separate account, to be entitled "The Results Fees Account;" and the Guardians of such contributory Union shall in their account with the Electoral Divisions of such contributory Union debit each Electoral Division with its proportion of the said amount according to the net annual value for the time being of the property rateable to the rates for the relief of the destitute poor in each such division."

---

## No. 6.—National School Teachers (Ireland) Act.

Local Government Board, Dublin,
18th November, 1875.

Sir,

With reference to the Resolution of the Board of Guardians of Union, passed in accordance with the 5th sec. of "The National School Teachers (Ireland) Act, 1875," to become a contributory Union under the provisions of that Act, the Local Government Board for Ireland now transmit to you to be laid before the Board of Guardians a copy of an Order under their seal, which has been issued in pursuance of the provisions of the 8th sec. assessing the sum payable by each contributory Union, the sum so assessed upon Union being £

A copy of the Order and a copy of the 9th sec. of the Act, which prescribes the mode in which the amount assessed is to be paid, have been forwarded to the Treasurer of the Union.

By order of the Board,

B. Banks, Secretary.

To the Clerk, Union.

---

## No. 7.—Results Fees in Workhouse National Schools.

Local Government Board, Dublin,
2nd December, 1875.

Sir,

The Local Government Board for Ireland having observed that in a few instances resolutions have been passed by Boards of Guardians on the subject of the payment of Results Fees to the Teachers of the Workhouse Schools, the Board think it advisable to draw attention to those provisions of the National School Teachers Act of last session which relate to the Teachers of Poor Law Union National Schools, and they accordingly annex to this Circular a copy of the 12th section of the Act, in which those provisions are contained.

By this section it will be seen:—

That the Guardians may, after due notice, resolve that "in any year" payment may be made out of the Poor Rates by way of Results Fees to the Teachers of the Workhouse Schools, where those schools are in connexion with the National Education Board.

That such payment can be made on receiving a certificate of results from the Commissioners of National Education.

That the payment may be of such amount as the Guardians determine, provided that it does not exceed the full amount which would be payable as Results Fees, under like circumstances in an ordinary National School.

It would appear from the above that any resolution which may be passed by the Guardians to pay Results Fees to the Workhouse Teachers will be operative only for the year in which it is passed, and must be renewed from year to year if the Guardians wish to continue the payment; and also that the payment must be made from the Poor Rate, no provision having been made for any contribution towards Results Fees to Workhouse School Teachers from Imperial Funds as in the case of ordinary National Schools.

By order of the Board,

B. Banks, Secretary.

To the Clerk of each Union.

---

Copy of Sec. 12 of "The National School Teachers (Ireland) Act," (38 & 39 Vic., c. 96).

The Guardians of any Union duly assembled after fourteen days' notice has been given in the manner required by the regulations of the Local Government Board may, by a majority of their number, resolve that in any year a sum may be given out of the rates for the relief of the destitute poor by way of fees to the Teachers of the Poor Law Union National Schools in such Union, in respect of results ascertained to have been effected in their respective schools, and thereupon the same shall be paid to such teachers by the Guardians, on receiving a certificate of the results from the Commissioners of Education: Provided always, that the amount of any such payment shall not exceed the full amount which would be payable under the like circumstances to such teachers of such Poor Law Union National Schools if they were teachers of other National Schools in such Union.

## No. 8.—LUNATIC ASYLUMS (IRELAND) ACT, 1875.

Local Government Board, Dublin,
18th September, 1875.

SIR,

The Local Government Board for Ireland forward to you herewith, for the information of the Board of Guardians, the annexed Extracts from the Lunatic Asylums (Ireland) Act, 1875, which received the Royal Assent on the 2nd August last.

By these Extracts it will be seen that the Guardians may, subject to the conditions set forth in sec. 9 of the Act, receive into the Workhouse from the District Lunatic Asylum any chronic lunatic who is not dangerous, upon such terms as may be agreed upon between the Guardians and the Governors of the Asylum, the expenses incurred in respect of such lunatic in the Workhouse to be deemed part of the expenses of the asylum, and to be paid by the Governors out of the moneys applicable to the payment of such expenses.

Under sec. 11 pauper patients, when discharged from an asylum, may be forwarded to the Workhouse from which they were sent to the asylum, and the Guardians are to repay to the Governors of the Asylum the expense of the removal.

By sec. 14 it will be seen that provision is now made for payment of expenses incurred in the examination of persons alleged to be dangerous lunatics, including the remuneration of the Medical Officers who may be called on by the Justices to examine such persons.

By order of the Board,

B. BANKS, Secretary.

To the Clerk of each Union.

---

### ENCLOSURE.

EXTRACTS from "The Lunatic Asylums (Ireland) Act, 1875," 38 and 39 Vic., c. 67.

Sec. 9. The Guardians of any Poor Law Union in Ireland may, with the consent of the Local Government Board and the inspectors of lunatics, and subject to such regulations as they shall respectively prescribe, receive into the workhouse of such Union any chronic lunatic, not being dangerous, who may have been received into a District Lunatic Asylum, and selected by the resident medical superintendent thereof and certified by him to be fit and proper so to be removed, upon such terms as may be agreed upon between the said Guardians and the Board of Governors of any such asylum, and thereupon every such lunatic, so long as he shall remain in such workhouse, shall continue a patient on the books of the asylum for and in respect of all the provisions of an Act passed in the session of Parliament held in the first and second years of the reign of His late Majesty King George the Fourth, intituled "An Act to make more effectual provision for the establishment of asylums for the lunatic poor, and for the custody of insane persons charged with offences in Ireland," and the Acts amending the same, so far as they relate to lunatics and insane persons received into District Lunatic Asylums; and any expenses incurred by the Board of Governors in respect of such lunatic in such workhouse shall be deemed part of the expenses of such District Lunatic Asylum, and shall be paid by the Governors out of the moneys applicable to the payment of such expenses.

Sec. 11. Whenever any person being a pauper patient in any District Lunatic Asylum may be lawfully discharged from any such asylum, the Board of Governors of such asylum shall, unless such patient be otherwise discharged, forward such patient to the workhouse of the Union from which he was sent to such asylum, and shall pay the expenses of such removal, and the Guardians of the said Union shall repay to the said Board of Governors the expenses so paid by them as aforesaid.

Sec. 14. Notwithstanding anything in section 10 of the Act of the session of Parliament held in the thirtieth and thirty-first years of the reign of Her present Majesty, chapter one hundred and eighteen, to the contrary, it shall be lawful for any two justices causing any person to be examined by any medical officer as therein mentioned, if they think fit so to do, to make an order under their hands and seals upon the Guardians of the Union to which such person belongs, for the reasonable remuneration to such medical officer and for the payment of all other reasonable expenses in or about the examination of such person, not exceeding in the whole the sum of two pounds.

All moneys so ordered to be paid by the Guardians of such Union shall respectively be advanced, paid, and raised in like manner as any other moneys required for supporting and maintaining the destitute poor of such union.

---

# APPENDIX B.

## CIRCULARS OF INSTRUCTION UNDER THE MEDICAL CHARITIES ACT AND THE VACCINATION ACTS.

### No. 1.—Annual Appointment of Dispensary Committees and Wardens.

Local Government Board, Dublin,
4th April, 1876.

Sir,

The Local Government Board for Ireland desire to call your attention to the circular of the Poor Law Commissioners dated the 21st of March, 1862, relating to the annual appointment of dispensary committees and wardens, and to the extracts from previous circulars appended thereto; and they request that you will take the necessary steps, as pointed out in the circular referred to, to place before the Board of Guardians, after the annual election, a correct list of the members of the Board entitled to be members of the respective dispensary committees in the union.

*This ought to be done by distinct resolution and recorded on the minutes.*

As soon as the committee shall have been completed for any dispensary district, the guardians should fix a day for the first meeting of such committee, *for the special purpose of appointing their honorary officers for the current year*, in accordance with articles 6 and 7 of the Dispensary Regulations, and you should give notice thereof to each member of the dispensary committee, in accordance with articles 11 and 13 of the Dispensary Regulations.

A form for the return of officers of the several dispensary committees in the union will be forwarded to you in due course.

By order of the Board,

B. Banks, Secretary.

To the Clerk of the Board of Guardians
of each Union.

## No. 2.—Return of Officers of Dispensary Committees.

Local Government Board, Dublin,
Sir, 7th April, 1876.

With reference to their circular of the 4th instant, relating to the annual appointment of dispensary committees and wardens, the Local Government Board for Ireland enclose herewith a form for the return of officers of the several dispensary committees in the union.

In the circular above referred to the Board recommended that as soon as the committee should have been completed for any dispensary district, the guardians should fix a day for the first meeting of such committee, *for the special purpose of appointing their honorary officers for the current year*, in accordance with the dispensary regulations, and that you should give notice thereof to each member of the dispensary committee, in accordance with those regulations; and if this recommendation has not been acted upon in the case of any dispensary district in the union, the Board request that you will bring the matter again under the notice of the Board of Guardians.

Articles 6 and 7 of the Dispensary Regulations of 29th November, 1869, relate to the appointment of the honorary officers, and articles 11 and 13 relate to the notice of meeting.

The Board enclose three copies of the form, so as to enable you to make the return in *duplicate* to this Office, and to retain a copy for the use of the Board; and they request that you will procure the necessary information with the least practicable delay, and then forward your return to this Office.

By order of the Board,

B. Banks, Secretary.

To the Clerk of the Board of Guardians of each Union.

---

## No. 3.—Examination of Dangerous Lunatics.

Local Government Board, Dublin,
Sir, 18th September, 1875.

Adverting to the Circular Letters addressed to Dispensary Medical Officers by the Poor Law Commissioners on the 7th January and 8th March, 1868,* on the subject of the examination of Dangerous Lunatics, the Local Government Board for Ireland forward to you, annexed, a copy of the 14th section of the Lunatic Asylums (Ireland) Act, 1875, by which you will perceive that the Justices are now authorized, if they think fit so to do, to order payment of the expenses of such examination, including reasonable remuneration to the Medical Officer.

By order of the Board,

B. Banks, Secretary.

To each Dispensary Medical Officer.

---

Lunatic Asylums (Ireland) Act, 1875. (38 & 39 Vic., c. 67.)

Sec. 14. Notwithstanding anything in section 10 of the Act of the session of Parliament held in the thirtieth and thirty-first years of the reign of Her present Majesty, chapter one hundred and eighteen, to the contrary, it shall be lawful for any two justices causing any person to be examined by any medical officer as therein mentioned, if they think fit so to do, to make an order under their hands

* Annual Report of Poor Law Commissioners for 1868, Appendix C, No. 2, p. 148, and C, No. 3, p. 149.

and seals upon the guardians of the union to which such person belongs, for the reasonable remuneration to such medical officer and for the payment of all other reasonable expenses in or about the examination of such person, not exceeding in the whole the sum of two pounds.

All moneys so ordered to be paid by the guardians of such union shall respectively be advanced, paid, and raised in like manner as any other moneys required for supporting and maintaining the destitute poor of such union.

---

# APPENDIX C.

## ORDERS, INSTRUCTIONAL CIRCULARS, AND CORRESPONDENCE UNDER THE LOCAL GOVERNMENT ACTS AND THE PUBLIC HEALTH ACT.

### I.—ORDERS.

### No. 1.—ORDER amending the GENERAL SANITARY ORDERS of 9th September, 1874, in reference to the TOWN of YOUGHAL.

To the GUARDIANS of the YOUGHAL UNION; to the MEDICAL OFFICERS of the WORKHOUSE and of the DISPENSARY DISTRICTS therein; to the CLERK and other paid OFFICERS thereof; to the TOWN COMMISSIONERS of the TOWN of YOUGHAL; and to all whom it may concern.

WHEREAS, by General Orders under our seal, bearing date the 9th day of September, 1874, We, the Local Government Board for Ireland, did issue rules and regulations under the Public Health (Ireland) Act, 1874, for the sanitary organization of Rural Sanitary Districts and Urban Sanitary Districts, the said General Orders being numbered and described as follows, that is to say:—

Sanitary Order No I., relating to Rural Sanitary Districts consisting of entire Unions;

Sanitary Order No. II., relating to Rural Sanitary Districts consisting of parts of Unions of which other parts are Urban Sanitary Districts;

Sanitary Order No. III., relating to Urban Sanitary Districts.

AND WHEREAS, the Youghal Union is named in the Schedule to the said General Order No. II.; and the town of Youghal is named in the Schedule to the said Order No. III.:

AND WHEREAS, it has been represented to us by the Town Commissioners of the town of Youghal that the population of the town within the limits or boundaries of the municipal borough under the jurisdiction of the Commissioners is under 6,000, according to the Parliamentary census of the population of the townlands, parts of townlands, streets, or places within the said limits; and the Commissioners for taking the census of Ireland have, after inquiry, confirmed the same, by which it appears that the population of the town of Youghal, as published in the census of the county of Cork, included the enumeration of the population of places not within the limits of the municipal borough, and the said town of Youghal does not therefore constitute an Urban Sanitary District as defined by the Public Health (Ireland) Act, 1874 but is part of the Youghal Union Sanitary District:

AND WHEREAS, it is therefore expedient to amend the said General Orders of the 9th day of September, 1874, with respect to the Youghal Union and the town of Youghal:

Now, THEREFORE, WE do hereby declare as follows, anything in the said General Orders to the contrary notwithstanding, that the said General Order No. I. shall apply to and be in force in the Youghal Union Sanitary District, including the town of Youghal, as fully and effectually as if the said Union was named in the Schedule to the said General Order, and the Guardians of the Union shall be the Sanitary authority for the said District; and the said General Orders No. II. and No. III. shall not apply to the said Union, nor to the town of Youghal—and in all other respects We do hereby confirm the said Orders.

Sealed with our seal, this First day of April, in the Year of our Lord One Thousand Eight Hundred and Seventy-five.

(Signed,)

A. POWER, *Vice-President.*
J. M'DONNELL, } *Commissioners.*
R. M. BELLEW, }

ABERCORN.

I, JAMES, DUKE OF ABERCORN, Lord Lieutenant-General and General Governor of Ireland, do approve this Order.

By command of His Grace,

T. H. BURKE

---

## No. 2.—ORDER amending the GENERAL SANITARY ORDERS of 9th September, 1874, in reference to the TOWN of BANDON.

To the GUARDIANS of the BANDON UNION; to the MEDICAL OFFICERS of the WORKHOUSE and of the DISPENSARY DISTRICTS therein; to the CLERK and other paid OFFICERS thereof; to the TOWN COMMISSIONERS of the TOWN of BANDON; and to all whom it may concern:

WHEREAS, by General Orders under our Seal, bearing date the 9th day of September, 1874, We, the Local Government Board for Ireland, did issue Rules and Regulations under the "Public Health (Ireland) Act, 1874," for the sanitary organization of rural sanitary districts and urban sanitary districts, the said General Orders being numbered and described as follows, that is to say—

Sanitary Order, No. I., relating to rural sanitary districts consisting of entire unions;

Sanitary Order No. II., relating to rural sanitary districts consisting of parts of unions of which other parts are urban sanitary districts;

Sanitary Order No. III., relating to urban sanitary districts.

AND WHEREAS, the Bandon Union is named in the Schedule to the said General Order No. II.; and the town of Bandon is named in the Schedule to the said Order No. III.:

AND WHEREAS, it has been represented to us by the Town Commissioners of the town of Bandon that the population of the town within the limits or boundaries of the municipal borough under the jurisdiction of the Commissioners is under 6,000, according to the Parliamentary Census of the population of the townlands, parts of townlands, streets, or places within the said limits; and the Commissioners for taking the Census of Ireland, have, after inquiry, confirmed the same, by which it appears that the population of the town of Bandon, as published in the Census of the county of Cork, included the enumeration of the population of places not within the limits of the municipal borough, and the said town of Bandon does not therefore constitute an urban sanitary district as defined by the "Public Health (Ireland) Act, 1874," but is part of the Bandon Union sanitary district:

AND WHEREAS, it is therefore expedient to amend the said General Orders of the 9th day of September, 1874, with respect to the Bandon Union and the town of Bandon:

NOW, THEREFORE, WE do hereby declare as follows, anything in the said General Orders to the contrary notwithstanding, that the said General Order No. I. shall apply to and be in force in the Bandon Union sanitary district, including the town of Bandon, as fully and effectually as if the said union was named in the Schedule to the said General Order, and the Guardians of the Union shall be the sanitary authority for the said district; and the said General Orders No. II. and No. III. shall not apply to the said union, nor to the town of Bandon—and in all other respects except as to the amendment of the said Orders by a General Order under our Seal, bearing date the 1st day of April last, relating to the Youghal Union and to the town of Youghal, We do hereby confirm the said Orders.

Sealed with our Seal, this Twenty-sixth day of July, in the Year of Our Lord One Thousand Eight Hundred and Seventy-five.

(Signed), A. POWER, *Vice-President.*
R. M. BELLEW, *Commissioner.*

J. T. BALL.

We, the LORDS JUSTICES, General Governors of Ireland, do approve this Order.

By Command of the Lords Justices,
T. H. BURKE.

---

## II.—CIRCULARS.

### No. 1.—PREVENTION OF FILTH DISEASES.

Local Government Board, Dublin,
9th August, 1875.

SIR,

The Local Government Board for Ireland send herewith for the use of the sanitary authority and its sanitary officers, one copy of a recent Report of the Medical Officer of the Local Government Board in England, with an appendix containing several special reports of the English Medical Inspectors. This volume is the latest of a series giving the results of many years' continuous scientific inquiry, under the English Privy Council and the English Local Government Board, into various causes of preventible disease, especially such as are connected with accumulations of filth, and the pollution of water used for drinking; and it cannot but be valuable as a book of reference to the consulting officer and the sanitary officers acting in the district which is under the control of each sanitary authority in Ireland.

The researches comprised in this volume are limited to filth and filth diseases, and their prevention, excluding some of an equally dangerous and fatal character arising from other causes than accumulated filth, and yet preventible; such, for example, as diseases originating in, or actively promoted by, the vitiated air of over-crowded rooms, which are referred to as belonging to a separate branch of inquiry.

The prevention of filth diseases is obviously to be effected only by a systematic prompt removal of the filth, in whatever form presented, and resolves itself into two branches; the *water-closet system*, and the removal of excremental refuse by other conveniences, generally outside the dwelling.

The water-closet, as self-acting, is the most reliable, when served with a sufficient and constant supply of water, and the most prompt of all removing appliances. The other class, unfortunately, at present usually consists of the common midden and cess-pool, or privy and ash-pit, whence prompt and regular removal is seldom practised, and no removal at all is sometimes the prevailing rule.

The water-closet, however, is by no means represented as a *summum bonum* in comparison with other expedients, but as possessing peculiar dangers of its own to life and health, more insidious and often more fatal than the visible and palpable depositories of accumulated filth; and the science of prevention of filth disease thus becomes applicable to the one quite as much as to the other; the former acting by poisonous ferments not always perceptible to smell; the latter chiefly through the pollution of water, afterwards applied to drinking purposes, by overflow on the surface, or soakage through the soil.

The peculiar types of fever engendered by those causes are all classed under the head of enteric fever, including diarrhœa, and seem allied, in some sense, to Asiatic cholera; and their endemic or epidemic forms are thought to depend on similar modes of introduction and propagation, as the disease of cholera.

The newest and most striking of the facts exhibited in this volume are those relating to the effects of polluted water when distributed in milk supply, the certainty of which is most exhaustively demonstrated in three of the six Inspectors' reports contained in the appendix. It may readily be supposed that if polluted water so distributed were capable of disseminating enteric fever, an outbreak from that cause would be open to detection by careful inquiry, and no one who studies these three reports can be otherwise than convinced of the truth in each case by the evidence presented.

There is one point which all these milk cases seem to possess in common—namely, the pollution of the dairyman's well by sewage presumed to contain alvine excreta from some patient known to have been under the specific influence of enteric fever.

The most practically useful part, perhaps, of the matters contained in the Medical Officers' Report relates to the improved forms of appliances by which excremental filth can be promptly removed from the dwellings of the lower classes in towns and villages.

Leaving the better-to-do classes in exclusive enjoyment of their luxurious appliance, the water-closet, and to the responsibility of providing against the dangers which accompany its incautious use, or defective construction, we have here before us the great extended field of labour in which, for many years past, the employés of the English Privy Council and Local Government Board have been engaged in a noble struggle against filth diseases arising from non-removal of filth, for the benefit of the poorer classes more especially.

We are here introduced to an improved system of removal appliances, all distinguished from the bad arrangements in most general use, the midden and cess-pool, by the characteristic of a receptacle not admitting of communication with the soil, and, therefore, not of percolation through its pores into adjacent wells or running streams of water.

Among these rank in the gradation assigned to them in the Report—

1. Pail-Privies.
2. Ash-Privies.
3. Earth-Privies.
4. Charcoal-Privies.

The indispensable adjunct to the use of any of these plans is held to be a systematic regular course of emptying and removal, such as can be secured only by the vigilant attention, through its officers and servants, of the sanitary authority itself.

It is impossible to attempt to epitomize the contents of Mr. Simon's Report, and all which is above stated is meant to give a general idea of the scope and character of its teachings.

The Appendices are seven in number :—

No. I. A Tabulated Illustration, derived from Inspectors' Reports during the last four years, of the "*circumstances in which Enteric Fever is commonly found prevalent.*" The localities reported on are no less than 150 in number.

No. II. Report by Dr. Blaxall on an outbreak of Enteric Fever in the town of Sherbourne, Dorsetshire.

No. III. Report by Dr. Buchanan on an outbreak of Enteric Fever in Caius College, Cambridge.

No. IV. Report by Dr. Ballard on an outbreak of Enteric Fever at Armley, in the borough of Leeds. (This is the first of the Milk Reports.)

No. V. Report by Dr. Ballard on an outbreak of Enteric Fever at Moseley and Balsall Heath, near Birmingham. (The second Milk report.)

No. VI. Report by Mr. J. Netten Radcliffe and Mr. W. H. Power on an outbreak of Enteric Fever in Marylebone and adjoining parts of London. (The third Milk Report.)

No. VII. Report by Mr. J. Netten Radcliffe on certain means of preventing excremental nuisances in towns and villages.

The latter report is of great practical value as describing the various towns in Great Britain in which the recently adopted contrivances for receiving and removing excremental deposits, are in practical operation.

The one great lesson expounded on the subject of these contrivances is, that whatever apparatus be in general use, the prompt removal of excrement by a thorough system of scavenging, or scavenge, as it is called, is indispensably necessary to the security of the public health; and that such a system cannot be expected to be maintained without unintermitting attention on the part of the sanitary authority through its officers and servants.

There is one mode of excrement removal, too recently invented to have a place in Mr. Simon's Report, which has, however, assumed a position of progress in public opinion which will justify its being mentioned in this circular—Captain Liernur's *System of Pneumatic Drainage.*

This, as the name implies, is removal by atmospheric pressure through a system of pipes terminating at one centre, where a vacuum is made by a steam-engine. All is removed through the pipes simultaneously, or nearly so, without offence to sight or smell, once in twenty-four hours, and, water being excluded as far as practicable, no sewer gas ever escapes to the closet, and through it into the dwelling. At the central terminus all is removed, after being dried by heat, each twenty-four hours, in barrels to its destination in the country, where experiment has shown that it has a substantial commercial value. The liquid sewage is dealt with by a separate system of drainage, and is sent away comparatively unpolluted. In towns whose situation is not so near to tidal waters as to afford facility for the removal of sewage to the depths of the sea, this system must soon become an object of interest and inquiry.

It has already been tried with alleged success in certain towns in Holland, as Leyden and Amsterdam, but nowhere yet in Great Britain or Ireland.

The great discouragement to the adoption of this system is the first expense of establishing the works; their subsequent repair and permanent working expenses being comparatively light, and no more than may be covered or exceeded probably by the profits; but the system, adopted for sanitary purposes in this country, of Treasury Loans for long periods at moderate interest affords facilities for large initiatory outlays which do not exist abroad.

Urban sanitary authorities in Ireland will do well to inform themselves of the Liernur process, and to watch the results of the first trials of it in Great Britain.

By Order of the Board,

B. BANKS, Secretary.

To the Executive Officer of each
Sanitary Authority in Ireland.

---

## No. 2.—SALE OF FOOD AND DRUGS ACT, 1875.

Local Government Board, Dublin,
3rd November, 1875.

SIR,

The Local Government Board for Ireland desire to draw the attention of the Sanitary Authority to those provisions of the Act of last session, relating to the Sale of Food and Drugs, which prescribe the mode of proceeding to obtain an analysis of any article of food or of any drug, and a certificate of the result of such analysis; upon which, if it shall appear that an offence has been committed against any of the provisions of the Act, proceedings for the recovery of the penalty imposed for such offence may be taken.

Extracts from the Act (sections 12 to 17) are accordingly annexed hereto; and with reference to the 13th section, which enables certain officers and other persons under the direction and at the cost of the Local Authority appointing them or charged with the execution of the Act, to procure any sample of food or drugs if they shall suspect the same to have been sold contrary to any provision of the Act, and to submit the same to be analysed, the Board desire to state that they consider the words "Medical Officer of Health," and the words "Inspector of Nuisances," as used in that section, to include the "Sanitary Officers" and the "Sub-Sanitary Officers" under the Public Health Act, 1874.

By order of the Board,

B. BANKS, Secretary.

To each Urban Sanitary Authority
and each Rural Sanitary Authority.

EXTRACTS from the "Act to repeal the Adulteration of Food Acts and to make better provision for the Sale of Food and Drugs in a pure state." (38 & 39 Vic., c. 63.)

Sec 12. Any purchaser of an article of food or of a drug in any place being a district, county, city, or borough where there is any analyst appointed under this or any Act hereby repealed, shall be entitled, on payment to such analyst of a sum not exceeding ten shillings and sixpence, or if there be no such analyst then acting for such place, to the analyst of another place, of such sum as may be agreed upon between such person and the analyst, to have such article analysed by such analyst, and to receive from him a certificate of the result of his analysis.

Sec. 13. Any medical officer of health, inspector of nuisances, or inspector of weights and measures, or any inspector of a market, or any police constable under the direction and at the cost of the local authority appointing such officer, inspector, or constable, or charged with the execution of this Act, may procure any sample of food or drugs, and if he suspect the same to have been sold to him contrary to any provision of this Act, shall submit the same to be analysed by the analyst of the district or place for which he acts, or if there be no such analyst then acting for such place, to the analyst of another place, and such analyst shall, upon receiving payment as is provided in the last section, with all convenient speed analyse the same, and give a certificate to such officer, wherein he shall specify the result of the analysis.

Sec. 14. The person purchasing any article with the intention of submitting the same to analysis shall, after the purchase shall have been completed, forthwith notify to the seller or his agent selling the article his intention to have the same analysed by the public analyst, and shall offer to divide the article into three parts, to be then and there separated, and each part to be marked and sealed, or fastened up in such manner as its nature will permit, and shall, if required to do so, proceed accordingly, and shall deliver one of the parts to the seller or his agent.

He shall afterwards retain one of the said parts for future comparison, and submit the third part, if he deems it right to have the article analysed, to the analyst.

Sec. 15. If the seller or his agent do not accept the offer of the purchaser to divide the article purchased in his presence, the analyst receiving the article for analysis shall divide the same into two parts, and shall seal or fasten up one of those parts, and shall cause it to be delivered, either upon receipt of the sample or when he supplies his certificate to the purchaser, who shall retain the same for production in case proceedings shall afterwards be taken in the matter.

Sec. 16. If the analyst do not reside within two miles of the residence of the person requiring the article to be analysed, such article may be forwarded to the analyst through the post office as a registered letter, subject to any regulations which the Postmaster-General may make in reference to the carrying and delivery of such article, and the charge for the postage of such article shall be deemed one of the charges of this Act, or of the prosecution, as the case may be.

Sec. 17. If any such officer, inspector, or constable, as above described, shall apply to purchase any article of food or any drug exposed to sale, or on sale by retail on any premises or in any shop or stores, and shall tender the price for the quantity which he shall require for the purpose of analysis, not being more than shall be reasonably requisite, and the person exposing the same for sale shall refuse to sell the same to such officer, inspector, or constable, such person shall be liable to a penalty not exceeding ten pounds.

---

## No. 3.—COMMON LODGING HOUSES.

Local Government Board, Dublin,
6th September, 1875.

SIR,

The Local Government Board for Ireland have had referred to them from the office of the Chief Secretary of the Lord Lieutenant a report from a resident magistrate of an investigation made by him into certain occurrences which took place in a lodging house in the county of Westmeath, in which he makes the following observation :—

"This case compels me to call the attention of Government to the disgraceful indecency—to say the least—which must result from the manner in which persons of both sexes are permitted to huddle together in one wretched room, with a mere hole as a window, in such lodging houses (and I know they are numerous) as the above described."

The power of regulating common lodging houses, and thus preventing such a state of things as above described, being vested in the sanitary authorities, the Board think it right to draw their attention to the powers which they possess under the Common Lodging Houses Act, and to recommend them to take active steps for bringing all common lodging houses which are within their jurisdiction under proper regulation and control.

The Board are aware that in some instances regulations have been made, and a system of inspection established, but they think it right nevertheless to draw attention to the subject, with a view to such measures being more generally adopted in rural as well as in urban districts, the powers and duties of the various local authorities under the Common Lodging Houses Acts having been transferred by the 7th section of "The Public Health Act, 1874," to the sanitary authorities.

The Board desire, therefore, to draw attention to the circular letter of the Poor Law Commissioners, of the 30th June, 1860, printed in the Annual Report for 1861, page 25, and to request that the subject may be taken into consideration by the sanitary authorities, with the view of enforcing the registration of common lodging houses in their district, the making of suitable by-laws, and the inspection of such houses.

A copy of the Common Lodging Houses Acts is enclosed, together with a copy of a set of by-laws which were settled by counsel some time since, and which may, subject to the approval of the Local Government Board, be adopted either entirely or with any modifications that may be thought advisable.

By order of the Board,

B. BANKS, Secretary.

To each Executive Sanitary Officer.

---

ENCLOSURE.

BY-LAWS made by the SANITARY AUTHORITY, in pursuance of the provisions of "The Common Lodging Houses Act, Ireland, 1860," for the well ordering of such houses—for the separation of the Sexes therein—for fixing the Number and Sex of the Lodgers who may be received into each such house, and for promoting Cleanliness and Ventilation therein.

1. A copy of the by-laws shall be placed in a conspicuous part in each room or apartment of every common lodging house within the said Union, and shall not be defaced nor removed, and shall be delivered to the inspector or other authorized officer when thereunto required.

2. No keeper of a common lodging house shall accommodate a greater number of lodgers or other persons than that mentioned in the entry of said house in the register of common lodging houses.

3. Every common lodging house shall be swept or brushed out daily, and not later than 10 o'clock, A.M., washed at least once in each week, limewashed twice each year, and all filth shall be removed from the premises in a covered tin bucket twice daily, viz., before 7 o'clock, A.M., and after 10 o'clock, P.M., and the windows of such lodging houses shall be kept open for at least two hours daily.

4. Males and females shall occupy separate sleeping rooms; but where there may be only one sleeping apartment for lodgers, such lodging house shall be registered as a common lodging house for males or females, or for one married couple, as the keeper of such lodging house may select, and the keeper shall not receive any other but those for the reception of whom the said lodging house is registered.

5. No house shall be registered as a common lodging house unless there shall be appurtenant thereto the use of a water-closet or privy or be furnished with a night-chair, nor unless each sleeping room shall have an external window made to open.

6. If any lodger in any common lodging house be attacked with illness, the keeper of the lodging house shall report the same to the Inspector of Lodging Houses or to the Relieving Officer and the Sanitary Officer of the District; and in all cases where a person ill of fever or any infectious disease is removed therefrom, or becomes convalescent, or dies therein, such lodging house shall be thoroughly cleansed and limewashed, and shall be purified by using a disinfecting process.

7. No horse, ass, mule, horned cattle, sheep, or swine shall be kept or fed in any common lodging house.

8. The keeper of every common lodging house shall always have a good supply of pure fresh water for the use and accommodation of lodgers, and shall at all times have a basin and towel for each sleeping room in such lodging house.

9. The yards and area of every common lodging house shall be thoroughly swept and cleansed once at least every day, and no stagnant or foul water or other offensive matter shall be allowed to remain in any such yards or areas.

10. The keeper of every common lodging house shall, before admitting any applicant for lodging, ascertain the name and last place of residence of such applicant or applicants, his or their usual occupation, trade, or calling; and every common lodging house keeper shall keep a book in which shall be entered the name of every person as aforesaid, and the day of the month each person commenced lodging, and also the day of the month each person ceased to be a lodger in such lodging house; and the keeper of every common lodging house shall produce at all times when so required said book to the Inspector of Common Lodging Houses or other authorized officer, who is hereby empowered to take a copy of any and every entry made therein.

——— Chairman.

——— Executive Sanitary Officer.

These By-laws confirmed by the Local Government Board for Ireland, this day of 187 .

{ *Seal of the Local Government Board.* }

---

NOTICE.

If the keeper of a common lodging house, or any other persons having or acting in the care or management thereof, offend against any of the provisions of the Common Lodging Houses Acts, or against any of the foregoing by-laws, every person so offending will for every such offence be liable to a penalty not exceeding five pounds, and to a further penalty not exceeding forty shillings for every day during which the offence continues, and such penalties are recoverable before the Justices at Petty Sessions (14 & 15 Vic., cap. 28, section 14, and 23 Vic., cap. 26, section 6).

——— Chairman.

——— Executive Sanitary Officer.

## No. 4.—Regulation and Inspection of Common Lodging Houses.

Local Government Board, Dublin,
9th February, 1876.

Sir,

Adverting to their circular letter of the 6th September last, on the subject of the adoption of by-laws by the sanitary authorities, for the regulation of common lodging houses under the provisions of the Common Lodging Houses Acts, the Local Government Board for Ireland desire to acquaint you that having received a communication from a rural sanitary authority, by which the by-laws which accompanied that letter had been adopted, suggesting that the services of the Royal Irish Constabulary should be made available in carrying out their provisions, the Board brought the subject under the consideration of His Grace the Lord Lieutenant, and the matter having been referred to the Inspector-General of Royal Irish Constabulary, it appears to be considered by him that for the police to carry out these by-laws would occupy too much of their time, but that there is no objection to their enforcing the rule which provides that no keeper of a common lodging house shall accommodate a greater number of lodgers or other persons than that mentioned in the entry of said house in the register of common lodging houses.

It is doubtful, however, whether the constabulary have power to enter common lodging houses at all times, and therefore, if the sanitary authority desire to avail themselves of the services of the constabulary in this respect, to the extent above stated, which the Board would recommend them to do, they should make a new by-law under the 4th section of the Common Lodging Houses (Ireland) Act, 1860, providing for the employment of the constabulary as officers to make entry and inspection at all hours, and providing a penalty in case of refusal or obstruction. A draft of such a by-law is annexed.

Should the proposed by-law be adopted, the sub-inspector or constable in charge should be informed of the authorized number of lodgers for each house.

By order of the Board,

B. Banks, Secretary.

To each Urban Sanitary Authority and each
Rural Sanitary Authority.

---

### Common Lodging Houses Acts.

*14 & 15 Vic., c. 28; 16 & 17 Vic., c. 41; 23 Vic., c. 26.*

Whereas the* sanitary authority have, in pursuance of the powers vested in them in that behalf, made by-laws respecting common lodging houses within their district, for the well ordering of such houses and for the separation of the sexes therein, and for fixing the number and sex of the lodgers who may be received into each such house, and for promoting cleanliness and ventilation therein, and such by-laws have been duly approved in accordance with the provisions of the above-mentioned Acts, and it is expedient to provide, by a by-law to be made in pursuance of the powers aforesaid, for the inspection of such houses:

Now, Therefore, We hereby make the following by-law in addition to the by-laws so made and approved as aforesaid:—

"The keeper of every common lodging house shall give access to the same, at all times when required by the Sanitary Officer, or by any Sub-Sanitary

* Insert the word "Urban" or "Rural," as the case may be, and the name of the district.

Officer of the District, or by any member of the Royal Irish Constabulary who shall be authorized by the sanitary authority to enter such common lodging house for any of the purposes of the said Acts. And any person who shall refuse so to admit any such Sanitary Officer, Sub-Sanitary Officer, or member of the Royal Irish Constabulary, or shall offer any obstruction to his or their entrance, shall be liable to the penalties provided by the said Acts for offences against by-laws made under the provisions thereof."

(Signed), ——— Chairman.
——— Executive Sanitary Officer.
(Date) ———, 1876.

This by-law confirmed by the Local Government Board for Ireland, this day of 1876.

[Seal].

---

## No. 5.—LOANS from PUBLIC WORKS LOAN COMMISSIONERS.

Local Government Board, Dublin,
3rd November, 1875.

SIR,

The Local Government Board for Ireland have received a communication from the Chief Secretary's office intimating the desire of His Grace the Lord Lieutenant that certain provisions of the Public Works Loans Act of last session (38 and 39 Vic., c. 89), should be communicated to the several Boards of Guardians, Towns Improvement Commissioners, and other bodies which are required by law to procure the sanction of this Board for the purpose of obtaining loans.

The Board accordingly desire to state that the 13th section of the Act provides that, for the purpose of passing an annual Act of Parliament granting money for the purpose of loans by the Public Works Loan Commissioners, every intending borrower shall send to those Commissioners, on or before the 31st day of December in every year, a statement of the new loan, or instalment of a loan already granted, which the sender will probably apply for during the ensuing financial year (that is, the year commencing on the 1st April). These statements are to be submitted to the Treasury by the Loan Commissioners, with such information as may be necessary for enabling the Treasury to lay before the House of Commons an estimate of the amount required to be granted for the purpose of loans by the Loan Commissioners, who will not have power, except with permission of the Treasury, to grant any loan or advance any instalment of a loan which has not been included in such a statement as above mentioned.

The Board are informed that the first measure for this purpose will be laid before Parliament in its next session, the 1st of April next being the date fixed for the commencement of the new system, and that it is therefore necessary, under the 54th section of the Act, that the Treasury should at once obtain materials for an estimate, any body or person not sending to the Public Works Loan Commissioners, on or before the 31st day of December next, an estimate of the loans out of the Consolidated Fund for which they will make application under the Public Works Loan Acts, will not be entitled to any loan out of the Consolidated Fund in the course of the financial year commencing the 1st day of April, 1876, even though they may fulfil all the other conditions which Parliament has prescribed.

It is right at the same time to observe that the 57th section provides that the Act shall not affect the issue of money for the purposes of Loans by the Commissioners of Public Works in Ireland, in accordance with the Act 29 and 30 Vic., c. 73, and that the sums mentioned in that Act may be issued in like manner as if the present Act had not been passed.

It appears, therefore, that the new enactment, so far as regards Ireland, applies only to those loans which are made by the English Public Works Loan Board, and does not affect loans which may be advanced by the Commissioners of Public Works in Ireland.

By order of the Board,

B. Banks, Secretary.

To each Board of Guardians
and each Governing Body of a town in Ireland.

---

III.—CORRESPONDENCE WITH THE BOARD OF GUARDIANS OF THE WATERFORD UNION, ON THE SUBJECT OF THE SALARIES OF SANITARY OFFICERS UNDER THE PUBLIC HEALTH ACT.

(In continuation of the correspondence printed in the Annual Report for 1875, App. C. III.)

### No. 1.—Extract from Minutes of Proceedings of the Board of Guardians, on Wednesday, 7th April, 1875.

Ordered in reference to Clerk's Report of last Board day concerning the payment of the salaries due to the Officers under the Public Health Act, which were fixed by the Local Government Board.

That this Board is prepared to pay these Sanitary salaries according to the scale fixed by this Board itself.

Moved by Mr. Conn, seconded by Mr. Clampett—passed with two dissentients.

---

### No. 2.—Extract from Minutes of Proceedings of the Board of Guardians, on 30th June, 1875.

Clerk's Report.

The usual Meeting of the Finance Committee was held yesterday. The Bills of the Sanitary Officers were presented, calculated according to the scale fixed by the Local Government Board. The Committee rejected them, and directed the Clerk to acquaint those Officers that the Committee is ready to pay their salaries as Sanitary Officers, at the scale fixed by the Board of Guardians.

Approved.

---

### No. 3.—Letter from the Local Government Board to the Board of Guardians.

Local Government Board, Dublin,
6th July, 1875.

Sir,

The Local Government Board for Ireland acknowledge the receipt of the Minutes of Proceedings of the Board of Guardians of the Waterford Union on the 30th ult., from which it appears that the Sanitary Officers' accounts, calculated in accordance with the scale fixed by the Order of the Local Government Board, were presented to the Finance Committee, but were rejected in consequence of their not being made out according to the sums fixed by the Guardians; and in reference thereto the Board desire to point out that the Guardians are liable to be sued for the legal salaries as fixed by the Local Government Board.

By order of the Board,

B. Banks, Secretary.

To the Clerk of Waterford Union.

---

## No. 4.—Extract from Minutes of Proceedings of the Board of Guardians, on 8th September, 1875.

Read letter from Messrs. Dobbyn and Tandy, solicitors, forwarding case submitted to counsel on behalf of Sir R. J. Paul, Bart., as Chairman of the Waterford Union, in reference to the powers of the Local Government Board to fix the salaries of the Sanitary Officers at a higher figure than that agreed upon by the Board of Guardians.

1. Counsel stated in reply to inquiries—"That in his opinion the effect of the Public Health Act, 1874, established by the decision of the Queen's Bench upon an earlier statute (Reg. *v.* Guardians of Bantry Union), is to empower the Local Government Board to compel the payment of the salaries approved by the Board. The sealed Order will not authorize the Treasurer to make the payment but if the Guardians should refuse to sanction the salary directed by the Board, a mandamus can be obtained by application to the Queen's Bench enforcing the payment of the salary fixed by the Order notwithstanding the opposition of the Guardians.

2. The medical officers cannot, in counsel's opinion, sue by action for their salaries, but they, as interested parties, can apply for the writ of mandamus to enforce payment of the sum which has been approved by the Local Government Board.

3. The Chairman is only one member of the Board of Guardians. He cannot be enforced in any way to obey the Orders of the Local Government Board, in signing cheques or otherwise, contrary to the vote of the majority of the Guardians, but the whole body of Guardians can be compelled by mandamus to pay the approved salary.

4. The same difference of opinion arose in many Poor Law Unions. I believe that the opinion I have given above has been given by other counsel, and acted on by the Guardians elsewhere. Inquiry might well be made as to this, because if it has been determined in any other Union to contest the matter, the Waterford Guardians might be unwilling to yield, until a general decision has been obtained, but I cannot advise litigation, and I would recommend the Guardians to pass a resolution under protest, yielding to the sealed Order, and directing the payment of the approved salaries.

Gerald FitzGibbon.

Board to be summoned specially, to take the foregoing into consideration this day week.

## No. 5.—Extracts from Minutes of Proceedings of the Board of Guardians on 22nd September, 1875.

The following letter was read from Sir R. J. Paul, Chairman:—

Ballyglan, Waterford,
September 21, 1875.

Dear Sir,

In answer to your circular, with query whether I would act as an *ex-officio* Guardian for the ensuing year, I regret that I feel constrained to answer in the negative. My decision has not been caused altogether by the late difference with the Local Government Board, but I can see that the general drift of the current of authority is towards central management. I, as a country gentleman, would always have been glad to assist in the relief of the poor, and to use any local knowledge that I possess for the furtherance of that object; but I could not afford to waste my time in acting merely as the medium for carrying out what I and the majority of the Board consider to be injudicious measures.

If the Local Government Board disapprove of the opinion held by the Board of Guardians in respect to vital questions of charges on the rates, they ought to appoint their own paid Guardians, and take the responsibility off the Local Guardians.

I also perceive that every day matters outside the relief of the poor are added to the duties of the Guardians and to the amount of the rate.

I hope that you will convey to the Board my sincere thanks for their kindness and good-will to me during the many years that I have had the honour of being the chairman.

I ought also to express my opinion that there should be no further opposition to paying the amount of salary named by the Local Government Board—that is, assuming that the Board of Guardians continue to act.

Permit me also to thank you individually for the assistance that you have always given to me.

Believe me yours faithfully,

R. J. Paul.

To John Mackey, esq.

Moved by Alderman Jacob, v.c., seconded by Mr. Bloomfield, J.P.:—

Resolved—That the Board has heard with deep regret the letter addressed by their valued Chairman, Sir R. J. Paul, to the Clerk, declining to act as an *ex-officio* Guardian during the coming year. Entirely uniting and sympathising with his views as expressed therein, yet they earnestly and unanimously entreat him to reconsider his determination and not withdraw himself from the chairmanship of the Board which has so loved and respected him.

Passed unanimously.

Read letter No. 1,610, 17th September, 1875, for return of salaries of officers under "The Public Health Act, 1874," to be signed by the presiding Chairman and Executive Sanitary Officer.

The Executive Sanitary Officer prepared the return as directed, and submitted it for the presiding Chairman's signature; but on a division, the Board decided, by 11 to 6 votes, to postpone the consideration of this return, as also the counsel's opinion upon the subject of the payment of the sanitary salaries fixed by sealed order of the Local Government Board for a fortnight.

## No. 6.—Extract from Minutes of Proceedings of the Board of Guardians on 27th October, 1875.

The Board having proceeded to the consideration of counsel's opinion upon the subject of the payment of the sanitary salaries fixed by the Local Government Board, &c., &c.—

Mr. Clampett moved, and Mr. Halley seconded—That this Board of Guardians adheres to its former resolution to pay the salaries of the Sanitary Officers as fixed by themselves.

Passed on a division by 8 to 2 votes.

The presiding Chairman accordingly declined to sign the return prepared by the Executive Sanitary Officer of the Sanitary Officers' salaries, the amount stated therein as the salaries of the Rural Sanitary Officers being in accordance with the sealed order of the Local Government Board.

---

## No. 7.—Letter from the Local Government Board to the Board of Guardians.

Local Government Board, Dublin,
8th November, 1875.

Sir,

The Local Government Board for Ireland have had before them the Minutes of Proceedings of the Board of Guardians of the Waterford Union on the 27th ult., when the opinion of counsel upon the subject of the payment of the salaries fixed by order of the Local Government Board was under consideration, and the following resolution was adopted :—

"That this Board of Guardians adheres to its former resolution to pay the salaries of the Sanitary Officers as fixed by themselves."

In reference thereto I am directed to state that the Local Government Board desire to learn whether, in face of the opinion given to them by the learned and eminent counsel whom they have consulted, the Guardians of Waterford Union are prepared to oppose a deliberate resistance to the law.

A specific statement of their intention to do so, or, on the other hand, to pay the Sanitary Officers what they are legally entitled to receive, must be promptly given, if the Guardians have any desire to avoid legal proceedings.

By order of the Board,

B. Banks, Secretary.

To the Clerk, Waterford Union.

---

## No. 8.—Extract from Minutes of Proceedings of the Board of Guardians, on 1st December, 1875.

In accordance with his adjourned motion Mr. Barron Newell moved, and Captain Power, v.c., seconded :—

1. That the Order of the Local Government Board be carried out as regards the salaries of our Sanitary Officers to avoid the threatened legal proceedings, at the same time this Board protesting against the arbitrary and coercive policy of the Local Government Board.

To this, the first resolution of Mr. Newell's motion, the Hon. Mr. Fortescue moved, and Alderman St. George Freeman seconded, an amendment.

That all the words in Mr. B. Newell's motion after "Legal proceedings" be postponed and considered in a separate resolution.

Amendment lost on a division by 8 to 4 votes. The original motion then put and carried by 8 to 2 votes.

The second resolution as follows, in the motion by Mr. Newell :—

"That we call on the members of Parliament for the county and city of Waterford to introduce a Bill into Parliament next session to amend and limit the excessive powers of the Local Government Board, particularly as regards the regulation of salaries, this Board considering that from local and personal knowledge, they must be the best judges of suitable amount of salaries," was withdrawn.

IV.—Statement of Orders issued under the 15th Section of the Public Health Act, 1874, determining the Area of Charge on which the Special Expenses mentioned in each Order respectively shall be chargeable.

| Name of Union, and Town, Village, or Place | Date of Order | Purposes for which Incurred or to be Incurred | | Area of Charge. |
|---|---|---|---|---|
| | | Water Supply, &c. | Sewerage, &c. | |
| Armagh Union: | | | | |
| Keady Town, . . | 22nd September, 1874, . | Supply of water, . . | — | The Townlands of Carganaghan, Crossdened, and Racarbry, situate in the Keady Electoral Division, and the Townlands of [illegible] and Dunlarg, situate in the [illegible] Electoral Division. |
| Bailieborough Union: | | | | |
| Kingscourt Town, . . | 23rd December, 1875, . | Do., . | — | The Kingscourt Electoral Division. |
| Ballina Union: | | | | |
| Ballina Town, | 2nd March, 1876, . | — | Sewerage. | Estimated expense, £8,207, of which £1,114, with interest thereon, to be charged to the Townlands of Ballina, Cloonanass, Gortern, Kilmoremoy, Knockbanagh, and Mullauns, situate in the Ballina Electoral Division, and the Townlands of Abbey Half-quarter, Ardnaree or Shanaghy, Bunree, Carrowcushlaun West, Garden, and Knockanelo or Downhill, situate in the Ardnaree South Electoral Division, and £466, with interest thereon, to be charged to the several Electoral Divisions of the Union. |
| Ballinrobe Union: | | | | |
| Ballinrobe Town, . | 23rd September, 1875, | — | Sewers in Cornmarket Townland. | The Townland of Cornmarket, situate in Ballinrobe Electoral Division. |
| Ballymoney Union: | | | | |
| Ballymoney Town, . | 18th December, 1875, . | — | Sewerage, . . . | The Townlands of Townparks and Glebe, situate in the Ballymoney Electoral Division. |
| Ballyshannon Union: | | | | |
| Ballyshannon Town, . | 18th March, 1876. . | — | Do., . . . | All the Townlands comprised in the Ballyshannon Electoral Division. |
| Ballyshannon „ . | — | Supply of water and a pump. | New Sewerage and cleansing old drains. | The Townlands of Camp, Cooloney and Townparks, situate in Ballyshannon Electoral Division, and the Townlands of Carrickboy and Portnason, situate in Carrickboy Electoral Division. |
| Belleek „ . | — | Do., . . | — | The Townlands of Finner and Rathmore, situate in Belleek Electoral Division. |
| Ballyvaghan Union: | | | | |
| Ballyvaghan Town, . . | 27th October, 1874, . | Supply of water, . . | — | £150, with interest thereon, to be charged to the several Electoral Divisions of the Union. |
| Ballyvaghan Workhouse. | Do., . | Do., . . | — | £360, with interest thereon, to be charged to the several Electoral Divisions of the Union. |

IV.—Statement of Orders issued under the 13th Section of the Public Health Act, 1874, determining the Area of Charge on which the Special Expenses mentioned in such Orders respectively shall be chargeable—*continued*.

| Name of Union, and Town, Village, or Place. | Date of Order. | Purposes for which incurred or to be incurred. | | Area of Charge. |
|---|---|---|---|---|
| | | Water Supply, &c. | Sewerage, &c. | |
| Balrothery Union: | | | | |
| Balbriggan Town, | 12th July, 1875, | — | Sewerage. | The Townlands of Balbriggan and Tankardstown, and "Balbriggan Demesne." |
| Rush " | 9th August, 1875, | Supply of water, | — | The Townlands of Rush and Rush Demesne, situate in the Lusk Electoral Division. |
| Kinsaley Townland, | 9th September, 1875, | Do., | — | The Townland of Kinsaley, situate in the Kinsaley Electoral Division. |
| Baltinglass Union: | | | | |
| Baltinglass Town, | 16th September, 1874, | Do. | — | The Townland of Baltinglass East, situate in the Baltinglass Electoral Division. |
| Banbridge Union: | | | | |
| Banbridge Town, | 20th June, 1874, | Do., | Sewerage, and removal of nuisances, &c. | The Townlands of Ballyvally, Edenderry, and Tullyear, situate in the Banbridge Electoral Division. |
| Dromore " | Do., | Do., | Do., | The Townlands of Ballymacormick, Ballymaganlis, Ballyvicknacally, and Drumbroneth, situate in the Dromore Electoral Division, and the Townland of Balleny, situate in the Quilly Electoral Division. |
| Gilford " | Do., | Do., | Do., | The Townlands of Drumaran and Loughans, situate in the Tullylish Electoral Division. |
| Tanderagee " | Do., | Do. | Do., | The Townlands of Ballymore, Cargans, Derryallen, Drumanaghy, Lisbane, and Tullyhugh, situate in the Tanderagee Electoral Division, and the Townland of Cordrain, situate in the Mullahead Electoral Division. |
| Belfast Union: | | | | |
| Holywood Town, | 20th August, 1875, | Do., | — | The Townlands of Holywood and Ballykeel, situate in Holywood Electoral Division. |
| Cahersiveen Union: | | | | |
| Cahersiveen Town, | 27th January, 1874, | Repairing public wells, and providing pipes at Quay street. | | The Townland of Cahirsiveen, situate in the Caher Electoral Division. |
| Carrick-on-Suir Union: | | | | |
| Ballyneill, | 12th August, 1875, | Supply of water, | — | The Electoral Division of Kilmurry, together with the Townlands of Figlash and Mullagh, situate in the Carrick-on-Suir Electoral Division, and the Townland of Moanmore, in the Newtown Electoral Division. |

| | | | | |
|---|---|---|---|---|
| CASTLEDERG UNION: | | | | |
| Castlederg Town, | 24th October, 1874, | Do., | Sewerage, | The Townland of Churchtown, situate in the Castlederg Electoral Division. |
| CAVAN UNION: | | | | |
| Kilnaleck Town, | 22nd September, 1874, | — | Do., | Kilnaleck Electoral Division. |
| Belturbet " | Do., | — | Do., | The Townland of Corporation Lands, in the Belturbet Electoral Division. |
| Cavan, " | Do., | Analysis of water supplied by public pumps. | Repairs of watercourse at Half Acre. | The Cavan Electoral Division. |
| Abbeyland, " | Do., | — | Sewerage, | The Townland of Abbeyland, in the Cavan Electoral Division. |
| CELBRIDGE UNION: | | | | |
| Ballymakealy Town, | 20th May, 1875, | Supply of water, | — | The Townlands of Ballymakealy Upper and Killadoon, situate in the Celbridge Electoral Division. |
| Lucan " | Do., | Do., | — | The Townlands of Lucan and Pettycanon and Lucan Demesne, situate in the Lucan Electoral Division. |
| Rathcoole " | Do., | Do., | — | The Townland of Rathcoole, situate in the Rathcoole Electoral Division. |
| Saggart " | Do., | Do., | — | The Townland of Saggart situate in the Saggart Electoral Division. |
| Rathcoffey " | 17th August, 1875, | Do., | — | The Townlands of Rathcoffey North and South, Rathcoffey Demesne, and Mooretown, situate in Balraheen Electoral Division. |
| Maynooth " | 16th November, 1875, | Supply of water, and keeping pump in order. | — | The Townlands of Maynooth, College Land, Mariavilla, and Greenfield, situate in Maynooth Electoral Division. |
| Celbridge " | Do., | Do., | — | The Townlands of Celbridge, Celbridge Abbey, Oakley Park, and Castletown, in the Celbridge Electoral Division. |
| Leixlip " | Do., | Do., | — | The Townlands of Leixlip and Newtown, situate in the Leixlip Electoral Division. |
| Newcastle " | 20th January, 1876, | Repairing a public pump, | — | The Townland of Newcastle South, situate in the Newcastle Electoral Division. |
| CLAREMORRIS UNION: | | | | |
| Claremorris Town, | 20th May, 1875, | — | Cleansing a sewer, | The Townland of Clare, situate in the Claremorris Electoral Division. |
| Ballyhaunis " | 10th January, 1876, | Cleansing and repairing a public well. | — | The Townlands of Hazelhill, Abbeyquarter, Friarsquarter, Carrowreaggans, and Pollinaroughy, situate in the Ballyhaunis Electoral Division. |
| CLONAKILTY UNION: | | | | |
| Clonakilty Town, | 15th April, 1875, | Supply of water, | — | The Townlands of Desert, Clogheen (Kilgarriff Parish), [illegible], [illegible], Tawnies Upper, Tawnies Lower, and Youghals (Kilgarriff Parish) situate in the Clonakilty Electoral Division. |
| Courtmacsherry, " | 10th June, 1875, | Do., | — | The Townlands of Courtmacsherry, Cullenagh, and Meelmane, situate in the Courtmacsherry Electoral Division. |

IV.—STATEMENT of ORDERS issued under the 13th Section of the PUBLIC HEALTH ACT, 1874, determining the AREA of CHARGE on which the SPECIAL EXPENSES mentioned in such Orders respectively shall be chargeable—*continued.*

| NAME OF UNION, AND TOWN, VILLAGE, OR PLACE. | Date of Order | Purposes for which Incurred or to be Incurred. | | AREA OF CHARGE. |
|---|---|---|---|---|
| | | Water Supply, &c. | Sewerage, &c. | |
| COLERAINE UNION: | | | | |
| Clifton terrace in Townland of Coleraine and Suburbs. | 22nd October, 1875. | — | Constructing sewer, | The Townland of Coleraine and Suburbs, situate in the Coleraine Electoral Division, except such portion of the Townland as is included within the Coleraine Urban Sanitary District |
| COOTEHILL UNION | | | | |
| Cootehill Town, | 8th November, 1875, | — | Cleansing sewers, &c. | The Townlands of Magheranure, Mounthill, Drumeril North, Killycrampa, and Bellamont Forest, situate in the Cootehill Electoral Division |
| CORK UNION | | | | |
| Passage West Town, | 19th August, 1875, | Supply of water, | Sewerage, | The Townlands of Monkstown, Pembroke, and Lackaroe, in the Monkstown Electoral Division. |
| DELVIN UNION | | | | |
| Delvin Town, | 18th October, 1875, | Do., and repairing pump. | Do., | The Delvin Electoral Division |
| Castlepollard | Do. | Repairing pump, | Do., | The Kinturk Electoral Division. |
| DONEGAL UNION | | | | |
| Donegal Town, | 14th October, 1875, | Supply of water, | Do. | The Townland of Donegal, situate in the Donegal Electoral Division |
| DOWNPATRICK UNION | | | | |
| Castlewellan Town, | 4th December, 1875, | — | Do. | The Townland of Castlewellan, situate in the Castlewellan Electoral Division |
| Killough | Do., | — | Do., | The Townland of Killough, situate in the Killough Electoral Division |
| DROGHEDA UNION | | | | |
| Bettystown Village, | 24th November, 1875, | Supply of water, | — | The Julianstown and St. Mary's Electoral Divisions, except such portion of St Mary's Division as is included within the Drogheda Urban Sanitary District. |
| Clogherhead, | 22nd February, 1876, | Do. | — | The St. Peter's Electoral Division, except the portion included within the Drogheda Urban Sanitary District. |

| | | | | |
|---|---|---|---|---|
| DUBLIN NORTH UNION: | | | | |
| River Tolka, at Ballybough Bridge. | 18th November, 1875, | — | Cleansing the river, &c. | The Drumcondra Electoral Division, except such portion as is included within the Clontarf Urban Sanitary District. |
| Blackhorse-lane, in Townlands of Ashtown and Cabragh | 20th December, 1875, | — | Sewerage, | The Castleknock Electoral Division. |
| Artane Village, | 9th February, 1876, | Supply of water, | — | The Clontarf and Drumcondra Electoral Divisions, except the portions comprised within the Clontarf Urban Sanitary District. |
| DUBLIN SOUTH UNION. | | | | |
| Saint-Laurence Townland, | 2nd June, 1876, | Do. | — | The Townland of Saint Laurence, situate in the Palmerstown Electoral Division |
| DUNGANNON UNION. | | | | |
| Dungannon Town, | 20th September, 1875, | Do. | Do. | The Electoral Division of Dungannon. |
| Coal Island | Do. | Construction of a new well, and the cleansing of the present pump well. | — | The Townlands of Brackaville, Derry, Gortgonis, and Gortnaskea, situate in the Electoral Division of Tullyniskan, and the Townland of Annagher, situate in the Electoral Division of Mullaghmore; one-half of the expenses to be charged to the said Townland of Brackaville, and the other half to be charged to the said Townlands of Derry, Gortgonis, Gortnaskea, and Annagher. |
| ENNISCORTHY UNION. | | | | |
| Enniscorthy Town, | 28th September, 1875, | — | Cleansing sewers, | The Townlands of Enniscorthy, Templeshannon, and Killagoley, situate in the Enniscorthy Electoral Division. |
| ENNISTYMON UNION. | | | | |
| Miltown-Malbay Town, | 7th October, 1875, | Supply of water, | Sewerage, | The Miltown-Malbay Electoral Division. |
| Lisdoonvarna | Do. | Do. | — | The Lisdoonvarna Electoral Division. |
| Kilfenora | Do. | Do. | — | The Kilfenora Electoral Division. |
| GLENNAMADDY UNION. | | | | |
| Glennamaddy Town, | 12th January, 1876, | Supply of water, | — | The Townlands of Glennamaddy, Cloonmore West, Gortnagier West, and Scotland, situate in the Glennamaddy Electoral Division. |
| Ballymoe | — | Do. | — | The Townlands of Derrew and Cloonee, situate in the Ballymoe Electoral Division. |
| Kilkerrin Village, | — | Do. | — | The Townlands of Carrowkeane and Tullinlaun, situate in the Shankill Electoral Division. |
| GLENTIES UNION. | | | | |
| Dunglow Town, | 6th March, 1876, | — | Sewerage, | The Townlands of Dunglow and Meenmore, situate in the Dunglow Electoral Division. |

IV.—Statement of Orders issued under the 15th Section of the Public Health Act, 1874, determining the Area of Charge on which the Special Expenses mentioned in such Orders respectively shall be chargeable—*continued.*

| Name of Union, and Town, Village, or Place. | Date of Order | Purposes for which incurred or to be incurred. | | Area of Charge. |
|---|---|---|---|---|
| | | Water Supply, &c. | Sewerage, &c. | |
| Granard Union: | | | | |
| Granard Town, | 31st December, 1878, | — | Do. | The Townlands of Granard, Granardkill, and Rathcronan, situate in the Granard Electoral Division. |
| Do. | 18th March, 1879, | — | Do. | The Townlands of Granard and Rathcronan, situate in the Granard Electoral Division. |
| Abbeylara Village, | 31st December, 1878, | Improving a well, | — | The Townlands of Abbeylara and Kilbride, situate in Abbeylara Electoral Division and the Townland of [illegible], situate in [illegible] Electoral Division. |
| [illegible] Union: | | | | |
| [illegible] Town, | 17th September, 1878, | Supply of water, | — | The Townland of [illegible], situate in the [illegible] Electoral Division. |
| [illegible] Union: | | | | |
| [illegible] Town, | 16th January, 1878, | Do. | — | The Electoral Divisions of [illegible], [illegible] Park, [illegible], Bally[illegible], and [illegible]town. |
| Killarney Union: | | | | |
| Killarney Town, | 8th October, 1878, | Repairing and keeping in repair public pumps | — | The Townlands of [illegible], [illegible], Avenue, Bally[illegible], Bally[illegible], [illegible], [illegible], [illegible], Killarney, [illegible], [illegible], [illegible], [illegible], and [illegible], situate in the Killarney Electoral Division. |
| Milltown Town, | Do. | Supply of water, | — | The Townlands of [illegible], Ballymacomaly, Ballyoughtragh North, Ballyoughtragh South, [illegible], [illegible], [illegible], [illegible], [illegible], Kilderry North, Kilderry South, [illegible], [illegible], [illegible], Milltown, [illegible] East, and [illegible] West, situate in the Milltown Electoral Division. |
| Gneeveguilla Village, | Do. | Do. | — | The Townlands of [illegible], Gneeveguilla, [illegible] East, [illegible] West, [illegible] and [illegible], situate in the [illegible] Electoral Division and the Townlands of [illegible], [illegible], and [illegible], situate in the Rathmore Electoral Division. |
| Kinsale Union: | | | | |
| Carrigaline Town (part of) | 10th April, 1878, | Do. | — | The Townland of [illegible], situate in the Carrigaline Electoral Division, and the Townland of [illegible], situate in the Liscleary Electoral Division. |

| | | | | |
|---|---|---|---|---|
| **Larne Union:** | | | | |
| Carrickfergus Town, . | 3rd September, 1875, | — | Cleansing and repairing sewers. | The Carrickfergus Electoral Division. |
| Larne, . . | Do. . | Providing a new pump, and repairing fountains and water pipes. | Repairing a sewer, | The Townlands of [illegible] and [illegible], situate in the Larne Electoral Division. |
| **Lismore Union.** | | | | |
| Tallow Town, . . . | 23rd September, 1875, | — | Sewerage, . . | One-half the expenses to be charged to the Townland of Tallow, and the other half to be charged to the several other townlands comprised in the Tallow Electoral Division. |
| **Listowel Union:** | | | | |
| Ballylongford Town, . | 20th November, 1875, | — | Do. | The Lisloughtin Electoral Division. |
| **Loughrea Union:** | | | | |
| Athenry Town, . . | 13th April, 1876, . | Supply of water | — | The Athenry Electoral Division. |
| **[illegible] Union:** | | | | |
| [illegible] Town, . . | 12th January, 1876, . | Improving a public well and providing a new pump. | — | The Townlands of [illegible] East and West, situate in the [illegible] Electoral Division. |
| **Macroom Union:** | | | | |
| Macroom Town and Workhouse. | 24th April, 1876, . | Supply of water, . . | — | Three-fourths of the total amount of expenses to be charged to the Townlands of Lackaduff, Sleveen East, Sleveen West, [illegible], [illegible], and [illegible], situate in the Macroom Electoral Division, in respect of the Town of Macroom, and one-fourth in respect of the Workhouse, to be charged on the several Electoral Divisions of the Macroom Union, including the Macroom Electoral Division. |
| **Mohill Union:** | | | | |
| Cloone Town, . . . | 9th April, 1877, . | Do. . | — | The Townland of Cloone, situate in the Cloone Electoral Division. |
| **[illegible] Union:** | | | | |
| [illegible] Village, . | 17th September, 1875, | Pumps to be kept in order. | Sewerage, . | The Townlands of [illegible] or The Dorlas, and [illegible], situate in the [illegible] Electoral Division. |
| Springfield, in Townland of [illegible]. | Do. . . | New well and pump, . | — | The Townlands of [illegible], [illegible], [illegible], and [illegible], situate in the [illegible] Electoral Division, and the Townland of [illegible], situate in the [illegible] Electoral Division. |
| [illegible]-road, in Townland of Lough. | Do. . . | New well and pump, | — | The Townland of Lough, situate in the [illegible] Electoral Division. |
| [illegible] Village. | Do. . | Well and pump to be put in order | — | The Townland of [illegible], situate in the [illegible] Electoral Division. |
| [illegible] Village, . | Do. . | New pump, . . . | — | The Townland of [illegible], situate in the [illegible] Electoral Division. |
| [illegible] Village. | Do. . . | Well and pump to be put in order | — | The Townlands of [illegible] and [illegible], situate in the [illegible] Electoral Division. |

IV.—Statement of Orders issued under the 13th Section of the Public Health Act, 1874, determining the Area of Charge on which the Special Expenses mentioned in such Orders respectively shall be chargeable—*continued*.

| Name of Union, and Town, Village, or Place. | Date of Order. | Purposes for which Incurred or to be Incurred: Water Supply, &c. | Purposes for which Incurred or to be Incurred: Sewerage, &c. | Area of Charge. |
|---|---|---|---|---|
| Mountmellick Union—*continued*. | | | | |
| Mountmellick Town, . | 13th September, 1876, | Two new pumps; all other pumps to be kept in order | Survey and map of streets. | The Townland of Townparks, situate in the Mountmellick Electoral Division, and the Townland of Ballycullenbeg, situate in the Dangans Electoral Division. |
| Acragar, . . . . | Do., . . | Present well to be sunk and put in order | — | The Townland of Acragar, situate in the Mountmellick Electoral Division. |
| Maryborough Town, | Do., . . | Wells to be sunk and pumps put down at Portlaoise and at the new road, well at railway bridge to be put in order; all the pumps to be kept in order, and survey and map of town to be made | — | The Townlands of Bearla Little, Clonminam, Kylekiproe, and Maryborough, situate in the Maryborough Electoral Division. |
| Mountrath Town, . . | Do., . . | Three wells to be sunk and three pumps erected, survey and map of the town to be made. | Sewer-drains to be put in order. | The Townland of Dysartbeagh and the two Townlands of Mountrath, situate in the Mountrath Electoral Division. |
| Portarlington Town, part situate in the Queen's County | Do., . . | Repairing pump and providing new well and pump in Bracklone-street, and proportion of expenses for survey and map of town. | Paving channel at Market square, and cleansing old canal. | The Townland of Cooltederry, situate in the Portarlington South Electoral Division. |
| Portarlington Town, part situate in the King's County | Do., . . | New pump at Kilmalogue, and proportion of expenses for survey and map of town. | — | The Townland of Kilmalogue, situate in the Portarlington North Electoral Division. |
| Mullingar Union: | | | | |
| Ballynacarrigy Townland | 2nd July, 1875, . . | Enclosing a public well, | — | The Townlands of Ballynacarrigy and Balliabon, situate in the Kilbixy Electoral Division. |
| Naas Union: | | | | |
| Ballymore Eustace Town, | 4th February, 1876, . | — | Sewerage, | Ballymore Eustace Electoral Division. |
| Clane " | Do., . . | — | Do., . . | Clane do. |

| | | | | |
|---|---|---|---|---|
| Kildare, | Do., | Supply of water, and repairing pumps. | — | Kildare do. |
| Kilteel | Do., | Supply of water, | — | Kilteel do. |
| Naas | Do., | Supply of water, and repairing pumps. | Sewerage, | Naas do. |
| Newbridge | Do., | Do., | Cleansing sewers, | Newbridge and Harristown[illegible] Electoral Divisions. |
| **Navan Union:** | | | | |
| Navan Town, | 20th December, 1875, | Providing a pump, | — | The Townlands of Abbeyland, Abbeyland South, Athlumney, Blackcastle, Blackcastle Demesne, Dillonsland, Limekiln Hill, and Townparks, situate in the Electoral Division of Navan. |
| Johnstown Town, | Do., | Do., | — | The Townlands of Ardbraccan, [illegible] Grange, [illegible], Oognastown, and Tankardstown, situate in the Ardbraccan Electoral Division. |
| Boyerstown Village, | Do., | Do., | — | The Ardbraccan Electoral Division. |
| Rathdrinagh Village, | Do., | Do., | — | The Townlands of Cabine, Gillstown, [illegible], Newtown, Rathdrinagh, [illegible], [illegible], and Thurstianstown, situate in the Painestown Electoral Division. |
| Gormanstown Townland, | 3rd January, 1876, | Supply of water, | — | The Townland of Gormanstown, situate in the Stackallen Electoral Division. |
| **Newry Union:** | | | | |
| Newry Town, | 17th November, 1875, | — | Sewerage, | Estimated expense, £1,[illegible], to be borrowed in two sums of £[illegible] and £[illegible] respectively—the sum of £[illegible], with interest thereon, to be charged to the Newry Electoral Division, and the sum of £[illegible], with interest thereon to be charged to the other Twenty-[illegible] Electoral Divisions of the Union, namely—Abbeyglen, Aghaderradia, Ardaveny, Bullina, Ballymacrea, Ballymacdermott, Ballyconnell, Bessbrook, Carrickagehan, Castletown, Derrymore, Dalla, Greenbank, Kilcurreny, Kilkeel, Killeavy, Killmore, [illegible], Killmorth, Kelly's Loughs, Loughgall, [illegible], Newpark, Tandragee, and Tonaghmore. |
| **Newcastle Union:** | | | | |
| Athea Village, | 2nd August, 1875, | Supply of water, | — | The Glensharrow and Rathronan Electoral Divisions. |
| **Newtownbarry Union:** | | | | |
| Loughgeorge Town, | 14th March, 1876, | Supply of water and a pump. | — | The Townland of Townparks of Loughgeorge, situate in the Loughgeorge Electoral Division. |
| Kilmuckridge, | Do., | Do., | — | The Townland of Kilmuckridge, situate in the Kilmuckridge Electoral Division. |
| **Oldcastle Union:** | | | | |
| Oldcastle Town, | 22nd May, 1876, | Supply of water, | — | The Townland of Oldcastle, situate in the Oldcastle Electoral Division. |
| Ballyjamesduff, | 4th July, 1876, | Do., | — | The Townlands of Carnakilly and Moodoge, situate in the Ballyjamesduff Electoral Division. |

IV.—STATEMENT of ORDERS issued under the 13th Section of the PUBLIC HEALTH ACT, 1874, determining the AREA of CHARGE on which the SPECIAL EXPENSES mentioned in such Orders respectively shall be chargeable—*continued*.

| NAME OF UNION, AND TOWN, VILLAGE, OR PLACE. | Date of Order. | Purposes for which Incurred or to be Incurred. | | AREA OF CHARGE. |
|---|---|---|---|---|
| | | Water Supply, &c. | Sewerage, &c. | |
| RATHDOWN UNION: | | | | |
| Kilbogget and Loughlinstown Townlands. | 10th November, 1875, | Supply of water and erecting a fountain in Cabinteely Village. | — | The under-named Townlands, situate in the Killiney Electoral Division, that is to say, the Townlands of Ballinclea, Ballybrack, Mackamstown, Kilbogget, Killiney, Loughlinstown, Loughlinstown Commons, Rochestown, and the Townland of Scalpwilliam or Hermit Magna, except that part which is situate within the Township of Dalkey in the said Union. |
| RATHDRUM UNION: | | | | |
| Wicklow Town (Irish-town portion). | 4th October, 1875, . | Supply of water, . . | — | The under-named Townlands, that is to say, the Townlands of Corporation Land 1st Division, Corporation Land 2nd Division, Corporation Murrough, Ballynerrin South, Glebe, Friarshill and Wicklow, in the Parish of Rathnew, Corporation Lands in the Parish of Kilpoole, and Ballynerrin Lower, in the Parish of Drumkay, all which Townlands being situate in the Wicklow Electoral Division. |
| SHILLELAGH UNION. | | | | |
| Tinahely Town, | 15th November, 1875, | Do., . . | — | The Townland of Tinahely, situate in the Tinahely Electoral Division. |
| SKIBBEREEN UNION: | | | | |
| Skibbereen Town, . | 29th May, 1874, . . | Do., . . | — | The Skibbereen Dispensary District. |
| Drimoleague " . . | Do., . . | Do., . . | — | The Drimoleague Dispensary District. |
| Skibbereen " . . | 9th March, 1876, . . | — | Sewerage, . . . | The under-named Townlands viz.:—Ennisvegune, situate in Aghadown North Electoral Division, Farranagilla (Castletown Parish), Farranagilla (Abbeystrowry Parish), Kilnahera, Letterscanlan, Lisheenroe, Lissaniskea, and Rea, situate in Castlehaven North Electoral Division, Drumnea, Lahertidaly, Lisheenagreine, and Lissaveaghy situate in Cloghdonnell Electoral Division; Gortnaclohy, situate in Kilfinnagh Electoral Division; Abbeystrowry, Bunlick, Carrigfadda, Coolnagarrane, Cunnaigowry, Creagh, Curragh, Dereenatra, Derreenlunnig, Derrygereen, Derrygoole, Drishane, Gortnaclohy, Gortnabrouchog, Knockalaggart, Licknavar, Lurriga, Mallavoge (Aghadown Parish), Mallavoge (Abbeystrowry Parish), Marsh, Mealbeg, Poundlick, Rossnagh, Smorane (Castlehaven Parish), Smorane (Creagh Parish), Tooreennaguirenma, situate in Skibbereen Electoral Division, Kilnadasha, situate in Woodfort Electoral Division. |

| | | | | |
|---|---|---|---|---|
| **Stranorlar Union:** | | | | |
| Stranorlar Town, . | 21st May, 1875, . . | Supply of water, . . | Improving the sewerage. | The Townland of Stranorlar, situate in the Stranorlar Electoral Division. |
| Ballybofey . . . | Do. . . | Do. . . | Do. | The Townland of Ballybofey, situate in the Stranorlar Electoral Division. |
| **[illegible] Union:** | | | | |
| Ballaghy Town. . . | 6th September, 1874, . | Enclosing a well, . . | Constructing a sewer. | The Townland of Ballaghy, situate in the [illegible] West Electoral Division. |
| **Trim Union:** | | | | |
| Athboy Town, . . . | 2nd November, 1875, . | — | Sewerage. . . | The Townlands of Townparks, [illegible], Eighty-eight-Acres, and [illegible], situate in the Athboy Electoral Division; and the Townland of [illegible], situate in the [illegible] Electoral Division. |
| Kildalkey . . . | Do. . . | Supply of water, . . | — | The Townlands of Kildalkey, [illegible], and [illegible], situate in the Kildalkey Electoral Division. |
| Longwood . . . | Do. . . | Do. . . | — | The two Townlands of Longwood, situate in the [illegible] Electoral Division. |
| Summerhill . . . | Do. . . | Do. . . | — | The Townlands of Summerhill and Summerhill Demesne, situate in the Summerhill Electoral Division. |
| **[illegible] Union.** | | | | |
| [illegible] . . . | 3rd December, 1875, . | Repairing and putting a well in order, | — | The Townlands of [illegible] and [illegible], situate in [illegible] Electoral Division, and the Townlands of [illegible] Lower and [illegible] ([illegible]), situate in the [illegible] Electoral Division. |
| Beggars-Inn Village, . | 10th March, 1876, . | Repairing a pump, . | — | The Townlands of [illegible], [illegible], and [illegible] ([illegible] Parish), situate in the [illegible] Electoral Division. |
| [illegible], . . . | Do. . | Supply of Water and completing pump. | — | All the Townlands comprised in the [illegible] Electoral Division, the Townlands of [illegible] and [illegible], situate in [illegible] Electoral Division, and the Townland of [illegible], situate in the [illegible] Electoral Division. |
| **Westport Union:** | | | | |
| Louisburgh Town, . . | 5th April, 1876, . . | — | Constructing a sewer. | The Townland of [illegible], situate in the Louisburgh Electoral Division. |
| Westport . . . | 26th August, 1875, | Supply of water at High-street | — | The Townland of [illegible], situate in the Westport Electoral Division. |
| **Youghal Union:** | | | | |
| Williamstown, . . . | 23rd July, 1875, . . | — | Repairing a drain, . | The Townlands of [illegible], Dysart, and Williamstown, situate in the Youghal Electoral Division. |

V. Letter addressed by the Chief Secretary by direction of His Grace the Lord Lieutenant to Dr. M'Donnell, on his retirement from the Office of Medical Commissioner.

Dublin Castle,
2nd February, 1876.

Sir,

With reference to your letter of the 30th December last, resigning your office of Medical Commissioner of the Local Government Board, I am directed by the Lord Lieutenant to acquaint you that the Lords Commissioners of Her Majesty's Treasury have been pleased to award you a retired allowance of £620 a year, and that their Lordships have instructed the Paymaster-General to pay you from the 6th ultimo inclusive.

I am to add that His Grace desires at the same time to express to you his high sense of the valuable services you have rendered to the Irish Government and the public during your long and honourable connection with Poor Law and Local Government Boards.

I am, sir, your obedient servant,

M. E. Hicks Beach.

J. M'Donnell, esq. M.D.,
Local Government Board.

# APPENDIX D.

## TABLES CONNECTED WITH POOR RELIEF AND EXPENDITURE.

No. 1.—A RETURN (in pursuance of the 29th Section of the Act 10 Vic., c. 31) of the and Out of the Workhouse, together with the RECEIPTS in each UNION in IRELAND, for Charities, Registration, Sanitary, Burial Grounds, Superannuation, and Cattle Plague

PART 1.—RETURN showing the Receipts and Expenditure

| NAMES OF COUNTIES AND UNIONS. | Receipts. | | | | | Expenditure. | | | | | |
|---|---|---|---|---|---|---|---|---|---|---|---|
| | Amount of Poor Rate Lodged. | Parliamentary Grant. | Repayment of Relief. | Other Receipts. | Total Receipts during the Year. | In-Maintenance. | Out-Relief. | Maintenance of Blind and Deaf and Dumb, in Asylums, and cost of Relief in Extern Hospitals. | Salaries and Rations of Officers. | Emigration Expenses. | All other Poor Relief Expenses. |
| PROVINCE OF ULSTER. | £ | £ | £ | £ | £ | £ | £ | £ | £ | £ | £ |
| ANTRIM. | | | | | | | | | | | |
| Antrim, . . | 5,344 | 640 | 35 | 63 | 5,082 | 2,174 | 539 | 44 | 830 | - | 851 |
| Ballycastle, . | 2,349 | 290 | 6 | 13 | 2,604 | 023 | 1 | - | 474 | - | 373 |
| Ballymena, . | 7,018 | 612 | 17 | 14 | 7,661 | 2,106 | 1,233 | 94 | 908 | - | 877 |
| Ballymoney, . | 3,039 | 453 | 27 | 34 | 3,553 | 834 | 606 | 40 | 596 | - | 294 |
| Belfast, . . | 37,164 | 2,448 | 46 | - | 39,657 | 20,208 | 1,209 | 386 | 4,466 | 6 | 6,363 |
| Larne, . . | 4,593 | 446 | 6 | 41 | 5,086 | 1,805 | 370 | - | 779 | - | 731 |
| Lisburn, . | 5,199 | 675 | 34 | 10 | 5,918 | 1,790 | 506 | 140 | 797 | - | 677 |
| ARMAGH. | | | | | | | | | | | |
| Armagh, . . | 4,770 | 786 | 8 | 143 | 5,715 | 2,403 | 84 | 11 | 817 | - | 1,279 |
| Lurgan, . . | 8,622 | 677 | 16 | 91 | 0,406 | 3,370 | 242 | 29 | 024 | - | 1,082 |
| CAVAN. | | | | | | | | | | | |
| Bailieborough, | 2,895 | 287 | 22 | 8 | 3,212 | 1,275 | 184 | 16 | 400 | - | 439 |
| Bawnboy, . | 3,313 | 268 | 6 | 8 | 3,506 | 1,046 | 633 | 29 | 443 | - | 327 |
| Cavan, . . | 5,942 | 684 | 5 | 20 | 6,651 | 3,037 | 593 | 60 | 782 | 17 | 848 |
| Cootehill, . | 2,440 | 341 | - | 13 | 2,794 | 987 | 74 | 18 | 457 | - | 416 |
| DONEGAL. | | | | | | | | | | | |
| Ballyshannon, | 2,446 | 322 | 13 | 2 | 2,783 | 1,220 | - | 15 | 414 | 3 | 270 |
| Donegal, . | 1,758 | 363 | 3 | 15 | 2,149 | 605 | 84 | 16 | 425 | - | 272 |
| Dunfanaghy, . | 1,578 | 237 | 2 | - | 1,817 | 314 | - | - | 337 | - | 144 |
| Glenties, . | 2,231 | 482 | 11 | 17 | 2,601 | 752 | 204 | 16 | 413 | - | 266 |
| Inishowen, . | 3,786 | 440 | 9 | 25 | 4,202 | 080 | 302 | 34 | 331 | - | 358 |
| Letterkenny, . | 2,217 | 271 | - | 30 | 2,518 | 054 | 5 | 34 | 438 | - | 382 |
| Milford, . . | 2,030 | 348 | 2 | 22 | 2,411 | 687 | 132 | - | 407 | - | 270 |
| Stranorlar, . | 1,365 | 320 | 2 | 12 | 1,509 | 367 | 7 | 16 | 457 | - | 273 |
| DOWN. | | | | | | | | | | | |
| Banbridge, . | 5,514 | 558 | 7 | 33 | 6,112 | 1,806 | 763 | 14 | 848 | - | 889 |
| Downpatrick, . | 5,065 | 579 | 27 | 59 | 5,730 | 1,013 | 94 | 12 | 772 | - | 740 |
| Kilkeel, . . | 1,734 | 292 | - | 11 | 2,037 | 619 | 16 | 15 | 326 | - | 294 |
| Newry, . . | 8,271 | 901 | 16 | 58 | 0,246 | 2,034 | 867 | 145 | 1,008 | - | 1,029 |
| Newtownards, | 7,034 | 646 | 21 | 106 | 7,807 | 2,066 | 1,323 | 48 | 880 | - | 885 |
| FERMANAGH. | | | | | | | | | | | |
| Enniskillen, . | 4,072 | 515 | 13 | 11 | 4,011 | 2,061 | 24 | 16 | 712 | - | 702 |
| Irvinestown, . | 2,440 | 292 | 3 | 6 | 2,746 | 804 | 34 | - | 415 | - | 345 |
| Lisnaskea, . | 2,320 | 321 | 4 | 16 | 2,069 | 634 | 241 | - | 430 | - | 456 |
| LONDONDERRY. | | | | | | | | | | | |
| Coleraine, . | 5,215 | 474 | 14 | 6 | 5,700 | 1,654 | 832 | 6 | 052 | 8 | 760 |
| Limavady, . | 2,496 | 407 | 20 | 19 | 2,942 | 946 | 23 | 27 | 557 | 16 | 453 |
| Londonderry, | 6,725 | 808 | 13 | 3 | 7,540 | 2,350 | 161 | 186 | 722 | - | 806 |
| Magherafelt, . | 4,107 | 487 | 1 | 41 | 4,706 | 1,599 | 14 | 101 | 670 | - | 567 |
| MONAGHAN. | | | | | | | | | | | |
| Carrickmacross | 2,308 | 267 | 34 | 22 | 2,631 | 1,011 | 19 | 116 | 458 | 4 | 369 |
| Castleblayney, | 3,113 | 375 | 6 | 20 | 3,514 | 1,064 | 216 | 20 | 584 | - | 510 |
| Clones, . . | 1,711 | 212 | 2 | 14 | 1,980 | 646 | 18 | 9 | 414 | - | 321 |
| Monaghan, . . | 3,120 | 529 | 16 | 257 | 3,922 | 1,176 | - | 49 | 589 | - | 674 |
| TYRONE. | | | | | | | | | | | |
| Castlederg, . | 1,114 | 207 | 11 | 3 | 1,335 | 351 | - | 15 | 369 | - | 176 |
| Clogher, . . | 2,328 | 270 | - | 23 | 2,621 | 826 | 226 | - | 431 | - | 451 |
| Cookstown, . | 1,737 | 310 | 1 | 17 | 2,065 | 791 | 76 | - | 447 | - | 263 |
| Dungannon, . | 4,241 | 440 | 11 | 33 | 4,725 | 1,540 | 611 | 19 | 626 | - | 617 |
| Gortin, . . | 1,233 | 102 | 2 | 13 | 1,438 | 387 | 35 | 16 | 306 | - | 190 |
| Omagh, . . | 3,196 | 508 | 10 | 31 | 3,745 | 1,258 | 132 | - | 720 | - | 468 |
| Strabane, . | 5,565 | 551 | 10 | 46 | 6,170 | 1,013 | 558 | 18 | 672 | - | 501 |
| Total, ULSTER, 1875, | 194,880 | 21,317 | 510 | 1,435 | 218,142 | 79,060 | 13,142 | 1,835 | 30,128 | 64 | 30,982 |
| Total, ULSTER, 1874, | 192,786 | 21,071 | 630 | 1,562 | 215,948 | 85,892 | 12,590 | 1,891 | 30,107 | 61 | 33,306 |
| Increase, . | 2,096 | 246 | - | - | 2,194 | - | 552 | - | 21 | 3 | - |
| Decrease, . | - | - | 20 | 127 | - | 6,833 | - | 56 | - | - | 2,324 |

EXPENDITURE on the RELIEF of the POOR, and of the TOTAL NUMBERS RELIEVED In the Year ended 29th September, 1875; also showing the EXPENSES under Medical Acts, and TOTAL EXPENDITURE out of the Poor Rates during the Year.

of Unions during the Year ended 29th September, 1875.

| Expenditure. | | | | | | | | | Poundage on the Valuation: | | |
|---|---|---|---|---|---|---|---|---|---|---|---|
| Total Poor Relief Expenditure. | Expenses under Medical Charities and Vaccination Acts. | Expenses under the Acts for Registration of Births, Deaths, and Marriages. | Expenses under the Sanitary Acts. | Expenses under Burial Grounds Acts, paid out of the Poor Rate. | Expenses under the Superannuation Acts. | Expenses under Cattle Plague Act. | Total Expenditure during the Year. | Valuation on 29th Sept., 1875. | Of the Expenditure on the Relief of the Poor. | Of Total Expenditure. | NAMES OF COUNTIES AND UNIONS. |
| £ | £ | £ | £ | £ | £ | £ | £ | £ | s. d. | s. d. | PROVINCE OF ULSTER. |
| | | | | | | | | | | | ANTRIM. |
| 4,447 | 848 | 88 | 155 | 10 | 24 | - | 5,572 | 123,086 | 0 8½ | 0 1[illegible] | Antrim. |
| 1,771 | 471 | 38 | 94 | - | - | - | 2,374 | 44,125 | 0 9½ | 1 [illegible] | Ballycastle. |
| 5,310 | 1,169 | 167 | 170 | 122 | 18 | 130 | 7,096 | 125,618 | 0 10½ | 1 [illegible] | Ballymena. |
| 2,370 | 816 | 75 | 153 | - | - | - | 3,414 | 82,266 | 0 7 | 0 1[illegible] | Ballymoney. |
| 34,750 | 3,997 | 690 | 406 | - | 194 | - | 40,037 | 593,741 | 1 2 | 1 4[illegible] | Belfast. |
| 3,666 | 846 | 87 | 281 | - | 32 | - | 4,831 | 94,733 | 0 9 | 1 0[illegible] | Larne. |
| 3,019 | 1,183 | 148 | 189 | - | - | 175 | 5,515 | 169,462 | 0 5½ | 0 8 | Lisburn. |
| | | | | | | | | | | | ARMAGH. |
| 4,544 | 1,607 | 166 | 280 | - | 168 | 212 | 6,976 | 204,004 | 0 5½ | 0 8[illegible] | Armagh. |
| 5,556 | 1,338 | 163 | 214 | 120 | 13 | - | 7,401 | 140,823 | 0 9½ | 1 0[illegible] | Lurgan. |
| | | | | | | | | | | | CAVAN. |
| 2,373 | 586 | 45 | 150 | 50 | 18 | - | 3,221 | 39,972 | 1 2½ | 1 7½ | Bailieborough. |
| 2,378 | 538 | 60 | 109 | 51 | - | - | 3,136 | 39,654 | 1 2½ | 1 7 | Bawnboy. |
| 4,935 | 1,136 | 111 | 485 | 73 | 90 | - | 6,829 | 112,674 | 0 10½ | 1 2½ | Cavan. |
| 1,981 | 609 | 63 | 172 | 31 | 42 | - | 2,897 | 72,367 | 0 6½ | 0 9½ | Cootehill. |
| | | | | | | | | | | | DONEGAL. |
| 1,922 | 567 | 37 | 135 | - | 45 | - | 2,736 | 50,530 | 0 9½ | 1 1 | Ballyshannon. |
| 1,107 | 721 | 55 | 146 | 6 | 6 | - | 2,040 | 34,030 | 0 9½ | 1 4½ | Donegal. |
| 795 | 371 | 35 | 58 | - | 53 | 12 | 1,324 | 11,506 | 1 4½ | 2 3½ | Dunfanaghy. |
| 1,652 | 946 | 78 | 147 | - | 36 | - | 2,658 | 20,010 | 1 7½ | 2 10½ | Glenties. |
| 2,296 | 947 | 80 | 240 | - | - | 40 | 3,608 | 39,064 | 1 2 | 1 10 | Inishowen. |
| 1,764 | 563 | 36 | 80 | 3 | 27 | - | 2,470 | 31,000 | 1 1½ | 1 7½ | Letterkenny. |
| 1,456 | 791 | 61 | 130 | 20 | 3 | - | 2,461 | 29,784 | 0 11½ | 1 7½ | Milford. |
| 1,100 | 466 | 35 | 98 | - | 42 | - | 1,750 | 30,083 | 0 8½ | 1 2 | Stranorlar. |
| | | | | | | | | | | | DOWN. |
| 4,204 | 1,036 | 143 | 450 | 9 | 67 | - | 5,950 | 159,090 | 0 6½ | 0 9 | Banbridge. |
| 3,631 | 1,193 | 114 | 227 | - | 54 | - | 5,119 | 176,530 | 0 4½ | 0 7 | Downpatrick. |
| 1,262 | 352 | 49 | 109 | 6 | 50 | - | 2,028 | 41,944 | 0 7½ | 0 11½ | Kilkeel. |
| 5,037 | 1,894 | 170 | 340 | 22 | 70 | - | 8,338 | 163,340 | 0 6½ | 1 0½ | Newry. |
| 6,042 | 1,163 | 125 | 257 | - | - | - | 7,577 | 136,620 | 0 10½ | 1 1½ | Newtownards. |
| | | | | | | | | | | | FERMANAGH. |
| 3,518 | 979 | 91 | 181 | 30 | 118 | - | 4,914 | 105,408 | 0 8 | 0 11½ | Enniskillen. |
| 1,596 | 628 | 35 | 110 | - | 11 | - | 2,280 | 48,717 | 0 7½ | 0 11½ | Irvinestown. |
| 1,961 | 643 | 37 | 94 | - | 55 | - | 2,788 | 57,085 | 0 8 | 0 11½ | Lisnaskea. |
| | | | | | | | | | | | LONDONDERRY. |
| 4,152 | 909 | 91 | 226 | - | 46 | 102 | 5,526 | 99,055 | 0 10 | 1 1½ | Coleraine. |
| 1,929 | 742 | 56 | 126 | - | 9 | - | 2,855 | 68,710 | 0 6½ | 0 10 | Limavady. |
| 4,247 | 1,712 | 134 | 246 | 16 | 102 | - | 6,457 | 152,438 | 0 6½ | 0 10½ | Londonderry. |
| 2,951 | 853 | 119 | 126 | 441 | - | - | 4,490 | 91,640 | 0 7½ | 0 11½ | Magherafelt. |
| | | | | | | | | | | | MONAGHAN. |
| 1,969 | 496 | 40 | 82 | 4 | - | - | 2,591 | 50,105 | 0 9½ | 1 0½ | Carrickmacross. |
| 2,418 | 766 | 67 | 145 | - | - | - | 3,106 | 75,310 | 0 7½ | 0 10½ | Castleblayney. |
| 1,406 | 461 | 39 | 95 | - | - | - | 1,906 | 57,097 | 0 6 | 0 8½ | Clones. |
| 2,488 | 920 | 79 | 170 | - | - | 98 | 3,764 | 94,029 | 0 6½ | 0 9½ | Monaghan. |
| | | | | | | | | | | | TYRONE. |
| 911 | 347 | 32 | 75 | - | - | - | 1,365 | 26,200 | 0 8½ | 1 0½ | Castlederg. |
| 1,934 | 560 | 59 | 113 | - | 43 | - | 2,790 | 56,224 | 0 8½ | 0 11½ | Clogher. |
| 1,597 | 580 | 73 | 161 | 2 | - | - | 2,413 | 63,408 | 0 6 | 0 9½ | Cookstown. |
| 3,312 | 876 | 93 | 254 | - | - | - | 4,535 | 93,623 | 0 8½ | 0 11½ | Dungannon. |
| 913 | 357 | 32 | 44 | 1 | 46 | - | 1,393 | 19,850 | 0 11½ | 1 5 | Gortin. |
| 2,852 | 988 | 100 | 277 | - | 74 | - | 4,101 | 93,820 | 0 8½ | 0 10½ | Omagh. |
| 3,749 | 939 | 78 | 360 | 10 | 202 | - | 5,328 | 96,607 | 0 9 | 1 1 | Strabane. |
| 155,950 | 39,632 | 4,187 | 8,179 | 1,037 | 1,785 | 770 | 210,950 | 4,116,200 | 0 9 | 1 0½ | 1875, } Total, ULSTER. |
| 163,837 | 40,334 | 3,993 | 1,160 | 1,151 | 1,715 | 3,469 | 215,650 | 4,092,628 | 0 9½ | 1 0½ | 1874, } Total, ULSTER. |
| - | - | 104 | 7,019 | - | 70 | - | - | 23,572 | - | - | Increase. |
| 8,037 | 502 | - | - | 121 | - | 2,699 | 4,670 | - | 0 0½ | 0 0½ | Decrease. |

No. 1. Part 1.—Return showing the Receipts and Expenditure

| Names of Counties and Unions. | Receipts. | | | | | Expenditure. | | | | | |
|---|---|---|---|---|---|---|---|---|---|---|---|
| | Amount of Poor Rate Lodged. | Parliamentary Grant. | Repayment of Relief. | Other Receipts. | Total Receipts during the Year. | In-Maintenance. | Out-Relief. | Maintenance of Blind and Deaf and Dumb in Asylums, and cost of Relief in Extern Hospitals. | Salaries and Rations of Officers. | Emigration Expenses. | All other Poor Relief Expenses. |
| PROVINCE OF MUNSTER. | £ | £ | £ | £ | £ | £ | £ | £ | £ | £ | £ |
| Clare. | | | | | | | | | | | |
| Ballyvaghan, | 2,478 | 136 | 2 | 33 | 2,747 | 1,361 | 34 | - | 330 | - | 372 |
| Corrofin, | 2,104 | 135 | - | - | 2,329 | 1,120 | 231 | 13 | 342 | 7 | 230 |
| Ennis, | 6,842 | 547 | 30 | - | 7,419 | 3,043 | 638 | 24 | 031 | 8 | 1,030 |
| Ennistymon, | 4,086 | 313 | 6 | 20 | 5,631 | 2,591 | 279 | 36 | 535 | 2 | 808 |
| Killadysert, | 2,007 | 163 | 3 | - | 2,703 | 1,324 | 289 | 2 | 415 | 5 | 530 |
| Kilrush, | 6,026 | 540 | 20 | - | 6,502 | 2,802 | 637 | 8 | 800 | 4 | 590 |
| Scariff, | 2,515 | 300 | 17 | 1 | 2,833 | 1,535 | 3 | 30 | 539 | 60 | 323 |
| Tulla, | 3,980 | 327 | 2 | 21 | 4,330 | 2,145 | 218 | 15 | 535 | - | 474 |
| Cork. | | | | | | | | | | | |
| Bandon, | 3,606 | 441 | 31 | 3 | 4,170 | 1,700 | 5 | 00 | 596 | - | 548 |
| Bantry, | 1,991 | 241 | 33 | - | 2,265 | 986 | 50 | 10 | 374 | - | 214 |
| Castletown, | 1,516 | 185 | 3 | 37 | 1,743 | 952 | 67 | - | 372 | 5 | 204 |
| Clonakilty, | 3,464 | 251 | 14 | - | 3,959 | 1,800 | 16 | 20 | 432 | - | 342 |
| Cork, | 30,987 | 2,364 | 69 | 334 | 42,602 | 20,410 | 2,600 | 1,001 | 3,777 | 63 | 4,556 |
| Dunmanway, | 2,870 | 270 | 6 | - | 3,156 | 1,301 | 93 | 15 | 417 | - | 234 |
| Fermoy, | 6,288 | 610 | 21 | 58 | 8,808 | 2,255 | 37 | 42 | 1,025 | - | 611 |
| Kanturk, | 7,490 | 590 | 47 | 17 | 8,194 | 4,076 | 1,258 | 63 | 802 | 10 | 854 |
| Kinsale, | 2,077 | 367 | 12 | 2 | 2,458 | 1,116 | 10 | - | 531 | - | 297 |
| Macroom, | 4,349 | 403 | 46 | - | 4,701 | 2,307 | 187 | 90 | 590 | - | 512 |
| Mallow, | 8,759 | 434 | 16 | 27 | 9,186 | 3,031 | 1,013 | 74 | 845 | 6 | 909 |
| Midleton, | 6,068 | 530 | 6 | 15 | 6,510 | 2,431 | 107 | 65 | 630 | - | 795 |
| Millstreet, | 6,020 | 228 | 28 | 13 | 6,294 | 2,540 | 236 | 41 | 520 | 25 | 509 |
| Mitchelstown, | 2,346 | 314 | 8 | 12 | 3,680 | 1,771 | 33 | 32 | 643 | - | 306 |
| Skibbereen, | 5,302 | 416 | - | - | 3,778 | 2,407 | 154 | 35 | 018 | 54 | 684 |
| Skull, | 1,686 | 166 | 5 | 4 | 1,861 | 810 | 49 | 7 | 301 | - | 175 |
| Youghal, | 5,874 | 456 | 9 | 21 | 6,363 | 1,926 | 482 | 62 | 622 | - | 603 |
| Kerry. | | | | | | | | | | | |
| Cahirciveen, | 3,378 | 411 | 6 | - | 3,792 | 1,147 | 415 | 15 | 483 | 6 | 519 |
| Dingle, | 2,744 | 401 | 1 | 40 | 3,186 | 1,287 | 17 | 10 | 543 | - | 238 |
| Kenmare, | 2,330 | 321 | 13 | - | 2,664 | 872 | 103 | 4 | 510 | - | 318 |
| Killarney, | 9,686 | 638 | 41 | - | 10,267 | 3,461 | 1,238 | 238 | 1,120 | 13 | 929 |
| Listowel, | 2,627 | 319 | 16 | 30 | 3,078 | 1,114 | 1 | 25 | 685 | - | 396 |
| Tralee, | 8,393 | 607 | 33 | 98 | 9,101 | 4,148 | 18 | 221 | 1,070 | 18 | 2,442 |
| Limerick. | | | | | | | | | | | |
| Croom, | 4,217 | 374 | 17 | - | 4,608 | 2,134 | 491 | 75 | 633 | - | 688 |
| Glin, | 2,756 | 270 | 2 | 37 | 3,070 | 1,317 | 277 | 81 | 551 | - | 283 |
| Kilmallock, | 12,606 | 076 | 25 | 200 | 13,807 | 5,897 | 1,791 | 107 | 1,115 | 14 | 1,325 |
| Limerick, | 24,241 | 1,433 | 98 | 4 | 25,776 | 14,270 | 2,061 | 148 | 2,284 | 3 | 3,127 |
| Newcastle, | 7,134 | 504 | 12 | 7 | 7,657 | 2,738 | 886 | 30 | 925 | 20 | 884 |
| Rathkeale, | 6,091 | 431 | - | 11 | 6,533 | 1,686 | 1,857 | 38 | 780 | 10 | 668 |
| Tipperary. | | | | | | | | | | | |
| Borrisokane, | 2,028 | 271 | - | 5 | 2,304 | 961 | 4 | 1 | 402 | - | 275 |
| Car.-on-Suir, | 5,346 | 499 | 13 | 19 | 5,877 | 2,262 | 550 | 30 | 976 | - | 762 |
| Cashel, | 7,384 | 534 | 38 | 1 | 7,967 | 3,820 | 1,378 | 43 | 935 | 3 | 911 |
| Clogheen, | 4,186 | 340 | 31 | 49 | 4,011 | 2,303 | - | 46 | 028 | - | 521 |
| Clonmel, | 6,881 | 647 | 48 | 10 | 8,386 | 4,735 | 476 | 71 | 1,083 | 3 | 1,284 |
| Nenagh, | 7,045 | 539 | 80 | - | 7,804 | 3,800 | 1,166 | 51 | 749 | 4 | 994 |
| Roscrea, | 3,825 | 352 | 1 | 192 | 4,370 | 1,338 | 409 | 4 | 720 | 45 | 515 |
| Thurles, | 4,173 | 506 | 22 | - | 4,701 | 1,944 | 134 | 88 | 642 | 5 | 504 |
| Tipperary, | 9,377 | 613 | 24 | 1 | 10,015 | 6,034 | 968 | 32 | 851 | 63 | 1,118 |
| Waterford. | | | | | | | | | | | |
| Dungarvan, | 7,457 | 419 | 10 | 35 | 7,922 | 3,629 | 648 | 73 | 881 | 58 | 936 |
| Kilmacthomas, | 3,373 | 236 | 6 | 16 | 3,640 | 1,519 | 413 | - | 801 | 20 | 486 |
| Lismore, | 3,858 | 370 | 15 | 617 | 4,760 | 1,493 | 278 | 33 | 681 | 5 | 561 |
| Waterford, | 13,707 | 901 | 00 | 42 | 14,746 | 8,229 | 2,177 | 72 | 1,422 | - | 1,425 |
| Total Munster, 1875, | 308,188 | 23,893 | 1,076 | 1,923 | 334,780 | 148,533 | 27,614 | 3,317 | 39,577 | 683 | 38,802 |
| Total Munster, 1874, | 317,363 | 21,250 | 1,024 | 2,682 | 344,279 | 166,353 | 27,465 | 3,296 | 39,866 | 1,291 | 40,111 |
| Increase, | - | 343 | 62 | - | - | - | 149 | 21 | - | - | - |
| Decrease, | 9,105 | - | - | 720 | 9,499 | 17,820 | - | - | 289 | 728 | 1,209 |

of Unions during the Year ended 29th September, 1875—*continued.*

| Expenditure: Total Poor Relief Expenditure. | Expenditure: Expenses under Medical Charities and Vaccination Acts. | Expenditure: Expenses under the Acts for Registration of Births, Deaths, and Marriages. | Expenditure: Expenses under the Sanitary Acts. | Expenditure: Expenses under Burial Grounds Acts, paid out of the Poor Rate. | Expenditure: Expenses under the Superannuation Acts. | Expenditure: Expenses under Cattle Plague Act. | Expenditure: Total Expenditure during the Year. | Valuation on 29th Sept., 1875. | Poundage on the Valuation: Of the Expenditure on the Relief of the Poor. | Poundage on the Valuation: Of Total Expenditure. | Names of Counties and Unions. |
|---|---|---|---|---|---|---|---|---|---|---|---|
| £ | £ | £ | £ | £ | £ | £ | £ | £ | s. d. | s. d. | PROVINCE OF MUNSTER. |
| | | | | | | | | | | | CLARE. |
| 2,287 | 100 | 18 | 60 | – | 53 | – | 2,583 | 10,460 | 2 4½ | 2 7½ | Ballyvaghan. |
| 1,984 | 158 | 12 | 42 | – | 6 | – | 2,202 | 20,426 | 1 11½ | 2 1½ | Corrofin. |
| 6,381 | 711 | 56 | 184 | – | 38 | – | 7,275 | 73,567 | 1 8¾ | [illegible] 11¾ | Ennis. |
| 4,340 | 553 | 49 | 214 | 6 | – | – | 5,164 | 36,843 | 2 4¼ | 2 9¾ | Ennistymon. |
| 2,425 | 286 | 26 | 76 | – | – | 20 | 2,843 | 25,322 | 1 11 | 2 2½ | Killadysert. |
| 5,007 | 738 | 81 | 202 | – | 67 | – | 6,095 | 52,510 | 1 11 | 2 3¾ | Kilrush. |
| 2,483 | 432 | 28 | 133 | – | 76 | – | 3,154 | 25,736 | 1 11¼ | 2 5¼ | Scariff. |
| 3,417 | 506 | 26 | 131 | 68 | – | – | 4,148 | 32,742 | 2 1 | 2 6¾ | Tulla. |
| | | | | | | | | | | | CORK. |
| 3,001 | 743 | 57 | 137 | – | 65 | – | 4,003 | 73,490 | 0 9¾ | 1 1 | Bandon. |
| 1,562 | 428 | 32 | 104 | 80 | – | – | 2,223 | 21,563 | 1 5¼ | 2 0¾ | Bantry. |
| 1,600 | 381 | 36 | 78 | 13 | 38 | – | 2,146 | 14,850 | 2 1¾ | 2 10¾ | Castletown. |
| 2,810 | 317 | 58 | 101 | – | 36 | – | 3,320 | 60,903 | 1 0¾ | 1 3¾ | Clonakilty. |
| 32,446 | 4,829 | 578 | 1,070 | 347 | 258 | – | 39,128 | 335,820 | 1 11¼ | 2 4 | Cork. |
| 2,063 | 494 | 41 | 128 | – | 40 | 34 | 2,800 | 32,134 | 1 3 | 1 8¾ | Dunmanway. |
| 3,970 | 944 | 80 | 188 | 14 | 77 | – | 5,269 | 103,390 | 0 0¾ | 1 0¾ | Fermoy. |
| 7,282 | 909 | 77 | 318 | 58 | 60 | – | 8,704 | 77,040 | 1 10¾ | 2 3 | Kanturk. |
| 1,954 | 656 | 56 | 153 | – | – | – | 2,819 | 59,215 | 0 8 | 0 11¼ | Kinsale. |
| 3,576 | 743 | 69 | 148 | – | 92 | – | 4,628 | 63,470 | 1 1¼ | 1 5¾ | Macroom. |
| 5,878 | 1,195 | 69 | 320 | 11 | 60 | – | 7,533 | 105,975 | 1 1¼ | 1 5 | Mallow. |
| 5,098 | 1,007 | 68 | 306 | 1 | 90 | – | 6,560 | 91,215 | 1 1 | 1 4¾ | Midleton. |
| 3,873 | 389 | 35 | 158 | 14 | 51 | – | 4,460 | 27,477 | 2 9¾ | 3 3 | Millstreet. |
| 2,787 | 314 | 47 | 90 | – | – | – | 3,438 | 49,110 | 1 1¼ | 1 4¾ | Mitchelstown. |
| 4,012 | 785 | 67 | 179 | 55 | 120 | – | 5,218 | 45,930 | 1 9 | 2 3¼ | Skibbereen. |
| 1,380 | 317 | 29 | 43 | – | 0 | – | 1,780 | 16,011 | 1 10¾ | 2 2¾ | Skull. |
| 3,937 | 780 | 46 | 200 | – | 77 | – | 5,050 | 60,700 | 1 3¾ | 1 8 | Youghal. |
| | | | | | | | | | | | KERRY. |
| 2,838 | 787 | 64 | 141 | 113 | 74 | – | 3,747 | 22,566 | 2 3¼ | 3 3¼ | Cahirciveen. |
| 2,123 | 734 | 48 | 163 | – | 33 | – | 3,121 | 22,700 | 1 10¾ | 2 9 | Dingle. |
| 1,867 | 639 | 43 | 152 | 20 | 132 | 20 | 2,873 | 19,210 | 1 11¼ | 3 0 | Kenmare. |
| 6,989 | 949 | 113 | 302 | 46 | 149 | – | 8,540 | 75,728 | 1 10¼ | 2 3 | Killarney. |
| 2,121 | 718 | 82 | 260 | – | 20 | – | 3,210 | 52,006 | 0 9¾ | 1 2¾ | Listowel. |
| 7,917 | 1,066 | 118 | 280 | 496 | 247 | – | 10,130 | 85,772 | 1 10¼ | 2 4¼ | Tralee. |
| | | | | | | | | | | | LIMERICK. |
| 3,891 | 638 | 35 | 145 | – | 217 | – | 4,920 | 64,006 | 1 2¾ | 1 3¼ | Croom. |
| 2,509 | 374 | 37 | 86 | – | 20 | 30 | 3,036 | 28,390 | 1 9¼ | 2 1¾ | Glin. |
| 10,249 | 1,377 | 92 | 350 | 3 | 39 | 142 | 12,252 | 136,740 | 1 6 | 1 9¼ | Kilmallock. |
| 21,802 | 1,752 | 193 | 202 | 158 | 422 | – | 24,689 | 194,763 | 2 3 | 2 [illegible] | Limerick. |
| 5,466 | 893 | 76 | 180 | – | 98 | – | 6,718 | 61,464 | 1 9¼ | 2 [illegible] | Newcastle. |
| 5,022 | 686 | 38 | 179 | – | 93 | – | 6,020 | 56,115 | 1 9¾ | 2 [illegible] | Rathkeale. |
| | | | | | | | | | | | TIPPERARY. |
| 1,643 | 456 | 20 | 60 | – | 7 | – | 2,186 | 41,600 | 0 9¼ | 1 [illegible] | Borrisokane. |
| 4,856 | 705 | 63 | 186 | – | 27 | 83 | 5,614 | 79,436 | 1 1¼ | 1 [illegible] | Carrick-on-Suir |
| 7,039 | 967 | 68 | 193 | – | 37 | – | 8,324 | 107,647 | 1 3¾ | 1 [illegible] | Cashel. |
| 3,522 | 565 | 49 | 110 | – | 9 | – | 4,195 | 64,062 | 1 1¼ | 1 [illegible] | Clogheen. |
| 7,282 | 886 | 56 | 369 | – | 83 | 73 | 8,751 | 70,362 | 2 0¾ | 2 [illegible] | Clonmel. |
| 5,874 | 899 | 69 | 190 | – | 317 | – | 7,349 | 93,885 | 1 3 | 1 [illegible] | Nenagh. |
| 3,039 | 603 | 36 | 134 | 1 | – | – | 3,803 | 71,633 | 0 10¼ | 1 0¾ | Roscrea. |
| 3,705 | 934 | 66 | 189 | 25 | – | – | 4,919 | 90,036 | 0 10 | 1 1 | Thurles. |
| 8,067 | 1,193 | 99 | 243 | 24 | 94 | – | 9,720 | 141,940 | 1 1¾ | 1 4¼ | Tipperary. |
| | | | | | | | | | | | WATERFORD. |
| 6,425 | 800 | 67 | 236 | 2 | – | – | 7,528 | 53,830 | 2 4¾ | 2 9¼ | Dungarvan. |
| 3,050 | 361 | 31 | 122 | – | 8 | 36 | 3,608 | 34,473 | 1 9¼ | 2 1 | Kilmacthomas. |
| 3,039 | 568 | 42 | 297 | 5 | 70 | 52 | 4,104 | 49,834 | 1 2¾ | 1 8 | Lismore. |
| 13,325 | 1,831 | 163 | 180 | 314 | 5 | 156 | 15,674 | 161,068 | 1 9¾ | 2 1 | Waterford. |
| 258,506 | 40,089 | 3,288 | 9,797 | 1,870 | 3,523 | 652 | 317,605 | 3,387,800 | 1 6¼ | 1 10¾ | 1875, Total, Munster. |
| 278,382 | 39,682 | 3,336 | 3,303 | 1,412 | 3,010 | 2,391 | 331,456 | 3,384,797 | 1 7¾ | 1 11¾ | 1874, Total, Munster. |
| – | 407 | – | 6,494 | 458 | 513 | – | – | 3,063 | – | – | Increase. |
| 19,876 | – | 48 | – | – | – | 1,739 | 13,791 | – | 0 1¼ | 0 1 | Decrease |

[*continued.*

No. 1. Part 1.—Return showing the Receipts and Expenditure

| Names of Counties and Unions. | Receipts. | | | | | Expenditure. | | | | | |
|---|---|---|---|---|---|---|---|---|---|---|---|
| | Amount of Poor Rate Lodged. | Parliamentary Grant. | Repayment of Relief. | Other Receipts. | Total Receipts during the Year. | In-Maintenance. | Out-Relief. | Maintenance of Blind and Deaf and Dumb in Asylums, and cost of Relief in Extern Hospitals. | Salaries and Rations of Officers. | Emigration Expenses. | All other Poor Relief Expenses. |
| PROVINCE OF LEINSTER. | £ | £ | £ | £ | £ | £ | £ | £ | £ | £ | £ |
| Carlow. | | | | | | | | | | | |
| Carlow, . . | 10,785 | 839 | 69 | 89 | 11,782 | 3,406 | 2,372 | 42 | 830 | 42 | 1,881 |
| Dublin. | | | | | | | | | | | |
| Balrothery, . | 4,858 | 553 | 1 | 67 | 5,479 | 1,304 | 661 | 15 | 697 | – | 489 |
| Dublin, North, | 30,817 | 2,287 | 52 | 38 | 33,194 | 17,311 | 1,015 | 402 | 3,862 | 16 | 4,213 |
| Dublin, South, | 51,130 | 2,319 | 122 | 12 | 51,583 | 31,568 | 2,422 | 671 | 6,426 | 3 | 7,741 |
| Rathdown, . | 12,408 | 089 | 13 | 144 | 13,644 | 6,578 | 71 | 207 | 1,216 | – | 2,850 |
| Kildare. | | | | | | | | | | | |
| Athy, . . | 9,569 | 628 | 21 | 1 | 10,219 | 3,075 | 1,427 | 60 | 965 | 5 | 1,442 |
| Celbridge, . | 4,089 | 417 | 1 | 57 | 5,404 | 1,918 | 1,012 | 46 | 815 | – | 734 |
| Naas, . . | 9,685 | 798 | 20 | 36 | 10,479 | 3,280 | 1,968 | 105 | 1,039 | – | 1,198 |
| Kilkenny. | | | | | | | | | | | |
| Callan, . . | 5,508 | 373 | 1 | – | 5,882 | 2,088 | 868 | 31 | 787 | 16 | 689 |
| Castlecomer, . | 3,677 | 328 | 10 | – | 4,015 | 1,608 | 780 | 40 | 768 | – | 618 |
| Kilkenny, . | 12,118 | 701 | 88 | 187 | 13,094 | 4,962 | 1,937 | 3 | 1,442 | 8 | 1,473 |
| Thomastown, . | 5,213 | 320 | 4 | 40 | 5,577 | 2,018 | 663 | 22 | 647 | 8 | 440 |
| Urlingford, . | 3,343 | 322 | 2 | 8 | 3,675 | 1,425 | 365 | 10 | 517 | 12 | 281 |
| King's Co. | | | | | | | | | | | |
| Edenderry, . | 3,642 | 526 | 3 | 14 | 4,185 | 1,746 | 323 | 18 | 601 | 13 | 448 |
| Parsonstown, | 4,614 | 527 | 61 | 31 | 5,233 | 2,203 | 11 | 68 | 887 | 1 | 660 |
| Tullamore, . | 5,330 | 470 | 0 | – | 5,818 | 2,729 | 1,430 | 06 | 666 | – | 503 |
| Longford. | | | | | | | | | | | |
| Ballymahon, . | 3,019 | 262 | 2 | – | 3,283 | 1,151 | 207 | 13 | 318 | 6 | 414 |
| Granard, . | 6,040 | 409 | 22 | 10 | 6,471 | 1,974 | 1,486 | 30 | 691 | 7 | 606 |
| Longford, . | 6,806 | 323 | 7 | 51 | 6,189 | 2,265 | 633 | 61 | 732 | 5 | 591 |
| Louth. | | | | | | | | | | | |
| Ardee, . . | 7,771 | 517 | 26 | 76 | 8,391 | 2,475 | 1,935 | 69 | 806 | – | 887 |
| Drogheda, . | 9,418 | 506 | 23 | 27 | 10,974 | 3,430 | 2,440 | 78 | 931 | – | 1,270 |
| Dundalk, . | 6,171 | 577 | 3 | 67 | 6,818 | 2,085 | 1,443 | 40 | 864 | – | 884 |
| Meath. | | | | | | | | | | | |
| Dunshaughlin, | 4,814 | 361 | – | 25 | 5,100 | 1,844 | 845 | – | 693 | – | 497 |
| Kells, . . | 6,775 | 476 | 10 | 87 | 7,348 | 2,151 | 929 | 37 | 795 | – | 640 |
| Navan, . . | 7,017 | 361 | 11 | 10 | 7,399 | 2,456 | 1,819 | 17 | 848 | – | 889 |
| Oldcastle, . | 3,643 | 332 | 41 | 27 | 4,043 | 1,942 | 61 | 26 | 620 | – | 537 |
| Trim, . . | 6,218 | 430 | – | 33 | 6,681 | 2,387 | 1,103 | 15 | 741 | 8 | 1,008 |
| Queen's Co. | | | | | | | | | | | |
| Abbeyleix, . | 4,208 | 378 | 5 | 68 | 4,653 | 1,661 | 810 | 45 | 659 | 23 | 662 |
| Donaghmore, . | 3,029 | 226 | 15 | 1 | 3,271 | 1,300 | 251 | 10 | 651 | – | 440 |
| Mountmellick, | 8,036 | 544 | 26 | 166 | 8,765 | 3,446 | 2,012 | 7 | 688 | 5 | 655 |
| Westmeath. | | | | | | | | | | | |
| Athlone, . | 5,120 | 637 | 62 | 17 | 5,845 | 2,037 | 331 | 3 | 781 | – | 705 |
| Delvin, . . | 2,862 | 275 | 15 | 1 | 3,353 | 931 | 379 | 1 | 471 | – | 279 |
| Mullingar, . | 10,075 | 682 | 4 | 104 | 10,786 | 3,281 | 1,916 | 80 | 1,071 | 29 | 915 |
| Wexford. | | | | | | | | | | | |
| Enniscorthy, . | 8,353 | 621 | 23 | – | 8,997 | 2,757 | 1,812 | 54 | 885 | – | 715 |
| Gorey, . . | 4,512 | 431 | 17 | 43 | 5,003 | 2,042 | 182 | 3 | 646 | 5 | 520 |
| New Ross, . | 8,130 | 572 | 12 | 4 | 8,718 | 3,998 | 1,700 | 18 | 792 | 2 | 891 |
| Wexford, . | 10,426 | 653 | 3 | 39 | 11,121 | 4,860 | 1,667 | 36 | 1,019 | – | 1,102 |
| Wicklow. | | | | | | | | | | | |
| Baltinglass, . | 5,619 | 403 | 22 | 26 | 6,070 | 2,065 | 1,426 | 61 | 814 | – | 620 |
| Rathdrum, . | 8,631 | 782 | – | 91 | 9,494 | 2,985 | 1,698 | 30 | 851 | – | 1,033 |
| Shillelagh, . | 3,087 | 261 | 6 | – | 3,354 | 1,779 | 125 | 16 | 562 | – | 441 |
| Total Leinster 1875 | 327,105 | 23,516 | 786 | 1,666 | 353,070 | 145,020 | 46,022 | 2,566 | 39,396 | 210 | 42,286 |
| Total Leinster 1874 | 332,506 | 23,355 | 770 | 1,739 | 358,370 | 158,488 | 45,694 | 2,575 | 40,290 | 386 | 41,066 |
| Increase, | – | 161 | 16 | – | – | – | 328 | – | – | – | 1,220 |
| Decrease, . | 5,400 | – | – | 74 | 5,300 | 13,468 | – | 9 | 894 | 176 | – |

of Unions during the Year ended 29th September, 1875—*continued.*

| Expenditure. | | | | | | | | Valuation on 29th Sept., 1875. | Poundage on the Valuation: | | Names of Counties and Unions. |
|---|---|---|---|---|---|---|---|---|---|---|---|
| Total Poor Relief Expenditure. | Expenses under Medical Charities and Vaccination Acts. | Expenses under the Acts for Registration of Births, Deaths, and Marriages. | Expenses under the Sanitary Acts. | Expenses under Burial Grounds Acts, paid out of the Poor Rate. | Expenses under the Superannuation Acts. | Expenses under Cattle Plague Act. | Total Expenditure during the Year. | | Of the Expenditure on the Relief of the Poor. | Of Total Expenditure. | |
| £ | £ | £ | £ | £ | £ | £ | £ | £ | s. d. | s. d. | PROVINCE OF LEINSTER. |
| | | | | | | | | | | | CARLOW. |
| 8,575 | 1,476 | 112 | 239 | 111 | - | - | 10,507 | 150,320 | 1 1¾ | 1 4¾ | Carlow. |
| | | | | | | | | | | | DUBLIN. |
| 3,146 | 1,140 | 65 | 414 | 147 | 60 | - | 4,955 | 96,062 | 0 8 | 1 0¼ | Balrothery. |
| 27,421 | 3,341 | 427 | 656 | - | 537 | - | 32,382 | 360,252 | 1 6¼ | 1 9¼ | Dublin, North. |
| 47,830 | 3,818 | 665 | 1,118 | 10 | 496 | - | 53,837 | 616,355 | 1 6¾ | 1 9 | Dublin, South. |
| 10,431 | 2,058 | 133 | 753 | - | 291 | - | 13,666 | 248,204 | 0 10 | 1 1¼ | Rathdown. |
| | | | | | | | | | | | KILDARE. |
| 6,964 | 1,235 | 66 | 306 | 181 | - | 114 | 8,868 | 109,697 | 1 3¼ | 1 7¼ | Athy. |
| 4,555 | 863 | 36 | 151 | 125 | - | - | 5,735 | 114,574 | 0 9¼ | 1 0 | Celbridge. |
| 7,991 | 1,474 | 98 | 400 | - | 143 | - | 9,706 | 162,573 | 1 0 | 1 3¼ | Naas. |
| | | | | | | | | | | | KILKENNY. |
| 5,068 | 659 | 60 | 196 | 68 | 17 | - | 5,991 | 73,436 | 1 4¾ | 1 7¼ | Callan. |
| 3,820 | 619 | 35 | 148 | - | 93 | - | 4,615 | 32,438 | 2 4¼ | 2 10¼ | Castlecomer. |
| 9,825 | 1,107 | 60 | 211 | 174 | 32 | - | 11,409 | 100,277 | 1 11½ | 2 3¼ | Kilkenny. |
| 3,798 | 532 | 42 | 252 | 1 | 152 | - | 4,777 | 65,962 | 1 1¾ | 1 5¼ | Thomastown. |
| 2,590 | 624 | 25 | 135 | 17 | 26 | - | 3,311 | 45,490 | 1 1¾ | 1 5¾ | Urlingford. |
| | | | | | | | | | | | KING'S CO. |
| 3,143 | 963 | 46 | 208 | - | 142 | - | 4,496 | 96,540 | 0 8 | 0 11¼ | Edenderry. |
| 3,690 | 1,106 | 66 | 293 | - | 20 | - | 5,115 | 102,550 | 0 8¼ | 1 0 | Parsonstown. |
| 5,714 | 855 | 58 | 253 | - | 10 | - | 6,890 | 83,075 | 1 4½ | 1 8 | Tullamore. |
| | | | | | | | | | | | LONGFORD. |
| 2,399 | 446 | 40 | 164 | - | 47 | - | 3,096 | 61,910 | 0 9¼ | 1 0 | Ballymahon. |
| 5,194 | 866 | 76 | 173 | 25 | 8 | - | 6,342 | 85,415 | 1 2¾ | 1 5¼ | Granard. |
| 4,527 | 502 | 61 | 140 | 94 | - | - | 5,284 | 60,105 | 1 6 | 1 9 | Longford. |
| | | | | | | | | | | | LOUTH. |
| 6,171 | 899 | 51 | 220 | 4 | - | 68 | 7,443 | 94,145 | 1 3¾ | 1 7 | Ardea. |
| 8,158 | 1,120 | 76 | 284 | 0 | 75 | - | 9,726 | 124,810 | 1 3¾ | 1 6¾ | Drogbeda. |
| 5,456 | 1,192 | 106 | 192 | - | - | - | 6,946 | 105,303 | 1 0¼ | 1 3¾ | Dundalk. |
| | | | | | | | | | | | MEATH. |
| 3,809 | 646 | 26 | 140 | - | 164 | - | 4,778 | 106,614 | 0 8¾ | 0 10¾ | Dunshaughlin. |
| 4,553 | 911 | 44 | 130 | 6 | 103 | - | 5,736 | 65,465 | 0 11¾ | 1 9¾ | Kells. |
| 6,029 | 672 | 46 | 123 | 16 | 23 | 102 | 7,010 | 97,990 | 1 2¾ | 1 5¼ | Navan. |
| 3,066 | 618 | 49 | 121 | 1 | 84 | - | 3,950 | 62,320 | 1 0 | 1 3¾ | Oldcastle. |
| 5,256 | 796 | 42 | 193 | - | 25 | - | 6,314 | 106,930 | 0 11¾ | 1 2 | Trim. |
| | | | | | | | | | | | QUEEN'S CO. |
| 3,752 | 802 | 47 | 168 | 117 | 20 | - | 4,606 | 67,297 | 1 1¼ | 1 5¼ | Abbeyleix. |
| 2,652 | 282 | 14 | 126 | - | 14 | 43 | 3,131 | 40,864 | 1 3¾ | 1 6¼ | Donaghmore. |
| 7,115 | 978 | 81 | 324 | - | 16 | - | 8,516 | 103,296 | 1 4½ | 1 8 | Mountmellick. |
| | | | | | | | | | | | WESTMEATH. |
| 3,797 | 1,121 | 70 | 196 | - | 113 | - | 5,296 | 88,396 | 0 10¼ | 1 2¾ | Athlone. |
| 1,952 | 427 | 25 | 220 | - | - | - | 2,624 | 53,113 | 0 8¾ | 0 11¾ | Delvin. |
| 7,957 | 1,133 | 82 | 262 | - | 70 | 164 | 9,978 | 157,550 | 0 11 | 1 1¾ | Mullingar. |
| | | | | | | | | | | | WEXFORD. |
| 6,223 | 1,161 | 87 | 177 | - | 127 | - | 7,775 | 110,360 | 1 1¼ | 1 5 | Enniscorthy. |
| 3,440 | 733 | 50 | 136 | - | 42 | 83 | 4,484 | 80,120 | 0 10¼ | 1 1¼ | Gorey. |
| 7,380 | 1,211 | 86 | 169 | - | 11 | - | 8,890 | 104,395 | 1 5 | 1 8¼ | New Ross. |
| 8,695 | 1,099 | 164 | 140 | 34 | - | 113 | 10,160 | 107,620 | 1 7¼ | 1 10¾ | Wexford. |
| | | | | | | | | | | | WICKLOW. |
| 4,962 | 768 | 59 | 108 | - | 20 | - | 5,947 | 73,864 | 1 4¼ | 1 7¼ | Baltinglass. |
| 6,526 | 1,346 | 77 | 503 | - | 3 | 140 | 8,698 | 133,790 | 0 11¾ | 1 3¼ | Rathdrum. |
| 2,943 | 415 | 46 | 101 | - | 32 | - | 3,531 | 50,814 | 1 2 | 1 4¾ | Shillelagh. |
| 275,490 | 41,743 | 3,310 | 10,275 | 1,073 | 2,996 | 856 | 335,752 | 4,618,320 | 1 2¾ | 1 5¼ | 1875, Total, LEINSTER. |
| 288,496 | 41,533 | 3,223 | 2,694 | 1,655 | 2,612 | 3,780 | 344,424 | 4,611,805 | 1 3 | 1 6 | 1874, Total, LEINSTER. |
| - | - | 87 | 7,581 | - | 384 | - | - | 6,515 | - | - | Increase. |
| 12,960 | 210 | - | - | 582 | - | 2,933 | 8,672 | - | 0 0¾ | 0 0¾ | Decrease. |

[*continued.*

No. 1. Part I.—Return showing the Receipts and Expenditure

| Names of Counties and Unions. | Receipts. | | | | | Expenditure. | | | | | |
|---|---|---|---|---|---|---|---|---|---|---|---|
| | Amount of Poor Rate Lodged. | Parliamentary Grant. | Repayment of Relief. | Other Receipts. | Total Receipts during the Year. | In-Maintenance. | Out-Relief. | Maintenance of Blind and Deaf and Dumb, in Asylums, and cost of Relief in Extern Hospitals. | Salaries and Rations of Officers. | Emigration Expenses. | All other Poor Relief Expenses. |
| **PROVINCE OF CONNAUGHT.** | £ | £ | £ | £ | £ | £ | £ | £ | £ | £ | £ |
| Galway. | | | | | | | | | | | |
| Ballinasloe, | 4,209 | 598 | 0 | 15 | 5,431 | 2,025 | 30 | 57 | 720 | 2 | 840 |
| Clifden, | 2,700 | 392 | – | 10 | 3,108 | 148 | 121 | 30 | 492 | – | 318 |
| Galway, | 6,947 | 714 | 31 | 25 | 7,747 | 3,104 | 214 | 30 | 1,029 | 6 | 809 |
| Glennamaddy, | 3,130 | 233 | 1 | 8 | 3,381 | 1,217 | 208 | 1 | 413 | 10 | 415 |
| Gort, | 3,100 | 347 | 49 | – | 3,550 | 1,194 | 35 | 25 | 531 | 10 | 458 |
| Loughrea, | 2,679 | 342 | 14 | 76 | 3,111 | 1,087 | 250 | 12 | 510 | 5 | 404 |
| Mountbellew, | 2,478 | 309 | 23 | 21 | 2,831 | 953 | 28 | 15 | 417 | 8 | 244 |
| Oughterard, | 2,103 | 308 | 10 | – | 2,425 | 072 | 40 | – | 358 | – | 279 |
| Portumna, | 2,323 | 243 | – | 4 | 2,570 | 1,235 | 04 | – | 427 | 8 | 292 |
| Tuam, | 5,812 | 546 | 20 | 8 | 6,386 | 2,340 | 787 | 30 | 745 | 6 | 679 |
| Leitrim. | | | | | | | | | | | |
| Car.-on-Shan., | 4,233 | 381 | 1 | 54 | 4,671 | 1,697 | 261 | 30 | 705 | – | 560 |
| Manorhamilton | 2,670 | 337 | – | 18 | 3,027 | 1,076 | – | 40 | 434 | – | 270 |
| Mohill, | 4,045 | 378 | 35 | 25 | 4,484 | 1,598 | 553 | 25 | 707 | 13 | 399 |
| Mayo. | | | | | | | | | | | |
| Ballina, | 2,744 | 290 | 11 | 31 | 3,076 | 1,210 | 83 | 15 | 595 | 10 | 418 |
| Ballinrobe, | 3,819 | 445 | 36 | 29 | 4,318 | 1,619 | 372 | 6 | 675 | 12 | 452 |
| Belmullet, | 1,814 | 206 | 5 | 1 | 2,026 | 1,058 | 70 | 5 | 416 | – | 304 |
| Castlebar, | 2,955 | 250 | 12 | 21 | 3,238 | 848 | 330 | – | 491 | – | 404 |
| Claremorris, | 2,605 | 281 | 21 | 1 | 2,908 | 1,160 | 201 | 56 | 518 | 2 | 326 |
| Killala, | 1,582 | 185 | 6 | 9 | 1,782 | 679 | 131 | – | 308 | – | 234 |
| Newport, | 1,837 | 273 | – | 1 | 2,111 | 700 | 25 | – | 441 | – | 203 |
| Swineford, | 3,276 | 410 | 20 | 9 | 3,715 | 1,451 | 180 | 23 | 460 | – | 387 |
| Westport, | 2,434 | 316 | – | 26 | 2,776 | 1,344 | 93 | 33 | 541 | 20 | 311 |
| Roscommon. | | | | | | | | | | | |
| Boyle, | 6,149 | 602 | 22 | 59 | 6,830 | 1,894 | 554 | 26 | 834 | – | 954 |
| Castlerea, | 2,824 | 385 | 51 | 7 | 3,267 | 1,253 | 163 | 25 | 504 | – | 650 |
| Roscommon, | 5,634 | 373 | 58 | 14 | 6,079 | 2,968 | 710 | 27 | 704 | 6 | 661 |
| Strokestown, | 4,151 | 381 | 28 | – | 4,560 | 1,647 | 633 | 47 | 592 | 9 | 493 |
| Sligo. | | | | | | | | | | | |
| Dromore, West, | 2,047 | 217 | 4 | 34 | 2,302 | 680 | 28 | 30 | 393 | – | 211 |
| Sligo, | 7,009 | 627 | 31 | 64 | 7,731 | 2,911 | 930 | 14 | 961 | 8 | 1,001 |
| Tobercurry, | 2,532 | 314 | 3 | 20 | 2,909 | 805 | 581 | 64 | 536 | – | 399 |
| Total, Connaught 1875, | 100,706 | 10,841 | 504 | 583 | 112,433 | 43,560 | 7,997 | 672 | 16,575 | 140 | 13,404 |
| Total, Connaught 1874, | 98,648 | 10,325 | 357 | 670 | 110,009 | 47,211 | 7,837 | 639 | 16,507 | 342 | 14,028 |
| Increase, | 2,058 | 316 | 147 | – | 2,424 | – | 160 | 33 | 68 | – | – |
| Decrease, | – | – | – | 87 | – | 3,651 | – | – | – | 202 | 624 |

SUMMARY OF

| | | | | | | | | | | | |
|---|---|---|---|---|---|---|---|---|---|---|---|
| Ulster, | 194,880 | 21,317 | 510 | 1,436 | 218,143 | 79,069 | 13,142 | 1,835 | 30,128 | 54 | 30,962 |
| Munster, | 308,188 | 23,593 | 1,076 | 1,973 | 334,730 | 148,583 | 27,614 | 3,317 | 39,577 | 663 | 38,902 |
| Leinster, | 327,193 | 23,516 | 796 | 1,565 | 353,070 | 145,020 | 46,023 | 2,566 | 39,300 | 210 | 42,286 |
| Connaught, | 100,706 | 10,841 | 591 | 583 | 112,433 | 43,560 | 7,997 | 672 | 16,575 | 140 | 13,404 |
| Total, Ireland, 1875, | 930,877 | 79,067 | 2,876 | 5,005 | 1,018,425 | 416,172 | 94,776 | 8,390 | 125,676 | 967 | 120,574 |
| Total, Ireland, 1874, | 941,292 | 78,001 | 2,681 | 6,532 | 1,028,606 | 457,944 | 93,586 | 8,401 | 120,769 | 2,070 | 128,511 |
| Increase, | – | 1,066 | 195 | – | – | – | 1,189 | – | – | – | – |
| Decrease, | 10,415 | – | – | 1,027 | 10,181 | 41,772 | – | 11 | 1,094 | 1,103 | 7,937 |

of Unions during the Year ended 29th September, 1875—*continued.*

| Expenditure. | | | | | | | | Valuation on 29th Sept., 1875. | Poundage on the Valuation: | | Names of Counties and Unions. |
|---|---|---|---|---|---|---|---|---|---|---|---|
| Total Poor Relief Expenditure. | Expenses under Medical Charities and Vaccination Acts. | Expenses under the Acts for Registration of Births, Deaths, and Marriages. | Expenses under the Sanitary Acts. | Expenses under Burial Grounds Acts, paid out of the Poor Rate. | Expenses under the Superannuation Acts. | Expenses under Cattle Plague Act. | Total Expenditure during the Year. | | Of the Expenditure on the Relief of the Poor. | Of Total Expenditure. | |
| £ | £ | £ | £ | £ | £ | £ | £ | £ | s. d. | s. d. | PROVINCE OF CONNAUGHT. |
| | | | | | | | | | | | GALWAY. |
| 4,274 | 857 | 46 | 161 | - | 13 | 82 | 5,433 | 73,376 | 1 1 | 1 4½ | Ballinasloe. |
| 1,949 | 783 | 36 | 161 | 30 | 60 | - | 3,019 | 17,730 | 2 2½ | 3 4½ | Clifden. |
| 5,421 | 1,339 | 103 | 297 | - | 155 | - | 7,315 | 55,350 | 1 7½ | 2 2½ | Galway. |
| 2,369 | 419 | 45 | 107 | 34 | - | - | 2,967 | 31,808 | 1 5½ | 1 10½ | Glennamaddy. |
| 2,302 | 558 | 48 | 72 | 23 | 38 | 45 | 3,044 | 44,212 | 1 0½ | 1 4½ | Gort. |
| 2,289 | 601 | 50 | 497 | 8 | 10 | - | 3,434 | 76,916 | 0 7½ | 0 10½ | Loughrea. |
| 1,735 | 675 | 40 | 97 | - | - | - | 2,448 | 40,450 | 0 10½ | 1 2½ | Mountbellew. |
| 1,580 | 737 | 42 | 108 | - | 12 | - | 2,488 | 15,064 | 2 1½ | 3 3½ | Oughterard. |
| 2,133 | 362 | 30 | 63 | 28 | - | - | 2,616 | 35,840 | 1 2½ | 1 5½ | Portumna. |
| 4,025 | 297 | 86 | 225 | 283 | 17 | - | 6,934 | 78,714 | 1 2½ | 1 7½ | Tuam. |
| | | | | | | | | | | | LEITRIM. |
| 3,253 | 645 | 61 | 185 | - | - | - | 4,144 | 48,160 | 1 4½ | 1 8½ | Car.-on-Shan. |
| 1,890 | 641 | 69 | 145 | - | 67 | - | 2,749 | 43,418 | 0 10 | 1 3½ | Manorhamilton. |
| 3,295 | 632 | 56 | 113 | 10 | 128 | - | 4,234 | 39,587 | 1 8 | 2 1½ | Mohill. |
| | | | | | | | | | | | MAYO. |
| 2,334 | 506 | 65 | 129 | - | 50 | - | 3,075 | 48,424 | 0 11½ | 1 3½ | Ballina. |
| 3,328 | 792 | 63 | 303 | - | 35 | - | 4,521 | 59,445 | 1 1½ | 1 6 | Ballinrobe. |
| 1,858 | 338 | 24 | 67 | - | - | - | 2,287 | 10,940 | 3 4½ | 4 2½ | Belmullet. |
| 2,073 | 593 | 66 | 102 | - | 20 | 44 | 2,962 | 46,270 | 0 10½ | 1 3½ | Castlebar. |
| 2,305 | 574 | 75 | 277 | - | 5 | - | 3,236 | 42,108 | 1 1½ | 1 7 | Claremorris. |
| 1,389 | 473 | 93 | 63 | - | - | - | 1,011 | 28,664 | 1 5½ | 1 10½ | Killala. |
| 1,369 | 464 | 34 | 95 | - | 145 | - | 2,107 | 12,105 | 2 1 | 3 2½ | Newport. |
| 2,535 | 856 | 128 | 206 | - | 33 | - | 3,756 | 40,786 | 1 3 | 1 10 | Swineford. |
| 2,183 | 519 | 59 | 167 | - | 21 | - | 2,948 | 31,112 | 1 4½ | 1 10½ | Westport. |
| | | | | | | | | | | | ROSCOMMON. |
| 4,362 | 1,157 | 82 | 167 | 10 | 78 | - | 5,856 | 73,022 | 1 2½ | 1 7 | Boyle. |
| 3,255 | 689 | 89 | 141 | - | 104 | - | 4,278 | 71,870 | 0 10½ | 1 2½ | Castlerea. |
| 5,095 | 516 | 54 | 112 | - | - | - | 5,777 | 64,432 | 1 7 | 1 9½ | Roscommon. |
| 3,641 | 575 | 49 | 193 | 34 | - | 53 | 4,476 | 50,778 | 1 5½ | 1 9½ | Strokestown. |
| | | | | | | | | | | | SLIGO. |
| 1,342 | 462 | 32 | 83 | - | 106 | - | 2,094 | 36,853 | 0 8½ | 1 1½ | Dromore, West. |
| 5,911 | 1,557 | 100 | 295 | 2 | 215 | | 8,010 | 97,806 | 1 2½ | 1 7½ | Sligo. |
| 2,485 | 552 | 67 | 140 | 13 | - | 42 | 3,199 | 40,635 | 1 2½ | 1 7 | Tubbercurry. |
| 82,368 | 19,848 | 1,712 | 4,083 | 475 | 1,311 | 270 | 110,047 | 1,363,220 | 1 2½ | 1 7½ | 1875, Total, Connaught. |
| 86,584 | 19,013 | 1,729 | 761 | 395 | 845 | 1,143 | 110,450 | 1,360,323 | 1 3½ | 1 7½ | 1874, Total, Connaught. |
| - | 835 | - | 3,322 | 80 | 466 | - | 197 | 2,897 | - | - | Increase. |
| 4,216 | - | 17 | - | - | - | 873 | - | - | 0 0½ | - | Decrease. |

PROVINCES.

| Total Poor Relief Expenditure. | Medical Charities and Vaccination Acts. | Registration Acts. | Sanitary Acts. | Burial Grounds Acts. | Superannuation Acts. | Cattle Plague Act. | Total Expenditure during the Year. | Valuation on 29th Sept., 1875. | Of the Expenditure on the Relief of the Poor. | Of Total Expenditure. | Names |
|---|---|---|---|---|---|---|---|---|---|---|---|
| 165,290 | 30,839 | 4,167 | 8,179 | 1,027 | 1,785 | 770 | 210,980 | 4,116,200 | 0 9 | 1 0½ | ULSTER. |
| 236,506 | 60,028 | 3,288 | 9,797 | 1,870 | 3,083 | 658 | 317,605 | 3,387,860 | 1 5½ | 1 10½ | MUNSTER. |
| 275,499 | 41,743 | 3,310 | 10,275 | 1,073 | 2,996 | 855 | 336,752 | 4,618,320 | 1 2½ | 1 5½ | LEINSTER. |
| 82,348 | 19,848 | 1,712 | 4,083 | 475 | 1,311 | 270 | 110,647 | 1,363,220 | 1 2½ | 1 7½ | CONNAUGHT. |
| 771,553 | 141,458 | 12,497 | 32,934 | 4,445 | 9,615 | 2,548 | 975,044 | 13,485,600 | 1 1½ | 1 5½ | 1875, Total, Ireland. |
| 817,281 | 140,922 | 12,281 | 7,918 | 4,613 | 8,182 | 10,792 | 1,001,989 | 13,449,553 | 1 2½ | 1 6 | 1874, Total, Ireland. |
| - | 530 | 216 | 25,016 | - | 1,433 | - | - | 36,047 | - | - | Increase. |
| 45,728 | - | - | - | 168 | - | 8,244 | 26,945 | - | 0 0½ | 0 0½ | Decrease. |

No. 1. Part 2.—Return of the Number of Persons who received Poor Relief during the Year ended 29th September, 1875, together with the Expenditure for Provisions, Necessaries, and Clothing of Workhouse Inmates during the Year, and the average Weekly Cost per head in the Workhouse.

| Names of Counties and Unions. | Number of Persons who received Relief under the Poor Relief Acts during the Year: In Workhouse. | Out-door. | In Blind and Deaf and Dumb Asylums. | Total. | Collective Number of Days for all Persons Relieved in the Workhouse during the Year. | Average Number of Days of Relief to each Person in Workhouse. | Average Daily Number of Persons in Workhouse. | Cost of Provisions, Necessaries, and Clothing: Provisions and Necessaries. | Clothing. | Total. | Average Weekly cost per head: Provisions and Necessaries. | Clothing. | Total. |
|---|---|---|---|---|---|---|---|---|---|---|---|---|---|
| PROVINCE OF ULSTER | | | | | | | | £ | £ | £ | s. d. | s. d. | s. d. |
| Antrim. | | | | | | | | | | | | | |
| Antrim, | 1,065 | 163 | 9 | 1,236 | 91,299 | 84 | 250 | 1,793 | 381 | 2,174 | 2 9 | 0 7 | 3 4 |
| Ballycastle, | 426 | 1 | – | 430 | 38,164 | 89 | 105 | 780 | 173 | 953 | 2 9½ | 0 7¼ | 3 4¾ |
| Ballymena, | 1,684 | 810 | 8 | 2,402 | 104,641 | 71 | 287 | 1,671 | 487 | 2,158 | 2 2½ | 0 7 | 2 9½ |
| Ballymoney, | 987 | 349 | 3 | 1,339 | 47,444 | 50 | 130 | 686 | 218 | 884 | 1 10 | 0 7¼ | 2 5¼ |
| Belfast, | 10,081 | 276 | 26 | 10,404 | 864,198 | 88 | 2,468 | 16,540 | 3,720 | 20,260 | 2 7 | 0 7 | 3 2 |
| Larne, | 939 | 215 | – | 1,154 | 76,977 | 82 | 211 | 1,488 | 343 | 1,700 | 2 8 | 0 7½ | 3 3½ |
| Lisburn, | 1,590 | 269 | 10 | 1,869 | 88,543 | 48 | 242 | 1,402 | 308 | 1,710 | 2 2 | 0 7 | 2 10 |
| Armagh. | | | | | | | | | | | | | |
| Armagh, | 1,167 | 38 | 1 | 1,206 | 110,856 | 95 | 303 | 1,964 | 429 | 2,180 | 2 6 | 0 8½ | 3 0½ |
| Lurgan, | 2,601 | 45 | 8 | 2,654 | 141,369 | 54 | 387 | 2,914 | 405 | 3,319 | 2 10½ | 0 3½ | 3 4½ |
| Cavan. | | | | | | | | | | | | | |
| Bailieborough, | 772 | 75 | 1 | 848 | 62,019 | 87 | 145 | 1,300 | 175 | 1,475 | 3 11½ | 0 6½ | 3 6½ |
| Bawnboy, | 850 | 466 | 6 | 1,322 | 44,004 | 58 | 120 | 803 | 144 | 1,040 | 2 10½ | 0 5½ | 3 4 |
| Cavan, | 1,729 | 411 | 6 | 2,146 | 117,042 | 108 | 321 | 2,152 | 480 | 2,637 | 2 7½ | 0 5½ | 3 1¼ |
| Cootehill, | 650 | 95 | 3 | 847 | 47,010 | 74 | 129 | 848 | 124 | 967 | 2 8½ | 0 5 | 2 11½ |
| Donegal. | | | | | | | | | | | | | |
| Ballyshannon, | 614 | – | 1 | 615 | 61,085 | 89 | 167 | 1,008 | 212 | 1,220 | 2 3½ | 0 8 | 2 9½ |
| Donegal, | 386 | 50 | 1 | 436 | 35,345 | 101 | 97 | 845 | 66 | 505 | 2 1½ | 0 8 | 2 4½ |
| Dunfanaghy, | 105 | – | – | 105 | 12,473 | 118 | 34 | 277 | 37 | 314 | 2 1½ | 0 5 | 2 6½ |
| Glenties, | 332 | 100 | 1 | 430 | 40,089 | 122 | 110 | 637 | 55 | 692 | 2 3½ | 0 4 | 2 7½ |
| Inishowen, | 408 | 188 | 3 | 597 | 50,738 | 125 | 193 | 653 | 227 | 880 | 2 4½ | 0 4½ | 2 9¼ |
| Letterkenny, | 397 | 1 | – | 398 | 38,050 | 96 | 107 | 481 | 123 | 604 | 2 11½ | 0 5½ | 2 6½ |

| | | | | | | | | | | | | | |
|---|---|---|---|---|---|---|---|---|---|---|---|---|---|
| Milford, . . | 248 | 47 | – | 287 | 39,157 | 131 | 80 | 494 | 66 | 587 | 2 4½ | 0 5½ | 2 9½ |
| Stranorlar, . . | 284 | 5 | 1 | 290 | 19,408 | 74 | 53 | 318 | 48 | 337 | 2 5 | 0 8½ | 2 6½ |
| Down. | | | | | | | | | | | | | |
| Banbridge, . . | 1,783 | 497 | 3 | 2,284 | 77,658 | 46 | 213 | 1,873 | 353 | 1,889 | 2 10 | 0 7 | 3 5 |
| Downpatrick, . . | 1,672 | 131 | 1 | 1,804 | 67,315 | 51 | 230 | 1,483 | 300 | 1,913 | 2 0¼ | 0 7½ | 2 0¾ |
| Kilkeel, . . | 408 | 88 | 1 | 497 | 33,474 | 73 | 123 | 326 | 85 | 619 | 2 2½ | 0 4½ | 2 7 |
| Newry, . . | 2,626 | 900 | 9 | 3,536 | 137,236 | 48 | 578 | 2,496 | 560 | 3,064 | 2 5½ | 0 6½ | 3 11½ |
| Newtownards, . . | 1,707 | 815 | 4 | 2,526 | 130,364 | 79 | 308 | 2,344 | 682 | 3,066 | 2 6½ | 0 8 | 3 2½ |
| Fermanagh. | | | | | | | | | | | | | |
| Enniskillen, . . | 940 | 34 | 1 | 975 | 94,401 | 100 | 209 | 1,776 | 286 | 2,061 | 2 7½ | 0 5 | 3 0½ |
| Irvinestown, . . | 501 | 3 | – | 508 | 37,280 | 73 | 208 | 680 | 108 | 806 | 2 7½ | 0 4½ | 3 0 |
| Lisnaskea, . . | 570 | 174 | – | 718 | 30,856 | 42 | 64 | 677 | 157 | 834 | 5 1½ | 0 3½ | 5 10 |
| Londonderry. | | | | | | | | | | | | | |
| Coleraine, . . | 1,636 | 231 | 1 | 1,868 | 60,837 | 33 | 235 | 1,466 | 238 | 1,704 | 2 3½ | 0 7 | 3 0½ |
| Limavady, . . | 1,030 | 5 | 1 | 1,046 | 41,636 | 42 | 181 | 666 | 211 | 847 | 1 10½ | 0 7½ | 2 6½ |
| Londonderry, . . | 2,128 | 26 | 6 | 2,159 | 152,098 | 66 | 385 | 1,763 | 636 | 2,409 | 1 9½ | 0 7½ | 2 5½ |
| Magherafelt, . . | 1,606 | 9 | 5 | 1,611 | 70,243 | 79 | 217 | 1,391 | 248 | 1,609 | 2 4½ | 0 9½ | 2 10 |
| Monaghan. | | | | | | | | | | | | | |
| Carrickmacross, . . | 686 | 7 | 6 | 679 | 41,119 | 62 | 113 | 858 | 183 | 1,041 | 3 11 | 0 5½ | 3 4½ |
| Castleblayney, . . | 785 | 236 | 1 | 988 | 64,074 | 75 | 130 | 714 | 170 | 1,084 | 2 1 | 0 5½ | 2 6½ |
| Clones, . . | 727 | 3 | – | 730 | 32,256 | 44 | 59 | 673 | 73 | 548 | 2 9½ | 0 5½ | 3 3½ |
| Monaghan, . . | 906 | – | 5 | 593 | 60,818 | 102 | 164 | 1,031 | 145 | 1,176 | 3 9 | 0 6 | 3 9 |
| Tyrone. | | | | | | | | | | | | | |
| Castlederg, . . | 838 | – | 1 | 639 | 26,011 | 79 | 71 | 500 | 61 | 561 | 1 7½ | 0 6½ | 1 10½ |
| Clogher, . . | 439 | 60 | – | 941 | 57,128 | 93 | 102 | 840 | 110 | 830 | 2 7 | 0 3½ | 3 1½ |
| Cookstown, . . | 636 | 24 | – | 660 | 43,108 | 67 | 117 | 763 | 69 | 791 | 2 3½ | 0 3½ | 3 7 |
| Dungannon, . . | 1,232 | 342 | 2 | 1,574 | 74,484 | 46 | 284 | 1,306 | 220 | 1,516 | 2 9½ | 0 3½ | 3 10½ |
| Gortin, . . | 163 | 10 | 1 | 537 | 36,496 | 84 | 84 | 383 | 74 | 363 | 2 3½ | 0 6½ | 2 9½ |
| Omagh, . . | 1,176 | 21 | – | 1,237 | 75,530 | 60 | 211 | 1,161 | 97 | 1,236 | 2 1½ | 0 2 | 3 4½ |
| Strabane, . . | 1,979 | 465 | 1 | 2,166 | 66,878 | 31 | 234 | 1,339 | 235 | 1,565 | 2 6½ | 0 7 | 3 1½ |
| Total Ulster, 1875, | 61,080 | 7,428 | 227 | 66,939 | 3,808,260 | 72 | 10,046 | 62,223 | 13,777 | 76,060 | 2 6 | 0 8½ | 3 0½ |
| Do. do. 1874, | 69,160 | 7,743 | 213 | 67,028 | 3,737,114 | 64 | 10,240 | 71,289 | 13,901 | 85,091 | 2 8½ | 0 3½ | 3 3½ |
| Increase, . . | – | – | 14 | – | – | 9 | – | – | – | – | – | – | – |
| Decrease, . . | 8,080 | 315 | – | 8,368 | 71,146 | – | 195 | 9,766 | 127 | 6,233 | 0 2½ | – | 0 9½ |

G

[continued.

| Names of Counties and Unions. | Number of Persons who received Relief under the Poor Relief Acts during the Year: In Workhouse. | Out-door. | In Blind and Deaf and Dumb Asylums. | Total. | Collective Number of Days for all Persons Relieved in the Workhouse during the Year. | Average Number of Days of Relief to each Pauper in Workhouse. | Average Daily Number of Paupers in Workhouse. | Cost of Provisions, Necessaries, and Clothing: Provisions and Necessaries. | Clothing. | Total. | Average Weekly Cost per head: Provisions and Necessaries. | Clothing. | Total. |
|---|---|---|---|---|---|---|---|---|---|---|---|---|---|
| PROVINCE OF MUNSTER. | | | | | | | | £ | £ | £ | s. d. | s. d. | s. d. |
| Clare. | | | | | | | | | | | | | |
| Ballyvaughan, | 309 | 59 | – | 368 | 50,841 | 109 | 158 | 1,231 | 130 | 1,351 | 2 11 | 0 9 | 3 8 |
| Corofin, | 411 | 206 | 1 | 618 | 45,488 | 111 | 125 | 990 | 140 | 1,130 | 3 0½ | 0 5½ | 3 5½ |
| Ennis, | 1,371 | 469 | 1 | 1,841 | 148,818 | 107 | 407 | 3,114 | 529 | 3,643 | 2 11½ | 0 6 | 3 4½ |
| Ennistymon, | 872 | 326 | 4 | 1,202 | 95,144 | 106 | 277 | 2,300 | 301 | 2,601 | 3 0½ | 0 7 | 3 10½ |
| Kildysart, | 416 | 137 | 1 | 554 | 71,102 | 179 | 144 | 1,616 | 180 | 1,781 | 2 11½ | 0 7½ | 3 7 |
| Kilrush, | 1,018 | 966 | 1 | 2,005 | 184,766 | 119 | 374 | 2,340 | 434 | 2,814 | 2 11 | 0 7½ | 3 6½ |
| Scarriff, | 334 | 6 | 4 | 343 | 67,544 | 202 | 189 | 1,375 | 160 | 1,535 | 2 9½ | 0 5½ | 3 3½ |
| Tulla, | 832 | 309 | 1 | 1,142 | 85,867 | 86 | 234 | 1,460 | 283 | 1,743 | 2 1½ | 0 5 | 3 6½ |
| Cork. | | | | | | | | | | | | | |
| Bandon, | 639 | – | 3 | 642 | 74,019 | 231 | 206 | 1,473 | 219 | 1,700 | 2 9½ | 0 7 | 3 4½ |
| Bantry, | 334 | 79 | 1 | 403 | 36,[illegible] | 140 | 110 | 604 | 91 | 695 | 2 [illegible] | 0 8 | 3 [illegible] |
| Castletown, | 402 | 56 | – | 846 | 68,701 | 90 | 199 | [illegible] | 126 | 963 | 2 4½ | 0 4½ | 2 8½ |
| Clonakilty, | 636 | 2 | 2 | 630 | 84,024 | 134 | 241 | 1,531 | 256 | 1,465 | 2 3½ | 0 3½ | 3 10½ |
| Cork, | 8,830 | 2,373 | 60 | 11,308 | 777,770 | 56 | 2,047 | 16,010 | 3,045 | 22,440 | 3 0½ | 0 8½ | 3 9½ |
| Dunmanway, | 617 | 131 | 1 | 749 | 68,694 | 165 | 188 | 1,061 | 251 | 1,401 | 2 7½ | 0 0½ | 3 3 |
| Fermoy, | 1,407 | 32 | 3 | 1,443 | 100,[illegible] | 73 | 282 | 2,018 | 337 | 2,356 | 2 7½ | 0 3½ | 3 0½ |
| Kanturk, | 1,430 | 1,136 | 7 | 4,017 | 158,[illegible] | 111 | 435 | 3,744 | 313 | 4,076 | 3 10½ | 0 6½ | 3 7 |
| Kinsale, | 678 | 6 | – | 681 | 47,477 | 70 | 130 | 946 | 168 | 1,114 | 2 10½ | 0 3½ | 3 3½ |
| Macroom, | 491 | 66 | 6 | 563 | [illegible] | 160 | 241 | 1,440 | 367 | 1,807 | 2 11 | 0 7 | 3 6 |
| Mallow, | 1,536 | 1,114 | 7 | 2,657 | 141,484 | 73 | 388 | 2,715 | 316 | 3,031 | 2 5½ | 0 3½ | 3 0 |
| Midleton, | 1,909 | 777 | 5 | 2,691 | 197,539 | 103 | 539 | 6,045 | 556 | 6,601 | 3 6 | 0 5 | 3 9 |
| Millstreet, | 1,140 | 208 | 0 | 1,348 | 101,[illegible] | 90 | 270 | 2,208 | 232 | 2,440 | 3 0½ | 0 3½ | 3 3½ |
| Mitchelstown, | 1,019 | 900 | 3 | 1,922 | [illegible] | 93 | 257 | 1,420 | 340 | 1,761 | 2 2 | 0 7 | 2 9 |
| Skibbereen, | 978 | 138 | 3 | 1,119 | 112,164 | 114 | 308 | 2,156 | 301 | 2,457 | 2 8½ | 0 4½ | 3 1 |

| | | | | | | | | | | | | | |
|---|---|---|---|---|---|---|---|---|---|---|---|---|---|
| Skull, . . | 326 | 22 | 1 | 302 | 46,006 | 157 | 196 | 718 | 96 | 310 | 2 2½ | 0 6½ | 2 6½ |
| Youghal, . | 906 | 487 | 5 | 1,394 | 85,905 | 306 | 268 | 1,460 | 668 | 1,365 | 2 3½ | 0 7 | 2 10½ |
| KERRY. | | | | | | | | | | | | | |
| Cahersiveen, . | 636 | 208 | 1 | 844 | 65,803 | 72 | 139 | 1,003 | 144 | 1,147 | 2 0½ | 0 5½ | 3 6 |
| Dingle, . . | 445 | 2 | 2 | 449 | 61,819 | 176 | 170 | 1,148 | 169 | 1,317 | 2 7½ | 0 3½ | 2 11 |
| Kenmare, . | 469 | 198 | – | 663 | 64,136 | 57 | 129 | 789 | 130 | 919 | 2 1½ | 0 4½ | 2 6½ |
| Killarney, . | 1,077 | 854 | 5 | 1,930 | 143,110 | 114 | 837 | 3,067 | 404 | 3,461 | 3 4½ | 0 5½ | 2 11½ |
| Listowel, . | 854 | 1 | 2 | 857 | 84,348 | 85 | 141 | 984 | 130 | 1,114 | 2 8½ | 0 4 | 2 0½ |
| Tralee, . . | 2,034 | 48 | 16 | 2,098 | 100,886 | 49 | 552 | 3,550 | 195 | 4,145 | 2 7½ | 0 7 | 3 0½ |
| LIMERICK. | | | | | | | | | | | | | |
| Croom, . . | 934 | 420 | 4 | 1,363 | 84,748 | 55 | 222 | 1,860 | 266 | 2,134 | 3 1 | 0 8½ | 3 6½ |
| Glin, . . | 317 | 753 | 7 | 677 | 48,650 | 84 | 136 | 1,083 | 234 | 1,317 | 3 1½ | 0 5 | 3 1½ |
| Kilmallock, . | 2,713 | 1,758 | 10 | 3,681 | 267,073 | 57 | 536 | 4,990 | 307 | 5,297 | 2 11½ | 0 6½ | 3 5½ |
| Limerick, . | 5,717 | 1,437 | 11 | 7,165 | 446,141 | 97 | 1,383 | 11,880 | 2,346 | 14,276 | 3 9 | 0 7½ | 3 7½ |
| Newcastle, . | 1,195 | 804 | 2 | 1,961 | 165,401 | 80 | 200 | 2,501 | 247 | 2,780 | 3 2 | 0 8½ | 3 7½ |
| Rathkeale, . | 780 | 787 | 8 | 1,589 | 60,196 | 60 | 301 | 1,479 | 207 | 1,796 | 3 1½ | 0 9½ | 3 8½ |
| TIPPERARY. | | | | | | | | | | | | | |
| Borrisokane . | 391 | 2 | – | 394 | 40,899 | 70 | 107 | 630 | 148 | 781 | 2 11½ | 0 6 | 3 6½ |
| Carrick-on-Suir, | 1,875 | 487 | 2 | 2,184 | 82,556 | 71 | 204 | 1,787 | 445 | 2,232 | 2 8½ | 0 5 | 3 4½ |
| Cashel, . . | 1,449 | 1,137 | 4 | 2,609 | 131,586 | 109 | 415 | 2,775 | 384 | 3,159 | 3 9½ | 0 6½ | 3 4½ |
| Clogheen, . | 984 | – | 3 | 987 | 80,685 | 92 | 245 | 1,839 | 324 | 2,157 | 3 9 | 0 0 | 3 8 |
| Clonmel, . | 2,449 | 469 | 7 | 2,879 | 125,416 | 76 | 405 | 3,465 | 730 | 4,195 | 3 3½ | 0 6½ | 3 9 |
| Nenagh, . | 1,148 | 919 | 4 | 2,181 | 121,688 | 111 | 720 | 2,418 | 487 | 2,905 | 3 9 | 0 6½ | 3 8½ |
| Roscrea, . | 564 | 204 | – | 768 | 51,144 | 92 | 160 | 1,006 | 284 | 1,290 | 2 11½ | 0 6½ | 3 8 |
| Thurles, . | 773 | 232 | 2 | 970 | 16,096 | 113 | 205 | 1,578 | 379 | 1,944 | 3 3 | 0 8 | 3 1 |
| Tipperary, . | 2,097 | 1,316 | 1 | 3,383 | 152,471 | 69 | 608 | 4,150 | 789 | 5,134 | 3 3 | 0 7 | 3 10 |
| WATERFORD. | | | | | | | | | | | | | |
| Dungarvan, . | 1,650 | 686 | 4 | 2,339 | 128,413 | 10 | 353 | 2,974 | 630 | 3,620 | 3 8½ | 0 8½ | 3 11 |
| Kilmacthomas, | 1,080 | 328 | – | 1,408 | 96,140 | 61 | 144 | 1,286 | 234 | 1,518 | 3 4 | 0 6½ | 4 0½ |
| Lismore, . | 850 | 251 | 2 | 1,133 | 64,203 | 70 | 176 | 1,320 | 156 | 1,488 | 3 8 | 0 7 | 3 9 |
| Waterford, . | 4,809 | 1,286 | 7 | 6,018 | 262,831 | 64 | 939 | 7,107 | 1,062 | 8,219 | 3 11 | 0 6½ | 3 4½ |
| Total Munster, 1875, | 62,561 | 25,875 | 242 | 88,561 | 6,059,150 | 83 | 16,580 | 131,878 | 23,660 | 146,546 | 3 10½ | 0 6½ | 3 6½ |
| Do. do. 1874, | 78,240 | 25,666 | 264 | 100,178 | 6,226,276 | 85 | 17,036 | 143,007 | 23,396 | 166,315 | 3 9½ | 0 6½ | 3 6½ |
| Increase, . . | – | 209 | – | – | – | 11 | – | – | 264 | – | – | 0 0½ | – |
| Decrease, . . | 15,679 | – | 22 | 10,572 | 167,116 | – | 456 | 16,061 | – | 17,570 | 0 8½ | – | 0 1½ |

No. 1. Part 2.—Return of the Number of Persons who received Poor Relief during the Year ended 29th September, 1875, together with the Expenditure for Provisions, Necessaries, and Clothing of Workhouse Inmates during the Year, &c.—continued.

| Names of Counties and Unions. | Number of Persons who received Relief under the Poor Relief Acts during the year: In Workhouse | Out-door | In Blind and Deaf and Dumb Asylums | Total. | Collective Number of Days for all Paupers Relieved in the Workhouse during the Year | Average Number of Days of Relief to each Pauper in Workhouse | Average Daily Number of Paupers in Workhouse | Cost of Provisions, Necessaries, and Clothing: Provisions and Necessaries. | Clothing. | Total. | Average Weekly Cost per head: Provisions and Necessaries. | Clothing. | Total. |
|---|---|---|---|---|---|---|---|---|---|---|---|---|---|
| PROVINCE OF LEINSTER. | | | | | | | | £ | £ | £ | s. d. | s. d. | s. d. |
| Carlow | | | | | | | | | | | | | |
| Carlow, . . | 1,382 | 1,419 | 3 | 2,804 | 120,317 | 87 | 330 | 2,779 | 640 | 3,409 | 3 9½ | 0 8¾ | 3 11¼ |
| Dublin. | | | | | | | | | | | | | |
| Balrothery, . . | 1,757 | 345 | 1 | 2,103 | 47,116 | 66 | 129 | 1,205 | 109 | 1,304 | 3 8½ | 0 7 | 3 10½ |
| Dublin, North, . | 6,093 | 224 | 21 | 6,338 | 664,438 | 104 | 1,678 | 15,194 | 2,117 | 17,311 | 3 1½ | 0 6½ | 3 8½ |
| Dublin, South, . | 9,871 | 4,146 | 24 | 14,041 | 1,075,247 | 110 | 2,900 | 26,172 | 5,307 | 31,479 | 3 4½ | 0 8½ | 4 1½ |
| Rathdown, . . | 2,539 | 152 | 17 | 2,698 | 198,317 | 70 | 545 | 5,437 | 1,144 | 6,579 | 3 10 | 0 9½ | 4 7½ |
| Kildare. | | | | | | | | | | | | | |
| Athy, . . . | 2,296 | 1,034 | 6 | 3,344 | 96,893 | 43 | 265 | 2,572 | 494 | 3,076 | 3 10½ | 0 7 | 4 5½ |
| Celbridge, . . | 845 | 493 | 3 | 1,356 | 53,750 | 61 | 147 | 1,506 | 313 | 1,919 | 4 9½ | 0 9½ | 5 6 |
| Naas, . . . | 2,311 | 1,303 | 7 | 3,621 | 110,915 | 50 | 304 | 2,569 | 489 | 3,059 | 3 7½ | 0 6½ | 4 1½ |
| Kilkenny. | | | | | | | | | | | | | |
| Callan, . . | 1,578 | 651 | 1 | 2,230 | 107,213 | 79 | 294 | 2,241 | 447 | 2,688 | 2 11 | 0 7 | 3 6 |
| Castlecomer, . | 875 | 400 | 6 | 1,281 | 59,735 | 64 | 166 | 1,378 | 230 | 1,608 | 3 4½ | 0 10½ | 4 3½ |
| Kilkenny, . . | 2,880 | 1,301 | — | 4,181 | 193,151 | 65 | 530 | 4,006 | 566 | 4,562 | 2 11½ | 0 7½ | 3 7½ |
| Thomastown, . | 1,080 | 515 | 9 | 1,604 | 81,296 | 75 | 222 | 1,664 | 354 | 2,018 | 2 10½ | 0 7½ | 3 5½ |
| Urlingford, . . | 444 | 234 | 1 | 679 | 52,567 | 99 | 144 | 1,116 | 100 | 1,225 | 3 5 | 0 3½ | 3 8½ |
| King's Co. | | | | | | | | | | | | | |
| Edenderry, . . | 2,056 | 372 | 1 | 2,644 | 67,235 | 33 | 184 | 1,519 | 227 | 1,746 | 3 3 | 0 3½ | 3 7½ |
| Parsonstown, . | 845 | 23 | 8 | 876 | 88,806 | 94 | 242 | 1,962 | 301 | 2,263 | 3 0 | 0 5½ | 3 5½ |
| Tullamore, . . | 1,408 | 760 | 5 | 2,167 | 301,325 | 55 | 834 | 2,290 | 445 | 2,735 | 2 11½ | 0 7 | 3 6½ |

| | | | | | | | | | | | | | |
|---|---|---|---|---|---|---|---|---|---|---|---|---|---|
| **Longford.** | | | | | | | | | | | | | |
| Ballymahon, . . | 690 | 363 | 1 | 306 | 43,134 | 90 | 117 | 971 | 290 | 1,151 | 3 2½ | 0 7 | 3 9½ |
| Granard, . . | 731 | 1,006 | 3 | 1,032 | 79,109 | 107 | 217 | 1,708 | 250 | 1,974 | 3 0½ | 0 3½ | 3 5½ |
| Longford, . . | 1,383 | 536 | 4 | 1,899 | 201,884 | 78 | 277 | 2,620 | 260 | 2,284 | 9 3½ | 0 4½ | 3 2 |
| **Louth.** | | | | | | | | | | | | | |
| Ardee, . . | 2,212 | 1,178 | 5 | 3,390 | 75,869 | 86 | 317 | 3,148 | 330 | 2,478 | 3 9½ | 0 7 | 4 4½ |
| Drogheda, . . | 3,887 | 1,790 | 6 | 5,382 | 139,870 | 97 | 836 | 8,062 | 364 | 8,430 | 3 1½ | 0 8½ | 3 8½ |
| Dundalk, . . | 2,180 | 966 | 3 | 3,122 | 97,444 | 45 | 896 | 1,630 | 200 | 2,006 | 3 7½ | 0 4½ | 3 0½ |
| **Meath.** | | | | | | | | | | | | | |
| Dunshaughlin, . | 2,639 | 611 | – | 3,160 | 68,548 | 28 | 160 | 1,879 | 295 | 2,044 | 3 9½ | 0 7½ | 4 5 |
| Kells, . . | 1,043 | 348 | 6 | 1,390 | 88,448 | 73 | 286 | 1,634 | 317 | 2,101 | 3 1½ | 0 8½ | 3 7½ |
| Navan, . . | 3,406 | 610 | 7 | 4,389 | 84,786 | 28 | 284 | 2,023 | 435 | 2,458 | 3 4½ | 0 8½ | 4 0½ |
| Oldcastle, . . | 1,106 | 73 | 3 | 1,171 | 70,431 | 94 | 198 | 1,550 | 497 | 1,949 | 3 0½ | 0 8½ | 3 10½ |
| Trim, . . | 3,474 | 680 | 1 | 5,154 | 87,811 | 97 | 164 | 1,806 | 481 | 2,287 | 4 0½ | 0 10½ | 4 11½ |
| **Queen's Co.** | | | | | | | | | | | | | |
| Abbeyleix, . . | 984 | 360 | 6 | 1,351 | 60,865 | 98 | 186 | 1,350 | 211 | 1,561 | 3 8½ | 0 7 | 4 3½ |
| Donaghmore, . | 450 | 120 | 1 | 570 | 30,452 | 59 | 48 | 1,108 | 192 | 1,300 | 4 1½ | 0 1½ | 3 11½ |
| Mountmellick, . | 1,800 | 964 | 1 | 2,961 | 186,255 | 79 | 868 | 3,004 | 444 | 3,448 | 3 4 | 0 8½ | 3 9½ |
| **Westmeath.** | | | | | | | | | | | | | |
| Athlone, . . | 1,389 | 254 | 1 | 1,648 | 59,853 | 96 | 946 | 1,706 | 333 | 2,037 | 3 8 | 0 4½ | 3 3½ |
| Delvin, . . | 1,440 | 185 | 1 | 1,628 | 38,156 | 23 | 66 | 796 | 136 | 932 | 3 8½ | 0 7 | 4 0½ |
| Mullingar, . . | 1,947 | 996 | 3 | 2,945 | 117,489 | 97 | 232 | 3,019 | 542 | 3,561 | 3 1½ | 0 8½ | 3 10½ |
| **Wexford.** | | | | | | | | | | | | | |
| Enniscorthy . . | 1,806 | 1,639 | 5 | 3,448 | 112,190 | 59 | 307 | 2,294 | 484 | 2,737 | 3 10½ | 0 1 | 3 5½ |
| Gorey . . | 849 | 988 | – | 1,828 | 98,370 | 87 | 238 | 1,729 | 343 | 2,052 | 3 11½ | 0 1 | 3 8½ |
| New Ross, . . | 1,374 | 984 | 1 | 2,360 | 153,207 | 113 | 490 | 3,356 | 540 | 3,996 | 3 0½ | 0 1 | 3 7½ |
| Wexford, . . | 2,107 | 1,674 | 4 | 3,785 | 191,947 | 91 | 335 | 4,003 | 600 | 4,460 | 2 11½ | 0 7 | 3 3½ |
| **Wicklow.** | | | | | | | | | | | | | |
| Baltinglass, . . | 1,496 | 979 | 4 | 2,478 | 71,806 | 49 | 197 | 1,600 | 462 | 2,060 | 3 1½ | 0 10½ | 4 0½ |
| Rathdrum, . . | 1,018 | 1,280 | – | 2,290 | 97,389 | 59 | 280 | 2,218 | 609 | 2,828 | 3 4 | 0 10½ | 4 2½ |
| Shillelagh, . . | 960 | 69 | 2 | 931 | 61,302 | 76 | 173 | 1,480 | 290 | 1,773 | 3 4 | 0 8½ | 4 0½ |
| Total Leinster, 1875, | 75,607 | 28,375 | 184 | 107,148 | 5,961,180 | 57 | 14,227 | 122,061 | 22,169 | 146,020 | 3 3 | 0 7½ | 3 10½ |
| Do. do. 1874, | 93,047 | 28,347 | 202 | 124,560 | 5,887,286 | 36 | 14,708 | 133,686 | 22,804 | 158,480 | 3 6½ | 0 7½ | 4 1½ |
| Increase, . . | – | 28 | – | – | – | 21 | – | – | 306 | – | – | 0 0½ | – |
| Decrease, . . | 17,440 | – | 18 | 17,427 | 116,186 | – | 212 | 10,973 | – | 12,460 | 0 3½ | – | 0 3½ |

[continued.

No. 1. Part 2.—Return of the Number of Persons who received Poor Relief during the Year ended 29th September, 1875, together with the Expenditure for Provisions, Necessaries, and Clothing of Workhouse Inmates during the Year, &c.—continued.

| Names of Counties and Unions. | Number of Persons who received Relief under the Poor Relief Acts during the year. In Workhouse. | Outdoor. | In Blind and Deaf and Dumb Asylums. | Total. | Collective Number of Days for all Persons Relieved in the Workhouse during the Year. | Average Number of Days of Relief to each Person in Workhouse. | Average Daily Number of Persons in Workhouse. | Cost of Provisions, Necessaries, and Clothing. Provisions and Necessaries. | Clothing. | Total. | Average Weekly Cost per head. Provisions and Necessaries. | Clothing. | Total. |
|---|---|---|---|---|---|---|---|---|---|---|---|---|---|
| PROVINCE OF CONNAUGHT. | | | | | | | | £ | £ | £ | s. d. | s. d. | s. d. |
| Galway. | | | | | | | | | | | | | |
| Ballinasloe, | 993 | 30 | 6 | 1,029 | 96,190 | 99 | 264 | 2,116 | 508 | 2,626 | 3 4 | 0 6¼ | 4 1½ |
| Clifden, | 491 | 201 | 3 | 704 | 44,780 | 112 | 145 | 801 | 187 | 988 | 3 9 | 0 5 | 4 2 |
| Galway, | 1,236 | 237 | 2 | 1,484 | 143,156 | 117 | 392 | 2,894 | 300 | 3,194 | 2 10 | 0 3½ | 3 1½ |
| Glennamaddy, | 781 | 398 | — | 1,180 | 66,840 | 85 | 187 | 1,073 | 144 | 1,217 | 2 2¼ | 0 3¼ | 2 6 |
| Gort, | 382 | 14 | 2 | 398 | 37,970 | 90 | 104 | 1,030 | 164 | 1,194 | 3 9½ | 0 5½ | 4 3 |
| Loughrea, | 648 | 352 | 1 | 1,001 | 48,100 | 75 | 132 | 961 | 120 | 1,081 | 2 9¼ | 0 4½ | 3 2 |
| Mount Bellew, | 443 | 88 | 1 | 532 | 35,147 | 79 | 99 | 878 | 75 | 953 | 3 4½ | 0 4½ | 3 8½ |
| Oughterard, | 276 | 160 | — | 436 | 45,710 | 166 | 125 | 873 | 97 | 970 | 2 2½ | 0 3½ | 2 11½ |
| Portumna, | 608 | 85 | — | 693 | 63,217 | 104 | 145 | 1,174 | 161 | 1,335 | 3 1½ | 0 5½ | 3 6¼ |
| Tuam, | 908 | 494 | 2 | 1,404 | 75,083 | 78 | 206 | 1,948 | 302 | 2,250 | 3 8½ | 0 5½ | 4 3½ |
| Leitrim. | | | | | | | | | | | | | |
| Carrick on Shannon, | 697 | 445 | 4 | 1,149 | 72,480 | 81 | 199 | 1,461 | 286 | 1,747 | 2 9 | 0 6½ | 3 3½ |
| Manorhamilton, | 496 | — | 4 | 500 | 68,142 | 93 | 186 | 875 | 201 | 1,076 | 2 2 | 0 7½ | 2 9½ |
| Mohill, | 847 | 416 | 2 | 1,265 | 56,298 | 78 | 144 | 1,330 | 254 | 1,584 | 2 0¾ | 0 5¾ | 2 6¾ |
| Mayo. | | | | | | | | | | | | | |
| Ballina, | 739 | 137 | 1 | 877 | 54,010 | 74 | 150 | 1,063 | 156 | 1,219 | 2 8½ | 0 4½ | 3 1½ |
| Ballinrobe, | 896 | 180 | 1 | [illegible] | 66,001 | 76 | 181 | [illegible] | 218 | [illegible] | 2 4½ | 0 3½ | 2 10 |
| Belmullet, | 283 | 729 | 1 | 1,013 | 37,973 | 135 | 104 | 904 | 151 | 1,055 | 2 4½ | 0 4½ | 2 9 |
| Castlebar, | 475 | 281 | — | 756 | 41,509 | 87 | 114 | 730 | 116 | 846 | 2 5½ | 0 4½ | 2 10½ |
| Claremorris, | 580 | 290 | 5 | 881 | 48,148 | 80 | 131 | 1,034 | 116 | 1,150 | 3 0 | 0 4 | 3 4 |
| Killala, | 237 | 191 | — | 539 | 29,707 | 127 | 81 | 617 | 60 | 677 | 4 11 | 0 3½ | 3 8½ |
| Newport, | 318 | 21 | — | 339 | 33,168 | 107 | 93 | 556 | 144 | 700 | 2 5 | 0 7½ | 3 0½ |
| Swineford, | 769 | 266 | 8 | 1,043 | 62,710 | 82 | 172 | 1,176 | 275 | 1,451 | 2 7½ | 0 7½ | 3 2½ |
| Westport, | 630 | 11 | 2 | 643 | 48,689 | 91 | 160 | 1,087 | 257 | 1,344 | 2 6 | 0 5 | 2 11 |

| | | | | | | | | | | | | | |
|---|---|---|---|---|---|---|---|---|---|---|---|---|---|
| ROSCOMMON. | | | | | | | | | | | | | |
| Boyle, . . . | 176 | 460 | 4 | 1,279 | 81,286 | 108 | 285 | 7,759 | 830 | 3,864 | 3 6 | 0 4¾ | 3 4¾ |
| Castlerea, . . | 780 | 204 | 8 | 948 | 77,179 | 103 | 212 | 1,771 | 187 | 1,918 | 3 2¼ | 0 4 | 3 0¾ |
| Roscommon, . . | 816 | 304 | 6 | 1,121 | 97,080 | 130 | 269 | 6,687 | 291 | 2,982 | 3 10 | 0 0¼ | 4 2¼ |
| Strokestown, | 820 | 360 | 6 | 1,183 | 61,600 | 98 | 187 | 1,439 | 279 | 2,647 | 3 4 | 0 6 | 3 10 |
| SLIGO. | | | | | | | | | | | | | |
| Dromore, West, . | 272 | 94 | 2 | 898 | 20,631 | 118 | 64 | 618 | 64 | 680 | 2 0¾ | 0 3¼ | 2 11 |
| Sligo, . . . | 1,186 | 649 | 2 | 1,847 | 138,103 | 108 | 884 | 8,604 | 309 | 9,911 | 0 10 | 0 4 | 1 2 |
| Tobercurry, . . | 519 | 278 | 2 | 800 | 44,278 | 78 | 131 | 502 | 92 | 563 | 1 0¼ | 0 0¼ | 2 10 |
| Total Connaught, 1875, | 18,961 | 7,063 | 58 | 26,024 | 1,798,361 | 94 | 4,903 | 37,842 | 3,715 | 49,380 | 2 11¼ | 0 0¾ | 3 3 |
| Total Connaught, 1874, | 21,739 | 6,573 | 55 | 28,280 | 1,830,481 | 84 | 4,988 | 41,185 | 3,720 | 47,211 | 3 3½ | 0 0¾ | 3 7½ |
| Increase, . . | – | 490 | 3 | – | – | 10 | – | – | – | – | – | 0 0¼ | – |
| Decrease, . . | 2,778 | – | – | 2,317 | 31,697 | – | 80 | 3,843 | 5 | 5,831 | 0 3½ | – | 0 3¾ |

SUMMARY OF PROVINCES

| | | | | | | | | | | | | | |
|---|---|---|---|---|---|---|---|---|---|---|---|---|---|
| ULSTER, . . | 51,290 | 7,424 | 137 | 58,533 | 3,676,980 | 78 | 10,044 | 66,292 | 28,777 | 79,850 | 2 6 | 0 4¾ | 2 0¾ |
| MUNSTER, . . | 66,281 | 20,773 | 242 | 87,306 | 6,089,180 | 93 | 16,800 | 124,975 | 23,580 | 146,535 | 2 10¾ | 0 3¼ | 3 4¾ |
| LEINSTER, . . | 78,097 | 28,279 | 188 | 107,188 | 5,391,177 | 67 | 14,387 | 121,681 | 22,009 | 143,680 | 1 3 | 0 7¼ | 3 10¾ |
| CONNAUGHT, . | 18,961 | 7,063 | 58 | 26,024 | 1,798,364 | 94 | 4,903 | 37,842 | 3,715 | 49,580 | 2 11¼ | 0 3¼ | 3 3 |
| Total Ireland, 1875, | 214,629 | 63,714 | 625 | 281,308 | 16,755,810 | 78 | 46,236 | 350,148 | 66,084 | 410,172 | 2 11 | 0 8¼ | 3 4¾ |
| Do. do. 1874, | 252,180 | 66,326 | 653 | 300,150 | 17,361,779 | 68 | 46,281 | 362,154 | 65,760 | 437,944 | 2 2¼ | 0 4¾ | 3 2 |
| Increase, . . | – | 396 | – | – | – | 10 | – | – | 324 | – | – | 0 0¼ | – |
| Decrease, . . | 38,163 | – | 28 | 38,904 | 125,460 | – | 1,068 | 12,906 | – | 41,772 | 0 3¾ | – | 0 1¼ |

No. 2.—Classification of Persons Relieved in the Union Workhouses in Ireland, during the Year ended 29th September, 1875.

| | Classes of Persons Relieved in the Workhouses. | No. in the Half-year ended 25th March, 1875. | No. in the Half-year ended 29th September, 1875. |
|---|---|---|---|
| | **ABLE-BODIED AND THEIR CHILDREN.** | | |
| 1 | Adults, Married Couples, Males, | 2,405 | 1,696 |
| 2 | Adults, Married Couples, Females, | 2,405 | 1,696 |
| 3 | Adults, Other Males, | 29,207 | 19,657 |
| 4 | Adults, Other Females, | 23,185 | 23,060 |
| 5 | Children under 15, of Able-bodied Inmates, Illegitimate, | 8,000 | 8,482 |
| 6 | Children under 15, of Able-bodied Inmates, Other Children, | 14,755 | 14,135 |
| | **NOT ABLE-BODIED.** | | |
| 7 | Adults, Married Couples, Males, | 659 | 552 |
| 8 | Adults, Married Couples, Females, | 659 | 552 |
| 9 | Adults, Other Males, | 22,667 | 22,232 |
| 10 | Adults, Other Females, | 18,864 | 19,707 |
| 11 | Children under 15, Of Parents not able-bodied being Inmates, Illegitimate, | 642 | 679 |
| 12 | Children under 15, Of Parents not able-bodied being Inmates, Other Children, | 1,857 | 1,869 |
| 13 | Children under 15, Orphans, or other Children, relieved without Parents, | 8,730 | 9,213 |
| | **LUNATICS, INSANE PERSONS, AND IDIOTS.** | | |
| 14 | Adult Males, | 1,279 | 1,266 |
| 15 | Adult Females, | 1,592 | 1,731 |
| 16 | Children under 15, | 93 | 99 |
| 17 | Total number of Males, | 56,217 | 45,403 |
| 18 | Do. Females, | 46,705 | 46,746 |
| 19 | Do. Children under 15, | 34,077 | 34,497 |
| 20 | Grand Total, | 136,995 | 126,646 |

No. 3.—Classification of Persons Relieved out of the Workhouses in Unions in Ireland, during the Year ended 29th September, 1875, including Persons relieved in Blind and Deaf and Dumb Asylums.

| | Classes of Persons Relieved. | Number in the Half-year ended 25th March, 1875. | Number in the Half-year ended 29th Sept., 1875. |
|---|---|---|---|
| 1 | Blind Persons maintained in Asylums, Males, | 62 | 72 |
| 2 | Blind Persons maintained in Asylums, Females, | 137 | 139 |
| 3 | Deaf and Dumb Persons maintained in Asylums, Males, | 205 | 210 |
| 4 | Deaf and Dumb Persons maintained in Asylums, Females, | 148 | 158 |
| | Total, | 552 | 579 |
| | RELIEVED UNDER 10 VIC., C. 31, SEC. 1. | | |
| 5 | Adult Males permanently disabled by old age or infirmity, | 4,374 | 4,375 |
| 6 | Families of Adult Males under heading 5, Wives, | 2,221 | 2,139 |
| 7 | Families of Adult Males under heading 5, Children under 15, | 973 | 974 |
| 8 | Adult Males relieved in cases of their own sickness or accident, | 4,299 | 3,930 |
| 9 | Families of Adult Males under heading 8, Wives, | 3,197 | 2,855 |
| 10 | Families of Adult Males under heading 8, Children under 15, | 8,421 | 7,568 |
| 11 | Adult Women permanently disabled by old age or infirmity, | 10,419 | 10,499 |
| 12 | Children under 15, of Women under heading 11, Legitimate, | 170 | 196 |
| 13 | Children under 15, of Women under heading 11, Illegitimate, | 22 | 20 |
| 14 | Adult Women relieved in cases of sickness or accident, | 2,815 | 2,538 |
| 15 | Children under 15, of Women under heading 14, Legitimate, | 1,642 | 1,468 |
| 16 | Children under 15, of Women under heading 14, Illegitimate, | 109 | 64 |
| 17 | Able-bodied Widows, having two or more legitimate children dependent on them, | 1,810 | 2,013 |
| 18 | Children under 15, dependent on Widows under heading 17, | 6,495 | 7,012 |
| 19 | Lunatics, Insane Persons, and Idiots, Males, | 34 | 39 |
| 20 | Lunatics, Insane Persons, and Idiots, Females, | 44 | 44 |
| 21 | Lunatics, Insane Persons, and Idiots, Children under 15, | 9 | 19 |
| | Total, | 47,054 | 45,753 |
| | PERSONS RELIEVED UNDER 10 VIC., C. 31, NOT RELIEVABLE UNDER SEC. 1. | | |
| 22 | Adult Males, married or single, relieved on account of want of work, | 2 | – |
| 23 | Families of Adult Males under heading 22, Wives, | 2 | – |
| 24 | Families of Adult Males under heading 22, Children under 15, | 7 | – |
| 25 | Able-bodied Women, Unmarried, | – | – |
| 26 | Able-bodied Women, Widows not relievable under sec. 1, | – | – |
| 27 | Children of Women under headings 25 and 26, Legitimate, | – | – |
| 28 | Children of Women under headings 25 and 26, Illegitimate, | – | – |
| | *Families Relieved without Husband or Father.* | | |
| 29 | Husband or Father in Gaol, Wives, | – | – |
| 30 | Husband or Father in Gaol, Children under 15, | – | – |
| 31 | Husband or Father on service in Army or Navy, Wives, | – | – |
| 32 | Husband or Father on service in Army or Navy, Children under 15, | – | – |
| 33 | Deserted by Husband or Father, Wives, | – | – |
| 34 | Deserted by Husband or Father, Children under 15, | – | – |
| 35 | Orphans and children relieved without either parent, | – | – |
| 36 | Number of persons relieved provisionally, and not included in the foregoing columns, | 1,331 | 1,198 |
| | Total, | 1,332 | 1,198 |
| 37 | Orphans or Deserted Children out at Nurse under sec. 9 of 25 and 26 Vic., c. 83, | 1,761 | 1,694 |
| | Grand Total, | 50,147 | 48,645 |

No. 4.—Summary of Returns from Clerks of Unions, showing for each Province, and for all Ireland, the Number of Persons admitted to the Workhouses during the Year ended 29th September, 1875, distinguishing the Number admitted in Sickness; also the Number of Births and Deaths in the Workhouses during the Year.

| Provinces. | Number of Persons admitted during the Year. Number admitted in Sickness. Suffering under Fever or other dangerous contagious diseases | Suffering under other diseases. | Suffering from accidental injury. | Total number admitted in sickness. | Number admitted who were not sick. | Total number admitted during the Year. | No. of Births in the Workhouses during the Year. | No. of Deaths in the Workhouses during the Year. |
|---|---|---|---|---|---|---|---|---|
| Ulster, . . | 1,904 | 7,315 | 561 | 9,780 | 31,815 | 41,595 | 479 | 2,733 |
| Munster, . . | 3,314 | 14,066 | 903 | 1 ,283 | 31,133 | 49,416 | 509 | 3,938 |
| Leinster, . . | 2,143 | 12,646 | 766 | 15,555 | 48,645 | 64,200 | 507 | 3,691 |
| Connaught, . . | 654 | 3,037 | 658 | 4,349 | 9,589 | 13,938 | 191 | 1,123 |
| Total, Ireland, | 8,018 | 37,064 | 2,888 | 47,967 | 121,162 | 169,149 | 1,759 | 11,470 |

No. 5.—Summary of Returns showing for each Province, and for all Ireland, the Number of Sick Persons who received Medical Treatment in the Workhouse Hospitals and Fever Hospitals, during the Year ended 29th September, 1875.

| Provinces. | Under treatment at the commencement of the Year. | | | | New Cases. | | | | Total Cases treated in Hospitals during the Year. | | | |
|---|---|---|---|---|---|---|---|---|---|---|---|---|
| | Fever or other dangerous contagious disease. | Other diseases. | Accidentally injured. | Total. | Fever or other dangerous contagious disease. | Other diseases. | Accidentally injured. | Total. | Fever or other dangerous contagious disease. | Other diseases. | Accidentally injured. | Total. |
| Ulster, . . | 203 | 2,333 | 75 | 2,611 | 2,721 | 13,123 | 573 | 16,417 | 2,924 | 15,456 | 618 | 19,028 |
| Munster, . . | 329 | 4,805 | 161 | 5,295 | 4,430 | 24,249 | 1,107 | 29,786 | 4,759 | 29,054 | 1,268 | 35,081 |
| Leinster, . . | 199 | 5,312 | 116 | 5,640 | 3,087 | 20,354 | 888 | 24,329 | 3,270 | 25,666 | 1,004 | 29,949 |
| Connaught, . . | 75 | 1,446 | 34 | 1,555 | 946 | 6,001 | 367 | 7,314 | 1,021 | 7,447 | 401 | 8,869 |
| Total, Ireland, | 809 | 13,296 | 376 | 15,081 | 11,184 | 63,727 | 2,935 | 77,846 | 11,993 | 77,623 | 3,311 | 92,927 |

No. 6.—Statement (in pursuance of Sec. 20 of 12 & 13 Vic., c. 104) relative to the Audit of Union Accounts:—(in continuation of Statement in Third Annual Report of the Local Government Board (Ireland), 1875, Appendix D., No. 6).

I. Date up to which the Accounts of Unions have been audited.

The Accounts of all the Unions have been audited up to 25th March, 1875, except those of Clifden, Glennamaddy, Portumna, Scariff, Tulla, and Oughterard, and up to 29th September, 1875, except those of Athlone, Athy, Ballina, Ballinasloe, Ballinrobe, Ballymahon, Belmullet, Castlebar, Castlerea, Claremorris, Clifden, Corrofin, Galway, Glennamaddy, Gort, Killala, Mount Bellew, Mullingar, Newport, Oughterard, Portumna, Rathdrum, Roscommon, Scariff, Swineford, Tuam, Tulla, Westport, and Wexford.

II. Sums disallowed or found due on Audit of the Accounts of Unions in Ireland, up to 29th September, 1875, and whether recovered or in course of Recovery from the Parties debited.

| Unions. | Half-year ended | Date of Audit. | Amount disallowed or found due. | Whether paid or in course of Recovery | Observations.—Nature of Sums disallowed, &c. |
|---|---|---|---|---|---|
| | | | £ s. d. | | |
| Abbeyleix, . . | 25 March, 1875, . | 18 Dec., 1875, . | 0 16 0 | Not enforced, . . . . | Charged by Relieving Officer as out-door relief without authority. |
| Armagh, . . | „ | 3 July, 1875, | 12 12 0 | Not enforced, . . . | Paid to temporary Medical Officer without sanction of Local Government Board. Debited to Guardians who signed the cheque. Sanction subsequently obtained. |
| „ . . | 29 Sept., 1875, . | 4 March, 1876, . | 0 16 8 | Paid, . . . . | Overpayment to Contractor. Charged to Clerk of the Union. |
| Athy, . . | 25 March, 1875, | 9 Sept., 1875, | 43 9 0 | In course of recovery, | Amount of defalcation of late Relieving Officer Ryan, who absconded, and has been dismissed by the Local Government Board. |
| „ . . | „ | „ | 0 15 1 | Paid, . . . . | Deficiency in stock of tea in charge of late Workhouse Master. |
| „ . . | „ | „ | 1 10 8 | Paid, . . . . | Overpaid Doctor O'Neill as Consulting Sanitary Officer. |
| Ballymoney, . | 29 Sept., 1875, | 12 Jan., 1876, . | 3 9 5 | Paid, . . . . | Overpayment to Workhouse Master by the Board of Guardians. Debited to his account. |
| Ballyshannon, . | 25 March, 1875, . | 9 June, 1875, . | 0 2 10 | Not enforced, . . . | Overcharge in weekly relief list. Surcharged to Workhouse Master. Corrected in subsequent half year. |
| Banbridge, . | 29 Sept., 1875, . | 25 Feb., 1876, | 0 10 0 | Not enforced, . . . | Out-door relief in money to a woman whose husband was in America. Debited to Guardian who authorized it. Not enforced under the circumstances. |
| Bawnboy, . . | 25 March, 1875, . | 8 July, 1875, . | 1 2 0 | Not enforced, . . . | Out-door relief to a married woman with six children, who refused to enter the Workhouse. Surcharged to Mr James Benson. It subsequently appeared that the woman was insane, and had been admitted to Sligo Lunatic Asylum. |
| „ . . | 29 Sept., 1875, . | 22 Dec., 1875, . | 0 5 0 | Not enforced, . . . | Out-door relief to a man apparently able-bodied. Surcharged to Mr Andrew Rogers, who subsequently forwarded a medical certificate showing that the man was permanently disabled. |

No. 6.—STATEMENT (in pursuance of Sec. 20 of 12 and 13 Vic., c. 104) relative to the AUDIT of UNION ACCOUNTS:—(in continuation of Statement in Third Annual Report of the Local Government Board (Ireland), 1875, Appendix D., No. 6)—continued.

II. Sums disallowed or found due on Audit of the Accounts of Unions in Ireland, up to 29th September, 1875, and whether recovered or in course of Recovery from the Parties debited—continued.

| Unions | Half-year ended | Date of Audit | Amount disallowed or found due. £ s. d. | Whether paid or in course of Recovery | Observations.—Nature of Sums disallowed, &c. |
|---|---|---|---|---|---|
| Callan, | 25 March, 1875, | 5 August, 1875, | 1 3 6 | Paid, | Cost of fittings for a blind man who was about being discharged from the Workhouse. Debited to Guardians who signed the cheque. |
| Cashel, | " | 26 August, 1875, | 0 14 6 | Paid, | Out-door relief illegally given. |
| " | 29 Sept., 1875, | 13 Dec., 1875, | 1 0 0 | Paid, | Same. |
| Castleblayney, | 25 March, 1875, | 13 Sept., 1875, | 8 8 1 | Not enforced, | Payment to temporary Medical Officer without the sanction of the Local Government Board. Debited to Guardians who signed the cheque. Sanction subsequently obtained. |
| Cavan, | " | 5 Sept., 1875, | 0 18 0 | Paid, | Out-door relief to a woman whose husband was in Scotland. Debited to Relieving Officer. |
| " | " | " | 0 18 0 | Not enforced, | Out-door relief to a healthy widow stated to have no children. Debited to Guardians who authorised it. Subsequently explained. |
| Celbridge, | " | 30 August, 1875, | 0 3 0 | Paid, | Out-door relief given without authority. |
| " | 29 Sept., 1875, | 6 Dec., 1875, | 0 4 5 | Not enforced, | Out-door relief given without authority. Not enforced, Guardians having explained. |
| Claremorris, | 25 March, 1875, | 16 July, 1875, | 0 8 3 | Not enforced, | An apparent overpayment in straw account. Surcharged to Clerk of Union, who has since satisfied the Board of Guardians that the entire quantity of straw paid for was received. |
| Cootehill, | " | 9 Sep., 1875, | 2 4 5 | Not enforced, | Out-door relief continued without authority. Debited to Relieving Officer. After correspondence with Local Government Board, payment was not enforced. |
| " | 29 Sept., 1875, | 7 Jan., 1876, | 15 0 3 | Not enforced, | Payment to temporary Medical Officer. Debited to Guardians who signed the cheque. Sanction subsequently obtained. |
| Cork, | " | 23 Feb., 1876, | 0 5 0 | Paid, | Out-door relief illegally given. Debited to Guardians who authorised it. |
| Downpatrick, | " | 29 Nov., 1875, | 0 17 7 | Paid, | Cash retained by the Honorary Secretary of the Killough Dispensary. Disallowed and charged to him. |
| Enniscorthy, | 25 March, 1875, | 18 Oct., 1875, | 3 13 6 | One-fourth paid; the remainder in course of recovery. | Out-door relief given by Relieving Officer Patrick Murphy without authority. |
| | 29 Sept., 1875, | 15 Jan., 1876, | 1 5 0 | Paid, | Amount given to a man on taking his two children from the Union, to enable him to release some articles in pawn. |

| | | | £ | s. | d. | | |
|---|---|---|---|---|---|---|---|
| Gorey, . | „ | 13 Jan., 1874, . | 50 | 6 | 6 | In course of recovery, . | Amount of deficiencies in stock of provisions and necessaries in charge of late Master of Workhouse, who has been discharged. |
| „ . . | „ | | 2 | 8 | 6 | In course of recovery, . | Illegal payment to late Schoolmaster on account of salary. |
| Kanturk, . . | „ | 26 Nov., 1873, . | 1 | 15 | 6 | Not enforced, . . | Expense of sending a pauper boy to Hibernian Military School. On explanation of the circumstances, the surcharge was remitted. |
| Kells, . . | „ | 19 Nov., 1873, . | 2 | 10 | 0 | Not enforced, . . | Amount of rate [illegible] paid for [illegible]. Debited to Relieving Officer. Explanation having been given, payment was not enforced. |
| Kenmare, . . | „ | 26 Nov., 1873, . | 1 | 8 | 0 | Paid, . . | Out-door relief illegally given. |
| Kilkeel, . . | 25 March, 1873, . | 10 July, 1873, . | 1 | 8 | 0 | In course of recovery, . | Out-door relief to a man apparently able bodied. Surcharged to Guardian who authorised it. |
| Mallow, . . | „ | 5 June, 1873, . | 14 | 10 | 8 | Paid, . . . . | Payment made for engrossing and advertising a congratulatory address presented by the Board of Guardians to the Right Rev. J. M'Carthy on his elevation to the episcopacy. Debited to Guardians who signed the cheque. |
| Manorhamilton, | 29 Sept., 1873, . | 19 Feb., 1874, . | 2 | 0 | 0 | Paid, . . | Amount included in cheque to late Medical Officer of Dispensary District for payment to owners of vaccination stations, for which receipts were not produced. Surcharged to late Medical Officer, who has since forwarded receipts to the Board of Guardians. |
| Mohill, . . | 25 March, 1873, . | 18 Sept., 1873, . | 0 | 5 | 0 | Paid, . . . . | Out-door relief given without authority. Surcharged to the Relieving Officer. |
| Monaghan, . | 29 Sept., 1873, . | 23 Feb., 1874, . | 6 | 4 | 5 | In course of recovery, . | Overcharge for sweet milk and buttermilk in provision account. Master surcharged. Master to pay 3s. 7d. cost of buttermilk—sweet milk substituted. |
| Mountmellick, | 25 March, 1874, . | 24 August, 1874, . | 2 | 13 | 3 | Not enforced, . . . | Out-door relief to a party in occupation of more than a quarter of a statute acre of land. |
| Naas, . . | „ | 11 Sept., 1873, . | 29 | 14 | 6 | Not enforced, . . . | Amount of costs paid Guardians' Attorney for witnessing execution of three Collectors' bonds and warrants of attorney, and marking judgment on the bonds. |
| Navan, . . | „ | 20 May, 1874, . | 1 | 17 | 6 | Paid, . . . . | Out-door relief given without authority. Surcharged to the Relieving Officer. |
| Roscrea, . . | „ | 13 August, 1873, | 2 | 8 | 0 | Not enforced, . . . | Out-door relief illegally given. Remitted on explanation of the circumstances of the case. |
| Strokestown, . | „ | 16 Sept., 1874, . | 1 | 0 | 0 | Paid, . . . | Money granted to enable a child to join its mother in Scotland. Surcharged to Guardians who authorised it. |
| Swineford, . | „ | 19 July, 1873, . | 0 | 9 | 6 | Paid, . . . | Overpayment in Medical Officer's account. Surcharged to Clerk of Union. |
| Thurles, . . | „ | 2 Sept., 1873, . | 1 | 7 | 8 | Paid, . . | Out-door relief illegally given. |
| Tulla, . . | 29 Sept., 1873, . | 15 Nov., 1873, . | 4 | 17 | 6 | Not enforced, . . . | Out-door relief illegally given. Remitted on explanation of the circumstances of the case. |
| Waterford, . | 25 March, 1873, . | 28 July, 1873, . | 1 | 14 | 2 | Paid, . . . . | Cost of printing and circulating a memorial addressed to the Lords Commissioners of Her Majesty's Treasury, which was distributed avowedly for the purpose of organising opposition to legitimate steps taken by the Local Government Board to bring the Public Health Act of 1874 into operation. Debited to Guardians who signed the cheque. |

No. 7.—Union Officers' Superannuation.—Statement of Allowances under the Superannuation Acts in force during any portion of the year ended 29th September, 1875; showing also the cases in which the Allowance had terminated during the year. (In continuation of Statement in the Third Report under Local Government Board (Ireland), 1875, Appendix D, No. 7.)

| Date of Commissioners' Sanction. | Union. | Name of Officer. | Office. | Age. | Period of Service as a Union Officer. | Cause of Retirement. | Annual Salary. | Annual Superannuation Allowance. | If terminated, date of termination. |
|---|---|---|---|---|---|---|---|---|---|
| | | | | | | | £ s. d. | £ s. d. | |
| 3 Aug. 1872 | Abbeyleix | Anne Plunkett | Schoolmistress | 60 | 13 | Infirmity of body | 40 10 0 | 20 0 0 | |
| 16 June, 1866 | Antrim | William Stone | Porter | 66 | 24 | Do. | 40 0 0 | 14 0 0 | 29 Nov., 1874 |
| 19 Nov. 1870 | Do. | Anne Neely | Matron of Workhouse | 63 | 27½ | Do. | 36 0 0 | 20 0 0 | |
| 7 Sept. 1860 | Armagh | Sarah Coll | Matron | 59 | 20 | Infirmity of mind and body | 42 0 0 | 14 0 0 | |
| 14 June, 1867 | Do. | Elizabeth M'Arthur | Infirmary Nurse | 64 | 10 | Infirmity of body | 16 0 0 | 10 0 0 | |
| 20 July, 1864 | Do. | Eleanor Walker | Schoolmistress | 50 | 12½ | Infirmity of mind | 20 0 0 | 10 0 0 | |
| 22 June, 1872 | Do. | James Leslie | Medical Officer | 65 | 30 | Infirmity of body | 150 0 0 | 100 0 0 | 2 Dec., 1874 |
| 13 Nov. 1873 | Do. | Malcolm M'Neill Johnston | Clerk | 67 | 29 | Do. | 100 0 0 | 100 0 0 | |
| 20 Dec. 1869 | Athlone | John O'Connell | Medical Officer of Dispensary District | 80 | [illegible] | Do. | 100 0 0 | 66 13 4 | 8 Aug., 1875 |
| 20 April, 1872 | Do. | Richard B. Cassidy | Relieving Officer | 56 | 24½ | Do. | 60 0 0 | 40 0 0 | |
| 13 Oct. 1870 | Do. | Elizabeth Cowley | Schoolmistress | 46 | 24½ | Do. | 34 0 7 | 24 0 0 | |
| 30 Jan. 1874 | Athy | Ellen Sandford | Cook | 60 | 10 | Do. | 12 10 10 | 4 0 0 | |
| 30 Nov. 1874 | Bailieborough | John Myers Aitkins | Medical Officer of Dispensary District | 70 | 23½ | Old age | 90 0 0 | 50 0 0 | |
| 12 April, 1875 | Ballina | Arthur C. Thompson | Do. | 80½ | 36 | Infirmity of body | 150 0 0 | 100 0 0 | |
| 16 Mar. 1872 | Ballinasloe | Catherine Keogh | Fever Hospital Nurse | 60 | 21 | Do. | 20 0 0 | 12 0 0 | |
| 27 June, 1868 | Ballinrobe | John Naher | Schoolmaster | 57 | 14 | Do. | 24 0 0 | 16 0 0 | |
| 30 Nov. 1871 | Do. | Cecilia O'Grady | Matron of Workhouse | 58 | 19 | Do. | 30 0 0 | 20 0 0 | |
| 2 Nov. 1868 | Ballymahon | Jas. Henry M'Manus | Medical Officer of Dispensary District | 72 | [illegible] | Do. | 80 0 0 | 60 0 0 | |
| 26 May, 1870 | Do. | Mary Smith | Hospital Nurse | 69 | [illegible] | Old age | 12 0 0 | [illegible] | |
| 14 July, 1875 | Ballymoney | James Jefferson | Medical Officer of Dispensary District | [illegible] | [illegible] | Infirmity of body | 60 0 0 | 40 0 0 | 17 Aug., 1875 |
| 3 Feb. 1873 | Ballyshannon | James Wilkin | Do. | 82 | 30½ | Old age | 90 0 0 | 73 0 0 | |
| 13 Dec. 1870 | Do. | William M'Fey | Porter | 63 | 18 | Infirmity of body | 15 0 0 | 12 0 0 | |
| 27 Jan. 1873 | Ballyvaghan | Ellen Hession | Matron of Workhouse | 65 | 22½ | Old age and infirmity | 20 0 0 | 13 0 0 | |
| 15 Oct. 1874 | Do. | Edmund Hogan | Master of Workhouse | 77 | [illegible] | Old age | 50 0 0 | 40 0 0 | |
| 6 Dec. 1871 | Balrothery | Emily L. Whelan | Fever Hospital Nurse | 67 | [illegible] | Infirmity of body | 20 0 0 | 10 0 0 | |
| 7 Dec. 1872 | Do. | Robert Smith | Clerk | 60 | [illegible] | Do. | 100 0 0 | 60 0 0 | |
| 21 April, 1874 | Baltinglass | Laurence Brennan | Tailor | 70 | 21 | Old age and infirmity | 30 7 6 | 20 0 0 | |

| | | | | | | | | | |
|---|---|---|---|---|---|---|---|---|---|
| 20 April, 1877 | Do | Mary Neale | Infirmary Nurse | 60 | 20½ | Old age | 15 0 0 | 5 0 0 | |
| 9 Jan. 1880 | Banbridge | Joseph Hickson | Clerk | 60 | 20 | Infirmity of mind and body | 100 0 0 | 66 13 4 | |
| 1 July, 1874 | Do | Fergus Osborne | Relieving Officer | 61 | 20 | Do | 70 0 0 | 40 0 0 | |
| 14 Oct. 1880 | Bandon | Samuel Holland | Porter | 64½ | 34 | Infirmity of body | 15 0 0 | 8 0 0 | |
| 21 June, 1879 | Do | William Nicolls | Master | 66 | 20 | Old age | 80 0 0 | 14 0 0 | |
| 11 Dec. 1870 | Do | James Fitzgerald | Relieving Officer | 60 | 25 | Do | 75 0 0 | 30 0 0 | |
| 20 Jan. 1880 | Belfast | David M'Elheron | Do | 54½ | 23½ | Infirmity of body | 150 0 0 | 70 0 0 | |
| 10 Dec. 1868 | Do | Ketlin Gordon | Do | 64 | 13½ | Do | 90 0 0 | 35 0 0 | |
| 6 May, 1867 | Do | Edward Long | Apothecary | 50 | 26 | Infirmity of body | 130 0 0 | 55 0 0 | |
| 7 April, 1877 | Do | Henry N. Johnston | Medical Officer of Workhouse | 65 | 30 (nearly) | Do | 180 0 0 | 80 0 0 | |
| 7 June, 1876 | Do | John Holden | Rate Collector | 79 | 34 | Infirmity of mind and body | [illegible] | [illegible] | |
| 7 Feb. 1870 | Balrothery | James Gibson | Relieving Officer | 62 | 6 | Do | 30 0 0 | [illegible] | |
| 21 June, 1873 | Do | Dominick Cosgrave | Porter | 72 | 12 | Infirmity of body | 20 0 0 | 5 0 0 | |
| 27 Feb. 1878 | [illegible] | Eliza Henley | Fever Hospital Nurse | 74 | 21½ | Old age | 20 0 0 | [illegible] | |
| 6 Nov. 1882 | Boyle | Alexander Fraser | Relieving Officer | 64 | 27 | Infirmity of body | 70 0 0 | 30 0 0 | |
| 14 Jan. 1856 | Do | Jane [illegible] | Infirmary Nurse | 49 | 8 | Do | 21 14 0 | 10 0 0 | |
| 21 May, 1864 | Do | Ellen Walsh | Matron of Workhouse | 60 | 19 | Do | 22 0 0 | 10 0 0 | |
| 29 Feb. 1876 | Do | Sarah Walsh | Fever Hospital Nurse | 50 | 16 | Do | 20 0 0 | 10 0 0 | |
| 18 Mar. 1865 | Do | George Petty | Relieving Officer | 66 | 17 | Infirmity of mind and body | 25 0 0 | 5 0 0 | 20 May, 1885 |
| 8 Oct. 1870 | Cahersiveen | Thomas M. Hartley | Medical Officer of Dispensary District | 60 | 24½ | Infirmity of body | 84 0 0 | 67 0 0 | |
| 15 Oct. 1871 | Do | Frances M'Clenaghan | Infirmary Nurse | 70 | 30 | Old age | 8 0 0 | 6 0 0 | |
| 24 April, 1866 | Do | Mary McIlroy | Fever Hospital Nurse | 75 | 25 | Old age and infirmity | 21 0 0 | 10 0 0 | |
| 22 May, 1869 | Callan | Richard Ryan | Porter | 64 | 23 | Do | 21 0 0 | 8 0 0 | |
| 6 May, 1877 | Do | John Kenney | Cook | [illegible] | [illegible] | Do | 25 0 0 | 6 13 4 | |
| 8 Aug. 1872 | Carrick-on-Suir | Mary Cahill | Infirmary Nurse | 58 | 21 | Do | 20 0 0 | 6 0 0 | |
| 26 Oct. 1864 | Do | Ellen Collins | Fever Hospital Nurse | 60 | 20 | Do | 8 0 0 | [illegible] | |
| 29 Jan. 1871 | Do | Christina Osborne | Do | 60 | 21 | Infirmity of body | 25 0 0 | 15 0 0 | |
| 4 May, 1870 | Cashel | E. A. Burke | Matron | 51 | 22 | Do | 40 0 0 | 20 0 0 | |
| 22 Oct. 1870 | Do | William Kennedy | Master Tailor | 75 | 20 | Old age and infirmity | 21 0 0 | 17 0 0 | |
| 1 June, 1871 | Castlebar | Mary Sinclair | Matron | 56 | 24½ | Infirmity of mind and body | 84 0 0 | 30 0 0 | |
| 16 Aug. 1876 | Castlecomer | John Wright Burns | Medical Officer of Dispensary District | 66 | 24 | Infirmity of body | 144 0 0 | 66 0 0 | |
| 7 May, 1866 | Do | Jane Henry | Infirmary Nurse | 45 | 21½ | Do | 15 0 0 | 10 0 0 | |
| 24 June, 1865 | Castlederg | Prudence Galbraith | Matron | 54 | 30 | Infirmity of body | 80 0 0 | 25 0 0 | |
| 22 April, 1871 | Do | Andrew Dalton | Medical Officer of Dispensary District | 63 | 19 | Do | 116 0 0 | 70 0 0 | |
| 16 Dec. 1873 | Do | John Crossan | Relieving Officer | 54 | 27½ | Do | 22 0 0 | 11 0 0 | |
| 4 Nov. 1874 | Castletown | Philip A. Armstrong | Medical Officer of Dispensary District | 69 | 34 | Old age | 100 0 0 | 60 0 0 | |
| 20 Nov. 1876 | Cavan | Hugh Fitzpatrick | Tailor | 66 | 26½ | Old age and infirmity | 20 0 0 | 17 0 0 | |
| 24 Jan. 1871 | Do | [illegible] Grier | Clerk | 57 | 21 | Do | 115 0 0 | [illegible] | |
| 11 July, 1871 | [illegible] | Bridget Fleming | Nurse in Infirmary and Fever Hospital | 60 | 20 | Infirmity of body | [illegible] | [illegible] | |

(continued.)

No. 7.—Union Officers' Superannuation.—Statement of Allowances under the Superannuation Acts in force during any portion of the year ended 29th September, 1875; showing also the cases in which the Allowances had terminated during the year. (In continuation of Statement in the Third Report under Local Government Board (Ireland), 1875, Appendix D, No. 7)—continued.

| Date of Commissioners' Consent. | Union. | Name of Officer. | Office. | Age. | Period of Service as a Union Officer. | Cause of Retirement. | Annual Salary. £ s. d. | Annual Superannuation Allowance. £ s. d. | If terminated, date of termination. |
|---|---|---|---|---|---|---|---|---|---|
| 17 Jan. 1872 | Clifden | Alex. Spear Hew | Medical Officer of Dispensary District. | 72 | 29 | Old age | 100 0 0 | 58 6 6 | |
| 6 Feb. 1870 | Clogher | Barber Twigg | Medical Officer of Workhouse. | 77 | 37 | Do. | 64 0 0 | 45 [illegible] 0 | |
| 5 July, 1866 | Clonakilty | Jane Hegarty | Nurse | 69 | 16½ | Infirmity of mind | 16 0 0 | 7 10 0 | 30 June, 1875 |
| 6 April, 1872 | Do. | Julia Duffy | Matron | 55 | 21 | Old age and infirmity | 45 0 0 | 22 0 0 | |
| 6 Nov. 1870 | Clonmel | John H. Fraser | Medical Officer of Dispensary District | 56 | 15 | Infirmity of body | 60 0 0 | 20 0 0 | |
| 26 May, 1872 | Do. | Mary Anne Murphy | Matron of Workhouse | 67 | 20 | Do. | 60 0 0 | 31 [illegible] 0 | |
| 16 Mar. 1869 | Coleraine | Isabella Hemphill | Matron | 64 | 15 | Old age and infirmity | 25 0 0 | 11 0 [illegible] | |
| 6 Oct. 1874 | Do. | John Shields | Schoolmaster | 55 | over 4 | Infirmity of mind and body | 30 [illegible] [illegible] | 12 [illegible] [illegible] | |
| 3 July, 1875 | Do. | John V. Fleming | Clerk of Union | 61 | 27 | Infirmity of body | 55 0 0 | 18 0 0 | |
| 24 July, 1874 | Do. | Margaret Moore | Fever Hospital Nurse | 60 | 20 | Do. | 16 0 0 | 12 0 0 | |
| 27 June, 1873 | Cootehill | William Stuart | Medical Officer of Dispensary District. | 67 | 15 | Infirmity of mind and body | 65 0 0 | 23 10 0 | |
| 26 Aug. 1868 | Cork | R. J. O'Shaughnessy | Clerk | 67 | 18 | Infirmity of body | 300 0 0 | 200 0 0 | 26 Jan., 1875 |
| 13 Mar. 1870 | Do. | Timothy Lane | Relieving Officer | 65 | 26 | Do. | 63 0 0 | 40 0 0 | 26 Mar., 1875 |
| 22 Aug. 1872 | Cork | Edw. Cardo Rowland | Relieving Officer and Sanitary Inspector | 74 | 25 | Old age and infirmity | 67 [illegible] 0 | 45 [illegible] 0 | |
| 26 April, 1874 | Do. | Jeremiah Leahy | Medical Officer of Dispensary District. | 80 | 31 | Do. | 130 0 0 | 60 0 0 | |
| 26 May, 1874 | Do. | John Popham | Medical Officer of Workhouse. | 77 | 35 | Old age and infirmity of body | 160 0 0 | 66 13 4 | |
| 12 May, 1873 | Do. | Cornelius Donoghue | Nurse | 67 | 17 | Infirmity of body | 26 13 0 | 10 [illegible] 0 | |
| 15 Sept. 1871 | Corofin | Frances M'Mahon | Relieving Officer, | 78 | 10 | Do. | 25 0 0 | 6 0 0 | |
| 24 May, 1872 | Croom | William C. Murphy | Medical Officer of Workhouse and Dispensary District. | 80 | 21 / 20 | Do. | 70 0 0 / 100 0 0 | 113 6 8 | |
| 9 July, 1874 | Do. | John Wessell | Medical Officer of Dispensary District | 64 | 30 | Do. | 100 0 0 | 50 0 0 | |
| 11 Aug. 1874 | Do. | James Lyons Nunan | Apothecary of Workhouse and Dispensary District | 73 | 42 | Old age and infirmity of body | 60 0 0 | 45 [illegible] 0 | |
| 22 Sept. 1866 | Dingle | Mary Grey | Matron | 66 | 20½ | Do. | 25 0 0 | 20 [illegible] 0 | |
| 15 Feb. 1872 | Donaghmore | Thomas Delaney | Porter of Workhouse | 50 | 21½ | Do. | 20 0 0 | 10 0 0 | |

| | | | | | | | | | | | | |
|---|---|---|---|---|---|---|---|---|---|---|---|---|
| 26 Sept 1866 | Downpatrick | George Patterson | Relieving Officer | 70 | 19 | Infirmity of body | 40 | 4 | 6 | 26 | 0 | 0 | |
| 20 Nov 1866 | Do. | Michael Savage | Relieving Officer and Sanitary Inspector | 76 | 26 | Old age | 64 | 10 | 0 | 30 | 0 | 0 | |
| 4 Jan 1869 | Drogheda | Maria Dillingham | Matron | 67 | 22½ | Do. | 30 | 0 | 0 | 20 | 0 | 0 | |
| 10 April 1872 | Do. | Nicholas Kelly | Relieving Officer and Sanitary Inspector | 58 | 21 | Infirmity of body | 44 | 0 | 0 | 25 | 0 | 0 | 6 Dec., 1874 |
| 24 June 1872 | Do. | Mary Anne Walsh | Fever Hospital Nurse | [illegible] | 20 | Do. | [illegible] | 15 | 0 | 20 | 10 | 0 | |
| 20 July 1874 | Do. | Neil M'Geavy | Apothecary of Workhouse | 61 | 19 | Do. | 75 | 0 | 0 | 34 | 0 | 0 | 26 Jan., 1880 |
| 13 Nov. 1874 | Do. | Sarah Hanlon | Infirmary Nurse | 66 | 11 | Old age and infirmity of body | 15 | 20 | 0 | 10 | 0 | 0 | |
| 27 May 1870 | Dromore, West | Catherine Coghrane | Matron | 60 | 19½ | Do. | 20 | 0 | 0 | 4 | 0 | 0 | |
| 18 Aug 1856 | Do. | James M'Mann | Medical Officer of Workhouse and Dispensary District | 54½ | 22½ | Do. | *192 | 14 | 10 | 100 | 0 | 0 | |
| 7 Sept. 1867 | Dublin, North | Jane Blake | Superintendent of Sheds | 69 | 24 | Do. | 91 | 0 | 0 | 27 | 0 | 0 | 7 Jan., 1874 |
| 14 Mar 1871 | Do. | Thomas Hamant | Relieving Officer | 71 | 10 | Do. | 94 | 0 | 0 | 60 | 0 | 0 | |
| 24 May 1872 | Do. | Daniel Gilligan | Relieving Officer | 74 | 20½ | Old age and infirmity | 60 | 0 | 0 | 26 | 0 | 0 | |
| 17 April 1872 | Do. | Frederick Hartford | Assistant Master | 60 | 17 | Infirmity of mind | *120 | 0 | 0 | 64 | 10 | 4 | |
| 20 April 1873 | Do. | Benjamin G. Danby | Medical Officer of Dispensary District | 66 | 26 | Old age | 125 | 0 | 0 | 86 | 0 | 0 | |
| 1 April 1873 | Do. | J. A. Crean | Assistant Clerk | 56 | 8 | Infirmity of body | 60 | 0 | 0 | 60 | 0 | 0 | |
| 24 April 1879 | Do. | George Thirimble | Gate Porter at Workhouse | 66 | 21½ | Do. | *70 | 0 | 0 | 37 | 0 | 0 | |
| 20 Oct. 1873 | Do. | Alexander Scarff | Gate Porter | 72 | 40 | Old age | *96 | 4 | 10 | 60 | 0 | 0 | |
| 7 July 1874 | Do. | Anne Scarff | Head Nurse of Workhouse | 55 | 21 | Infirmity of body | 273 | 4 | 0 | 30 | 0 | 0 | |
| 21 Dec. 1875 | Do. | Jane Jenkins | Assistant Schoolmistress | 74 | 25 | Do. | [illegible] | 15 | 2 | [illegible] | 0 | 0 | |
| 13 Feb. 1869 | Dublin, South | Henry Evans | Relieving Officer | 66 | 30 | Do. | 78 | 0 | 0 | 51 | 0 | 0 | |
| 16 Mar 1870<br>20 Mar 1870 | Do. | James Brien | Master Tailor | 60 | 20 | Old age and infirmity | 64 | 15 | 0 | 21<br>20 | 0<br>0 | 0<br>0 | |
| 24 Mar 1871 | Do. | Jane Dollard | Matron | 73 | 20 | Do. | 60 | 0 | 0 | 42 | 0 | 0 | |
| 27 April 1871 | Do. | John Johnston | Wardmaster | 66 | 26 | Do. | 15 | 0 | 0 | 20 | 15 | 4 | |
| 7 April 1877 | Do. | Catherine Scully | Infant Schoolmistress | 70 | 22 | Old age and infirmity of body | *40 | 0 | 4 | 40 | 0 | 0 | |
| 3 April 1874 | Do. | Edward M. Berry | Gate Porter | 69 | 19 | Infirmity of body | 40 | 15 | 0 | 27 | 0 | 0 | |
| 12 Jan 1871 | Dunfanaghy | Michael Diver | Porter of Dispensary | 66 | 25 | Do. | 8 | 0 | 0 | 5 | 0 | 0 | 6 July, 1872 |
| 11 Dec 1873 | Do. | Patrick Coll | Clerk of Union and Master of Workhouse | 66½ | 23 | Old age | *290 | 0 | 0 | 56 | 0 | 0 | |
| 24 May 1873 | Dunmanway | James Hagan | Clerk of Union and Master of Workhouse | 67 | 11 | Infirmity of mind and body | 60 | 0 | 0 | 60 | 0 | 0 | |
| 7 Feb. 1869 | Dunshaughlin | Wm. Chas. Byrne | Medical Officer of Workhouse Infirmary, and Medical Officer of Dispensary District | 50 | 17 7/12<br>17 1/12 | Infirmity of body | 67<br>86 | 10<br>0 | 0<br>0 | 75 | 0 | 0 | |
| 19 Mar 1856 | Do. | Laurence O'Reilly | Medical Officer of Dispensary District | 70 | 29 | Old age | *110 | 3 | 4 | 70 | 15 | 4 | |
| 26 May 1873 | Edenderry | Patrick O'Brien | Do. | 70 | 20 | Old age and infirmity | 100 | 0 | 0 | 60 | 10 | 4 | |
| 16 Aug 1870 | Do. | T. P. Edwards | Medical Officer | 64 | 23 | Infirmity of body | 120 | 0 | 0 | 75 | 0 | 0 | |

[continued.

H

No. 7.—Union Officers' Superannuation.—Statement of Allowances under the Superannuation Acts in force during any portion of the year ended 29th September, 1875, showing also the cases in which the Allowances had terminated during the year. (In continuation of Statement in the Third Report under Local Government Board (Ireland), 1875, Appendix D, No 7)—continued.

| Date of Commissioners' Consent. | Union. | Name of Officer. | Office. | Age. | Period of Service as a Union Officer. | Cause of Retirement. | Annual Salary. £ s. d. | Annual Superannuation Allowance. £ s. d. | If terminated, date of termination. |
|---|---|---|---|---|---|---|---|---|---|
| 30 Oct. 1869 | Ennis | R. J. M'Namara | Schoolmistress | 34 | 23 | Infirmity of body | 56 0 0 | 19 [illegible] 0 | |
| 30 Aug. 1871 | Do. | Honora Fay | Matron | 47 | 19 | Do. | 35 0 0 | 20 0 0 | |
| 22 Oct. 1867 | Enniscorthy | Margaret Harris | Schoolmistress | 60 | 20 | Do. | 30 0 0 | 10 0 0 | |
| 10 Feb. 1876 | Do. | Patrick O'Rourke | Medical Officer of Workhouse | 79 | 18½ | Do. | 104 0 0 | 60 13 6 | |
| 7 Aug. 1874 | Do. | John Taylor | Medical Officer of Dispensary District | 60 | 22 | Do. | 60 0 0 | 60 0 0 | |
| 11 Feb. 1870 | Enniskillen | Rebecca Cassen | Matron | 72 | 29 | Old age | 50 0 0 | 30 0 0 | |
| 1 Aug. 1872 | Do. | James Wilkin | Medical Officer of Dispensary District | 80 | 24 | Do. | 104 0 0 | 60 13 6 | |
| 12 Nov. 1872 | Do. | Eliza Jane Britton | Schoolmistress | 72 | 27 | Do. | *41 0 0 | 21 0 0 | |
| 9 Dec. 1868 | Fermoy | John F. Edgar | Medical Officer of Dispensary District | 79 | 17½ | Infirmity of body | 100 0 0 | 67 0 0 | |
| 10 April, 1873 | Do. | Ellen Crawford | Hospital Nurse | 60 | 23 | Do. | *47 0 0 | 21 0 0 | |
| 13 Sept. 1871 | Galway | Michael Cullinan | Medical Officer of Dispensary District | 64 | 30 | Do. | 90 0 0 | 50 0 0 | |
| 20 May, 1873 | Do. | Richard A. England | Medical Officer of Dispensary District and Apothecary of Workhouse | 60 | 8[illegible] | Do. | 100 0 0 | 34 0 0 | |
| 6 July, 1874 | Do. | Michael Colohan | Medical Officer of Workhouse | 60 | 13 | Do. | 90 0 0 | 60 0 0 | |
| 21 Jan. 1872 | Glenties | John Wadding | Medical Officer of Dispensary District | 74 | 13 | Infirmity of mind | *147 6 4 | 50 0 0 | |
| 29 Jan. 1861 | Glin | John Riordan | Assistant Medical Officer of Workhouse | 67 | 20½ | Infirmity and old age | 30 0 0 | 20 0 0 | |
| 19 May, 1870 | Gorey | Charles Somerton | Storekeeper | 60 | 14 | Old age | 20 11 8 | 14 0 0 | |
| 7 Dec. 1874 | Do. | Wm. Hugh Miller | Relieving Officer | 73 | 23[illegible] | Infirmity of mind and body | 31 1 0 | 22 0 0 | |
| 29 Nov. 1873 | Gort | Martin Donohoe | Porter | 70 | 21[illegible] | Old age | 8 0 0 | 5 0 0 | |
| 21 Nov. 1871 | Do. | James Forrest | Relieving Officer and Sanitary Inspector | 67 | 26 | Old age and infirmity | 22 0 0 | 10 0 0 | |
| 16 May, 1876 | Gortin | Daniel M'Farland | Clerk | 70 | 20 | Infirmity of mind and body | 60 0 0 | 40 0 0 | |
| 26 Mar. 1871 | Do. | Margaret M'Keane | Fever Hospital Nurse | 67 | 17[illegible] | Infirmity of body | 19 0 0 | 6 10 0 | |
| 24 May, 1870 | Granard | Patrick Sheil | Porter | 72 | 23 | Do. | 12 10 0 | 6 0 0 | |

| | | | | | | | | |
|---|---|---|---|---|---|---|---|---|
| 22 April, 1879 | Irvinestown . . | Charles Humphreys | Relieving Officer and Sub-Sanitary Officer | 62 | 29 | Do. . | 30 0 0 | 19 10 0 |
| 16 July, 1871 | Kanturk | Kate Clifford | Matron | 60 | 77½ | Do. | 60 0 0 | 21 0 0 |
| 6 Mar 1879 | Do. . . | John Clifford | Relieving Officer and Sanitary Inspector | 60 | 24 | Do. | 36 10 0 | 18 5 0 |
| 20 May, 1874 | Do. . | Anthony K. Sidley | Apothecary of Dispensary District | 71 | 79 | Old age . | 15 0 0 | 13 13 4 |
| 10 June, 1878 | Kells . | Henry Prendiand | Medical Officer of Dispensary District | 60 | 35 | Infirmity of body | 130 0 0 | 81 13 4 |
| 17 Sept 1877 | Do. | Margaret Baldwin | Matron of Workhouse | 50 | 20 | Do. . | 30 0 0 | 20 0 0 |
| 7 Nov 1878 | Do . . | Elizabeth Fisher | Infirmary Nurse . | 66 | 4½ | Do. . | 20 0 0 | 3 0 0 |
| 22 Jan 1875 | Do | George Latimer | Storemaker | 77 | 41 | Do . | 22 0 0 | 18 13 0 |
| 18 Dec. 1874 | Kenmare . | George A. Doran | Medical Officer of Dispensary District | 67 | 24 | Permanent infirmity | 150 0 0 | 75 0 0 |
| 5 April, 1876 | Do. | Adrian Taylor | Do. . | 64 | 22 | Infirmity of body . | 150 0 0 | 90 0 0 |
| 11 Aug. 1869 | Kilkeel . | John Boyd | Clerk . . | 40½ | 17 | Do | 75 0 0 | 15 0 0 |
| 17 Sept. 1866 | Kilkenny . | Smithwick Carpenter | Medical Officer of Dispensary District and Fever Hospital and Sanitary Officer | 64 | 17 1/12 | Permanent infirmity | 150 0 0 | 100 0 0 |
| 5 Dec. 1877 | Killarney . | J. D. Sullivan | Relieving Officer | 59 | 20 | Old age and infirmity . | 40 0 0 | 20 13 4 |
| 17 June, 1874 | Do. . | Thomas Sugrue | Medical Officer of Dispensary District | 61 | 33½ | Infirmity of body | *200 0 0 | 133 6 8 |
| 9 April, 1875 | Kilmacthomas . | Margaret Walsh | Matron . | 67 | 40 | Do. . | 25 0 0 | 16 0 0 |
| 3 Feb. 1866 | Kilmallock . | Thomas Broull | Relieving Officer | 67 | 15½ | Infirmity of mind and body | 20 0 0 | 10 0 0 |
| 7 April, 1878 | Do | Edmund Walsh | Do | 70 | 12 | Infirmity of body | 30 0 0 | 60 0 0 |
| 27 Dec. 1871 | Do. | Catherine Meade | Fever Hospital Nurse | 65 | 10½ | Do. | 18 0 0 | 7 12 0 |
| 15 Feb. 1862 | Kilrush | John Griffin | Dispensary Medical Officer | 66 | 20 1/12 | Do | 100 0 0 | 66 13 4 |
| 9 June, 1860 | Larne | Samuel J. Smiley | Relieving Officer | 66 | 11 | Do . | 40 0 0 | 15 0 0 |
| 26 Dec. 1872 | Do | Margaret Rogers | Fever Hospital Nurse . | 73½ | 15 1/12 | Old age . | 20 0 0 | 17 0 0 |
| 29 Dec. 1871 | Letterkenny . | William Graham | Master of Workhouse | 67 | 34½ | Old age and infirmity | 60 0 0 | 38 10 0 |
| 26 May, 1878 | Lismore . | Charles Gilmore | Porter and Agriculturist | 70 | 26½ | Old age | *18 10 0 | 11 0 0 |
| 11 April, 1867 | Limerick . | Patrick J. M'Inerney | Master | 52 | 26 | Infirmity of mind and body | 170 0 0 | 70 0 0 |
| 20 Feb. 1879 | Do. | James McNamara | Medical Officer of Dispensary District | 64 | 36 | Infirmity of body | 190 0 0 | 98 13 4 |
| 19 May, 1875 | Do. . | Patrick Hartigan | Relieving Officer . . | 60 | 21 | Old age and infirmity of body | 50 0 0 | 63 0 0 |
| 24 July, 1873 | Do. . . | Michael Scoddie | Medical Officer of Dispensary District & Workhouse | 70 | 22 | Old age . | *232 10 0 | 164 7 0 |
| 19 Nov 1870 | Do. . . | Julia Scully | Hospital Attendant | 71 | 19 | Infirmity of body . | 20 0 0 | 10 0 0 |
| 11 May, 1876 | Do. . | Mary Mahony | Fever Hospital Nurse | 65 | 20 | Old age | *22 11 0 | 20 0 0 |
| 8 Nov 1876 | Do. . | Johanna Flynn | Wardmistress | 60 | 20 | Infirmity of body | 30 0 0 | 20 0 0 |
| 4 Aug 1879 | Do | John Bowerman | Rate Collector | 62 | 24 | Infirmity of mind and body | 202 14 7 | 100 0 0 |
| 9 Feb. 1870 | Limavady . | F. M. Lettar | Medical Officer of Dispensary District | 64 | 2½ | Infirmity of body . | 100 0 0 | 20 0 0 |
| 13 April, 1873 | Do . . | Sarah C. Murray | Matron | 68 | 22 | Infirmity of mind | *60 0 0 | 27 0 0 |
| 23 Aug. 1869 | Lismore | James Bolton | Clerk | 61 | 29 1/2 | Infirmity of mind and body | 60 0 0 | 42 0 0 |

(continued.)

No. 7.—UNION OFFICERS' SUPERANNUATION.—Statement of Allowances under the Superannuation Acts in force during any portion of the year ended 29th September, 1875, showing also the cases in which the Allowances had terminated during the year. (In continuation of Statement in the Third Report under Local Government Board (Ireland), 1875, Appendix D, No. 7)—continued.

| Date of Commissioners' Consent. | Union. | Name of Officer. | Office. | Age. | Period of Service as a Union Officer. | Cause of Retirement. | Actual Salary. | Annual Superannuation Allowance. | If terminated, date of termination. |
|---|---|---|---|---|---|---|---|---|---|
| | | | | | | | £ s. d. | £ s. d. | |
| 9 Jan 1869 | Listowel | Garrett Fitzmaurice | Relieving Officer | 42 | 17 | Infirmity of mind and body | 24 0 0 | 10 0 0 | |
| 21 Nov 1870 | Londonderry | William Rogers | Master | 54 | 27½ | Infirmity of body | 70 0 0 | 40 0 0 | |
| 7 Feb 1870 | Do | John Harvey, M.D. | Medical Officer of Dispensary District | 67 | 30 1/6 | Do. | 100 0 0 | 66 13 4 | |
| 20 July, 1870 | Do | Ellen Cochrane | Matron | 66 | 25 | Do. | *24 0 0 | 20 0 0 | |
| 11 April, 1870 | Loughrea | James Stanton | Porter | 65 | 10 | Do. | 18 0 0 | 10 0 0 | |
| 16 May, 1873 | Lurgan | Alex. Carroll | Shoemaker | 77 | 8 1/12 | Do. | 21 0 0 | 13 0 0 | |
| 30 Oct 1873 | Macroom | Thomas Godfrey | Medical Officer of Dispensary District | 71 | 31 | Old age | *135 1 11 | 83 0 0 | |
| 2 July, 1870 | Magherafelt | Mary A. Henderson | Infirmary Nurse | 74 | 17½ | Infirmity of mind and body | *24 10 0 | 9 0 0 | |
| 9 Mar 1873 | Mallow | James P. Sheehan | Medical Officer of Dispensary District | 67 | 19½ | Infirmity of body | 98 0 0 | 60 0 0 | |
| Sept. 1870 | Manorhamilton | Thomas Davis | Medical Officer of Workhouse | 68 | 24 1/12 | Do | 100 0 0 | 66 13 4 | |
| 10 Dec 1870 | Midleton | John W. Barry | Medical Officer of Dispensary District | 78 | 31½ | Old age | *122 0 1 | 76 10 0 | |
| 9 Dec 1871 | Do. | Catherine Geary | Infirmary Nurse | 64 | 16½ | Old age and infirmity of body | 20 0 0 | 10 0 0 | |
| 11 May, 1870 | Do | Michael Riordan | Relieving Officer | 67 | 4½ | Infirmity of body | 20 0 0 | 12 0 0 | |
| 12 April, 1870 | Milford | William Young | Porter | 79 | 11½ | Do | 5 0 0 | 3 0 0 | 26 Mar 1875. |
| 30 Nov 1870 | Millstreet | Mary Leary | Infirmary Nurse | 60½ | 20 1/12 | Do. | 16 0 0 | 9 13 4 | |
| 26 Mar 1872 | Do | Eugene Riordan | Porter of Workhouse | 70 | 21 1/12 | Old age and infirmity | 8 0 0 | 5 0 0 | |
| 13 June, 1873 | Do | Daniel Crowley | Relieving Officer | 65 | 9 7/12 | Old age | 26 0 0 | 16 10 6 | |
| 10 Mar 1874 | Do | Thomas Barrett | Do. | 64 | 27 | Old age and infirmity | 42 10 0 | 27 10 0 | |
| 24 Oct 1865 | Mohill | Timothy Kelly | Porter | 70 | 25 | Infirmity of body | 15 0 0 | 10 0 0 | |
| 14 Aug 1872 | Do | Patrick Mulholland | Relieving Officer | 62 | 20 | Old age | 40 0 0 | 27 0 0 | |
| 24 Aug 1874 | Do. | Edward Sexton | Medical Officer of Dispensary District. | 69 | 25 | Infirmity of body. | *161 10 0 | 17 7 2 | |
| 6 April, 1871 | Mountmellick | Margaret Dunne | Matron | 56 | 23 1/12 | Infirmity of mind and body | 30 0 0 | 10 0 0 | |
| 9 April, 1872 | Mullingar | Alexander Fallon | Medical Officer of Dispensary District. | 75 | 19½ | Infirmity of body | 100 0 0 | 66 13 4 | 21 Nov. 1874. |
| 10 July, 1872 | Do. | John H. Pilkington | Relieving Officer | 60 | 24 | Do. | 46 0 0 | 30 0 0 | |
| 4 Feb 1874 | Do. | William Whaley | Weaver and Assistant in Workhouse | 70 | 25 | Old age and infirmity of body | *24 0 0 | 20 0 0 | |

| | | | | | | | | | | | | | |
|---|---|---|---|---|---|---|---|---|---|---|---|---|---|
| 6 Oct. 1874 | Naas | George Robinson | Medical Officer of Dispensary District | 72 | 40½ | Old age | 160 | 0 | 0 | 80 | 10 | 0 | |
| 10 Dec. 1874 | Do. | Rev George Dunney | R. C. Chaplain | 79 | 30 | Do. | 100 | 0 | 0 | 66 | 10 | 0 | |
| 24 Sept. 1876 | Do. | Rev Jeremiah Lowe | Chaplain (Irish Church Act, 1869) | 75 | 31½ | Do. | 53 | 0 | 0 | 35 | 0 | 0 | |
| 10 April, 1878 | Navan | Judith Reilly | Fever Hospital Nurse | 77 | 31½ | Do. | 20 | 0 | 0 | 15 | 0 | 0 | |
| 26 July, 1872 | Do. | Catherine Kennedy | Infirmary Nurse | 63 | 31 | Infirmity of body | 20 | 0 | 0 | 13 | 0 | 0 | |
| 7 Sept. 1879 | Do. | Clement Hamerton | Medical Officer of Dispensary District | 66 | 38 | Old age | 160 | 0 | 0 | 100 | 0 | 0 | |
| 24 Feb. 1867 | Nenagh | John Considine | Relieving Officer | 65 | 17 | Infirmity of body | 50 | 0 | 0 | 18 | 13 | 4 | 17 Jan. 1876 |
| 12 Sept. 1878 | Do. | Mary M'Glynn | Schoolmistress | 40 | 16⅚ | Do. | 36 | 0 | 0 | 12 | 0 | 0 | |
| 11 Dec. 1878 | Do. | Thomas Cleary | Baker | 47 | 15½ | Permanent infirmity | 27 | 0 | 0 | 15 | 0 | 0 | |
| 14 Jan. 1879 | Do. | Robert L. Rae | Medical Officer of Dispensary District | 54 | 30½ | Infirmity of body | 123 | 4 | 11 | 80 | 0 | 0 | |
| 15 May, 1873 | Do. | Rowan F. Cashel | Do. | 55 | 26⅚ | Permanent infirmity | 120 | 0 | 0 | 18 | 0 | 0 | |
| 15 June, 1874 | Do. | O'Neill Quin | Medical Officer of Workhouse and Dispensary District | 73 | 37 | Old age and infirmity of body | 214 | 10 | 0 | 146 | 0 | 0 | |
| 21 Sept. 1879 | Do. | Margaret Carroll | Infirmary Nurse | 56 | 27½ | Permanent infirmity | 25 | 0 | 0 | 20 | 0 | 0 | |
| 19 Dec. 1878 | Newcastle | Myles O'Brien | Apothecary of Workhouse and Dispensary District | 61 | 31 | Infirmity of body | 60 | 0 | 0 | 40 | 0 | 0 | |
| 17 Feb. 1879 | Do. | Thomas Ambrose | Medical Officer of Dispensary District | 64 | 40 | Old age and infirmity | 180 | 0 | 0 | 66 | 13 | 4 | |
| 6 Oct. 1876 | Newport | James Davis | Medical Officer of Workhouse and Dispensary District | 72 | 34½ | Old age | 217 | 3 | 10 | 144 | 15 | 11 | |
| 6 Oct. 1878 | New Ross | Bridget Keating | Midwife | 66 | 16 | Infirmity of body | 10 | 0 | 0 | 4 | 13 | 4 | |
| 15 May, 1875 | Do. | Catherine O'Shea | Assistant Schoolmistress | 43 | 20 | Do. | 15 | 0 | 0 | 11 | 0 | 0 | |
| 26 Aug. 1879 | Newry | Henry S. Gray | Medical Officer of Dispensary District | 66 | 19 | Do. | 90 | 0 | 0 | 40 | 0 | 0 | |
| 29 Jan. 1877 | Do. | James Harvey | Relieving Officer | 75 | 16½ | Do. | 55 | 0 | 0 | 24 | 13 | 4 | 4 Jan. 1878 |
| 25 Oct. 1876 | Oldcastle | John M. Atkin | Medical Officer of Dispensary District | 76 | 30 | Old age | 125 | 0 | 0 | 76 | 17 | 0 | |
| 19 Nov. 1874 | Do. | Frances Jenkins | Infirmary Nurse | 61 | 17 | Infirmity of body | 15 | 0 | 0 | 15 | 0 | 0 | |
| 4 Dec. 1861 | Omagh | Dorothea Wilkins | Midwife | 66 | 14 | Do. | 10 | 0 | 0 | 5 | 0 | 0 | |
| 25 June, 1866 | Do. | Rebecca M'Gowan | Fever Nurse | 60 | 17⅚ | Do. | 12 | 0 | 0 | 5 | 0 | 0 | |
| 13 Oct. 1876 | Do. | John Galbraith | Relieving Officer and Sanitary Inspector | 59½ | 20½ | Do. | 55 | 0 | 0 | 20 | 0 | 0 | |
| 1 April, 1875 | Do. | Samuel Cunningham | Relieving Officer and Sanitary Sub-Officer | 64½ | 27½ | Old age and infirmity of body | 56 | 10 | 0 | 45 | 0 | 0 | |
| 1 April, 1878 | Do. | John M'Elroy | Wardmaster and Agriculturist | 77½ | 30½ | Do. | 28 | 0 | 0 | 14 | 0 | 0 | |
| 4 Dec. 1873 | Oughterard | Matthew Moss | Relieving Officer | 64 | 16 | Old age and infirmity of body | 40 | 0 | 0 | 18 | 0 | 0 | |
| 4 Dec. 1872 | Parsonstown | Gertrude Doody | Matron | 66 | 22 | Infirmity of mind | 50 | 0 | 0 | 30 | 0 | 0 | |
| 10 Sept. 1878 | Rathdrum | Michael C. Brennan | Medical Officer of Dispensary District | 61 | 24 | Infirmity of body | 40 | 0 | 0 | 20 | 0 | 0 | |
| 21 Aug. 1871 | Do. | Joseph Ledwith | Do. | 65 | 26 | Do. | 110 | 0 | 0 | 70 | 0 | 0 | |
| 1 Sept. 1871 | Rathdown | Bernard M'Cabe | Master Shoemaker | 60 | 29 | Old age and infirmity | 26 | 0 | 0 | 20 | 0 | 0 | |

No. 7.—Union Officers' Superannuation.—Statement of Allowances under the Superannuation Acts in force during any portion of the year ended 29th September, 1875, showing also the cases in which the Allowances had terminated during the year (In continuation of Statement in the Third Report under Local Government Board (Ireland), 1875, Appendix D, No. 7)—continued.

| Date of Commissioners' Consent. | Union. | Name of Officer. | Office. | Age. | Period of Service as a Union Officer. | Cause of Retirement. | Annual Salary. | Annual Superannuation Allowance. | If terminated, date of termination. |
|---|---|---|---|---|---|---|---|---|---|
| | | | | | | | £ s. d. | £ s. d. | |
| [illegible] Nov. 187[illegible] | Rathdown | Frederick Hunter | Medical Officer of Dispensary District. | [illegible] | [illegible] | Old age | [illegible] | [illegible] | |
| [illegible] Mar. 187[illegible] | Do. | Wm. H. Franklin | Do. | [illegible] | [illegible] | Permanent infirmity | [illegible] | [illegible] | |
| [illegible] July, 187[illegible] | Do. | Patrick Gorman | Baker | [illegible] | [illegible] | Old age and infirmity of body | [illegible] | [illegible] | |
| [illegible] June, 187[illegible] | Rathdrum | John Walsh | Do. | [illegible] | nearly [illegible] | Infirmity of body | [illegible] | [illegible] | |
| [illegible] Mar. 18[illegible] | Rathkeale | John O'Donovan | Schoolmaster | [illegible] | [illegible] | Infirmity of body | [illegible] | [illegible] | |
| [illegible] Jan. 18[illegible] | Do. | Thomas [illegible] | Medical Officer of Workhouse | [illegible] | [illegible] | Old age | [illegible] | [illegible] | |
| [illegible] Mar. 18[illegible] | Scariff | Robert Lloyd [illegible] | Medical Officer of Dispensary District. | [illegible] | [illegible] | Infirmity of body | [illegible] | [illegible] | |
| [illegible] May, 18[illegible] | Shillelagh | Ellen Dowse | Matron | [illegible] | [illegible] | Infirmity | [illegible] | [illegible] | |
| [illegible] Oct. 187[illegible] | Do. | George Blake | Porter of Workhouse | [illegible] | [illegible] | Old age | [illegible] | [illegible] | |
| [illegible] Jan. 187[illegible] | Skibbereen | Daniel Donovan | Medical Officer of Workhouse | [illegible] | [illegible] | Do. | [illegible] | [illegible] | |
| [illegible] Mar. 18[illegible] | Do. | Daniel Donovan | Medical Officer of Dispensary | [illegible] | [illegible] | Infirmity of body | [illegible] | [illegible] | |
| [illegible] June, 187[illegible] | Skull | Ellen Holland | Hospital Nurse, | [illegible] | [illegible] | Old age and infirmity | [illegible] | [illegible] | |
| [illegible] Dec. 187[illegible] | Sligo | John Longford | Apothecary of Dispensary District | [illegible] | [illegible] | Infirmity of body | [illegible] | [illegible] | |
| [illegible] May, 187[illegible] | Do. | Michael M'Donnell | Relieving Officer | [illegible] | [illegible] | Old age | [illegible] | [illegible] | |
| [illegible] July, 18[illegible] | Do. | Thomas Burrowes, | Medical Officer of Dispensary District | [illegible] | [illegible] | Old age and infirmity | [illegible] | [illegible] | |
| [illegible] Oct. 187[illegible] | Do. | Bridget [illegible] | Assistant Hospital Nurse | [illegible] | [illegible] | Infirmity of body | [illegible] | [illegible] | |
| [illegible] Sept. 18[illegible] | Do. | Rose Conway | Fever Hospital Nurse | [illegible] | [illegible] | Old age and infirmity of body | [illegible] | [illegible] | |
| 14 June, 187[illegible] | Do. | Edward Powell | Medical Officer of Workhouse and Consulting Sanitary Officer | [illegible] | [illegible] | Infirmity of body | [illegible] | [illegible] | |
| [illegible] Dec. 18[illegible] | Strabane | John James | Ward Master and Fever Ward Steward | [illegible] | [illegible] | Do. | [illegible] | [illegible] | |
| 4 May, 1874 | Do. | Alex. Leney | Medical Officer of Workhouse and Dispensary Dist. | [illegible] | [illegible] / [illegible] | Old age | [illegible] / [illegible] | [illegible] / [illegible] | |
| [illegible] Sept. 18[illegible] | Do. | John Geo. Gregory | Relieving Officer | [illegible] | [illegible] | Old age and infirmity | [illegible] | [illegible] | |

| | | | | | | | | | | | | |
|---|---|---|---|---|---|---|---|---|---|---|---|---|
| 6 Jan 1878 | Do. | Ross M'Clintock | Medical Officer of Dispensary District | 80 | 34½ | Old age | *121 | 10 | 0 | 70 | 0 | 0 |
| 24 Nov 1874 | Stranorlar | Henry Alex. Walker | Medical Officer of Dispensary District | 60 | 27½ | Infirmity of body | 100 | 0 | 0 | 64 | 1 | 8 |
| 29 July, 1874 | Do. | Ellen Doherty | Fever Hospital Nurse | 67 | 19½ | Do. | 28 | 0 | 0 | 6 | 16 | 4 |
| 24 July, 1873 | Swineford | Cathrn Fitzpatrick | Schoolmistress | 50 | 18 | Do | 25 | 0 | 0 | 10 | 0 | 0 |
| 11 May, 1874 | Do. | Patrick M'Dermott | Relieving Officer and Sanitary Inspector | 78 | 30 | Old age | 80 | 0 | 0 | 14 | 18 | 5 |
| 12 Mar 1874 | Do. | Margaret Furey | Hospital Nurse | 60 | 21½ | Old age and infirmity of body | *20 | 0 | 0 | 12 | 0 | 0 |
| 15 Feb. 1873 | Thomastown | Thomas Bradley | Medical Officer of Dispensary District | 64 | 18½ | Infirmity of body | 80 | 0 | 0 | 40 | 0 | 0 |
| 14 Mar 1873 | Do. | Malcolm Perkins | Relieving Officer | 79 | 20½ | Old age | 40 | 0 | 0 | 24 | 0 | 0 |
| 30 April, 1873 | Do | W J Thompson | Medical Officer of Dispensary District | 55 | 31 | Do | *168 | 10 | 0 | 84 | 0 | 0 |
| 7 April, 1870 | Tipperary | Michael Reardon | Master | 49 | 19 | Infirmity of body | 70 | 0 | 0 | 46 | 10 | 4 |
| 3 April, 1873 | Do | Matthew Ryan | Porter | 72 | 21 | Old age and infirmity | 24 | 0 | 0 | 7 | 0 | 0 |
| 26 July, 1878 | Do. | Thomas B. Ryan | Medical Officer of Dispensary District | 54 | 19 | Infirmity of body | 100 | 0 | 0 | 44 | 0 | 0 |
| 4 Dec. 1873 | Tralee | Robert Fitzmaurice | Do | 48 | 22 | Do | *190 | 0 | 0 | 64 | 0 | 0 |
| 20 May, 1870 | Do | Margaret Walsh | Ward Mistress | 60 | 20 | Permanent infirmity | *40 | 0 | 0 | 16 | 0 | 0 |
| 27 May 1879 | Do. | David M Roche | Relieving Officer | 73 | 27 | Old age | 32 | 0 | 0 | 14 | 18 | 4 |
| 23 July, 1874 | Do | Myles Daly | Master of Workhouse | 67 | 24 | Infirmity of body | *251 | 10 | 0 | 100 | 0 | 0 |
| 23 Nov 1874 | Do | Mary Casey | Hospital Nurse | 66 | 27 | Old age | 44 | 0 | 0 | 20 | 0 | 0 |
| 1 Mar 1874 | Do. | Nancie Murphy | Fever Hospital Nurse | 60 | 20 | Old age and infirmity of body | *18 | 0 | 0 | 24 | 7 | 0 |
| 14 Oct. 1869 | Trim | Elizabeth Smith | Do. | 62 | 19 | Infirmary of body | 30 | 0 | 0 | 18 | 0 | 0 |
| 1 Oct. 1873 | Do. | Peter Byrne | Relieving Officer | 63 | 24 | Old age and infirmity of body | 34 | 0 | 0 | 18 | 0 | 0 |
| 27 Sept. 1869 | Tuam | Ellen Conn | Matron | 66 | 17½ | Infirmity of body | 20 | 0 | 0 | 13 | 13 | 4 |
| 14 Nov 1873 | Tullamore | Esther Quinn | Nurse in Fever Hospital | 77 | 20 | Old age | 16 | 0 | 0 | 11 | 0 | 0 |
| 13 April, 1873 | Urlingford | Ambrose Lane | Relieving Officer | 79 | 31 | Old age and infirmity of body | 30 | 0 | 0 | 24 | 0 | 0 |
| 3 Mar. 1871 | Waterford | Margaret Moriarty | Assistant Fever Hospital Nurse | 67½ | 10 | Old age | 9 | 4 | 0 | 4 | 0 | 0 |
| 17 June, 1869 | Westport | Miss H A Wilson | Matron | 50 | 11 | Infirmity of body | 41 | 10 | 0 | 21 | 0 | 4 |
| 14 June, 1873 | Youghal | William C Poole | Medical Officer of Dispensary District | 55 | 30 | Do | 194 | 0 | 0 | 91 | 13 | 4 |
| 30 Aug 1874 | Do. | Ellen Adams | Hospital Nurse | 64 | 27½ | Do | 28 | 0 | 0 | 14 | 0 | 0 |

* Including emoluments.

# APPENDIX E.

## TABULAR RETURNS IN CONNEXION WITH RELIEF UNDER THE MEDICAL CHARITIES ACT.

[Note.—In this series of Tables, the Unions are classed in the Counties and Provinces in which the chief or central place of the respective Unions is situate; but many of the Unions comprise parts of more than one County or Province. The total of Population and Area of the Unions in the respective Counties and Provinces, as arranged in these Tables, will not, therefore, agree with the summaries of those Counties and Provinces in the Census Returns. An Alphabetical Index List of the Dispensary Districts is annexed (No. 6), showing the name of the Union in which each District is situate, and referring to the table and page in which the particulars relating to each District are to be found.]

Statement of Alterations in Dispensary Districts in Unions in Ireland (arranged in Provinces and Counties) according to the Orders issued in pursuance of sec. 6 of 14 and 15 Vic., cap. 68:—(*since the completion of Table No. 1, Appendix E, in Third Annual Report of the Local Government Board.*)

| Name of Union. | Names of Dispensary Districts. | No. of Electoral Divisions in each. | Population: 1871. | Area: in Statute Acres. | Poor Law Valuation. | No. of Members of Committee of Management. | No. of Medical Officers authorized by Sealed Order. | Number of Apothecaries. | Number of Midwives. | Date of Order. |
|---|---|---|---|---|---|---|---|---|---|---|
| Column 1. | 2. | 3. | 4. | 5. | 6. | 7. | 8. | 9. | 10. | 11. |
| **PROVINCE OF ULSTER.** | | | | A. | £ | | | | | |
| County of Antrim. | | | | | | | | | | |
| Ballycastle, | Cushendall, | – | – | – | – | 16 | – | – | – | 15th Oct., 1875. |
| County of Donegal. | | | | | | | | | | |
| Milford, | Rathmelton, | – | – | – | – | 21 | – | – | – | 9th April, 1875. |
| County of Down. | | | | | | | | | | |
| Banbridge, | Cromgar, | – | – | – | – | 15 | – | – | – | 20th May, 1875. |
| Downpatrick, | Killough, | – | – | – | – | 21 | – | – | – | 24th " " |
| Newry, | Newry, | – | – | – | – | 26 | – | – | – | 3rd Nov., 1875. |
| County of Fermanagh. | | | | | | | | | | |
| Enniskillen, | Enniskillen, | – | – | – | – | 52 | – | – | – | 20th April, 1875. |
| Lisnaskea, | Lisnaskea, | – | – | – | – | 18 | – | – | – | 13th " " |
| County of Londonderry. | | | | | | | | | | |
| Limavady, | Limavady,* | – | – | – | – | – | – | – | – | 30th Sept., 1875. |
| **PROVINCE OF MUNSTER.** | | | | | | | | | | |
| County of Clare. | | | | | | | | | | |
| Kilrush, | Carrigaholt, | – | – | – | – | 16 | – | – | – | 14th April, 1875. |
| County of Cork. | | | | | | | | | | |
| Kanturk, | Boherboy, | – | – | – | – | 20 | – | – | – | 23rd April, 1875. |
| Do., | Newmarket, | – | – | – | – | 26 | – | – | – | " |
| County of Limerick. | | | | | | | | | | |
| Newcastle, | Abbeyfeale, | – | – | – | – | 27 | – | – | – | 7th May, 1875. |
| Do., | Ardagh, | – | – | – | – | 21 | – | – | – | " |
| Do., | Broadford, | – | – | – | – | 31 | – | – | – | " |
| Do., | Feenagh, | – | – | – | – | 31 | – | – | – | " |
| Do., | Newcastle, | – | – | – | – | 25 | – | – | – | " |
| County of Tipperary. | | | | | | | | | | |
| Cashel, | Cashel, | – | – | – | – | – | – | – | –† | 17th Aug., 1875. |
| Roscrea, | Shinrone, | – | – | – | – | – | – | – | 1 | 3rd Sept., 1875. |
| County of Waterford. | | | | | | | | | | |
| Waterford, | Ullid, | – | – | – | – | – | – | – | 1 | 21st July, 1875. |

* Name altered by this Order from Newtownlimavady.

† Rescinding Order of 27th January, 1871, authorizing the appointment of midwife.

## Statement of Alterations in Dispensary Districts—*continued.*

| Name of Union. | Names of Dispensary Districts. | No. of Electoral Divisions in each. | Population: 1871. | Area: in Statute Acres. | Poor Law Valuation. | No. of Members of Committee of Management. | No. of Medical Officers authorised by Sealed Order. | Number of Apothecaries. | Number of Midwives. | Date of Order. |
|---|---|---|---|---|---|---|---|---|---|---|
| Column 1. | 2. | 3. | 4. | 5. | 6. | 7. | 8. | 9. | 10. | 11. |
| **PROVINCE OF LEINSTER.** | | | | A. | £ | | | | | |
| County of Carlow. | | | | | | | | | | |
| Carlow, . | Leighlinbridge, | – | – | – | – | – | – | – | 1 | 25th June, 1875. |
| County of Dublin. | | | | | | | | | | |
| Balrothery, . | Kilsallaghan, . | – | – | – | – | – | – | – | 1 | 4th May, 1875. |
| Dublin, North | North City, . | – | – | – | – | 52 | – | – | – | 17th Dec., 1875. |
| Rathdown, . | Kingstown, . | – | – | – | – | – | – | – | 1* | 21st May, 1875. |
| County of Longford. | | | | | | | | | | |
| Ballymahon, . | Ballymore, . | – | – | – | – | 25 | – | – | – | 12th April, 1875. |
| County of Louth. | | | | | | | | | | |
| Dundalk, . | Louth, . . | – | – | – | – | – | – | – | 1 | 20th May, 1875. |
| County of Meath. | | | | | | | | | | |
| Dunshaughlin | Killeen, . . | – | – | – | – | – | – | – | 1 | 23rd Nov., 1875. |
| Trim, . . | Athboy, . . | – | – | – | – | – | – | – | 1 | 11th Jan., 1876. |
| Queen's County. | | | | | | | | | | |
| Donaghmore, | Rathdowney, . | – | – | – | – | 27 | – | – | – | 21st April, 1875. |
| County of Wicklow. | | | | | | | | | | |
| Rathdrum, . | Ashford,† . | – | – | – | – | – | – | – | – | 8th Dec., 1875. |
| **PROVINCE OF CONNAUGHT.** | | | | | | | | | | |
| County of Galway. | | | | | | | | | | |
| Ballinasloe, . | Ahascragh, . | – | – | – | – | – | – | – | 1 | 16th Dec., 1875. |
| County of Mayo. | | | | | | | | | | |
| Castlebar, . | Castlebar, . | – | – | – | – | – | – | – | 1 | 4th August, 1875. |
| County of Roscommon. | | | | | | | | | | |
| Boyle, . . | Boyle, . . | – | – | – | – | 38 | – | – | – | 10th May, 1875. |

* An additional midwife authorised for Kingstown District by this Order.
† Name altered to "Wicklow" by this Order.

## SUMMARY OF DISPENSARY DISTRICTS, ACCORDING TO TABLE No. 1, APPENDIX E, OF PREVIOUS REPORT, AS ALTERED BY THE FOREGOING TABLE UP TO THE 25TH MARCH, 1876.

| Provinces. | Number of Unions. | Number of Dispensary Districts. | Number of Electoral Divisions. | Population: 1871. | Area: in Statute Acres. | Poor Law Valuation, 29th Sept., 1875. | Number of Medical Officers, authorised by Sealed Order. | Number of Apothecaries. | Number of Midwives. |
|---|---|---|---|---|---|---|---|---|---|
| | | | | | | £ | | | |
| Ulster, . | 44 | 214 | 875 | 1,833,228 | 5,483,206 | 4,116,200 | 235 | 3 | 71 |
| Munster, . | 50 | 205 | 1,023 | 1,393,485 | 6,067,722 | 3,387,860 | 227 | 20 | 29 |
| Leinster, . | 40 | 203 | 944 | 1,339,451 | 4,876,934 | 4,618,320 | 229 | 12 | 96 |
| Connaught, . | 29 | 98 | 596 | 846,213 | 4,392,085 | 1,363,220 | 113 | 6 | 19 |
| Total, Ireland, | 163 | 720 | 3,438 | 5,412,377 | 20,819,947 | 13,485,600 | 804 | 41 | 215 |

No. 2.—FINANCIAL and RELIEF RETURNS.—LIST, in pursuance of § 20 of the Medical Charities Act (14 & 15 Vic., c. 68), of all DISPENSARY DISTRICTS in the several Unions in Ireland (arranged in Provinces and Counties)—showing the NUMBER of DISPENSARIES in each, and the EXPENSES of each Dispensary District for the Year ended 29th September, 1875; with a RETURN,—for the Year ended 30th September, 1875,—of the NUMBER of CASES of MEDICAL RELIEF afforded to Patients at the Dispensary and at their own Homes, respectively; the Number of TICKETS for Medical Relief CANCELLED by the Committee of Management, under § 9 of the Act, Number of Cases of VACCINATION; Number of DANGEROUS LUNATICS certified; of Patients attended to BRIDEWELLS, &c.

---

NOTE ON TABLE, No. 2.

Columns 1, 2, 4, 5 and 6 inclusive, are abstracted from the sealed Orders of the Commissioners.
Columns 3 and 7 to 15, inclusive, are abstracted from Returns received from the Clerks of Unions.
Columns 16 to 23, inclusive, are abstracted from Returns received from the Medical Officers of Dispensary Districts.
Column 8.—In various instances in which Rent does not appear in this Table as part of the Annual Expenses, the Dispensary of the District is held in a house which was used for a Dispensary under the late system, or in a court-house, or other public building, the use of which is obtained by the Guardians for the purpose, or in a house granted by the proprietor, rent free, or at a nominal rent.
Columns 4 and 10.—In some instances two Dispensary Districts, in different but adjoining Unions, are attended by the same Medical Officer.

| Name of Union | Names of Dispensary Districts | No. of Dispensaries | Med. Officers | Apothecaries | Midwives | Medicines and Medical Appliances | Rent of Dispensary Buildings | Books, Forms, Stationery and Printing | Salaries: Medical Officers | Salaries: Apothecaries | Vaccination Expenses | Vaccination Expenses (other) | [illegible] | Total Expenditure for the Year ended 29th Sept., 1875 | Dispensary Tickets | Visiting Tickets | Total | [illegible] | [illegible] | [illegible] | [illegible] | [illegible] |
|---|---|---|---|---|---|---|---|---|---|---|---|---|---|---|---|---|---|---|---|---|---|---|
| Column 1. | 2. | 3. | 4. | 5. | 6. | 7. | 8. | 9. | 10. | 11. | 12. | 13. | 14. | 15. | 16. | 17. | 18. | 19. | 20. | 21. | 22. | 23. |
| PROVINCE OF ULSTER. | | | | | | £ s. d. | £ s. d. | £ s. d. | £ s. d. | £ s. d. | £ s. d. | £ s. d. | £ s. d. | £ s. d. | | | | | | | | |
| COUNTY OF ANTRIM. | | | | | | | | | | | | | | | | | | | | | | |
| ANTRIM, | 1. Antrim, | [illegible] | [illegible] | [illegible] | [illegible] | [illegible] | [illegible] | [illegible] | [illegible] | – | [illegible] | [illegible] | [illegible] | [illegible] | [illegible] | [illegible] | [illegible] | – | [illegible] | 4 | [illegible] | [illegible] |
| | 2. Connor, | [illegible] | [illegible] | [illegible] | [illegible] | [illegible] | [illegible] | [illegible] | [illegible] | – | [illegible] | – | [illegible] | [illegible] | [illegible] | [illegible] | [illegible] | – | [illegible] | [illegible] | – | – |
| | 3. Crumlin, | [illegible] | [illegible] | [illegible] | [illegible] | [illegible] | [illegible] | [illegible] | [illegible] | – | [illegible] | [illegible] | [illegible] | [illegible] | [illegible] | [illegible] | [illegible] | – | [illegible] | [illegible] | – | – |
| | 4. Doagh, | [illegible] | [illegible] | [illegible] | [illegible] | [illegible] | [illegible] | [illegible] | [illegible] | – | [illegible] | – | [illegible] | [illegible] | [illegible] | [illegible] | [illegible] | – | [illegible] | – | – | – |
| | 5. Randalstown, | [illegible] | [illegible] | [illegible] | [illegible] | [illegible] | [illegible] | [illegible] | [illegible] | – | [illegible] | [illegible] | [illegible] | [illegible] | [illegible] | [illegible] | [illegible] | – | [illegible] | – | – | – |
| | 6. Templepatrick, | [illegible] | [illegible] | [illegible] | [illegible] | [illegible] | [illegible] | [illegible] | [illegible] | – | [illegible] | – | [illegible] | [illegible] | [illegible] | [illegible] | [illegible] | – | [illegible] | – | – | – |
| | | 6 | 6 | – | – | [illegible] | [illegible] | [illegible] | [illegible] | – | [illegible] | [illegible] | [illegible] | [illegible] | [illegible] | [illegible] | [illegible] | – | [illegible] | 11 | [illegible] | [illegible] |

| Union | Dispensary District | Figures |
|---|---|---|
| Ballycastle | 1. Ballycastle, | [illegible] |
| | 2. Croagh?, | [illegible] |
| | 3. Cushendall, | [illegible] |
| | Total | [illegible] |
| Ballymena | 1. Ahoghill, | [illegible] |
| | 2. Ballymena, | [illegible] |
| | 3. Broughshane, | [illegible] |
| | 4. Clough, | [illegible] |
| | 5. Dalgorm?, | [illegible] |
| | 6. Glenwhirry?, | [illegible] |
| | 7. Portglenone, | [illegible] |
| | 8. Toome, | [illegible] |
| | Total | [illegible] |
| Ballymoney | 1. Ballymoney, | [illegible] |
| | 2. [illegible] | [illegible] |
| | 3. Dervock, | [illegible] |
| | 4. [illegible] | [illegible] |
| | 5. Kilrea, | [illegible] |
| | Total | [illegible] |
| Belfast | 1. Belfast, | [illegible] |
| | 2. Castlereagh, | [illegible] |
| | Total | [illegible] |
| Larne | 1. Ballynure?, | [illegible] |
| | 2. Ballycarry?, | [illegible] |
| | 3. Carrickfergus, | [illegible] |
| | 4. Glenarm,* | [illegible] |
| | 5. Larne, | [illegible] |
| | Total | [illegible] |

* Larne Union. Glenarm Dispensary District—A second Medical Officer authorized for this District by Order dated 19th December, 1876.

[continued.]

**No. 2.—Dispensary Districts, with the Expenses, and Amount of Medical Relief afforded, in the several Unions—*continued.***

| Name of Union. | Names of Dispensary Districts. | No. of Dispensaries, or Dispensary Stations, in each District. | No. of Officers authorised by Sealed Order. Med. Officers. | Apothecaries. | Midwives. | Expenses of Year ended 29th September, 1875. Medicines and Medical Appliances. | Rent of Dispensary Buildings. | Books, Forms, Stationery, and Printing. | Salaries. Medical Officers. | Salaries. Apothecaries. | Vaccination Expenses. Amnt. of Fees paid to Medical Officers. | Other Expenses in carrying out the Vaccination Act. | Fuel and Attendance, Midwives' Salaries, and any Incidental Expenses not included in the foregoing Columns. | Total Expenditure for each Dispensary District for Year ended 29th Sept., 1875. | Medical Relief afforded in Year ended 30th September, 1875. Number of New Cases attended and registered during the year. Dispensary Tickets. | Visiting Tickets. | Total. | No. of Tickets for Medical Relief cancelled by Dispensary Committee during the year. | No. of Cases of Vaccination during the year. | No. of Dangerous Lunatics certified. | No. of Days on which Attendance given at Bridewell or House of Correction, under s. 15. | No. of Patients attended in Bridewell or House of Correction during year. |
|---|---|---|---|---|---|---|---|---|---|---|---|---|---|---|---|---|---|---|---|---|---|---|
| Column 1. | 2. | 3. | 4. | 5. | 6. | 7. | 8. | 9. | 10. | 11. | 12. | 13. | 14. | 15. | 16. | 17. | 18. | 19. | 20. | 21. | 22. | 23. |
| | | | | | | £ s. d. | £ s. d. | £ s. d. | £ s. d. | £ s. | £ s. d. | £ s. d. | £ s. d. | £ s. d. | | | | | | | | |
| PROVINCE OF ULSTER—*continued.* | | | | | | | | | | | | | | | | | | | | | | |
| COUNTY OF ANTRIM—*con.* | | | | | | | | | | | | | | | | | | | | | | |
| LISBURN, . | 1. Annahilt, . | 1 | 1 | – | – | 15 6 1 | 10 0 0 | 1 8 0 | 100 0 0 | – | 7 6 0 | – | 16 3 3 | 149 18 4 | 272 | 150 | 429 | – | 182 | – | – | – |
| | 2. Ballylesson, . | 1 | 1 | – | – | 13 3 4 | 10 10 0 | 0 18 6 | 100 0 0 | – | 6 5 0 | – | 4 0 0 | 134 16 10 | 249 | 263 | 512 | – | 122 | – | – | – |
| | 3. Dunmurry, . | 1 | 1 | – | – | 22 5 2 | 10 0 0 | 0 18 6 | 100 0 0 | – | 7 10 0 | – | 4 0 0 | 144 13 8 | 646 | 213 | 859 | – | 150 | – | – | – |
| | 4. Glenavy, . | 1 | 1 | – | – | 15 2 2 | 10 0 0 | 0 11 0 | 100 0 0 | – | 5 18 0 | 2 0 0 | 2 0 0 | 135 11 2 | 328 | 122 | 450 | – | 105 | – | – | – |
| | 5. Hillsborough, | 1 | 1 | – | – | 33 18 1 | 10 0 0 | 0 18 6 | 100 0 0 | – | 12 13 0 | – | 2 0 0 | 159 9 7 | 264 | 339 | 603 | – | 201 | – | – | – |
| | 6. Knocknadona, | 1 | 1 | – | – | 26 14 4 | 7 0 0 | 1 9 5 | 100 0 0 | – | 11 6 0 | 2 0 0 | 1 4 6 | 149 14 4 | 111 | 175 | 286 | – | 202 | 1 | – | – |
| | 7. Lisburn, . | 1 | 1 | – | – | 34 14 10 | 15 0 0 | 1 9 0 | 100 0 0 | – | 11 7 0 | 2 0 0 | 6 19 4 | 171 10 2 | 782 | 685 | 1,467 | – | 289 | 1 | – | – |
| | 8. Saintfield, . | 1 | 1 | – | – | 15 0 10 | 8 0 0 | 0 11 0 | 100 0 0 | – | 5 16 0 | 1 0 0 | 6 6 10 | 136 17 8 | 479 | 188 | 667 | – | 73 | – | – | – |
| | | 8 | 8 | – | – | 176 13 10 | 80 10 0 | 7 19 0 | 800 0 0 | – | 68 1 0 | 7 0 0 | 42 7 11 | 1182 11 9 | 3,131 | 2,135 | 5,266 | – | 1,324 | 2 | – | – |
| COUNTY OF ARMAGH. | | | | | | | | | | | | | | | | | | | | | | |
| ARMAGH, . | 1. Armagh, . | 1 | 1 | – | 1 | 17 7 10 | 15 0 0 | 3 3 6 | 150 0 0 | – | 13 3 0 | 2 0 0 | 61 15 9 | 261 10 1 | 1,514 | 672 | 2,186 | 3 | 250 | 3 | – | – |
| | 2. Blackwatertown | 2 | 1 | – | 1 | 41 9 2 | 14 10 0 | 1 13 0 | 141 0 0 | – | 4 14 0 | – | 11 15 0 | 215 1 8 | 413 | 111 | 524 | – | 93 | – | – | – |
| | 3. Caledon, . | 1 | 1 | – | – | 18 17 0 | 7 0 0 | 1 3 6 | 60 0 0 | – | 1 5 0 | – | 0 10 0 | 88 15 6 | 197 | 93 | 290 | – | 27 | – | – | – |
| | 4. Keady, . . | 1 | 1 | – | – | 25 14 9 | 7 0 0 | 1 18 5 | 128 8 0 | – | 17 6 0 | 2 0 0 | 3 0 0 | 185 7 2 | 582 | 248 | 830 | – | 330 | 1 | – | – |
| | 5. Loughgall, . | 1 | 1 | – | 1 | 56 2 6 | 6 0 0 | 1 11 5 | 120 0 0 | – | 10 5 0 | 3 0 0 | 24 0 3 | 230 19 2 | 446 | 292 | 738 | – | 188 | 1 | – | – |
| | 6. Markethill, . | 1 | 1 | – | 1 | 23 7 4 | 9 0 0 | 1 18 5 | 133 12 0 | – | 10 8 0 | 4 5 6 | 10 0 0 | 191 11 5 | 500 | 358 | 858 | – | 236 | – | – | – |
| | 7. Richhill, . | 1 | 1 | – | – | 24 12 2 | 6 0 0 | 1 8 5 | 120 0 0 | – | 6 2 0 | – | 17 6 2 | 175 8 9 | 668 | 251 | 919 | – | 121 | – | – | – |
| | 8. Tynan, . . | 1 | 1 | – | – | 79 9 5 | 8 10 0 | 1 13 6 | 164 18 1 | – | 4 15 0 | 1 0 0 | 7 12 9 | 267 18 9 | 308 | 151 | 459 | – | 96 | – | – | – |
| | | 9 | 8 | – | 4 | 287 0 2 | 73 0 0 | 13 10 8 | 1016 18 1 | – | 67 18 0 | 12 5 8 | 135 19 11 | 1606 12 6 | 4,558 | 2,206 | 6,764 | 3 | 1,352 | 5 | – | – |
| LURGAN, . | 1. Aghalee, . | 1 | 1 | – | – | 25 17 9 | 8 0 0 | 2 18 2 | 100 0 0 | – | 4 15 0 | 1 0 0 | 3 10 8 | 145 19 7 | 391 | 198 | 589 | 1 | 88 | – | – | – |
| | 2. Lurgan, . | 2 | 2 | – | – | 111 2 10 | 20 0 0 | 8 2 5 | 240 0 0 | – | 17 5 0 | – | 14 12 6 | 411 2 9 | 1,833 | 1,373 | 3,206 | – | 331 | 3 | – | – |
| | 3. Moira, . . | 1 | 1 | – | – | 29 5 2 | 8 0 0 | 4 5 8 | 137 0 0 | – | 7 1 0 | 4 0 0 | 4 15 1 | 194 6 11 | 621 | 301 | 922 | – | 129 | – | – | – |
| | 4. Portadown, . | 1 | 1 | – | 1 | 43 7 2 | 11 0 0 | 8 7 8 | 150 0 0 | – | 18 9 0 | 2 0 0 | 35 2 10 | 267 19 8 | 1,506 | 840 | 2,346 | – | 392 | 2 | – | – |
| | 5. Tartaraghan, | 1 | 1 | – | – | 17 4 6 | 10 0 0 | 3 17 9 | 100 0 0 | – | 12 5 0 | 4 0 0 | 9 1 6 | 156 8 9 | 596 | 296 | 892 | 4 | 372 | 2 | – | – |
| | 6. Waringstown, | 1 | 1 | – | – | 31 13 1 | 12 0 0 | 2 18 2 | 100 0 0 | – | 7 14 0 | 6 0 0 | 1 14 6 | 161 18 9 | 630 | 496 | 1,126 | 1 | 166 | 3 | – | – |
| | | 7 | 7 | – | 1 | 258 9 6 | 69 0 0 | 30 9 10 | 827 0 0 | – | 67 0 0 | 17 0 0 | 66 17 1 | 1337 16 5 | 5,627 | 3,504 | 9,131 | 6 | 1,308 | 10 | – | – |

| Union | Dispensary District | Figures |
|---|---|---|
| **County of Cavan** | | |
| Bailieborough, | 1. Bailieborough, | [illegible] |
| | 2. [illegible], | [illegible] |
| | 3. Kingscourt, | [illegible] |
| | 4. Shercock, | [illegible] |
| | 5. [illegible], | [illegible] |
| | Total | [illegible] |
| Bawnboy, | 1. [illegible], | [illegible] |
| | 2. [illegible], | [illegible] |
| | 3. [illegible], | [illegible] |
| | 4. [illegible], | [illegible] |
| | Total | [illegible] |
| Cavan, | 1. Arvagh, | [illegible] |
| | 2. Ballyhaise, | [illegible] |
| | 3. Ballyjamesduff, | [illegible] |
| | 4. Belturbet, | [illegible] |
| | 5. Cavan, | [illegible] |
| | 6. Killeshandra, | [illegible] |
| | 7. Kilnaleck, | [illegible] |
| | 8. Stradone, | [illegible] |
| | Total | [illegible] |
| Cootehill, | 1. Cootehill, | [illegible] |
| | 2. [illegible], | [illegible] |
| | 3. [illegible], | [illegible] |
| | 4. Tullyvin, | [illegible] |
| | Total | [illegible] |
| **County of Donegal** | | |
| Ballyshannon, | 1. Ballintra, | [illegible] |
| | 2. Ballyshannon, | [illegible] |
| | 3. Belleek, | [illegible] |
| | 4. Church Hill, | [illegible] |
| | 5. Kinlough, | [illegible] |
| | Total | [illegible] |

* Bawnboy Union. Ballinamore District.—[illegible] of Midwife appears not yet to have been made.

[continued.

| Name of Union | Names of Dispensary Districts | 3 | 4 | 5 | 6 | 7 | 8 | 9 | 10 | 11 | 12 | 13 | 14 | 15 | 16 | 17 | 18 | 19 | 20 | 21 | 22 | 23 |
|---|---|---|---|---|---|---|---|---|---|---|---|---|---|---|---|---|---|---|---|---|---|---|
| Column 1 | 2 | 3 | 4 | 5 | 6 | 7 | 8 | 9 | 10 | 11 | 12 | 13 | 14 | 15 | 16 | 17 | 18 | 19 | 20 | 21 | 22 | 23 |
| PROVINCE OF ULSTER—continued. County of Donegal—con. | | | | | | £ s. d. | £ s. d. | £ s. d. | £ s. d. | £ s. d. | £ s. | £ s. d. | £ s. d. | £ s. d. | | | | | | | | |
| Donegal, | 1. [illegible] | [illegible] | [illegible] | [illegible] | [illegible] | [illegible] | [illegible] | – | [illegible] | – | [illegible] | [illegible] | [illegible] | [illegible] | [illegible] | [illegible] | [illegible] | [illegible] | [illegible] | [illegible] | – | – |
| | 2. Dunkineely, | [illegible] | [illegible] | [illegible] | [illegible] | [illegible] | [illegible] | – | [illegible] | – | [illegible] | [illegible] | [illegible] | [illegible] | [illegible] | [illegible] | [illegible] | [illegible] | [illegible] | [illegible] | – | – |
| | 3. Laghy, | [illegible] | [illegible] | [illegible] | [illegible] | [illegible] | [illegible] | – | [illegible] | – | [illegible] | [illegible] | [illegible] | [illegible] | [illegible] | [illegible] | [illegible] | [illegible] | [illegible] | [illegible] | – | – |
| | 4. Mountcharles, | [illegible] | [illegible] | [illegible] | [illegible] | [illegible] | [illegible] | – | [illegible] | – | [illegible] | [illegible] | [illegible] | [illegible] | [illegible] | [illegible] | [illegible] | [illegible] | [illegible] | [illegible] | – | – |
| | 5. Pettigo, | [illegible] | [illegible] | [illegible] | [illegible] | [illegible] | [illegible] | – | [illegible] | – | [illegible] | [illegible] | [illegible] | [illegible] | [illegible] | [illegible] | [illegible] | [illegible] | [illegible] | [illegible] | – | – |
| | Total | [illegible] | [illegible] | | [illegible] | [illegible] | [illegible] | – | [illegible] | – | [illegible] | [illegible] | [illegible] | [illegible] | [illegible] | [illegible] | [illegible] | [illegible] | [illegible] | [illegible] | – | – |
| Dunfanaghy, | 1. Creeslough, | [illegible] | [illegible] | – | – | [illegible] | [illegible] | [illegible] | [illegible] | – | [illegible] | [illegible] | [illegible] | [illegible] | [illegible] | [illegible] | [illegible] | – | [illegible] | [illegible] | – | – |
| | 2. Dunfanaghy, | [illegible] | [illegible] | – | – | [illegible] | [illegible] | [illegible] | [illegible] | – | [illegible] | – | [illegible] | [illegible] | [illegible] | [illegible] | [illegible] | – | [illegible] | – | – | – |
| | Total | [illegible] | [illegible] | | – | [illegible] | [illegible] | [illegible] | [illegible] | – | [illegible] | [illegible] | [illegible] | [illegible] | [illegible] | [illegible] | [illegible] | – | [illegible] | [illegible] | – | – |
| Glenties, | 1. Ardara, | [illegible] | [illegible] | – | [illegible] | [illegible] | [illegible] | [illegible] | [illegible] | – | [illegible] | – | [illegible] | [illegible] | [illegible] | [illegible] | [illegible] | [illegible] | [illegible] | – | – | – |
| | 2. Carrick, | [illegible] | [illegible] | – | – | [illegible] | [illegible] | [illegible] | [illegible] | – | [illegible] | – | [illegible] | [illegible] | [illegible] | [illegible] | [illegible] | [illegible] | [illegible] | [illegible] | – | – |
| | 3. [illegible], | [illegible] | [illegible] | – | – | [illegible] | [illegible] | [illegible] | [illegible] | – | – | – | [illegible] | [illegible] | [illegible] | [illegible] | [illegible] | – | [illegible] | – | – | – |
| | 4. Dungloe, | [illegible] | [illegible] | – | – | [illegible] | [illegible] | [illegible] | [illegible] | – | [illegible] | – | [illegible] | [illegible] | [illegible] | [illegible] | [illegible] | [illegible] | [illegible] | [illegible] | – | – |
| | 5. Glenties, | [illegible] | [illegible] | – | – | [illegible] | [illegible] | [illegible] | [illegible] | – | [illegible] | – | – | [illegible] | [illegible] | [illegible] | [illegible] | – | [illegible] | – | – | – |
| | 6. Killybegs, | [illegible] | [illegible] | – | [illegible] | [illegible] | [illegible] | [illegible] | [illegible] | – | [illegible] | – | [illegible] | [illegible] | [illegible] | [illegible] | [illegible] | [illegible] | [illegible] | [illegible] | – | – |
| | Total | [illegible] | [illegible] | – | [illegible] | [illegible] | [illegible] | [illegible] | [illegible] | – | [illegible] | | [illegible] | [illegible] | [illegible] | [illegible] | [illegible] | [illegible] | [illegible] | [illegible] | – | – |
| Inishowen, | 1. Buncrana, | [illegible] | [illegible] | – | [illegible] | [illegible] | [illegible] | [illegible] | [illegible] | – | [illegible] | [illegible] | [illegible] | [illegible] | [illegible] | [illegible] | [illegible] | – | [illegible] | [illegible] | – | – |
| | 2. Carndonagh, | [illegible] | [illegible] | – | [illegible] | [illegible] | [illegible] | [illegible] | [illegible] | – | [illegible] | – | [illegible] | [illegible] | [illegible] | [illegible] | [illegible] | [illegible] | [illegible] | [illegible] | – | – |
| | 3. Clonmany, | [illegible] | [illegible] | – | [illegible] | [illegible] | [illegible] | [illegible] | [illegible] | – | [illegible] | – | [illegible] | [illegible] | [illegible] | [illegible] | [illegible] | [illegible] | [illegible] | [illegible] | – | – |
| | 4. Malin, | [illegible] | [illegible] | – | – | [illegible] | [illegible] | [illegible] | [illegible] | – | [illegible] | [illegible] | [illegible] | [illegible] | [illegible] | [illegible] | [illegible] | [illegible] | [illegible] | [illegible] | – | – |
| | 5. Moville, | [illegible] | [illegible] | – | [illegible] | [illegible] | [illegible] | [illegible] | [illegible] | – | [illegible] | – | [illegible] | [illegible] | [illegible] | [illegible] | [illegible] | – | [illegible] | [illegible] | – | – |
| | Total | [illegible] | [illegible] | – | [illegible] | [illegible] | [illegible] | [illegible] | [illegible] | – | [illegible] | [illegible] | [illegible] | [illegible] | 1,776 | [illegible] | [illegible] | [illegible] | [illegible] | [illegible] | – | – |

| Union | Dispensary District | Figures |
| --- | --- | --- |
| Letterkenny, | 1. Church Hill | [illegible] |
| | 2. Letterkenny | [illegible] |
| | 3. [illegible] | [illegible] |
| | Total | [illegible] |
| Milford, | 1. [illegible] | [illegible] |
| | 2. [illegible] and Milford | [illegible] |
| | 3. Rathmullan | [illegible] |
| | 4. Rathmelton | [illegible] |
| | 5. [illegible] | [illegible] |
| | Total | [illegible] |
| Stranorlar, | 1. [illegible] | [illegible] |
| | 2. [illegible] | [illegible] |
| | 3. [illegible] | [illegible] |
| | Total | [illegible] |
| County of Down. Banbridge, | 1. Ballyward, | [illegible] |
| | 2. Banbridge, | [illegible] |
| | 3. [illegible] | [illegible] |
| | 4. [illegible] | [illegible] |
| | 5. Loughbrickland | [illegible] |
| | 6. [illegible] | [illegible] |
| | Total | [illegible] |
| Downpatrick, | 1. Ballynahinch, | [illegible] |
| | 2. Clough | [illegible] |
| | 3. [illegible] | [illegible] |
| | 4. [illegible] | [illegible] |
| | 5. [illegible] | [illegible] |
| | 6. [illegible] | [illegible] |
| | 7. [illegible] | [illegible] |
| | 8. [illegible] | [illegible] |
| | Total | [illegible] |
| Kilkeel, | 1. [illegible] | [illegible] |
| | 2. Kilkeel, | [illegible] |
| | 3. Rostrevor, | [illegible] |
| | Total | [illegible] |

* [illegible] Union, [illegible] District.—No appointment of Midwife appears to have been made.
† [illegible] Union, [illegible] District.—No appointment of Midwife appears to have been made.

[continued.

## No. 2.—Dispensary Districts, with the Expenses, and Amount of Medical Relief afforded, in the several Unions—*continued*.

| Name of Union. | Names of Dispensary Districts. | No. of Dispensaries, or Dispensary Stations, in each District. | No. of Officers authorised by Sealed Order: Med. Officers. | No. of Officers authorised by Sealed Order: Apothecaries. | No. of Officers authorised by Sealed Order: Midwives. | Expenses of Year ended 29th September, 1875: Medicines and Medical Appliances. | Rent of Dispensary Buildings. | Books, Forms, Stationery, and Printing. | Salaries: Medical Officers. | Salaries: Apothecaries. | Vaccination Expenses: Amnt. of Fees paid to Medical Officers. | Vaccination Expenses: Other Expenses in carrying out the Vaccination Act. | Fuel and Attendance, Midwives' Salaries, and any Incidental Expenses not included in the foregoing Columns. | Total Expenditure for each Dispensary District for Year ended 29th Sept., 1875. | Medical Relief afforded in Year ended 30th September, 1875: Number of New Cases attended and registered during the year: Dispensary Tickets. | Visiting Tickets. | Total. | No. of Tickets for Medical Relief cancelled by Dispensary Committee during the year. | No. of Cases of Vaccination during the year. | No. of Dangerous Lunatics certified. | No. of Days on which Attendance given at Bridewell or House of Correction, under s. 15. | No. of Patients attended in Bridewell or House of Correction during year. |
|---|---|---|---|---|---|---|---|---|---|---|---|---|---|---|---|---|---|---|---|---|---|---|
| Column 1. | 2. | 3. | 4. | 5. | 6. | 7. | 8. | 9. | 10. | 11. | 12. | 13. | 14. | 15. | 16. | 17. | 18. | 19. | 20. | 21. | 22. | 23. |
| PROVINCE OF ULSTER—*continued*. | | | | | | £ s. d. | £ s. d. | £ s. d. | £ s. d. | £ s. d. | £ s. | £ s. d. | £ s. d. | £ s. d. | | | | | | | | |
| COUNTY OF DOWN—*con*. | | | | | | | | | | | | | | | | | | | | | | |
| NEWRY, . | 1. Donaghmore, | 1 | 1 | – | – | 16 3 9 | 10 0 0 | 1 15 6 | 120 0 0 | – | 4 10 0 | 1 0 0 | – | 163 9 3 | 342 | 110 | 452 | – | 77 | – | – | – |
| | 2. Forkhill, . | 1 | 1 | – | – | 23 16 11 | 8 10 0 | 1 5 6 | 120 0 0 | – | 5 16 0 | – | 3 19 6 | 163 7 11 | 233 | 125 | 358 | – | 123 | 1 | – | – |
| | 3. Meigh, . . | 1 | 1 | – | – | 21 11 7 | 6 0 0 | 1 10 6 | 120 0 0 | – | 10 1 0 | – | 6 0 0 | 167 3 1 | 378 | 314 | 692 | – | 178 | – | – | – |
| | 4. Mountnorris, | 2 | 1 | – | – | 7 1 8 | 16 0 0 | 1 14 10 | 120 0 0 | – | 5 0 0 | 0 8 0 | 7 4 7 | 157 9 1 | 232 | 108 | 340 | – | 110 | – | – | – |
| | 5. Mullaghglass, | 1 | 1 | – | 1 | 16 0 10 | 10 0 0 | 1 5 6 | 120 0 0 | – | 10 13 0 | – | 16 10 6 | 173 9 10 | 471 | 351 | 822 | – | 252 | 2 | – | – |
| | 6. Newry, . . | 1 | 2 | – | – | 60 9 0 | 16 0 0 | 3 12 4 | 240 0 0 | – | 21 7 0 | – | 15 5 5 | 356 6 9 | 1,059 | 623 | 1,682 | – | 435 | 4 | 6 | 6 |
| | 7. Pointzpass, . | 1 | 1 | – | – | 18 12 6 | 8 0 0 | 1 5 6 | 120 0 0 | – | 3 1 0 | – | – | 160 19 0 | 382 | 192 | 574 | – | 58 | – | – | – |
| | 8. Rathfriland, . | 1 | 1 | – | – | 21 3 0 | 10 10 0 | 1 13 0 | 120 0 0 | – | 14 9 0 | 0 16 0 | 6 7 4 | 163 18 1 | 231 | 271 | 502 | – | 341 | 2 | – | – |
| | 9. Warrenpoint, | 2 | 1 | – | 1 | 18 4 6 | 21 5 6 | 1 5 6 | 120 0 0 | – | 6 15 0 | – | 20 0 0 | 187 10 6 | 287 | 237 | 524 | 5 | 68 | – | – | – |
| | | 11 | 10 | – | 2 | 202 17 6 | 108 5 6 | 15 7 2 | 1,200 0 0 | – | 81 13 0 | 2 4 0 | 74 7 4 | 1,693 13 6 | 3,615 | 2,531 | 6,146 | 5 | 1,642 | 9 | 6 | 6 |
| NEWTOWNARDS, . | 1. Bangor, . | 1 | 1 | – | – | 73 16 2 | 14 0 0 | 0 16 0 | 110 0 0 | – | 7 0 0 | – | 5 2 6 | 210 14 8 | 1,397 | 336 | 1,733 | – | 117 | – | – | – |
| | 2. Comber, . | 1 | 1 | – | – | 35 0 10 | 8 0 0 | 0 19 1 | 100 0 0 | – | 9 18 0 | 1 0 0 | 5 13 4 | 160 11 10 | 616 | 324 | 940 | – | 166 | – | – | – |
| | 3. Donaghadee, | 1 | 1 | – | – | 20 6 0 | 7 0 0 | 1 3 6 | 100 0 0 | – | 8 6 0 | 0 13 0 | 4 9 8 | 141 18 2 | 477 | 324 | 801 | 1 | 148 | 2 | – | – |
| | 4. Grey Abbey, . | 3 | 1 | – | – | 62 13 10 | 9 0 0 | 4 10 10 | 110 0 0 | – | 4 0 0 | – | 13 8 3 | 203 12 11 | 1,270 | 290 | 1,560 | – | 193 | – | – | – |
| | 5. Kilmood, . | 1 | 1 | – | – | 24 8 10 | 9 10 0 | 0 15 10 | 100 0 0 | – | 8 2 0 | 0 15 0 | 13 14 8 | 165 6 4 | 193 | 308 | 501 | – | 123 | – | – | – |
| | 6. Newtownards, | 1 | 1 | – | – | 98 4 2 | 10 0 0 | 2 13 9 | 150 0 0 | – | 14 12 0 | – | 4 3 11 | 280 13 10 | 2,709 | 1,462 | 4,171 | 3 | 316 | – | – | – |
| | | 8 | 6 | – | – | 314 9 10 | 57 10 0 | 10 19 7 | 670 0 0 | – | 50 18 0 | 2 8 0 | 46 12 4 | 1,152 17 9 | 6,662 | 3,043 | 9,705 | 4 | 1,066 | 2 | – | – |
| COUNTY OF FERMANAGH. | | | | | | | | | | | | | | | | | | | | | | |
| ENNISKILLEN, . | 1. Ely, . . | 1 | 1 | – | – | 24 12 1 | 9 15 0 | 1 0 9 | 100 0 0 | – | 7 5 0 | 0 10 6 | 2 10 0 | 145 13 4 | 235 | 79 | 314 | 5 | 118 | – | – | – |
| | 2. Enniskillen, . | 1 | 1 | – | 1 | 80 10 8 | 14 10 0 | 1 17 8 | 100 0 0 | – | 8 14 0 | 0 10 6 | 35 7 10 | 247 10 3 | 958 | 833 | 1,791 | 12 | 242 | 5 | – | – |
| | 3. Florencecourt | 1 | 1 | – | 1 | 23 0 1 | 10 0 0 | 0 18 3 | 100 0 0 | – | 5 1 0 | 0 10 6 | 24 0 0 | 163 9 10 | 346 | 136 | 482 | – | 129 | – | – | – |
| | 4. Holywell, . | 2 | 1 | – | – | 11 5 10 | 10 10 0 | 1 11 1 | 110 0 0 | – | 14 2 0 | 0 10 6 | 22 4 0 | 170 3 5 | 792 | 249 | 1,041 | – | 241 | – | – | – |
| | 5. Lisbellaw, . | 1 | 1 | – | – | 3 12 6 | 7 10 0 | 1 4 9 | 90 0 0 | – | 3 1 0 | 0 10 6 | – | 104 18 9 | 102 | 104 | 206 | – | 48 | – | – | – |
| | 6. Tempo, . . | 2 | 1 | – | – | 23 18 6 | 13 0 0 | 0 17 7 | 100 0 0 | – | 6 10 0 | 0 10 6 | 2 2 0 | 146 16 7 | 184 | 181 | 365 | – | 134 | 2 | – | – |
| | | 8 | 6 | – | 2 | 172 19 3 | 65 5 0 | 7 10 1 | 600 0 0 | – | 43 13 0 | 3 3 0 | 86 3 10 | 978 14 2 | 2,617 | 1,582 | 4,199 | 17 | 912 | 7 | – | – |

| Union | Dispensary District | Returns |
|---|---|---|
| Inishowen, | 1 Clonmany, | [illegible] |
| | 2 Ederney, | [illegible] |
| | 3 Inishowen, | [illegible] |
| | Total | [illegible] |
| Letterkenny, | 1 Breachborough, | [illegible] |
| | 2 Derryveagh, | [illegible] |
| | 3 Letterkenny, | [illegible] |
| | 4 Manorcunningham, | [illegible] |
| | Total | [illegible] |
| County of Londonderry. Coleraine, | 1 Aghadowey, | [illegible] |
| | 2 Articlave, | [illegible] |
| | 3 Bushmills, | [illegible] |
| | 4 Coleraine, | [illegible] |
| | 5 Garvagh, | [illegible] |
| | Total | [illegible] |
| Limavady,† | 1 Ballykelly, | [illegible] |
| | 2 Bellarena, | [illegible] |
| | 3 Dungiven,* | [illegible] |
| | 4 Feeny, | [illegible] |
| | 5 Limavady, | [illegible] |
| | Total | [illegible] |
| Londonderry, | 1 Burt, | [illegible] |
| | 2 City of Londonderry, | [illegible] |
| | 3 Claudy, | [illegible] |
| | 4 Eglinton, | [illegible] |
| | 5 Glendermot, | [illegible] |
| | 6 Killea, | [illegible] |
| | 7 Killea, | [illegible] |
| | Total | [illegible] |

* Limavady Union. Dungiven Dispensary District.—No appointment of Midwife appears to have been made.

† Limavady Union. Limavady Dispensary District.—Name altered from Newtownlimavady.

[Continued.

| Name of Union. | Names of Dispensary Districts. | 3 | 4 | 5 | 6 | Medicines and Medical Appliances. | Rent of Dispensary Buildings. | Books, Forms, Stationery, and Printing. | Salaries: Medical Officers. | Salaries: Apothecaries. | Vaccination Expenses | | 14 | Total Expenditure for Year ended 29th Sept. 1873. | Number of New Cases during the year: Dispensary Tickets. | Visit Tickets. | Total. | 19 | 20 | 21 | 22 | 23 |
|---|---|---|---|---|---|---|---|---|---|---|---|---|---|---|---|---|---|---|---|---|---|---|
| Column 1. | 2. | 3. | 4. | 5. | 6. | 7. | 8. | 9. | 10. | 11. | 12. | 13. | 14. | 15. | 16. | 17. | 18. | 19. | 20. | 21. | 22. | 23. |
| | | | | | | £ s. d. | £ s. d. | £ s. d. | £ s. d. | £ s. d. | £ s. d. | £ s. d. | £ s. d. | £ s. d. | | | | | | | | |
| PROVINCE OF ULSTER—continued. | | | | | | | | | | | | | | | | | | | | | | |
| County of Londonderry—con. | | | | | | | | | | | | | | | | | | | | | | |
| Magherafelt. | 1. [illegible] | [illegible] | [illegible] | — | — | [illegible] | [illegible] | [illegible] | [illegible] | — | [illegible] | [illegible] | [illegible] | [illegible] | [illegible] | [illegible] | [illegible] | [illegible] | [illegible] | [illegible] | — | — |
| | 2. Draperstown, | [illegible] | [illegible] | — | — | [illegible] | [illegible] | [illegible] | [illegible] | — | [illegible] | [illegible] | [illegible] | [illegible] | [illegible] | [illegible] | [illegible] | [illegible] | [illegible] | [illegible] | — | — |
| | 3. Maghera, | [illegible] | [illegible] | — | — | [illegible] | [illegible] | [illegible] | [illegible] | — | [illegible] | [illegible] | [illegible] | [illegible] | [illegible] | [illegible] | [illegible] | [illegible] | [illegible] | [illegible] | — | — |
| | 4. Magherafelt, | [illegible] | [illegible] | — | — | [illegible] | [illegible] | [illegible] | [illegible] | — | [illegible] | [illegible] | [illegible] | [illegible] | [illegible] | [illegible] | [illegible] | [illegible] | [illegible] | [illegible] | [illegible] | [illegible] |
| | 5. Moneymore, | [illegible] | [illegible] | — | — | [illegible] | [illegible] | [illegible] | [illegible] | — | [illegible] | [illegible] | [illegible] | [illegible] | [illegible] | [illegible] | [illegible] | [illegible] | [illegible] | [illegible] | — | — |
| | | [illegible] | [illegible] | — | — | [illegible] | [illegible] | [illegible] | [illegible] | — | [illegible] | [illegible] | [illegible] | [illegible] | [illegible] | [illegible] | [illegible] | [illegible] | [illegible] | [illegible] | [illegible] | [illegible] |
| County of Monaghan. | | | | | | | | | | | | | | | | | | | | | | |
| Carrickmacross. | 1. Carrickmacross, | [illegible] | [illegible] | — | [illegible] | [illegible] | [illegible] | [illegible] | [illegible] | — | [illegible] | [illegible] | [illegible] | [illegible] | [illegible] | [illegible] | [illegible] | [illegible] | [illegible] | [illegible] | — | — |
| | 2. Donaghmoyne, | [illegible] | [illegible] | — | [illegible] | [illegible] | [illegible] | [illegible] | [illegible] | — | [illegible] | [illegible] | [illegible] | [illegible] | [illegible] | [illegible] | [illegible] | [illegible] | [illegible] | [illegible] | — | — |
| | 3. [illegible] | [illegible] | [illegible] | — | [illegible] | [illegible] | [illegible] | [illegible] | [illegible] | — | [illegible] | [illegible] | [illegible] | [illegible] | [illegible] | [illegible] | [illegible] | — | [illegible] | — | — | — |
| | | [illegible] | [illegible] | | [illegible] | [illegible] | [illegible] | [illegible] | [illegible] | — | [illegible] | [illegible] | [illegible] | [illegible] | [illegible] | [illegible] | [illegible] | [illegible] | [illegible] | [illegible] | — | — |
| Castleblayney. | 1. Ballybay, | [illegible] | [illegible] | | [illegible] | [illegible] | [illegible] | [illegible] | [illegible] | — | [illegible] | — | [illegible] | [illegible] | [illegible] | [illegible] | [illegible] | [illegible] | [illegible] | | — | — |
| | 2. Castleblayney, | [illegible] | [illegible] | — | [illegible] | [illegible] | [illegible] | [illegible] | [illegible] | — | [illegible] | [illegible] | [illegible] | [illegible] | [illegible] | [illegible] | [illegible] | [illegible] | [illegible] | [illegible] | [illegible] | [illegible] |
| | 3. [illegible] | [illegible] | [illegible] | — | [illegible] | [illegible] | [illegible] | [illegible] | [illegible] | — | [illegible] | — | [illegible] | [illegible] | [illegible] | [illegible] | [illegible] | — | [illegible] | — | | — |
| | 4. Newtownhamilton, | [illegible] | [illegible] | — | — | [illegible] | [illegible] | [illegible] | [illegible] | — | [illegible] | [illegible] | [illegible] | [illegible] | [illegible] | [illegible] | [illegible] | [illegible] | [illegible] | [illegible] | — | — |
| | | [illegible] | [illegible] | | [illegible] | [illegible] | [illegible] | [illegible] | [illegible] | — | [illegible] | [illegible] | [illegible] | [illegible] | [illegible] | [illegible] | [illegible] | [illegible] | [illegible] | [illegible] | [illegible] | [illegible] |
| Clones. | 1. Clones, | [illegible] | [illegible] | — | — | [illegible] | [illegible] | [illegible] | [illegible] | — | [illegible] | [illegible] | [illegible] | [illegible] | [illegible] | [illegible] | [illegible] | — | [illegible] | [illegible] | [illegible] | [illegible] |
| | 2. [illegible] | [illegible] | [illegible] | — | — | [illegible] | [illegible] | [illegible] | [illegible] | — | [illegible] | [illegible] | [illegible] | [illegible] | [illegible] | [illegible] | [illegible] | — | [illegible] | — | — | — |
| | 3. [illegible] | [illegible] | [illegible] | — | — | [illegible] | [illegible] | [illegible] | [illegible] | — | [illegible] | [illegible] | — | [illegible] | [illegible] | [illegible] | [illegible] | — | [illegible] | — | — | — |
| | | [illegible] | [illegible] | — | — | [illegible] | [illegible] | [illegible] | [illegible] | — | [illegible] | [illegible] | [illegible] | [illegible] | [illegible] | [illegible] | [illegible] | — | [illegible] | [illegible] | [illegible] | [illegible] |

| Union | Dispensary District | Data |
|---|---|---|
| MONAGHAN, | 1. Castleshane, | [illegible] |
| | 2. Glaslough, | [illegible] |
| | 3. Emyvale, | [illegible] |
| | 4. Monaghan, | [illegible] |
| | 5. Scotstown, | [illegible] |
| | | [illegible] |
| COUNTY OF TYRONE. CASTLEDERG,† | 1. Castlederg and Killeter, | [illegible] |
| | 2. Drumquin, | [illegible] |
| | | [illegible] |
| CLOGHER, | 1. Augher, | [illegible] |
| | 2. Ballygawley, | [illegible] |
| | 3. Clogher, | [illegible] |
| | 4. Fivemiletown, | [illegible] |
| | | [illegible] |
| COOKSTOWN, | 1. Coagh, | [illegible] |
| | 2. Cookstown, | [illegible] |
| | 3. Pomeroy, | [illegible] |
| | 4. Stewartstown, | [illegible] |
| | | [illegible] |
| DUNGANNON, | 1. Ballygawley, | [illegible] |
| | 2. Benburb, | [illegible] |
| | 3. Clonavrilly, | [illegible] |
| | 4. Coalisland, | [illegible] |
| | 5. Dungannon, | [illegible] |
| | | [illegible] |
| GORTIN,‡ | 1. Gortin, | [illegible] |
| | 2. Plumb Bridge, | [illegible] |
| | | [illegible] |

* Castleblayney Union.—Midwives—One person acts for the three Districts.
† Castlederg Union. Castlederg District.—No appointment of Midwife appears to have been made.
‡ Gortin Union. Gortin Dispensary District.—No appointment of Midwife appears to have been made.

[continued.

No. 2.—Dispensary Districts, with the Expenses, and Amount of Medical Relief afforded, in the several Unions—continued.

| Name of Union | Names of Dispensary Districts | 3 | 4a | 4b | 5 | Medicines and Medical Appliances (7) | Rent of Dispensary Buildings (8) | Books, Forms, Stationery and Printing (9) | Salaries: Medical Officers (10) | Salaries: Apothecaries (11) | Vaccination Expenses (12) | Vaccination Expenses (13) | 14 | Total Expenditure for each Dispensary District (15) | Dispensary Tickets (16) | Visiting Tickets (17) | Total (18) | 19 | 20 | 21 | 22 | 23 |
|---|---|---|---|---|---|---|---|---|---|---|---|---|---|---|---|---|---|---|---|---|---|---|
| Column 1 | 2 | 3 | 4a | 4b | 5 | 7 | 8 | 9 | 10 | 11 | 12 | 13 | 14 | 15 | 16 | 17 | 18 | 19 | 20 | 21 | 22 | 23 |
| PROVINCE OF ULSTER—continued. County of Tyrone—con. | | | | | | £ s. d. | £ s. d. | £ s. d. | £ s. d. | £ s. d. | £ s. d. | £ s. d. | £ s. d. | £ s. d. | | | | | | | | |
| Omagh, | 1. [illegible] | [illegible] | [illegible] | – | [illegible] | [illegible] | [illegible] | [illegible] | [illegible] | – | [illegible] | [illegible] | [illegible] | [illegible] | [illegible] | [illegible] | [illegible] | – | [illegible] | [illegible] | – | – |
| | 2. Drumquin, | [illegible] | [illegible] | – | [illegible] | [illegible] | [illegible] | [illegible] | [illegible] | – | [illegible] | [illegible] | [illegible] | [illegible] | [illegible] | [illegible] | [illegible] | – | 77 | [illegible] | – | – |
| | 3. Fintona, | [illegible] | [illegible] | – | [illegible] | [illegible] | [illegible] | [illegible] | [illegible] | | [illegible] | [illegible] | [illegible] | [illegible] | [illegible] | [illegible] | [illegible] | – | [illegible] | [illegible] | – | – |
| | 4. [illegible] | [illegible] | [illegible] | – | [illegible] | [illegible] | [illegible] | [illegible] | [illegible] | – | [illegible] | [illegible] | [illegible] | [illegible] | [illegible] | [illegible] | [illegible] | – | [illegible] | [illegible] | – | – |
| | 5. [illegible] | [illegible] | [illegible] | – | [illegible] | [illegible] | [illegible] | [illegible] | [illegible] | | [illegible] | [illegible] | [illegible] | [illegible] | [illegible] | [illegible] | [illegible] | – | [illegible] | [illegible] | – | – |
| | | 9 | [illegible] | – | 5 | [illegible] | [illegible] | [illegible] | [illegible] | – | [illegible] | [illegible] | [illegible] | [illegible] | [illegible] | [illegible] | [illegible] | – | [illegible] | [illegible] | – | – |
| Strabane, | 1. Castle Finn, | [illegible] | [illegible] | – | [illegible] | [illegible] | [illegible] | [illegible] | [illegible] | – | – | [illegible] | [illegible] | [illegible] | [illegible] | [illegible] | [illegible] | – | [illegible] | [illegible] | – | – |
| | 2. [illegible] | [illegible] | [illegible] | – | [illegible] | [illegible] | [illegible] | [illegible] | [illegible] | – | [illegible] | [illegible] | [illegible] | [illegible] | [illegible] | [illegible] | [illegible] | 1 | [illegible] | [illegible] | – | – |
| | 3. Newtown Stewart, | [illegible] | [illegible] | – | [illegible] | [illegible] | [illegible] | [illegible] | [illegible] | – | [illegible] | [illegible] | [illegible] | [illegible] | [illegible] | [illegible] | [illegible] | – | [illegible] | [illegible] | – | – |
| | 4. Raphoe, | [illegible] | [illegible] | – | [illegible] | [illegible] | [illegible] | [illegible] | [illegible] | – | [illegible] | | [illegible] | [illegible] | [illegible] | [illegible] | [illegible] | 1 | [illegible] | [illegible] | – | – |
| | 5. Strabane, | [illegible] | [illegible] | | [illegible] | [illegible] | [illegible] | [illegible] | [illegible] | – | [illegible] | [illegible] | [illegible] | [illegible] | [illegible] | [illegible] | [illegible] | | [illegible] | [illegible] | – | – |
| | | 9 | [illegible] | – | 10 | [illegible] | [illegible] | [illegible] | [illegible] | – | [illegible] | [illegible] | [illegible] | [illegible] | [illegible] | [illegible] | [illegible] | 2 | [illegible] | [illegible] | – | – |
| PROVINCE OF MUNSTER. County of Clare. | | | | | | | | | | | | | | | | | | | | | | |
| Ballyvaghan, | 1. Ballyvaghan, | 2 | 1 | – | – | [illegible] | [illegible] | – | 100 0 0 | – | [illegible] | – | [illegible] | [illegible] | [illegible] | [illegible] | [illegible] | – | [illegible] | 1 | – | – |
| | | 2 | 1 | | – | [illegible] | [illegible] | – | 100 0 0 | – | [illegible] | | [illegible] | [illegible] | [illegible] | [illegible] | [illegible] | – | [illegible] | 1 | – | – |
| Corrofin, | 1. Corrofin, | [illegible] | 1 | – | – | [illegible] | [illegible] | – | [illegible] | – | [illegible] | – | [illegible] | [illegible] | [illegible] | [illegible] | [illegible] | – | [illegible] | 1 | – | – |
| | | [illegible] | [illegible] | – | – | [illegible] | [illegible] | | [illegible] | – | [illegible] | – | [illegible] | [illegible] | [illegible] | [illegible] | [illegible] | – | [illegible] | 1 | – | – |

| Union | Dispensary District | Figures |
|---|---|---|
| Ennis, | 1. [illegible], | [illegible] |
| | 2. Ennis, | [illegible] |
| | 3. [illegible], | [illegible] |
| | 4. Newmarket, | [illegible] |
| | | [illegible] |
| Ennistymon, | 1. Ennistymon, | [illegible] |
| | 2. [illegible], | [illegible] |
| | 3. [illegible], | [illegible] |
| | | [illegible] |
| Killadysert, | 1. Ballynacally, | [illegible] |
| | 2. [illegible], | [illegible] |
| | | [illegible] |
| Kilrush, | 1. Carrigaholt, | [illegible] |
| | 2. [illegible], | [illegible] |
| | 3. Kilkee, | [illegible] |
| | 4. [illegible], | [illegible] |
| | 5. Kilrush, | [illegible] |
| | | [illegible] |
| Scariff, | 1. [illegible], | [illegible] |
| | 2. Feakle, | [illegible] |
| | 3. [illegible], | [illegible] |
| | | [illegible] |
| Tulla, | 1. Killaloe, | [illegible] |
| | 2. Quin, | [illegible] |
| | 3. Tulla, | [illegible] |
| | | [illegible] |
| County of Cork. | | |
| Bandon, | 1. Bandon, | [illegible] |
| | 2. Innishannon, | [illegible] |
| | 3. [illegible], | [illegible] |
| | 4. [illegible], | [illegible] |
| | 5. Templemartin, | [illegible] |
| | | [illegible] |

* [illegible] Union [illegible] District.—No appointment of Midwife appears to have been made.
† Ennis Union Ennis Dispensary District.—No appointment of Midwife appears to have been made.
‡ Kilrush Union Kilrush District.—No appointment of Midwife appears to have been made.
§ Tulla Union Killaloe District.—No appointment of Midwife appears to have been made.

[continued.

No 5.—Dispensary Districts, with the Expenses, and Amount of Medical Relief afforded, in the several Unions—continued.

| Name of Union | Names of Dispensary Districts | No. of ... | No. of Officers appointed by Sealed Order: Med. Officers | Apothecaries | Midwives | Expenses of Year ended ... September, 1874: Medicines and Medical Appliances | Rent of Dispensary Buildings | Books, Forms, Stationery, and Printing | Salaries: Medical Officers | Salaries: Apothecaries | Vaccination Expenses | Vaccination Expenses | ... | Total Expenditure ... | Medical Relief afforded in Year ended ... September, 1875: Dispensary Tickets | Visiting Tickets | Total | ... | ... | ... | ... | ... |
|---|---|---|---|---|---|---|---|---|---|---|---|---|---|---|---|---|---|---|---|---|---|---|
| Column 1. | 2. | 3. | 4. | 5. | 6. | 7. | 8. | 9. | 10. | 11. | 12. | 13. | 14. | 15. | 16. | 17. | 18. | 19. | 20. | 21. | 22. | 23. |
| PROVINCE OF MUNSTER—continued. | | | | | | £ s. d. | £ s. d. | £ s. d. | £ s. d. | £ s. d. | £ s. d. | £ s. d. | £ s. d. | £ s. d. | | | | | | | | |
| County of Cork—con. | | | | | | | | | | | | | | | | | | | | | | |
| Bantry, | 1 Bantry, | 1 | 1 | | – | [illegible] | | [illegible] | [illegible] | – | [illegible] | [illegible] | [illegible] | [illegible] | [illegible] | [illegible] | [illegible] | – | [illegible] | – | 3 | 3 |
| | 2 Durrus and Kilcrohane, | 1 | 1 | – | – | [illegible] | – | [illegible] | [illegible] | – | [illegible] | – | [illegible] | [illegible] | [illegible] | [illegible] | [illegible] | – | [illegible] | | – | – |
| | 3 Glengarriff, | 1 | 1 | – | – | [illegible] | [illegible] | [illegible] | [illegible] | | [illegible] | – | [illegible] | [illegible] | [illegible] | [illegible] | [illegible] | – | [illegible] | 1 | – | – |
| | | 3 | 3 | – | – | [illegible] | [illegible] | [illegible] | [illegible] | – | [illegible] | [illegible] | [illegible] | [illegible] | [illegible] | [illegible] | [illegible] | – | [illegible] | 1 | 3 | 3 |
| Castletown, | 1 Castletown, | [illegible] | [illegible] | – | – | [illegible] | [illegible] | | [illegible] | – | [illegible] | – | [illegible] | [illegible] | [illegible] | [illegible] | [illegible] | – | [illegible] | [illegible] | – | – |
| | 2 Kilcatherine, | [illegible] | [illegible] | – | – | [illegible] | [illegible] | – | [illegible] | – | [illegible] | – | [illegible] | [illegible] | [illegible] | [illegible] | [illegible] | – | [illegible] | – | – | – |
| | | [illegible] | [illegible] | – | – | [illegible] | [illegible] | | [illegible] | – | [illegible] | – | [illegible] | [illegible] | [illegible] | [illegible] | [illegible] | – | [illegible] | [illegible] | – | – |
| Clonakilty, | 1 Clonakilty, | 1 | 1 | – | – | [illegible] | [illegible] | – | [illegible] | – | [illegible] | [illegible] | [illegible] | [illegible] | [illegible] | [illegible] | [illegible] | – | [illegible] | [illegible] | – | – |
| | 2 Rosscarbery, | 1 | 1 | – | – | [illegible] | [illegible] | – | [illegible] | – | [illegible] | [illegible] | [illegible] | [illegible] | [illegible] | [illegible] | [illegible] | – | [illegible] | [illegible] | – | – |
| | 3 Timoleague, | 1 | 1 | – | – | [illegible] | [illegible] | – | [illegible] | – | [illegible] | [illegible] | [illegible] | [illegible] | [illegible] | [illegible] | [illegible] | – | [illegible] | [illegible] | – | – |
| | | 3 | 3 | – | – | [illegible] | [illegible] | – | [illegible] | – | [illegible] | [illegible] | [illegible] | [illegible] | [illegible] | [illegible] | [illegible] | – | [illegible] | [illegible] | – | – |
| Cork, | 1 Ballincollig, | 1 | 1 | – | – | [illegible] | [illegible] | [illegible] | [illegible] | – | [illegible] | – | [illegible] | [illegible] | [illegible] | [illegible] | [illegible] | – | [illegible] | – | – | – |
| | 2 Ballygarvan, | 1 | 1 | – | – | [illegible] | [illegible] | – | [illegible] | – | [illegible] | – | [illegible] | [illegible] | [illegible] | [illegible] | [illegible] | – | [illegible] | – | – | – |
| | 3 Blarney, | 1 | 1 | – | – | [illegible] | [illegible] | – | [illegible] | – | [illegible] | – | [illegible] | [illegible] | [illegible] | [illegible] | [illegible] | – | [illegible] | – | – | – |
| | 4 Carrigaline, | 1 | 1 | – | 1 | [illegible] | [illegible] | [illegible] | [illegible] | – | [illegible] | – | [illegible] | [illegible] | [illegible] | [illegible] | [illegible] | 1 | [illegible] | – | – | – |
| | 5 Carrignavar, | 1 | 1 | – | – | [illegible] | [illegible] | [illegible] | [illegible] | – | [illegible] | – | [illegible] | [illegible] | [illegible] | [illegible] | [illegible] | – | [illegible] | – | – | – |
| | 6 Cork, | [illegible] | [illegible] | [illegible] | – | [illegible] | [illegible] | [illegible] | [illegible] | [illegible] | [illegible] | – | [illegible] | [illegible] | [illegible] | [illegible] | [illegible] | – | [illegible] | [illegible] | – | – |
| | 7 Douglas, | 1 | 1 | – | – | [illegible] | [illegible] | – | [illegible] | – | – | – | [illegible] | [illegible] | [illegible] | [illegible] | [illegible] | – | [illegible] | – | – | – |
| | 8 Dripsey, | 1 | 1 | – | – | [illegible] | [illegible] | – | [illegible] | – | [illegible] | – | [illegible] | [illegible] | [illegible] | [illegible] | [illegible] | [illegible] | [illegible] | – | – | – |
| | 9 Queenstown, | [illegible] | [illegible] | [illegible] | – | [illegible] | [illegible] | [illegible] | [illegible] | [illegible] | [illegible] | – | [illegible] | [illegible] | [illegible] | [illegible] | [illegible] | [illegible] | [illegible] | [illegible] | – | – |
| | 10 Whitechurch, | 1 | 1 | – | – | [illegible] | [illegible] | – | [illegible] | – | [illegible] | – | [illegible] | [illegible] | [illegible] | [illegible] | [illegible] | – | [illegible] | – | – | – |
| | | [illegible] | [illegible] | [illegible] | 1 | [illegible] | [illegible] | [illegible] | [illegible] | [illegible] | [illegible] | – | [illegible] | [illegible] | [illegible] | [illegible] | [illegible] | 21 | [illegible] | [illegible] | – | – |

| Union | Dispensary District | | | | | | | | | | | | | | | | | |
|---|---|---|---|---|---|---|---|---|---|---|---|---|---|---|---|---|---|---|
| [illegible] | [illegible] | [illegible] | [illegible] | [illegible] | [illegible] | [illegible] | [illegible] | [illegible] | [illegible] | [illegible] | [illegible] | [illegible] | [illegible] | [illegible] | [illegible] | [illegible] | [illegible] | [illegible] |
| Fermoy, | [illegible] | [illegible] | [illegible] | [illegible] | [illegible] | [illegible] | [illegible] | [illegible] | [illegible] | [illegible] | [illegible] | [illegible] | [illegible] | [illegible] | [illegible] | [illegible] | [illegible] | [illegible] |
| Kanturk, | [illegible] | [illegible] | [illegible] | [illegible] | [illegible] | [illegible] | [illegible] | [illegible] | [illegible] | [illegible] | [illegible] | [illegible] | [illegible] | [illegible] | [illegible] | [illegible] | [illegible] | [illegible] |
| [illegible] | [illegible] | [illegible] | [illegible] | [illegible] | [illegible] | [illegible] | [illegible] | [illegible] | [illegible] | [illegible] | [illegible] | [illegible] | [illegible] | [illegible] | [illegible] | [illegible] | [illegible] | [illegible] |
| [illegible] | [illegible] | [illegible] | [illegible] | [illegible] | [illegible] | [illegible] | [illegible] | [illegible] | [illegible] | [illegible] | [illegible] | [illegible] | [illegible] | [illegible] | [illegible] | [illegible] | [illegible] | [illegible] |
| Mallow, | [illegible] | [illegible] | [illegible] | [illegible] | [illegible] | [illegible] | [illegible] | [illegible] | [illegible] | [illegible] | [illegible] | [illegible] | [illegible] | [illegible] | [illegible] | [illegible] | [illegible] | [illegible] |

[continued.

| Name of Union. | Names of Dispensary Districts. | 3 | 4 | 5 | 6 | 7 | 8 | 9 | 10 | 11 | 12 | 13 | 14 | 15 | 16 | 17 | 18 | 19 | 20 | 21 | 22 | 23 |
|---|---|---|---|---|---|---|---|---|---|---|---|---|---|---|---|---|---|---|---|---|---|---|
| Column 1 | 2 | 3 | 4 | 5 | 6 | 7 | 8 | 9 | 10 | 11 | 12 | 13 | 14 | 15 | 16 | 17 | 18 | 19 | 20 | 21 | 22 | 23 |
| PROVINCE OF MUNSTER —continued. | | | | | | £ s. d. | £ s. d. | £ s. d. | £ s. d. | £ s. d. | £ s. d. | £ s. d. | £ s. d. | £ s. d. | | | | | | | | |
| County of Cork—con. Midleton, | 1. Aghada, | [illegible] | [illegible] | | - | [illegible] | [illegible] | [illegible] | [illegible] | - | [illegible] | - | [illegible] | [illegible] | [illegible] | [illegible] | [illegible] | - | [illegible] | [illegible] | - | - |
| | 2. Castlemartyr, | [illegible] | [illegible] | - | - | [illegible] | [illegible] | [illegible] | [illegible] | - | [illegible] | - | [illegible] | [illegible] | [illegible] | [illegible] | [illegible] | - | [illegible] | | | - |
| | 3. Cloyne, | [illegible] | [illegible] | - | - | [illegible] | [illegible] | [illegible] | [illegible] | - | [illegible] | - | [illegible] | [illegible] | [illegible] | [illegible] | 711 | 1 | [illegible] | 1 | - | - |
| | 4. Midleton, | [illegible] | [illegible] | - | - | [illegible] | [illegible] | [illegible] | [illegible] | - | [illegible] | - | [illegible] | [illegible] | [illegible] | [illegible] | [illegible] | - | [illegible] | - | 4 | 4 |
| | 5. Whitegate- more, East. | 1 | [illegible] | | - | [illegible] | [illegible] | [illegible] | [illegible] | - | [illegible] | - | [illegible] | [illegible] | [illegible] | [illegible] | [illegible] | | [illegible] | - | - | - |
| | | [illegible] | [illegible] | - | - | [illegible] | [illegible] | [illegible] | [illegible] | - | [illegible] | - | [illegible] | [illegible] | [illegible] | [illegible] | [illegible] | 1 | [illegible] | 3 | 4 | 4 |
| Millstreet | 1. Cullen, | 1 | [illegible] | - | - | [illegible] | [illegible] | [illegible] | [illegible] | - | [illegible] | - | [illegible] | [illegible] | [illegible] | [illegible] | [illegible] | - | [illegible] | - | - | - |
| | 2. Millstreet, | 1 | [illegible] | - | - | [illegible] | [illegible] | [illegible] | [illegible] | - | [illegible] | - | [illegible] | [illegible] | [illegible] | [illegible] | [illegible] | - | [illegible] | 1 | - | - |
| | | [illegible] | [illegible] | | - | [illegible] | [illegible] | [illegible] | [illegible] | - | [illegible] | | [illegible] | [illegible] | [illegible] | [illegible] | [illegible] | - | [illegible] | 1 | - | - |
| Mitchelstown, | 1. [illegible], | [illegible] | [illegible] | - | - | [illegible] | [illegible] | [illegible] | [illegible] | - | [illegible] | [illegible] | [illegible] | [illegible] | [illegible] | [illegible] | [illegible] | - | [illegible] | - | - | - |
| | 2. [illegible], | [illegible] | [illegible] | - | - | [illegible] | [illegible] | [illegible] | [illegible] | - | [illegible] | - | [illegible] | [illegible] | [illegible] | [illegible] | [illegible] | 1 | [illegible] | [illegible] | - | - |
| | 3. Mitchelstown, | [illegible] | [illegible] | - | [illegible] | [illegible] | [illegible] | [illegible] | [illegible] | - | [illegible] | - | [illegible] | [illegible] | [illegible] | [illegible] | [illegible] | - | [illegible] | [illegible] | - | - |
| | | [illegible] | [illegible] | - | 1 | [illegible] | [illegible] | [illegible] | [illegible] | - | [illegible] | [illegible] | [illegible] | [illegible] | [illegible] | [illegible] | [illegible] | 1 | [illegible] | [illegible] | - | - |
| Skibbereen, | 1. Drimoleague, | [illegible] | [illegible] | - | - | [illegible] | [illegible] | [illegible] | [illegible] | - | [illegible] | [illegible] | [illegible] | [illegible] | [illegible] | [illegible] | [illegible] | - | [illegible] | 1 | - | - |
| | 2. Skibbereen, | [illegible] | [illegible] | [illegible] | - | [illegible] | [illegible] | [illegible] | [illegible] | [illegible] | [illegible] | [illegible] | [illegible] | [illegible] | [illegible] | [illegible] | [illegible] | - | [illegible] | 1 | - | - |
| | 3. Tullagh, | [illegible] | [illegible] | - | - | [illegible] | [illegible] | [illegible] | [illegible] | - | [illegible] | [illegible] | [illegible] | [illegible] | [illegible] | [illegible] | [illegible] | [illegible] | [illegible] | 1 | - | - |
| | 4. Union Hosp., | [illegible] | [illegible] | - | - | [illegible] | [illegible] | [illegible] | [illegible] | - | [illegible] | [illegible] | [illegible] | [illegible] | [illegible] | [illegible] | [illegible] | - | [illegible] | [illegible] | - | - |
| | | [illegible] | [illegible] | [illegible] | - | [illegible] | [illegible] | [illegible] | [illegible] | [illegible] | [illegible] | [illegible] | [illegible] | [illegible] | [illegible] | [illegible] | [illegible] | [illegible] | [illegible] | [illegible] | - | - |

[illegible]

* Mitchelstown Union. Mitchelstown District.—Office of Midwife vacant.
† Dingle Union. Dingle and Ventry Districts.—A Midwife authorised for each district, but one acts for both.
‡ [illegible] Union. [illegible] District.—No appointment of Midwife appears to have been made.

No. 2.—Dispensary Districts, with the Expenses, and Amount of Medical Relief afforded, in the several Unions—*continued.*

| Name of Union. | Names of Dispensary Districts. | No. of Dispensaries, or Dispensary Stations, in each District. | No. of Officers authorized by Sealed Order: Med. Officers. | Apothecaries. | Midwives. | Expenses of Year ended 29th September, 1875: Medicines and Medical Appliances. | Rent of Dispensary Buildings. | Books, Forms, Stationery, and Printing. | Salaries: Medical Officers. | Salaries: Apothecaries. | Vaccination Expenses: Amount of Fees paid to Medical Officers. | Other Expenses in carrying out the Vaccination Act. | Fuel and Attendance, Midwives' Salaries, and any Incidental Expenses not included in the foregoing Columns. | Total Expenditure for each Dispensary District for Year ended 29th Sept., 1875. | Medical Relief afforded in Year ended 30th September, 1875: Number of New Cases attended and registered during the year: Dispensary Tickets. | Visiting Tickets. | Total. | No. of Tickets for Medical Relief cancelled by Dispensary Committee during the year. | No. of Cases of Vaccination during the year. | No. of Dangerous Lunatics certified. | No. of Days on which Attendance given at Bridewell or House of Correction, under s. 14. | No. of Patients attended in Bridewell or House of Correction during year. |
|---|---|---|---|---|---|---|---|---|---|---|---|---|---|---|---|---|---|---|---|---|---|---|
| Column 1. | 2. | 3. | 4. | 5. | 6. | 7. | 8. | 9. | 10. | 11. | 12. | 13. | 14. | 15. | 16. | 17. | 18. | 19. | 20. | 21. | 22. | 23. |
| PROVINCE OF MUNSTER —*continued.* | | | | | | £ s. d. | £ s. d. | £ s. d. | £ s. d. | £ s. d. | £ s. d. | £ s. d. | £ s. d. | £ s. d. | | | | | | | | |
| County of Kerry—*con.* | | | | | | | | | | | | | | | | | | | | | | |
| Tralee, | 1. Ardfert, | 2 | 1 | – | – | 34 5 9 | 16 0 0 | 0 10 5 | 100 0 0 | – | 19 3 0 | 3 4 3 | 8 10 0 | 176 13 8 | 335 | 171 | 506 | – | 186 | – | – | – |
| | 2. Brosna, | 3 | 1 | – | – | 16 4 1 | 18 0 0 | 0 5 3 | 100 0 0 | – | 13 18 0 | 3 10 6 | 13 9 2 | 164 5 0 | 848 | 109 | 957 | – | 228 | – | – | – |
| | 3. Castle Island, | 1 | 1 | – | – | 39 12 6 | 4 0 0 | 0 5 3 | 100 0 0 | – | 9 18 0 | 2 0 6 | 12 8 6 | 169 4 9 | 1,465 | 276 | 1,761 | – | 199 | – | – | – |
| | 4. Castlemaine, | 1 | 1 | – | – | 15 3 8 | 10 0 0 | 0 5 3 | 40 0 0 | – | 10 0 0 | 3 4 6 | 7 19 6 | 85 12 11 | 631 | 200 | 831 | – | 128 | 1 | – | – |
| | 5. Kilgobban, | 1 | 1 | – | – | 19 0 3 | 7 0 0 | 0 5 3 | 30 0 0 | – | 1 3 0 | 0 10 6 | 10 19 0 | 68 16 0 | 242 | 46 | 288 | – | 18 | – | – | – |
| | 6. Tralee, | 1 | 2 | – | – | 75 1 9 | 16 0 0 | 1 12 1 | 230 0 0 | – | 21 2 9 | 0 10 6 | 57 17 0 | 402 4 1 | 1,[illegible] | 1,007 | 2,[illegible] | – | 378 | 3 | 4 | 6 |
| | | 9 | 7 | – | – | 199 8 0 | 71 0 0 | 8 3 9 | 600 0 0 | – | 65 2 9 | 13 0 9 | 111 3 2 | 1,055 18 5 | 5,242 | 1,850 | 7,101 | – | 1,137 | 4 | 4 | 6 |
| County of Limerick. | | | | | | | | | | | | | | | | | | | | | | |
| Croom, | 1. Adare, | 2 | 1 | – | – | 18 5 3 | 18 0 0 | 0 0 2 | 120 0 0 | – | 1 16 0 | 0 10 6 | 6 9 9 | 185 7 8 | 477 | 161 | 638 | – | 71 | 2 | – | – |
| | 2. Castletown, | 2 | 1 | – | – | 54 16 3 | 14 0 0 | 1 10 2 | 120 0 0 | – | 9 3 0 | 2 10 6 | 8 2 0 | 210 1 11 | 363 | 185 | 548 | – | 179 | – | – | – |
| | 3. Croom, | 2 | 1 | 1 | – | 64 16 9 | 11 0 0 | 1 13 2 | 120 0 0 | 37 6 8 | 10 15 0 | 5 10 4 | 11 6 2 | 262 8 1 | 880 | 270 | 1,150 | – | 104 | – | – | – |
| | | 6 | 3 | 1 | – | 137 18 3 | 43 0 0 | 3 9 6 | 360 0 0 | 37 6 8 | 21 14 0 | 8 11 4 | 25 17 11 | 657 17 8 | 1,720 | 616 | 2,336 | – | 354 | 2 | – | – |
| Glin, | 1. Shanagolden, | 2 | 1 | – | – | 18 0 10 | 22 0 0 | 0 7 6 | 120 0 0 | – | 7 11 0 | – | 3 14 5 | 171 12 9 | 454 | 160 | 614 | – | 151 | 1 | – | – |
| | 2. Tarbert, | 2 | 2 | – | – | 13 18 2 | 8 0 0 | 1 2 6 | 160 0 0 | – | 14 19 0 | – | 4 5 7 | 202 6 3 | 660 | 507 | 1,167 | 1 | 278 | 1 | – | – |
| | | 4 | 3 | – | – | 31 19 0 | 30 0 0 | 1 10 0 | 280 0 0 | – | 22 10 0 | – | 8 0 0 | 373 19 0 | 1,114 | 667 | 1,781 | 1 | 429 | 2 | – | – |
| Kilmallock. | 1. Bruff, | 1 | 1 | 1 | 1 | 74 18 5 | 8 0 0 | 4 0 2 | 153 15 2 | 35 0 0 | 5 10 0 | 0 18 0 | 30 7 5 | 318 0 2 | 1,205 | 341 | 1,546 | – | 141 | – | 3 | 1 |
| | 2. Bruree, | 1 | 1 | – | – | 13 13 9 | 12 0 0 | 0 13 10 | 115 0 0 | – | 3 17 0 | 2 10 6 | 15 5 11 | 163 1 0 | 1,299 | 161 | 1,460 | – | 86 | – | – | – |
| | 3. Charleville, | 1 | 1 | 1 | – | 15 2 8 | – | 1 14 0 | 125 0 0 | 35 0 0 | 7 4 0 | 1 10 6 | 18 6 7 | 203 17 9 | 1,189 | 224 | 1,413 | – | 151 | 2 | 3 | 1 |
| | 4. Hospital, | 1 | 1 | – | – | 58 6 8 | 5 0 0 | 1 19 1 | 115 0 0 | – | 6 12 0 | 1 10 6 | 9 11 8 | 197 19 6 | 683 | 172 | 855 | – | 149 | 2 | – | – |
| | 5. Kilfinnane, | 1 | 1 | 1 | 1 | 46 17 6 | 9 0 0 | 2 18 6 | 149 9 0 | 36 0 0 | 10 19 0 | 1 0 6 | 37 4 7 | 292 9 1 | 1,765 | 336 | 2,101 | 1 | 240 | 2 | – | – |
| | 6. Kilmallock, | 1 | 1 | – | 1 | 24 3 7 | 6 0 0 | 3 8 0 | 115 0 0 | – | 6 17 0 | 2 5 6 | 43 10 10 | 201 4 11 | 1,162 | 258 | 1,420 | – | 141 | 1 | – | – |
| | | 6 | 6 | 3 | 3 | 233 2 2 | 40 0 0 | 14 13 7 | 773 4 2 | 106 0 0 | 40 10 0 | 9 15 6 | 160 7 0 | 1,376 12 5 | 7,201 | 1,494 | 8,795 | 1 | 908 | 7 | 5 | 2 |

| Union | Dispensary District | Figures |
|---|---|---|
| LIMERICK, | 1. Abbey city, | [illegible] |
| | 2. Bridgetown, | [illegible] |
| | 3. Caherconlish, | [illegible] |
| | 4. City of Limerick, | [illegible] |
| | 5. Glenroe, | [illegible] |
| | 6. Grobunny, | [illegible] |
| | 7. Murroe, | [illegible] |
| | | [illegible] |
| NEWCASTLE, | 1. Abbeyfeale, | [illegible] |
| | 2. Ardagh, | [illegible] |
| | 3. Broadford, | [illegible] |
| | 4. [illegible] | [illegible] |
| | 5. Newcastle, | [illegible] |
| | | [illegible] |
| RATHKEALE, | 1. Askeaton, | [illegible] |
| | 2. Ballingarry, | [illegible] |
| | 3. Rathkeale, | [illegible] |
| | | [illegible] |
| COUNTY OF TIPPERARY. BORRISOKANE, | 1. Borrisokane, | [illegible] |
| | 2. Cloughjordan, | [illegible] |
| | 3. Terryglass, | [illegible] |
| | | [illegible] |
| CARRICK-ON-SUIR, | 1. Carrick-on-Suir, | [illegible] |
| | 2. Garrangibbon, | [illegible] |
| | 3. Fiddown, | [illegible] |
| | 4. Portlaw, | [illegible] |
| | 5. Rathgormuck, | [illegible] |
| | | [illegible] |
| CASHEL, | 1. Cashel, | [illegible] |
| | 2. [illegible] | [illegible] |
| | 3. Killenaule, | [illegible] |
| | 4. Kilpatrick, | [illegible] |
| | 5. [illegible] | [illegible] |
| | | [illegible] |

* Cashel Union; [illegible] and Cashel Districts.—No appointment of Midwife has been made in these Districts. Cashel District—Order authorising the appointment of Midwife rescinded.

No. 2.—Dispensary Districts, with the Expenses, and Amount of Medical Relief afforded, in the several Unions—*continued*.

| Name of Union. | Names of Dispensary Districts. | No. of Dispensaries, or Dispensary Stations, in each District | No. of Officers authorized by Sealed Order: Med. Officers. | Apothecaries. | Midwives. | Expenses of Year ended 29th September, 1875: Medicines and Medical Appliances. | Rent of Dispensary Buildings. | Books, Forms, Stationery, and Printing. | Salaries: Medical Officers. | Salaries: Apothecaries. | Vaccination Expenses: Amnt. of Fees paid to Medical Officers. | Vaccination Expenses: Other Expenses in carrying out the Vaccination Act. | Fuel and Attendance, Midwives' Salaries, and any Incidental Expenses not included in the foregoing Columns. | Total Expenditure for each Dispensary District for Year ended 29th Sept., 1875. | Medical Relief afforded in Year ended 30th September, 1875: Number of New Cases attended and registered during the year: Dispensary Tickets. | Visiting Tickets. | Total. | No. of Tickets for Medical Relief cancelled by Dispensary Committee during the year. | No. of Cases of Vaccination during the year. | No. of Dangerous Lunatics certified. | No. of Days on which Attendance given at Bridewell or House of Correction, under s. 15. | No. of Patients attended in Bridewell or House of Correction during year. |
|---|---|---|---|---|---|---|---|---|---|---|---|---|---|---|---|---|---|---|---|---|---|---|
| Column 1. | 2. | 3. | 4. | 5. | 6. | 7. | 8. | 9. | 10. | 11. | 12. | 13. | 14. | 15. | 16. | 17. | 18. | 19. | 20. | 21. | 22. | 23. |
| | | | | | | £ s. d. | £ s. d. | £ s. d. | £ s. d. | £ s. d. | £ s. d. | £ s. d. | £ s. d. | £ s. d. | | | | | | | | |
| PROVINCE OF MUNSTER—*continued*. | | | | | | | | | | | | | | | | | | | | | | |
| COUNTY OF TIPPERARY—*con.* | | | | | | | | | | | | | | | | | | | | | | |
| CLOGHEEN, | 1. Ardfinnan, | 3 | 1 | - | - | 17 1 9 | 25 0 0 | 0 5 0 | 110 0 0 | - | 7 11 0 | 0 10 0 | 14 7 4 | 174 15 10 | 378 | 168 | 546 | - | 141 | 2 | - | - |
| | 2. Caher, | 1 | 1 | - | - | 13 10 5 | 10 0 0 | 0 10 9 | 120 0 0 | - | 9 4 0 | 1 0 0 | 2 19 4 | 157 4 6 | 810 | 241 | 1,051 | - | 183 | 1 | 5 | 2 |
| | 3. Clogheen, | 2 | 1 | - | *1 | 21 13 9 | 19 0 0 | 0 16 0 | 120 0 0 | - | 7 4 0 | - | 4 7 1 | 173 5 10 | 730 | 167 | 897 | - | 140 | 1 | - | - |
| | | 6 | 3 | - | 1 | 52 10 11 | 54 0 0 | 1 12 6 | 350 0 0 | - | 23 19 0 | 1 10 0 | 21 13 9 | 505 6 9 | 1,918 | 576 | 2,494 | - | 464 | 4 | 5 | 2 |
| CLONMEL, | 1. Ballymacarbry, | 1 | 1 | - | - | 11 5 2 | 4 0 0 | 0 11 8 | 70 0 0 | - | 1 11 0 | 0 10 6 | 5 3 1 | 93 1 5 | 157 | 53 | 210 | - | 60 | - | - | - |
| | 2. Clonmel and St. Mary's, | 1 | 2 | 1 | - | 68 0 2 | - | 3 10 7 | 210 0 0 | 65 0 0 | 7 7 0 | 0 10 6 | 22 6 8 | 366 14 11 | 3,500 | 978 | 4,478 | - | 265 | 6 | - | - |
| | 3. Kilsheelan, | 1 | 1 | - | - | 17 3 10 | 5 0 0 | 1 0 6 | 140 0 0 | - | 4 7 0 | 2 10 6 | 6 3 11 | 170 5 9 | 512 | 250 | 762 | - | 109 | 3 | | |
| | 4. Kiltinan, | 1 | 1 | - | - | 7 6 7 | 8 0 0 | 0 12 5 | 50 0 0 | - | 1 6 0 | 0 10 6 | 4 16 11 | 72 12 5 | 217 | 61 | 278 | 1 | 24 | 1 | - | - |
| | 5. Marlfield, | 2 | 1 | - | - | 4 14 11 | 15 0 0 | 0 13 0 | 140 0 0 | - | - | 0 10 6 | 10 4 10 | 177 3 3 | 316 | 185 | 450 | - | 53 | - | - | - |
| | | 6 | 6 | 1 | - | 98 10 8 | 32 0 0 | 6 8 2 | 610 0 0 | 65 0 0 | 14 11 0 | 4 12 6 | 54 15 5 | 885 17 0 | 4,797 | 1,465 | 6,262 | 1 | 504 | 10 | - | - |
| NENAGH, | 1. Nenagh, | 2 | 2 | - | - | 49 12 11 | 16 0 0 | 1 7 6 | 200 0 0 | - | 11 12 3 | 0 10 6 | 7 17 8 | 287 0 10 | 1,301 | 403 | 1,704 | - | 103 | - | - | - |
| | 2. Newport, | 1 | 1 | - | - | 37 5 9 | 10 0 0 | 0 17 6 | 100 0 0 | - | 8 18 0 | 0 10 6 | 4 0 0 | 161 11 9 | 559 | 201 | 760 | - | 166 | 3 | 20 | 5 |
| | 3. Portroe, | 2 | 1 | - | - | 7 5 7 | 16 0 0 | 0 17 6 | 100 0 0 | - | 6 18 0 | 2 10 6 | 0 7 6 | 133 19 1 | 201 | 129 | 330 | - | 136 | - | - | - |
| | 4. Silvermines, | 1 | 1 | - | - | 54 19 7 | 6 0 0 | 0 16 0 | 100 0 0 | - | 3 14 0 | 2 10 6 | 7 18 5 | 175 19 3 | 347 | 89 | 436 | - | 69 | - | - | - |
| | 5. Toomevara, | 1 | 1 | - | - | 9 7 11 | 10 0 0 | 0 17 6 | 100 0 0 | - | 13 16 0 | 0 10 6 | 6 1 11 | 140 13 10 | 472 | 203 | 675 | 2 | 133 | - | - | - |
| | | 7 | 6 | - | - | 158 11 9 | 58 0 0 | 4 18 9 | 600 0 0 | - | 44 18 3 | 6 12 6 | 26 5 6 | 899 4 9 | 2,880 | 1,025 | 3,905 | 2 | 609 | 3 | 20 | 5 |
| ROSCREA, | 1. Bourney, | 3 | 1 | - | - | 4 9 9 | 15 0 0 | 0 18 7 | 100 0 0 | - | - | 1 1 0 | 3 0 0 | 124 9 4 | 161 | 134 | 295 | - | 54 | - | - | - |
| | 2. Roscrea, | 2 | 2 | - | †1 | 46 14 8 | 5 0 0 | 2 18 7 | 195 18 0 | - | 8 6 0 | 1 1 0 | 28 0 0 | 287 18 3 | 683 | 243 | 926 | - | 170 | 4 | - | - |
| | 3. Shinrone, | 2 | 1 | - | †1 | 43 2 11 | 10 10 0 | 3 12 4 | 120 0 0 | - | 6 12 0 | 1 1 0 | 6 0 0 | 190 18 3 | 410 | 102 | 572 | - | 105 | 1 | - | - |
| | | 7 | 4 | - | 2 | 94 7 4 | 30 10 0 | 7 9 6 | 415 18 0 | - | 14 18 0 | 3 3 0 | 37 0 0 | 603 5 10 | 1,254 | 539 | 1,793 | - | 329 | 5 | - | - |

| Union | District | Returns |
|---|---|---|
| Thurles | 1. Borrisoleigh | [illegible] |
| | 2. Holycross | [illegible] |
| | 3. Littleton | [illegible] |
| | 4. Moyne | [illegible] |
| | 5. Templemore | [illegible] |
| | 6. Thurles | [illegible] |
| | Total | [illegible] |
| Tipperary | 1. Bansha | [illegible] |
| | 2. Cappagh | [illegible] |
| | 3. Emly | [illegible] |
| | 4. Galbally | [illegible] |
| | 5. Oola | [illegible] |
| | 6. Tipperary | [illegible] |
| | Total | [illegible] |
| County of Waterford. Dungarvan | 1. [illegible] | [illegible] |
| | 2. [illegible] | [illegible] |
| | 3. [illegible] | [illegible] |
| | 4. [illegible] | [illegible] |
| | Total | [illegible] |
| Kilmacthomas | 1. Bonmahon | [illegible] |
| | 2. Kilmacthomas | [illegible] |
| | Total | [illegible] |
| Lismore | 1. Ballyduff | [illegible] |
| | 2. Cappoquin | [illegible] |
| | 3. Lismore | [illegible] |
| | 4. Tallow | [illegible] |
| | Total | [illegible] |
| Waterford | 1. [illegible] | [illegible] |
| | 2. [illegible] | [illegible] |
| | 3. Tramore | [illegible] |
| | 4. [illegible] | [illegible] |
| | 5. Waterford | [illegible] |
| | 6. Woodstown | [illegible] |
| | Total | [illegible] |

* Clogheen Union. Clogheen District.—No appointment of Midwife appears to have been made.
† Roscrea Union. [illegible] Dispensary District.—A Midwife appointed to this District in addition to the Medical Officer, by Order dated 3rd September, [illegible].
‡ Thurles Union. Moyne and Templemore Divisions.—No appointment of Midwife appears to have been made. Thurles District.—Office of Apothecary not filled up.
§ Tipperary Union. Cappagh District.—No appointment of Midwife appears to have been made.

No. 3.—Dispensary Districts, with the Expenses, and Amount of Medical Relief afforded, in the several Unions—continued.



| Name of Union. | Names of Dispensary Districts. | [illegible] | No. of [illegible] Sealed Order: [illegible] | [illegible] | [illegible] | Expenses of Year ended 29th September: Medicines and Medical Appliances | Rent of Dispensary [illegible] | Books, Forms, Stationery, and Printing | Salaries: Medical Officers | Salaries: Apothecaries | Vaccination Expenses: [illegible] | Vaccination Expenses: [illegible] | [illegible] | Total Expenditure for Year ended 29th Sept. | Medical Relief afforded in Year ended 29th September: Dispensary Tickets | Visiting Tickets | Total | [illegible] | [illegible] | [illegible] | [illegible] | [illegible] |
|---|---|---|---|---|---|---|---|---|---|---|---|---|---|---|---|---|---|---|---|---|---|---|
| Column 1. | 2. | 3. | 4. | 5. | 6. | 7. | 8. | 9. | 10. | 11. | 12. | 13. | 14. | 15. | 16. | 17. | 18. | 19. | 20. | 21. | 22. | 23. |
| PROVINCE OF LEINSTER. County of Carlow. | | | | | | £ s. d. | £ s. d. | £ s. d. | £ s. d. | £ s. d. | £ s. d. | £ s. d. | £ s. d. | £ s. d. | | | | | | | | |
| Carlow, | 1. Bagenalstown, | [illegible] | [illegible] | [illegible] | [illegible] | [illegible] | [illegible] | [illegible] | [illegible] | [illegible] | [illegible] | [illegible] | [illegible] | [illegible] | [illegible] | [illegible] | [illegible] | [illegible] | [illegible] | [illegible] | [illegible] | [illegible] |
| | 2. Ballickmoyler and Newtown, | [illegible] | [illegible] | [illegible] | [illegible] | [illegible] | [illegible] | [illegible] | [illegible] | [illegible] | [illegible] | [illegible] | [illegible] | [illegible] | [illegible] | [illegible] | [illegible] | [illegible] | [illegible] | [illegible] | [illegible] | [illegible] |
| | 3. Borris, | [illegible] | [illegible] | [illegible] | [illegible] | [illegible] | [illegible] | [illegible] | [illegible] | [illegible] | [illegible] | [illegible] | [illegible] | [illegible] | [illegible] | [illegible] | [illegible] | [illegible] | [illegible] | [illegible] | [illegible] | [illegible] |
| | 4. Carlow, | [illegible] | [illegible] | [illegible] | [illegible] | [illegible] | [illegible] | [illegible] | [illegible] | [illegible] | [illegible] | [illegible] | [illegible] | [illegible] | [illegible] | [illegible] | [illegible] | [illegible] | [illegible] | [illegible] | [illegible] | [illegible] |
| | 5. Fenagh and Myshall, | [illegible] | [illegible] | [illegible] | [illegible] | [illegible] | [illegible] | [illegible] | [illegible] | [illegible] | [illegible] | [illegible] | [illegible] | [illegible] | [illegible] | [illegible] | [illegible] | [illegible] | [illegible] | [illegible] | [illegible] | [illegible] |
| | 6. Leighlinbridge, | [illegible] | [illegible] | [illegible] | [illegible] | [illegible] | [illegible] | [illegible] | [illegible] | [illegible] | [illegible] | [illegible] | [illegible] | [illegible] | [illegible] | [illegible] | [illegible] | [illegible] | [illegible] | [illegible] | [illegible] | [illegible] |
| | 7. Tullow, | [illegible] | [illegible] | [illegible] | [illegible] | [illegible] | [illegible] | [illegible] | [illegible] | [illegible] | [illegible] | [illegible] | [illegible] | [illegible] | [illegible] | [illegible] | [illegible] | [illegible] | [illegible] | [illegible] | [illegible] | [illegible] |
| | | [illegible] | [illegible] | [illegible] | [illegible] | [illegible] | [illegible] | [illegible] | [illegible] | [illegible] | [illegible] | [illegible] | [illegible] | [illegible] | [illegible] | [illegible] | [illegible] | [illegible] | [illegible] | [illegible] | [illegible] | [illegible] |
| County of Dublin. Balrothery, | 1. Balbriggan, | [illegible] | [illegible] | [illegible] | [illegible] | [illegible] | [illegible] | [illegible] | [illegible] | [illegible] | [illegible] | [illegible] | [illegible] | [illegible] | [illegible] | [illegible] | [illegible] | [illegible] | [illegible] | [illegible] | [illegible] | [illegible] |
| | 2. Holmpatrick, | [illegible] | [illegible] | [illegible] | [illegible] | [illegible] | [illegible] | [illegible] | [illegible] | [illegible] | [illegible] | [illegible] | [illegible] | [illegible] | [illegible] | [illegible] | [illegible] | [illegible] | [illegible] | [illegible] | [illegible] | [illegible] |
| | 3. [illegible], | [illegible] | [illegible] | [illegible] | [illegible] | [illegible] | [illegible] | [illegible] | [illegible] | [illegible] | [illegible] | [illegible] | [illegible] | [illegible] | [illegible] | [illegible] | [illegible] | [illegible] | [illegible] | [illegible] | [illegible] | [illegible] |
| | 4. Lusk, | [illegible] | [illegible] | [illegible] | [illegible] | [illegible] | [illegible] | [illegible] | [illegible] | [illegible] | [illegible] | [illegible] | [illegible] | [illegible] | [illegible] | [illegible] | [illegible] | [illegible] | [illegible] | [illegible] | [illegible] | [illegible] |
| | 5. Malahide, | [illegible] | [illegible] | [illegible] | [illegible] | [illegible] | [illegible] | [illegible] | [illegible] | [illegible] | [illegible] | [illegible] | [illegible] | [illegible] | [illegible] | [illegible] | [illegible] | [illegible] | [illegible] | [illegible] | [illegible] | [illegible] |
| | 6. Swords, | [illegible] | [illegible] | [illegible] | [illegible] | [illegible] | [illegible] | [illegible] | [illegible] | [illegible] | [illegible] | [illegible] | [illegible] | [illegible] | [illegible] | [illegible] | [illegible] | [illegible] | [illegible] | [illegible] | [illegible] | [illegible] |
| | | [illegible] | [illegible] | [illegible] | [illegible] | [illegible] | [illegible] | [illegible] | [illegible] | [illegible] | [illegible] | [illegible] | [illegible] | [illegible] | [illegible] | [illegible] | [illegible] | [illegible] | [illegible] | [illegible] | [illegible] | [illegible] |
| Dublin, North, | 1. Blanchardstown & Castleknock, | [illegible] | [illegible] | [illegible] | [illegible] | [illegible] | [illegible] | [illegible] | [illegible] | [illegible] | [illegible] | [illegible] | [illegible] | [illegible] | [illegible] | [illegible] | [illegible] | [illegible] | [illegible] | [illegible] | [illegible] | [illegible] |
| | 2. Clontarf and Howth, | [illegible] | [illegible] | [illegible] | [illegible] | [illegible] | [illegible] | [illegible] | [illegible] | [illegible] | [illegible] | [illegible] | [illegible] | [illegible] | [illegible] | [illegible] | [illegible] | [illegible] | [illegible] | [illegible] | [illegible] | [illegible] |
| | 3. Coolock and Drumcondra, | [illegible] | [illegible] | [illegible] | [illegible] | [illegible] | [illegible] | [illegible] | [illegible] | [illegible] | [illegible] | [illegible] | [illegible] | [illegible] | [illegible] | [illegible] | [illegible] | [illegible] | [illegible] | [illegible] | [illegible] | [illegible] |
| | 4. Finglas and Glasnevin, | [illegible] | [illegible] | [illegible] | [illegible] | [illegible] | [illegible] | [illegible] | [illegible] | [illegible] | [illegible] | [illegible] | [illegible] | [illegible] | [illegible] | [illegible] | [illegible] | [illegible] | [illegible] | [illegible] | [illegible] | [illegible] |
| | 5. North City, | [illegible] | [illegible] | [illegible] | [illegible] | [illegible] | [illegible] | [illegible] | [illegible] | [illegible] | [illegible] | [illegible] | [illegible] | [illegible] | [illegible] | [illegible] | [illegible] | [illegible] | [illegible] | [illegible] | [illegible] | [illegible] |
| | | [illegible] | [illegible] | [illegible] | [illegible] | [illegible] | [illegible] | [illegible] | [illegible] | [illegible] | [illegible] | [illegible] | [illegible] | [illegible] | [illegible] | [illegible] | [illegible] | [illegible] | [illegible] | [illegible] | [illegible] | [illegible] |

| | | | | | | |
|---|---|---|---|---|---|---|
| [illegible] | [illegible] | [illegible] | – | [illegible] | – | [illegible] |
| [illegible] | [illegible] | [illegible] | – | [illegible] | – | [illegible] |
| [illegible] | [illegible] | [illegible] | – | [illegible] | – | [illegible] |
| [illegible] | [illegible] | [illegible] | – | [illegible] | – | [illegible] |
| [illegible] | [illegible] | [illegible] | – | [illegible] | – | [illegible] |
| [illegible] | [illegible] | [illegible] | – | [illegible] | – | [illegible] |
| [illegible] | [illegible] | [illegible] | – | [illegible] | – | [illegible] |
| [illegible] | [illegible] | [illegible] | [illegible] | [illegible] | – | [illegible] |
| [illegible] | [illegible] | [illegible] | – | [illegible] | – | [illegible] |
| [illegible] | [illegible] | [illegible] | – | [illegible] | – | [illegible] |
| [illegible] | [illegible] | [illegible] | – | [illegible] | – | [illegible] |
| [illegible] | [illegible] | [illegible] | – | [illegible] | – | [illegible] |
| [illegible] | [illegible] | [illegible] | – | [illegible] | – | [illegible] |
| [illegible] | [illegible] | [illegible] | [illegible] | [illegible] | – | [illegible] |
| [illegible] | [illegible] | [illegible] | – | [illegible] | [illegible] | [illegible] |
| [illegible] | [illegible] | [illegible] | – | [illegible] | [illegible] | [illegible] |
| [illegible] | [illegible] | [illegible] | – | [illegible] | [illegible] | [illegible] |
| [illegible] | [illegible] | [illegible] | – | [illegible] | [illegible] | [illegible] |
| [illegible] | [illegible] | [illegible] | – | [illegible] | [illegible] | [illegible] |
| [illegible] | [illegible] | [illegible] | – | [illegible] | [illegible] | [illegible] |

No. 2.—Dispensary Districts, with the Expenses, and Amount of Medical Relief afforded, in the several Unions—*continued*.

| Name of Union. | Names of Dispensary Districts. | [illegible] | No. of Officers: Medical Officers | Apothecaries | Midwives | Expenses: Medicines and Medical Appliances | Rent of Dispensary Buildings | Books, Forms, Stationery, and Printing | Salaries: Medical Officers | Apothecaries | Vaccination Expenses | [illegible] | [illegible] | Total Expenditure | Medical Relief: [illegible] | [illegible] | [illegible] | [illegible] | [illegible] | [illegible] | [illegible] | [illegible] |
|---|---|---|---|---|---|---|---|---|---|---|---|---|---|---|---|---|---|---|---|---|---|---|
| Column 1 | 2 | 3 | 4 | 5 | 6 | 7 | 8 | 9 | 10 | 11 | 12 | 13 | 14 | 15 | 16 | 17 | 18 | 19 | 20 | 21 | 22 | 23 |
| | | | | | | £ s. d. | £ s. d. | £ s. d. | £ s. d. | £ s. d. | £ s. d. | £ s. d. | £ s. d. | £ s. d. | | | | | | | | |
| PROVINCE OF LEINSTER—continued. COUNTY OF KILDARE—con. | | | | | | | | | | | | | | | | | | | | | | |
| Naas, | 1. Blessington & Ballymore, | [illegible] | [illegible] | [illegible] | [illegible] | [illegible] | [illegible] | [illegible] | [illegible] | [illegible] | [illegible] | [illegible] | [illegible] | [illegible] | [illegible] | [illegible] | [illegible] | [illegible] | [illegible] | [illegible] | [illegible] | [illegible] |
| | 2. Clane and [illegible] | [illegible] | [illegible] | [illegible] | [illegible] | [illegible] | [illegible] | [illegible] | [illegible] | [illegible] | [illegible] | [illegible] | [illegible] | [illegible] | [illegible] | [illegible] | [illegible] | [illegible] | [illegible] | [illegible] | [illegible] | [illegible] |
| | 3. Kilcullen, | [illegible] | [illegible] | [illegible] | [illegible] | [illegible] | [illegible] | [illegible] | [illegible] | [illegible] | [illegible] | [illegible] | [illegible] | [illegible] | [illegible] | [illegible] | [illegible] | [illegible] | [illegible] | [illegible] | [illegible] | [illegible] |
| | 4. Kildare, | [illegible] | [illegible] | [illegible] | [illegible] | [illegible] | [illegible] | [illegible] | [illegible] | [illegible] | [illegible] | [illegible] | [illegible] | [illegible] | [illegible] | [illegible] | [illegible] | [illegible] | [illegible] | [illegible] | [illegible] | [illegible] |
| | 5. [illegible], | [illegible] | [illegible] | [illegible] | [illegible] | [illegible] | [illegible] | [illegible] | [illegible] | [illegible] | [illegible] | [illegible] | [illegible] | [illegible] | [illegible] | [illegible] | [illegible] | [illegible] | [illegible] | [illegible] | [illegible] | [illegible] |
| | 6. Newbridge, | [illegible] | [illegible] | [illegible] | [illegible] | [illegible] | [illegible] | [illegible] | [illegible] | [illegible] | [illegible] | [illegible] | [illegible] | [illegible] | [illegible] | [illegible] | [illegible] | [illegible] | [illegible] | [illegible] | [illegible] | [illegible] |
| | 7. [illegible] | [illegible] | [illegible] | [illegible] | [illegible] | [illegible] | [illegible] | [illegible] | [illegible] | [illegible] | [illegible] | [illegible] | [illegible] | [illegible] | [illegible] | [illegible] | [illegible] | [illegible] | [illegible] | [illegible] | [illegible] | [illegible] |
| | 8. Robertstown and [illegible] | [illegible] | [illegible] | [illegible] | [illegible] | [illegible] | [illegible] | [illegible] | [illegible] | [illegible] | [illegible] | [illegible] | [illegible] | [illegible] | [illegible] | [illegible] | [illegible] | [illegible] | [illegible] | [illegible] | [illegible] | [illegible] |
| | | [illegible] | [illegible] | [illegible] | [illegible] | [illegible] | [illegible] | [illegible] | [illegible] | [illegible] | [illegible] | [illegible] | [illegible] | [illegible] | [illegible] | [illegible] | [illegible] | [illegible] | [illegible] | [illegible] | [illegible] | [illegible] |
| COUNTY OF KILKENNY. | | | | | | | | | | | | | | | | | | | | | | |
| Callan, | 1. Ballingarry, | [illegible] | [illegible] | [illegible] | [illegible] | [illegible] | [illegible] | [illegible] | [illegible] | [illegible] | [illegible] | [illegible] | [illegible] | [illegible] | [illegible] | [illegible] | [illegible] | [illegible] | [illegible] | [illegible] | [illegible] | [illegible] |
| | 2. Callan, | [illegible] | [illegible] | [illegible] | [illegible] | [illegible] | [illegible] | [illegible] | [illegible] | [illegible] | [illegible] | [illegible] | [illegible] | [illegible] | [illegible] | [illegible] | [illegible] | [illegible] | [illegible] | [illegible] | [illegible] | [illegible] |
| | 3. [illegible], | [illegible] | [illegible] | [illegible] | [illegible] | [illegible] | [illegible] | [illegible] | [illegible] | [illegible] | [illegible] | [illegible] | [illegible] | [illegible] | [illegible] | [illegible] | [illegible] | [illegible] | [illegible] | [illegible] | [illegible] | [illegible] |
| | 4. Mullinahone, | [illegible] | [illegible] | [illegible] | [illegible] | [illegible] | [illegible] | [illegible] | [illegible] | [illegible] | [illegible] | [illegible] | [illegible] | [illegible] | [illegible] | [illegible] | [illegible] | [illegible] | [illegible] | [illegible] | [illegible] | [illegible] |
| | | [illegible] | [illegible] | [illegible] | [illegible] | [illegible] | [illegible] | [illegible] | [illegible] | [illegible] | [illegible] | [illegible] | [illegible] | [illegible] | [illegible] | [illegible] | [illegible] | [illegible] | [illegible] | [illegible] | [illegible] | [illegible] |
| Castlecomer, | 1. Ballyragget, | [illegible] | [illegible] | [illegible] | [illegible] | [illegible] | [illegible] | [illegible] | [illegible] | [illegible] | [illegible] | [illegible] | [illegible] | [illegible] | [illegible] | [illegible] | [illegible] | [illegible] | [illegible] | [illegible] | [illegible] | [illegible] |
| | 2. Castlecomer, | [illegible] | [illegible] | [illegible] | [illegible] | [illegible] | [illegible] | [illegible] | [illegible] | [illegible] | [illegible] | [illegible] | [illegible] | [illegible] | [illegible] | [illegible] | [illegible] | [illegible] | [illegible] | [illegible] | [illegible] | [illegible] |
| | | [illegible] | [illegible] | [illegible] | [illegible] | [illegible] | [illegible] | [illegible] | [illegible] | [illegible] | [illegible] | [illegible] | [illegible] | [illegible] | [illegible] | [illegible] | [illegible] | [illegible] | [illegible] | [illegible] | [illegible] | [illegible] |
| Kilkenny, | 1. Freshford, | [illegible] | [illegible] | [illegible] | [illegible] | [illegible] | [illegible] | [illegible] | [illegible] | [illegible] | [illegible] | [illegible] | [illegible] | [illegible] | [illegible] | [illegible] | [illegible] | [illegible] | [illegible] | [illegible] | [illegible] | [illegible] |
| | 2. Gowran, | [illegible] | [illegible] | [illegible] | [illegible] | [illegible] | [illegible] | [illegible] | [illegible] | [illegible] | [illegible] | [illegible] | [illegible] | [illegible] | [illegible] | [illegible] | [illegible] | [illegible] | [illegible] | [illegible] | [illegible] | [illegible] |

| Union | Dispensary District | Returns |
| --- | --- | --- |
| [illegible] | Kilkenny, | [illegible] |
| | Thomastown, | [illegible] |
| | Callan, | [illegible] |
| Thomastown, | Graiguenamanagh, | [illegible] |
| | Inistioge, | [illegible] |
| | Knocktopher, | [illegible] |
| | Thomastown, | [illegible] |
| Urlingford, | [illegible] | [illegible] |
| | Johnstown, | [illegible] |
| | [illegible] | [illegible] |
| | Urlingford, | [illegible] |
| King's County. Edenderry, | [illegible] | [illegible] |
| | [illegible] | [illegible] |
| | Edenderry, | [illegible] |
| | [illegible] | [illegible] |
| | [illegible] | [illegible] |
| Parsonstown, | Banagher, | [illegible] |
| | Ferbane, | [illegible] |
| | [illegible] | [illegible] |
| | Kilcormac, | [illegible] |
| | Kinnitty, | [illegible] |
| | Parsonstown, | [illegible] |
| | [illegible] | [illegible] |
| Tullamore, | Clara, | [illegible] |
| | [illegible] | [illegible] |
| | [illegible] | [illegible] |
| | Philipstown, | [illegible] |
| | Tullamore, | [illegible] |

* Kilkenny Union. [illegible] and Kilkenny Dispensary Districts.—No appointment of Midwife appears to have been made.
† Parsonstown Union, [illegible] Dispensary District.—A Midwife authorized for this District—[illegible]
‡ Tullamore Union, Clara Dispensary District.—A Midwife authorized for this District, but the appointment does not appear to have been made.

continued

No. 2.—Dispensary Districts, with the Expenses, and Amount of Medical Relief afforded, in the several Unions—*continued.*

| Name of Union. | Names of Dispensary Districts. | No. of Dispensaries, or Dispensary Stations, in each District. | No. of Officers authorised by Sealed Order: Med. Officers. | Apothecaries. | Midwives. | Expenses of Year ended 29th September, 1875: Medicines and Medical Appliances. | Rent of Dispensary Buildings. | Books, Forms, Stationery, and Printing. | Salaries: Medical Officers. | Salaries: Apothecaries. | Vaccination Expenses: Amnt. of Fees paid to Medical Officers. | Vaccination Expenses: Other Expenses in carrying out the Vaccination Act. | Fuel and Attendance, Midwives' Salaries, and any Incidental Expenses not included in the foregoing Columns. | Total Expenditure for each Dispensary District for Year ended 29th Sept., 1875. | Medical Relief afforded in Year ended 30th September, 1875: Number of New Cases attended and registered during the year: Dispensary Tickets. | Visiting Tickets. | Total. | No. of Tickets for Medical Relief cancelled by Dispensary Committee during the year. | No. of Cases of Vaccination during the year. | No. of Dangerous Lunatics certified. | No. of Days on which Attendance given at Bridewell or House of Correction, under s. 18. | No. of Patients attended in Bridewell or House of Correction during year. |
|---|---|---|---|---|---|---|---|---|---|---|---|---|---|---|---|---|---|---|---|---|---|---|
| Column 1. | 2. | 3. | 4. | 5. | 6. | 7. | 8. | 9. | 10. | 11. | 12. | 13. | 14. | 15. | 16. | 17. | 18. | 19. | 20. | 21. | 22. | 23. |
| | | | | | | £ s. d. | £ s. d. | £ s. d. | £ s. d. | £ s. d. | £ s. d. | £ s. d. | £ s. d. | £ s. d. | | | | | | | | |
| PROVINCE OF LEINSTER—*continued.* | | | | | | | | | | | | | | | | | | | | | | |
| County of Longford. | | | | | | | | | | | | | | | | | | | | | | |
| Ballymahon | 1. Abbeyshrule, | 1 | 1 | – | – | 20 9 9 | 10 0 0 | – | 100 0 0 | – | 5 13 0 | 0 10 0 | 4 0 0 | 141 17 9 | 479 | 349 | 828 | 4 | 153 | 2 | | – |
| | 2. Ballymahon, | 2 | 1 | – | *1 | 25 4 0 | 23 10 0 | – | 120 0 0 | – | 3 3 0 | 0 10 6 | 6 0 0 | 178 7 6 | 1,010 | 203 | 1,213 | 1 | 138 | 2 | – | – |
| | 3. Ballymore, | 1 | 1 | – | – | 9 0 4 | 10 0 0 | – | 100 0 0 | – | 5 2 0 | 0 10 6 | 1 10 0 | 126 2 10 | 545 | 113 | 655 | – | 107 | – | – | – |
| | | 5 | 3 | – | 1 | 54 14 1 | 43 10 0 | – | 320 0 0 | – | 14 18 0 | 1 16 0 | 11 10 0 | 446 8 1 | 2,027 | 665 | 2,692 | 5 | 398 | 4 | – | – |
| Granard, | 1. Ballinalee, | 1 | 1 | – | – | 39 13 4 | 9 0 0 | 0 4 0 | 100 0 0 | – | 6 18 0 | 2 0 0 | 5 2 0 | 165 17 4 | 379 | 211 | 590 | – | 134 | – | – | – |
| | 2. Coole, | 1 | 1 | – | – | 11 17 1 | 7 0 0 | 6 4 0 | 50 0 0 | – | 1 10 0 | – | 2 12 0 | 73 3 1 | 270 | 96 | 366 | – | 27 | – | – | – |
| | 3. Finnea, | 1 | 1 | – | – | 32 7 1 | 8 0 0 | 0 4 0 | 100 0 0 | – | 5 12 0 | 2 0 0 | 9 10 0 | 157 13 1 | 369 | 249 | 618 | – | 114 | 2 | – | – |
| | 4. Granard, | 1 | 1 | – | – | 27 8 0 | – | 0 4 0 | 123 0 0 | – | 9 8 0 | 5 0 0 | 7 17 0 | 172 17 0 | 365 | 255 | 620 | 2 | 143 | 1 | – | – |
| | 5. Scrabby, | 1 | 1 | – | – | 42 17 1 | 8 0 0 | 0 4 0 | 106 0 0 | – | 6 5 0 | 2 0 0 | 6 0 0 | 171 6 1 | 240 | 222 | 462 | – | 172 | – | – | – |
| | 6. Street, | 2 | 1 | – | – | 11 5 10 | 12 0 0 | 0 4 0 | 100 0 0 | – | 6 0 0 | – | 6 0 0 | 136 9 10 | 124 | 181 | 305 | – | 96 | 1 | – | – |
| | | 7 | 6 | – | – | 158 8 5 | 44 0 0 | 1 4 0 | 570 0 0 | – | 35 13 0 | 11 0 0 | 37 1 0 | 866 6 5 | 1,737 | 1,214 | 2,951 | 2 | 660 | 4 | – | – |
| Longford, | 1. Drumlish. | 1 | 1 | – | – | 53 0 9 | 12 0 0 | 3 16 6 | 104 16 11 | – | 11 17 0 | 4 0 0 | 10 0 9 | 200 0 11 | 900 | 153 | 1,053 | – | 272 | 2 | – | – |
| | 2. Killashee | 1 | 1 | – | – | 13 6 1 | 10 0 0 | 1 0 6 | 100 0 0 | – | 9 4 0 | – | 1 0 0 | 134 10 1 | 201 | 146 | 347 | 8 | 144 | – | – | – |
| | 3. Longford, | 2 | 1 | – | – | 61 7 3 | 19 0 0 | 5 18 8 | 92 17 10 | – | 9 8 0 | 1 0 0 | 7 9 6 | 197 1 3 | 1,670 | 449 | 2,119 | – | 140 | 2 | – | – |
| | | 4 | 3 | – | – | 128 3 1 | 41 0 0 | 10 15 2 | 297 14 9 | – | 30 9 0 | 5 0 0 | 18 10 3 | 531 12 3 | 2,771 | 748 | 3,519 | 8 | 556 | 4 | – | – |
| County of Louth. | | | | | | | | | | | | | | | | | | | | | | |
| Ardee, | 1. Ardee, | 2 | 1 | – | 1 | 41 4 10 | 6 5 0 | 3 18 6 | 150 0 0 | – | 9 5 0 | 0 10 6 | 46 1 0 | 256 4 10 | 857 | 535 | 1,392 | – | 160 | 2 | 6 | 4 |
| | 2. Castlebellingham, | 2 | 1 | – | – | 21 1 8 | 20 0 0 | 1 11 11 | 120 0 0 | – | 2 10 0 | 0 10 6 | – | 166 3 1 | 278 | 198 | 476 | 2 | 86 | – | – | – |
| | 3. Collon, | 2 | 1 | – | – | – | 13 0 0 | 1 6 3 | 120 0 0 | – | 2 14 0 | 0 10 6 | 5 15 0 | 142 5 9 | 168 | 111 | 279 | – | 49 | 1 | – | – |
| | 4. Drumcondra, | 2 | 1 | – | 1 | 9 3 4 | 11 10 0 | 2 3 9 | 120 0 0 | – | 5 1 0 | 0 10 6 | 25 10 0 | 174 18 7 | 331 | 217 | 548 | – | 117 | 2 | – | – |
| | 5. Dunleer, | 2 | 1 | – | – | 7 18 5 | 15 5 0 | 1 3 9 | 130 0 0 | – | 4 12 0 | 0 10 6 | 1 4 0 | 160 13 8 | 276 | 160 | 443 | – | 102 | – | – | – |
| | | 10 | 5 | – | 2 | 79 8 3 | 64 0 0 | 10 4 2 | 640 0 0 | – | 24 11 0 | 2 12 6 | 78 10 0 | 899 5 11 | 1,910 | 1,220 | 3,130 | 2 | 494 | 5 | 6 | 4 |

| Union | Dispensary District | Returns |
|---|---|---|
| Drogheda, | 1. Drogheda, | [illegible] |
| | 2. Duleek, | [illegible] |
| | 3. [illegible] | [illegible] |
| | 4. St. Mary's, | [illegible] |
| | 5. [illegible] | [illegible] |
| | 6. Termonfeckin, | [illegible] |
| | Total | [illegible] |
| Dundalk, | 1. [illegible] | [illegible] |
| | 2. Carlingford, | [illegible] |
| | 3. [illegible] | [illegible] |
| | 4. Dundalk, | [illegible] |
| | 5. Louth, | [illegible] |
| | 6. Ravensdale, | [illegible] |
| | Total | [illegible] |
| County of Meath — Dunshaughlin, | 1. Dunboyne, | [illegible] |
| | 2. [illegible] | [illegible] |
| | 3. [illegible] | [illegible] |
| | 4. [illegible] | [illegible] |
| | Total | [illegible] |
| Kells, | 1. Kells, | [illegible] |
| | 2. [illegible] | [illegible] |
| | 3. [illegible] | [illegible] |
| | 4. Nobber, | [illegible] |
| | Total | [illegible] |
| Navan, | 1. [illegible] | [illegible] |
| | 2. Navan, | [illegible] |
| | 3. [illegible] | [illegible] |
| | Total | [illegible] |
| Oldcastle, | 1. [illegible] | [illegible] |
| | 2. [illegible] | [illegible] |
| | 3. Oldcastle, | [illegible] |
| | 4. Virginia, | [illegible] |
| | Total | [illegible] |

* [illegible] Union. [illegible] Dispensary District.—A Midwife authorised for this District, but no appointment appears to have been made.
[illegible] Union. [illegible] Dispensary District.—No appointment of Midwife appears to have been made.
† Dundalk Union. Louth Dispensary District.—A Midwife authorised for this District by Order dated [illegible], but no appointment appears to have been made.
‡ Navan Union. Navan Dispensary District.—The office of Midwife appears to be vacant.
§ [illegible] Union. [illegible] Dispensary District.—A Midwife authorised for this District, but no appointment has been made.

[continued.

## No. 2.—Dispensary Districts, with the Expenses, and Amount of Medical Relief afforded, in the several Unions—*continued.*

| Name of Union. | Names of Dispensary Districts. | No. of Dispensaries, or Dispensary Stations, in each District | No. of Officers authorised by Sealed Order: Med. Officers. | No. of Officers authorised by Sealed Order: Apothecaries. | No. of Officers authorised by Sealed Order: Midwives. | Expenses of Year ended 29th September, 1875: Medicines and Medical Appliances. | Rent of Dispensary Buildings. | Books, Forms, Stationery, and Printing. | Salaries: Medical Officers. | Salaries: Apothecaries. | Vaccination Expenses: Amnt. of Fees paid to Medical Officers. | Vaccination Expenses: Other Expenses in carrying out the Vaccination Act. | Fuel and Attendance, Midwives' Salaries, and any Incidental Expenses not included in the foregoing Columns. | Total Expenditure for each Dispensary District for Year ended 29th Sept., 1875. | Medical Relief afforded in Year ended 29th September, 1875: Number of New Cases attended and registered during the year: Dispensary Tickets. | Visiting Tickets. | Total. | No. of Tickets for Medical Relief cancelled by Dispensary Committee during the year. | No. of Cases of Vaccination during the year. | No. of Dangerous Lunatics certified. | No. of Days on which Attendance given at Bridewell or House of Correction, under s. 15. | No. of Patients attended in Bridewell or House of Correction during year. |
|---|---|---|---|---|---|---|---|---|---|---|---|---|---|---|---|---|---|---|---|---|---|---|
| Column 1. | 2. | 3. | 4. | 5. | 6. | 7. | 8. | 9. | 10. | 11. | 12. | 13. | 14. | 16. | 16. | 17. | 18. | 19. | 20. | 21. | 22. | 23. |
| PROVINCE OF LEINSTER—*continued.* | | | | | | £ s. d. | £ s. d. | £ s. d. | £ s. d. | £ s. d. | £ s. d. | £ s. d. | £ s. d. | £ s. d. | | | | | | | | |
| COUNTY OF MEATH—*con.* | | | | | | | | | | | | | | | | | | | | | | |
| Trim, | 1. Athboy, | 2 | 1 | - | - | 58 3 5 | 20 0 0 | 2 9 5 | 120 0 0 | - | 4 16 0 | 1 1 0 | 0 4 11 | 206 16 9 | 570 | 217 | 787 | - | 55 | 1 | - | - |
| | 2. Innfield, | 2 | 1 | - | - | 36 11 4 | 20 0 0 | 0 18 5 | 120 0 0 | - | 3 16 0 | 1 1 0 | - | 182 6 9 | 625 | 170 | 795 | - | 75 | - | - | - |
| | 3. Summerhill, | 2 | 1 | - | 1 | 23 9 5 | 35 0 0 | 0 18 5 | 120 0 0 | - | 5 8 0 | 1 1 0 | 26 0 10 | 211 17 8 | 560 | 197 | 757 | - | 107 | - | - | - |
| | 4. Trim, | 1 | 1 | - | 1 | 31 7 1 | 10 0 0 | 1 10 11 | 120 0 0 | - | 4 12 0 | 1 1 0 | 28 5 8 | 196 16 8 | 560 | 180 | 740 | - | 84 | - | - | - |
| | | 7 | 4 | | 2 | 149 11 3 | 85 0 0 | 5 17 2 | 480 0 0 | - | 18 14 0 | 4 4 0 | 54 11 5 | 797 17 10 | 2,215 | 764 | 2,979 | - | 394 | 1 | - | - |
| QUEEN'S COUNTY. | | | | | | | | | | | | | | | | | | | | | | |
| Abbeyleix, | 1. Abbeyleix, | 1 | 1 | - | - | 4 16 9 | 10 10 0 | 1 17 10 | 100 0 0 | - | 5 7 0 | 1 1 0 | 4 15 0 | 198 7 7 | 677 | 126 | 803 | - | 95 | 1 | - | - |
| | 2. Ballinakill, | 2 | 1 | - | - | 12 10 8 | - | 3 2 3 | 103 17 7 | - | 1 17 0 | 1 1 0 | 15 3 0 | 137 11 6 | 247 | 121 | 368 | - | 67 | - | - | - |
| | 3. Ballyroan, | 2 | 1 | - | - | 47 17 4 | 9 5 0 | 3 6 3 | 108 1 6 | - | 3 7 0 | 1 1 0 | 17 5 11 | 189 4 0 | 469 | 137 | 606 | - | 57 | - | - | - |
| | 4. Castletown, | 1 | 1 | - | 1 | 34 18 5 | 6 0 0 | 0 16 3 | 100 0 0 | - | 3 0 0 | - | 28 2 0 | 179 15 8 | 307 | 111 | 418 | - | 63 | 2 | - | - |
| | 5. Durrow, | 1 | 1 | - | 1 | 30 3 7 | 12 0 0 | 1 10 2 | 100 0 0 | - | 7 3 0 | 1 1 0 | 22 12 2 | 174 9 11 | 423 | 151 | 574 | - | 82 | - | - | - |
| | | 7 | 5 | - | 2 | 130 6 9 | 37 15 0 | 10 11 9 | 511 19 1 | - | 19 14 0 | 4 4 0 | 87 18 1 | 802 8 8 | 2,123 | 646 | 2,769 | - | 365 | 3 | - | - |
| Donaghmore, | 1. Borris-in-Ossory, | 1 | 1 | - | - | - | 13 0 0 | - | 100 0 0 | - | - | 0 10 6 | 5 11 3 | 119 1 9 | 340 | 63 | 403 | - | 74 | 1 | - | - |
| | 2. Rathdowney, | 1 | 1 | - | 1 | - | 13 0 0 | - | 120 0 0 | - | 8 2 0 | 0 10 6 | 21 1 0 | 162 13 6 | 613 | 165 | 778 | 6 | 60 | - | - | - |
| | | 2 | 2 | - | 1 | - | 26 0 0 | - | 220 0 0 | - | 8 2 0 | 1 1 0 | 26 12 3 | 281 15 3 | 953 | 228 | 1,181 | 6 | 134 | 1 | - | - |
| Mountmellick, | 1. Clonaslee, | 1 | 1 | - | - | 7 14 3 | 7 0 0 | 0 15 0 | 100 0 0 | - | 2 10 0 | - | 0 1 8 | 118 0 11 | 483 | 189 | 672 | - | 75 | 2 | - | - |
| | 2. Clonygowan, | 2 | 1 | - | - | 42 11 3 | 14 0 0 | 0 15 0 | 100 0 0 | - | 5 18 0 | - | 3 3 4 | 168 7 7 | 507 | 311 | 818 | - | 90 | - | - | - |
| | 3. Coolrain, | 1 | 1 | - | - | 10 1 5 | 8 12 0 | 0 9 0 | 96 6 0 | - | 2 19 0 | - | 0 1 8 | 118 9 1 | 122 | 107 | 229 | - | 51 | - | - | - |
| | 4. Emo, | 2 | 1 | - | - | 24 5 6 | 10 0 0 | 0 15 0 | 100 0 0 | - | 5 16 0 | - | 0 3 4 | 140 19 10 | 786 | 233 | 1,019 | - | 118 | - | - | - |
| | 5. Maryborough, | 2 | 1 | - | - | 91 0 4 | 14 0 0 | 1 11 0 | 100 0 0 | - | 4 18 0 | - | 3 18 4 | 146 7 8 | 803 | 237 | 1,040 | - | 121 | - | - | - |

| Union | Dispensary District | Figures |
|---|---|---|
| | 6 [illegible], | [illegible] |
| | 7 Mountnugent, | [illegible] |
| | Total | [illegible] |
| COUNTY OF WESTMEATH. ATHLONE, | 1 Athlone, | [illegible] |
| | 2 [illegible], | [illegible] |
| | 3 Glasson, | [illegible] |
| | 4 Kiltoom, | [illegible] |
| | 5 Moate, | [illegible] |
| | Total | [illegible] |
| DELVIN, | 1 Castlepollard,* | [illegible] |
| | 2 Clonmellon,* | [illegible] |
| | 3 Delvin,* | [illegible] |
| | Total | [illegible] |
| MULLINGAR, | 1 Ballynacargy,† | [illegible] |
| | 2 Castletown Geoghegan, | [illegible] |
| | 3 [illegible], | [illegible] |
| | 4 [illegible], | [illegible] |
| | 5 Mullingar, | [illegible] |
| | 6 Multyfarnham, | [illegible] |
| | 7 Tyrrellspass, | [illegible] |
| | Total | [illegible] |
| COUNTY OF WEXFORD. ENNISCORTHY, | 1 Clonroche, | [illegible] |
| | 2 Enniscorthy, | [illegible] |
| | 3 Ferns, | [illegible] |
| | 4 Killann, | [illegible] |
| | 5 Newtownbarry, | [illegible] |
| | 6 Oulart, | [illegible] |
| | Total | [illegible] |
| GOREY, | 1 Camolin, | [illegible] |
| | 2 Coolgreany, | [illegible] |
| | 3 Gorey, | [illegible] |
| | 4 Killenagh and Wells, | [illegible] |
| | Total | [illegible] |

* Delvin Union. Castlepollard, Clonmellon and Delvin Dispensary Districts.—Order authorising Midwives for each of these Districts, dated 1st January, 1879, but no appointment appears to have been made in the Districts of Clonmellon and Delvin.

† Mullingar Union. Ballynacargy Dispensary District.—Midwife authorised for this District, but no appointment appears to have been made.

[continued

## No. 2.—Dispensary Districts, with the Expenses, and Amount of Medical Relief afforded, in the several Unions—*continued*

| Name of Union. | Names of Dispensary Districts. | No. of Dispensaries, or Dispensary Stations, in each District | No. of Officers authorised by Sealed Order: Med. Officers. | Apothecaries. | Midwives. | Expenses of Year ended 29th September, 1875: Medicines and Medical Appliances. | Rent of Dispensary Buildings. | Books, Forms, Stationery, and Printing. | Salaries: Medical Officers. | Salaries: Apothecaries. | Vaccination Expenses: Amount of Fees paid to Medical Officers. | Vaccination Expenses: Other Expenses in carrying out the Vaccination Act. | Fuel and Attendance, Midwives' Salaries, and any Incidental Expenses not included in the foregoing Columns. | Total Expenditure for each Dispensary District for Year ended 29th Sept., 1875. | Medical Relief afforded in Year ended 30th September, 1875: Number of New Cases attended and registered during the year: Dispensary Tickets. | Visiting Tickets. | Total. | No. of Tickets for Medical Relief cancelled by Dispensary Committee during the year. | No. of Cases of Vaccination during the year. | No. of Dangerous Lunatics certified. | No. of Days on which Attendance given at Bridewell or House of Correction, under s. 15. | No. of Patients attended in Bridewell or House of Correction during year. |
|---|---|---|---|---|---|---|---|---|---|---|---|---|---|---|---|---|---|---|---|---|---|---|
| Column 1. | 2. | 3. | 4. | 5. | 6. | 7. | 8. | 9. | 10. | 11. | 12. | 13. | 14. | 15. | 16. | 17. | 18. | 19. | 20. | 21. | 22. | 23. |
| | | | | | | £ s. d. | £ s. d. | £ s. d. | £ s. d. | £ s. d. | £ s. d. | £ s. d. | £ s. d. | £ s. d. | | | | | | | | |
| PROVINCE OF LEINSTER —*continued.* | | | | | | | | | | | | | | | | | | | | | | |
| COUNTY OF WEXFORD—*con.* | | | | | | | | | | | | | | | | | | | | | | |
| New Ross, | 1. Carrickbyrne, | 1 | 1 | – | 1 | 34 8 10 | 6 0 0 | – | 100 0 0 | – | 3 6 0 | – | 28 10 3 | 174 4 1 | 735 | 198 | 933 | – | 167 | – | – | – |
| | 2. Dysartmoon, | 3 | 1 | – | – | 16 4 2 | 18 2 6 | – | 105 0 0 | – | 4 10 0 | – | 29 7 8 | 172 4 9 | 197 | 128 | 325 | – | 74 | 3 | – | – |
| | 3. Fethard, | 3 | 2 | – | 2 | 30 3 7 | 18 0 0 | 0 18 0 | 200 0 0 | – | 9 13 0 | – | 45 7 6 | 305 0 1 | 311 | 270 | 581 | 1 | 158 | 1 | – | – |
| | 4. New Ross, | 1 | 1 | – | 1 | 24 16 6 | 4 0 0 | 0 3 0 | 100 0 0 | – | – | – | 32 18 0 | 161 17 8 | 713 | 506 | 1,219 | – | 163 | 1 | 1 | 1 |
| | 5. Old Ross, | 2 | 1 | – | 1 | 23 5 6 | 16 0 0 | – | 100 0 0 | – | – | – | 16 10 0 | 154 16 6 | 860 | 215 | 1,075 | – | 113 | 2 | – | – |
| | 6. St. Mullins, | 1 | 1 | – | 1 | – | 5 18 0 | 0 4 0 | 70 0 0 | – | 5 4 0 | – | 22 9 4 | 103 15 4 | 122 | 84 | 206 | – | 115 | – | – | – |
| | 7. Templeudigan, | 1 | 1 | – | – | 13 2 10 | 9 2 0 | – | 30 0 0 | – | 2 13 0 | – | 64 9 9 | 130 7 7 | 292 | 66 | 358 | – | 89 | – | – | – |
| | | 12 | 8 | – | 6 | 141 1 6 | 76 2 0 | 1 3 0 | 725 0 0 | – | 27 6 0 | – | 240 12 4 | 1,211 4 8 | 3,250 | 1,461 | 4,711 | 1 | 792 | 7 | 1 | 1 |
| Wexford, | 1. Bannow, | 1 | 1 | – | 2 | 20 1 2 | 8 0 0 | 0 6 0 | 100 0 0 | – | 5 12 6 | 1 0 0 | 24 5 0 | 168 4 9 | 648 | 219 | 867 | – | 103 | – | – | – |
| | 2. Bridgetown, | 2 | 1 | – | 1 | 12 6 7 | 9 0 0 | 0 18 0 | 100 0 0 | – | 4 18 0 | 1 0 0 | 38 14 7 | 166 17 2 | 408 | 161 | 569 | – | 93 | – | – | – |
| | 3. Broadway, | 2 | 1 | – | 1 | 29 1 11 | 12 17 6 | 0 6 0 | 100 0 0 | – | 4 3 0 | 0 10 0 | 21 12 9 | 168 11 2 | 170 | 133 | 303 | – | 90 | – | – | – |
| | 4. Crossabeg, | 1 | 1 | – | 1 | 14 5 4 | 10 0 0 | 0 6 0 | 80 0 0 | – | 0 15 0 | 2 0 0 | 22 0 0 | 129 6 4 | 238 | 168 | 406 | – | 63 | – | – | – |
| | 5. Taghmon and Glynn, | 2 | 1 | – | 1 | 17 15 3 | 11 10 0 | 0 6 0 | 100 0 0 | – | 3 5 0 | – | 25 6 3 | 158 2 6 | 450 | 167 | 617 | – | 96 | 1 | – | – |
| | 6. Wexford, | 1 | 1 | 1 | 1 | 65 17 6 | 15 0 0 | 1 13 0 | 120 0 0 | 40 0 0 | 16 10 0 | 1 0 0 | 39 7 0 | 298 7 5 | 563 | 746 | 1,309 | – | 318 | 2 | – | – |
| | | 9 | 6 | 1 | 7 | 168 7 9 | 66 7 6 | 3 15 0 | 600 0 0 | 40 0 0 | 34 3 6 | 5 10 0 | 171 5 7 | 1,089 0 4 | 2,477 | 1,593 | 4,070 | – | 763 | 3 | – | – |
| COUNTY OF WICKLOW. | | | | | | | | | | | | | | | | | | | | | | |
| Baltinglass, | 1. Baltinglass, | 3 | 1 | – | – | 31 15 9 | 26 0 0 | – | 140 0 0 | – | 5 11 0 | 0 10 6 | 1 0 0 | 224 17 3 | 380 | 256 | 636 | – | 92 | – | 60 | 41 |
| | 2. Dunlavin, | 3 | 1 | – | – | 20 17 8 | 28 0 0 | – | 120 0 0 | – | 5 10 0 | 0 10 6 | 4 4 0 | 179 8 0 | 430 | 166 | 595 | – | 108 | – | – | – |
| | 3. Kiltegan, | 2 | 1 | – | – | 35 16 6 | 18 0 0 | – | 120 0 0 | – | 6 2 0 | 0 10 6 | 4 1 4 | 184 10 4 | 217 | 113 | 330 | – | 108 | – | – | – |
| | 4. Rathvilly, | 2 | 1 | – | – | 34 0 5 | 19 0 0 | – | 120 0 0 | – | 3 7 0 | 0 10 6 | 2 5 0 | 179 2 11 | 262 | 188 | 450 | 1 | 64 | – | – | – |
| | | 10 | 4 | – | – | 122 10 2 | 91 0 0 | – | 500 0 0 | – | 20 10 0 | 2 2 0 | 11 10 4 | 767 12 6 | 1,289 | 722 | 2,011 | 1 | 372 | – | 60 | 41 |

| Union | Dispensary District | Figures |
|---|---|---|
| [illegible] | 1. Aughamore, | [illegible] |
| | 2. [illegible], | [illegible] |
| | 3. [illegible], | [illegible] |
| | 4. [illegible], | [illegible] |
| | 5. [illegible], | [illegible] |
| | 6. [illegible], | [illegible] |
| | 7. [illegible], | [illegible] |
| | 8. [illegible], | [illegible] |
| | Total | [illegible] |
| Castlereagh | 1. [illegible] and [illegible], | [illegible] |
| | 2. [illegible] and [illegible], | [illegible] |
| | 3. [illegible], | [illegible] |
| | Total | [illegible] |
| **PROVINCE OF CONNAUGHT** — County of Galway — Ballinasloe, | 1. Ahascragh, | [illegible] |
| | 2. Ballinasloe, | [illegible] |
| | 3. [illegible], | [illegible] |
| | 4. Killimor, | [illegible] |
| | 5. [illegible], | [illegible] |
| | 6. Laurencetown, | [illegible] |
| | Total | [illegible] |
| Clifden, | 1. Clifden, | [illegible] |
| | 2. [illegible], | [illegible] |
| | 3. Roundstone, | [illegible] |
| | Total | [illegible] |
| Galway, | 1. Arran, | [illegible] |
| | 2. Galway, | [illegible] |
| | 3. Moycullen, | [illegible] |
| | 4. Oranmore, | [illegible] |
| | 5. Spiddal, | [illegible] |
| | 6. [illegible], | [illegible] |
| | Total | [illegible] |

* [illegible] Union. [illegible] Dispensary District.—[illegible] discontinued—duty performed by Medical Officer.

(continued)

Nc. 2.—Dispensary Districts, with the Expenses, and Amount of Medical Relief afforded, in the several Unions—*continued.*

| Name of Union. | Names of Dispensary Districts. | No. of Dispensaries, or Dispensary Stations, in each District | No. of Officers authorised by Sealed Order: Med. Officers. | Apothecaries. | Midwives. | Expenses of Year ended 29th September, 1875: Medicines and Medical Appliances. | Rent of Dispensary Buildings. | Books, Forms, Stationery, and Printing. | Salaries: Medical Officers. | Salaries: Apothecaries. | Vaccination Expenses: Amnt. of Fees paid to Medical Officers. | Other Expenses in carrying out the Vaccination Act. | Fuel and Attendance Midwives' Salaries, and any Incidental Expenses not included in the foregoing Columns. | Total Expenditure for each Dispensary District for Year ended 29th Sept., 1875. | Medical Relief afforded in Year ended 30th September, 1875: Number of New Cases attended and registered during the year: Dispensary Tickets. | Visiting Tickets. | Total. | No. of Tickets for Medical Relief cancelled by Dispensary Committee during the year. | No. of Cases of Vaccination during the year. | No. of Dangerous Lunatics certified. | No. of Days on which Attendance given at Bridewell or House of Correction, under s. 14. | No. of Patients attended in Bridewell or House of Correction during year. |
|---|---|---|---|---|---|---|---|---|---|---|---|---|---|---|---|---|---|---|---|---|---|---|
| Column 1. | 2. | 3. | 4. | 5. | 6. | 7. | 8. | 9. | 10. | 11. | 12. | 13. | 14. | 15. | 16. | 17. | 18. | 19. | 20. | 21. | 22. | 23. |
| | | | | | | £ s. d. | £ s. d. | £ s. d. | £ s. d. | £ s. d. | £ s. d. | £ s. d. | £ s. d. | £ s. d. | | | | | | | | |
| PROVINCE OF CONNAUGHT—*continued.* County of Galway—*con.* | | | | | | | | | | | | | | | | | | | | | | |
| Glennamaddy, | 1. Dunmore, | 1 | 1 | – | – | 9 13 8 | 10 0 0 | 0 10 0 | 55 0 0 | – | 3 10 0 | 1 0 6 | 5 0 0 | 85 0 2 | 205 | 35 | 240 | 5 | 97 | – | – | – |
| | 2. Glennamaddy, | 1 | 1 | – | – | 25 0 2 | – | 0 10 0 | 100 0 0 | – | 2 13 0 | 2 10 6 | 12 8 0 | 143 1 8 | 330 | 72 | 402 | – | 206 | 4 | – | – |
| | 3. Williamstown, | 1 | 1 | – | – | 34 15 10 | 10 0 0 | 0 10 0 | 120 0 0 | – | 20 1 0 | 2 0 6 | 4 0 0 | 191 7 4 | 660 | 148 | 808 | – | 263 | – | – | – |
| | | 3 | 3 | – | – | 69 9 8 | 20 0 0 | 1 10 0 | 275 0 0 | – | 25 10 0 | 5 11 6 | 21 8 0 | 419 9 2 | 1,195 | 269 | 1,464 | 5 | 566 | 4 | – | – |
| Gort, | 1. Ardrahan, | 3 | 1 | – | – | 1 11 6 | 21 0 0 | 1 7 0 | 140 0 0 | – | 7 13 0 | 0 10 6 | – | 172 2 0 | 601 | 114 | 715 | – | 271 | – | – | – |
| | 2. Gort, | 1 | 1 | 1 | – | 28 9 7 | – | 0 12 0 | 100 0 0 | 40 0 0 | 8 11 6 | 0 10 6 | 0 3 0 | 178 7 1 | 613 | 302 | 915 | – | 262 | 2 | 2 | 2 |
| | 3. Kinvarra, | 1 | 1 | – | – | 41 2 2 | 8 0 0 | 3 18 7 | 129 11 0 | – | 22 5 0 | 0 10 6 | – | 205 7 3 | 719 | 190 | 909 | – | 300 | – | – | – |
| | | 5 | 3 | 1 | – | 71 3 3 | 29 0 0 | 5 17 7 | 369 11 0 | 40 0 0 | 38 9 6 | 1 11 6 | 0 3 0 | 555 16 4 | 1,933 | 606 | 2,539 | – | 833 | 2 | 2 | 2 |
| Loughrea, | 1. Athenry, | 2 | 1 | – | – | 29 1 10 | 16 0 0 | 0 18 4 | 100 0 0 | – | 10 6 0 | – | 5 0 0 | 178 4 2 | 309 | 178 | 487 | – | 486 | 2 | – | – |
| | 2. Bullaun, | 2 | 1 | – | – | 18 3 0 | 10 10 0 | 0 13 0 | 100 0 0 | – | 2 9 0 | – | 4 4 0 | 133 19 6 | 60 | 86 | 146 | – | 36 | 2 | – | – |
| | 3. Loughrea, | 2 | 1 | – | – | 16 13 5 | 9 0 0 | 0 13 2 | 100 0 0 | – | 18 17 0 | – | 4 0 0 | 149 3 7 | 219 | 195 | 414 | – | 502 | 3 | 3 | 3 |
| | 4. Woodford, | 3 | 1 | – | – | 22 13 5 | 9 0 0 | 0 13 2 | 100 0 0 | – | 12 1 0 | – | 1 0 0 | 145 7 7 | 105 | 104 | 209 | – | 229 | – | – | – |
| | | 9 | 4 | – | – | 86 11 8 | 44 10 0 | 2 17 8 | 400 0 0 | – | 43 13 0 | – | 14 4 0 | 600 14 4 | 693 | 563 | 1,256 | – | 1,253 | 7 | 3 | 3 |
| Mount Bellew, | 1. Clonbrock, | 1 | 1 | – | 1 | 39 9 1 | 5 0 0 | 1 17 9 | 141 0 0 | – | 15 16 0 | 2 0 6 | 10 4 0 | 215 7 4 | 967 | 170 | 1,137 | 2 | 257 | – | – | – |
| | 2. Killeroran, | 1 | 1 | – | 1 | 44 10 0 | 5 0 0 | 0 10 9 | 120 0 0 | – | 7 0 0 | 1 5 6 | 26 10 0 | 204 16 3 | 1,086 | 140 | 1,226 | – | 159 | 1 | – | – |
| | 3. Mount Bellew, | 1 | 1 | – | 1 | 10 0 8 | 6 0 0 | 0 10 9 | 120 0 0 | – | 10 0 0 | 2 0 6 | 6 15 0 | 155 6 11 | 861 | 170 | 1,031 | – | 157 | – | – | – |
| | | 3 | 3 | – | 3 | 93 19 9 | 16 0 0 | 2 19 3 | 381 0 0 | – | 32 16 0 | 5 6 6 | 43 9 0 | 575 10 6 | 2,914 | 480 | 3,394 | 2 | 573 | 1 | – | – |

| Union | Dispensary District | Returns |
|---|---|---|
| Oughterard, | 1. Clonbur,* | [illegible] |
| | 2. Leitrim, | [illegible] |
| | 3. Oughterard, | [illegible] |
| | | [illegible] |
| Portumna, | 1. Eyrecourt, | [illegible] |
| | 2. Portumna,† | [illegible] |
| | | [illegible] |
| Tuam, | 1. Abbey, | [illegible] |
| | 2. Dunmore, | [illegible] |
| | 3. Headford, | [illegible] |
| | 4. Tuam, | [illegible] |
| | | [illegible] |
| County of Leitrim. | | |
| Carrick-on-Shannon, | 1. Aughrim, | [illegible] |
| | 2. Drumshanbo,‡ | [illegible] |
| | 3. Jamestown, | [illegible] |
| | 4. Leitrim, | [illegible] |
| | | [illegible] |
| Manorhamilton, | 1. Dromahaire, | [illegible] |
| | 2. Drumkeeran, | [illegible] |
| | 3. Largydonnell, | [illegible] |
| | 4. Manorhamilton, | [illegible] |
| | | [illegible] |
| Mohill, | 1. Carrigallen, | [illegible] |
| | 2. Mohill, | [illegible] |
| | 3. Rooskey, | [illegible] |
| | 4. Fenagh, | [illegible] |
| | | [illegible] |
| County of Mayo. | | |
| Ballina, | 1. Ballina, | [illegible] |
| | 2. Crossmolina, | [illegible] |
| | | [illegible] |

* Oughterard Union: Clonbur Dispensary District.—No appointment of Midwife appears to have been made.
† Portumna Union: Portumna Dispensary District.—No appointment of Midwife appears to have been made.
‡ Carrick-on-Shannon Union: Drumshanbo Dispensary District.—Office of Midwife appears to be vacant.

[continued

No. 2.—Dispensary Districts, with the Expenses, and Amount of Medical Relief afforded, in the several Unions—*continued.*

| Name of Union. | Name of Dispensary District. | No. of Dispensaries, or Dispensary Stations, in each District. | No. of Officers authorized by Sealed Order: Med. Officers. | Apothecaries. | Midwives. | Expenses of Year ended 29th September, 1875: Medicines and Medical Appliances. | Rent of Dispensary Buildings. | Books, Forms, Stationery, and Printing. | Salaries: Medical Officers. | Salaries: Apothecaries. | Vaccination Expenses: Amnt. of Fees paid to Medical Officers. | Other Expenses in carrying out the Vaccination Act. | Fuel and Attendance, Midwives' Salaries, and any Incidental Expenses not included in the foregoing Columns. | Total Expenditure for each Dispensary District for Year ended 29th Sept., 1875. | Medical Relief afforded in Year ended 30th September, 1875: Number of New Cases attended and registered during the year: Dispensary Tickets. | Visiting Tickets. | Total. | No. of Tickets for Medical Relief cancelled by Dispensary Committees during the year. | No. of Cases of Vaccination during the year. | No. of Dangerous Lunatics certified. | No. of Days on which Attendance given at Bridewell or House of Correction, under s. 15. | No. of Patients attended in Bridewell or House of Correction during year. |
|---|---|---|---|---|---|---|---|---|---|---|---|---|---|---|---|---|---|---|---|---|---|---|
| Column 1. | 2. | 3. | 4. | 5. | 6. | 7. | 8. | 9. | 10. | 11. | 12. | 13. | 14. | 15. | 16. | 17. | 18. | 19. | 20. | 21. | 22. | 23. |
| | | | | | | £ s. d. | £ s. d. | £ s. d. | £ s. d. | £ s. d. | £ s. d. | £ s. d. | £ s. d. | £ s. d. | | | | | | | | |
| PROVINCE OF CONNAUGHT—*continued.* County of Mayo—*con.* | | | | | | | | | | | | | | | | | | | | | | |
| Ballinrobe | 1. Ballinrobe, | 2 | 2 | – | – | 41 5 1 | 8 0 0 | 1 9 8 | 200 0 0 | – | 70 9 0 | 1 0 0 | 16 17 10 | 338 1 7 | 1,764 | 383 | 2,147 | – | 1,398 | 5 | – | – |
| | 2. Cong, | 2 | 1 | – | – | 60 10 1 | 8 1 6 | 0 19 5 | 100 0 0 | – | 68 7 0 | – | 18 11 0 | 250 9 3 | 992 | 178 | 1,170 | – | 1,235 | – | – | – |
| | 3. Hollymount, | 1 | 1 | – | – | 38 17 5 | 8 0 0 | 0 18 8 | 100 0 0 | – | 43 18 0 | 1 0 0 | 9 7 7 | 202 2 8 | 545 | 197 | 742 | – | 884 | – | – | – |
| | | 5 | 4 | – | – | 140 12 7 | 24 1 6 | 3 9 9 | 400 0 0 | – | 178 14 0 | 2 0 0 | 44 16 5 | 791 13 6 | 3,301 | 758 | 4,059 | – | 3,517 | 5 | – | – |
| Belmullet, | 1. Bangor, | 2 | 1 | – | – | – | 15 0 0 | 2 12 11 | 125 0 0 | – | 11 6 0 | 5 11 6 | 4 12 10 | 164 3 3 | 187 | 89 | 276 | 1 | 817 | – | – | – |
| | 2. Binghamstown | 1 | 1 | – | – | 18 3 4 | 7 10 0 | 1 12 11 | 100 0 0 | – | 41 7 0 | 3 6 0 | 2 6 6 | 174 5 9 | 409 | 63 | 472 | – | 791 | – | – | – |
| | | 3 | 2 | – | – | 18 3 4 | 22 10 0 | 4 5 10 | 225 0 0 | – | 52 13 0 | 8 17 6 | 6 19 4 | 338 9 0 | 596 | 152 | 748 | 1 | 1,608 | – | – | – |
| Castlebar, | 1. Balla, | 2 | 1 | – | – | 3 0 0 | 17 0 0 | 4 0 0 | 110 0 0 | – | 19 13 0 | 0 13 0 | 9 18 6 | 164 3 6 | 110 | 117 | 227 | – | 338 | 3 | – | – |
| | 2. Castlebar, | 5 | 2 | – | *1 | 41 11 9 | 19 6 8 | 11 4 6 | 220 0 0 | – | 90 17 0 | 1 4 0 | 44 6 6 | 428 10 5 | 398 | 208 | 606 | – | 412 | – | – | – |
| | | 7 | 3 | – | 1 | 44 11 9 | 36 6 8 | 15 4 6 | 330 0 0 | – | 110 10 0 | 1 16 0 | 54 5 0 | 592 13 11 | 508 | 325 | 833 | – | 750 | 3 | – | – |
| Claremorris, | 1. Ballindine, | 1 | 1 | – | – | 41 12 7 | 6 0 0 | 1 7 3 | 100 0 0 | – | 45 3 0 | 2 8 0 | 9 0 0 | 206 10 10 | 351 | 193 | 544 | – | 778 | – | – | – |
| | 2. Ballyhaunis, | 1 | 1 | – | – | 26 16 5 | 8 0 0 | 1 7 3 | 133 8 0 | – | 64 18 0 | 2 2 0 | 5 12 0 | 243 3 8 | 798 | 172 | 970 | – | 1,488 | – | 5 | – |
| | 3. Claremorris, | 1 | 1 | – | – | 45 10 5 | – | 1 19 7 | 138 10 2 | – | 29 10 0 | 0 10 0 | 8 19 4 | 224 19 6 | 212 | 226 | 438 | – | 628 | – | – | – |
| | | 3 | 3 | – | – | 113 19 5 | 14 0 0 | 4 14 1 | 371 18 2 | – | 139 11 0 | 5 0 0 | 24 11 4 | 673 14 0 | 1,361 | 591 | 1,952 | – | 2,894 | – | 5 | – |
| Killala, | 1. Ballycastle, | 2 | 1 | – | – | 44 19 8 | 11 10 0 | 0 7 6 | 125 0 0 | – | 6 11 0 | – | 101 5 6 | 289 13 8 | 422 | 237 | 659 | – | 611 | – | – | – |
| | 2. Killala, | 1 | 1 | – | – | 54 5 8 | – | 1 8 6 | 100 0 0 | – | 8 9 0 | – | 19 11 10 | 183 15 0 | 288 | 96 | 384 | – | 154 | – | – | – |
| | | 3 | 2 | – | – | 99 5 4 | 11 10 0 | 1 16 0 | 225 0 0 | – | 15 0 0 | – | 120 17 4 | 473 8 8 | 710 | 333 | 1,043 | – | 765 | – | – | – |

| Union | Dispensary District | Returns |
| --- | --- | --- |
| Newport, | 1. Achill, | [illegible] |
| | 2. Newport, | [illegible] |
| | Total | [illegible] |
| Swinford, | 1. Foxford, | [illegible] |
| | 2. Kiltimagh, | [illegible] |
| | 3. Killasser, | [illegible] |
| | 4. Lowpark, | [illegible] |
| | 5. Swinford, | [illegible] |
| | Total | [illegible] |
| Westport, | 1. Islandeady, | [illegible] |
| | 2. Louisburgh, | [illegible] |
| | 3. Westport, | [illegible] |
| | Total | [illegible] |
| County of [illegible] — Boyle, | 1. Ballinameen, | [illegible] |
| | 2. Ballyfarnon, | [illegible] |
| | 3. Boyle, | [illegible] |
| | 4. [illegible] | [illegible] |
| | 5. Keadue, | [illegible] |
| | Total | [illegible] |
| Castlerea, | 1. Ballinlough, | [illegible] |
| | 2. Castleplunket, | [illegible] |
| | 3. Castlerea, | [illegible] |
| | 4. Frenchpark, | [illegible] |
| | Total | [illegible] |
| Roscommon, | 1. Athleague, | [illegible] |
| | 2. Ballintober, | [illegible] |
| | 3. Roscommon, | [illegible] |
| | Total | [illegible] |

* Castlebar Union. Castlebar Dispensary District.—A Midwife authorised for this District in addition to the Medical Officer, but no appointment appears to have been made.
† Newport Union. Newport and Achill Dispensary Districts.—No appointment of Midwife appears to have been made.

[continued.

No. 2.—Dispensary Districts, with the Expenses, and Amounts of Medical Relief afforded, in the several Unions—continued.

| Name of Union. | Name of Dispensary Districts. | No. of [illegible] | No. of Officers appointed by Board of Guardians: Med. Officers | Apothecaries | Midwives | Expenses of Year ended 29th September, 1874: Medicines and Medical Appliances | Rent of Dispensary Buildings | Books, Forms, Stationery, and Printing | Salaries: Medical Officers | Salaries: Apothecaries | Vaccination Expenses: [illegible] | Vaccination Expenses: [illegible] | [illegible] | Total Expenditure [illegible] for Year ended 29th Sept. 1874 | Medical Relief afforded in Year ended 29th September, 1874: Number of New Cases attended and registered during the year: Dispensary Tickets | Visiting Tickets | Total | [illegible] | [illegible] | [illegible] | [illegible] | [illegible] |
|---|---|---|---|---|---|---|---|---|---|---|---|---|---|---|---|---|---|---|---|---|---|---|
| Column 1. | 2 | 3 | 4 | 5 | 6 | 7 | 8 | 9 | 10 | 11 | 12 | 13 | 14 | 15 | 16 | 17 | 18 | 19 | 20 | 21 | 22 | 23 |
| | | | | | | £ s. d. | £ s. d. | £ s. d. | £ s. d. | £ s. d. | £ s. d. | £ s. d. | £ s. d. | £ s. d. | | | | | | | | |
| Province of Connaught—continued. County of Roscommon—continued. | | | | | | | | | | | | | | | | | | | | | | |
| Strokestown, | 1 Elphin | [illegible] | [illegible] | [illegible] | [illegible] | [illegible] | [illegible] | [illegible] | [illegible] | [illegible] | [illegible] | [illegible] | [illegible] | [illegible] | [illegible] | [illegible] | [illegible] | [illegible] | [illegible] | [illegible] | [illegible] | [illegible] |
| | 2 Roosky* | [illegible] | [illegible] | [illegible] | [illegible] | [illegible] | [illegible] | [illegible] | [illegible] | [illegible] | [illegible] | [illegible] | [illegible] | [illegible] | [illegible] | [illegible] | [illegible] | [illegible] | [illegible] | [illegible] | [illegible] | [illegible] |
| | 3 Strokestown, | [illegible] | [illegible] | [illegible] | [illegible] | [illegible] | [illegible] | [illegible] | [illegible] | [illegible] | [illegible] | [illegible] | [illegible] | [illegible] | [illegible] | [illegible] | [illegible] | [illegible] | [illegible] | [illegible] | [illegible] | [illegible] |
| | | [illegible] | [illegible] | [illegible] | [illegible] | [illegible] | [illegible] | [illegible] | [illegible] | [illegible] | [illegible] | [illegible] | [illegible] | [illegible] | [illegible] | [illegible] | [illegible] | [illegible] | [illegible] | [illegible] | [illegible] | [illegible] |
| County of Sligo. | | | | | | | | | | | | | | | | | | | | | | |
| Dromore West, | 1 Easkey‡ | [illegible] | [illegible] | [illegible] | [illegible] | [illegible] | [illegible] | [illegible] | [illegible] | [illegible] | [illegible] | [illegible] | [illegible] | [illegible] | [illegible] | [illegible] | [illegible] | [illegible] | [illegible] | [illegible] | [illegible] | [illegible] |
| | 2 Skreen | [illegible] | [illegible] | [illegible] | [illegible] | [illegible] | [illegible] | [illegible] | [illegible] | [illegible] | [illegible] | [illegible] | [illegible] | [illegible] | [illegible] | [illegible] | [illegible] | [illegible] | [illegible] | [illegible] | [illegible] | [illegible] |
| | | [illegible] | [illegible] | [illegible] | [illegible] | [illegible] | [illegible] | [illegible] | [illegible] | [illegible] | [illegible] | [illegible] | [illegible] | [illegible] | [illegible] | [illegible] | [illegible] | [illegible] | [illegible] | [illegible] | [illegible] | [illegible] |
| Sligo, | 1 Ballymote, | [illegible] | [illegible] | [illegible] | [illegible] | [illegible] | [illegible] | [illegible] | [illegible] | [illegible] | [illegible] | [illegible] | [illegible] | [illegible] | [illegible] | [illegible] | [illegible] | [illegible] | [illegible] | [illegible] | [illegible] | [illegible] |
| | 2 Geevagh | [illegible] | [illegible] | [illegible] | [illegible] | [illegible] | [illegible] | [illegible] | [illegible] | [illegible] | [illegible] | [illegible] | [illegible] | [illegible] | [illegible] | [illegible] | [illegible] | [illegible] | [illegible] | [illegible] | [illegible] | [illegible] |
| | 3 Collooney, | [illegible] | [illegible] | [illegible] | [illegible] | [illegible] | [illegible] | [illegible] | [illegible] | [illegible] | [illegible] | [illegible] | [illegible] | [illegible] | [illegible] | [illegible] | [illegible] | [illegible] | [illegible] | [illegible] | [illegible] | [illegible] |
| | 4 Riverstown, | [illegible] | [illegible] | [illegible] | [illegible] | [illegible] | [illegible] | [illegible] | [illegible] | [illegible] | [illegible] | [illegible] | [illegible] | [illegible] | [illegible] | [illegible] | [illegible] | [illegible] | [illegible] | [illegible] | [illegible] | [illegible] |
| | 5 Sligo, | [illegible] | [illegible] | [illegible] | [illegible] | [illegible] | [illegible] | [illegible] | [illegible] | [illegible] | [illegible] | [illegible] | [illegible] | [illegible] | [illegible] | [illegible] | [illegible] | [illegible] | [illegible] | [illegible] | [illegible] | [illegible] |
| | | [illegible] | [illegible] | [illegible] | [illegible] | [illegible] | [illegible] | [illegible] | [illegible] | [illegible] | [illegible] | [illegible] | [illegible] | [illegible] | [illegible] | [illegible] | [illegible] | [illegible] | [illegible] | [illegible] | [illegible] | [illegible] |
| Tobercurry, | 1 Achonry, | [illegible] | [illegible] | [illegible] | [illegible] | [illegible] | [illegible] | [illegible] | [illegible] | [illegible] | [illegible] | [illegible] | [illegible] | [illegible] | [illegible] | [illegible] | [illegible] | [illegible] | [illegible] | [illegible] | [illegible] | [illegible] |
| | 2 Coolaney | [illegible] | [illegible] | [illegible] | [illegible] | [illegible] | [illegible] | [illegible] | [illegible] | [illegible] | [illegible] | [illegible] | [illegible] | [illegible] | [illegible] | [illegible] | [illegible] | [illegible] | [illegible] | [illegible] | [illegible] | [illegible] |
| | 3 Tobercurry, | [illegible] | [illegible] | [illegible] | [illegible] | [illegible] | [illegible] | [illegible] | [illegible] | [illegible] | [illegible] | [illegible] | [illegible] | [illegible] | [illegible] | [illegible] | [illegible] | [illegible] | [illegible] | [illegible] | [illegible] | [illegible] |
| | | [illegible] | [illegible] | [illegible] | [illegible] | [illegible] | [illegible] | [illegible] | [illegible] | [illegible] | [illegible] | [illegible] | [illegible] | [illegible] | [illegible] | [illegible] | [illegible] | [illegible] | [illegible] | [illegible] | [illegible] | [illegible] |

* Strokestown Union. Roosky Dispensary District.—Office of Midwife vacant.
† Dromore West Union. Easkey and Skreen Dispensary Districts.—No appointment of Midwife appears to have been made for these Districts.
‡ " " Easkey and Castleconnor Dispensary Districts to have one Midwife, to be called The Easkey Dispensary District, by order dated December, 1874.

SUMMARY OF FOREGOING TABLE, No. 2.

| PROVINCES. | [illegible] | [illegible] | [illegible] | [illegible] | [illegible] | [illegible] | EXPENSES OF YEAR ENDED [illegible] SEPTEMBER, [illegible]. | | | | | | | | | MEDICAL RELIEF AFFORDED IN YEAR ENDED [illegible] SEPTEMBER, [illegible]. | | | | | | | |
|---|---|---|---|---|---|---|---|---|---|---|---|---|---|---|---|---|---|---|---|---|---|---|---|
| | | | | | | | Medicines and Medical Appliances. | Rent of Dispensary Buildings. | [illegible] | Salaries. Medical Officers. | Salaries. Apothecaries. | [illegible] | [illegible] | [illegible] | [illegible] | [illegible] | [illegible] | Total. | [illegible] | [illegible] | [illegible] | [illegible] | [illegible] |
| | | | | | | | £ s. d. | £ s. d. | £ s. d. | £ s. d. | £ s. d. | £ s. d. | £ s. d. | £ s. d. | £ s. d. | | | | | | | | |
| ULSTER | [illegible] | [illegible] | [illegible] | [illegible] | [illegible] | [illegible] | [illegible] | [illegible] | [illegible] | [illegible] | [illegible] | [illegible] | [illegible] | [illegible] | [illegible] | [illegible] | [illegible] | [illegible] | [illegible] | [illegible] | [illegible] | [illegible] | [illegible] |
| MUNSTER | [illegible] | [illegible] | [illegible] | [illegible] | [illegible] | [illegible] | [illegible] | [illegible] | [illegible] | [illegible] | [illegible] | [illegible] | [illegible] | [illegible] | [illegible] | [illegible] | [illegible] | [illegible] | [illegible] | [illegible] | [illegible] | [illegible] | [illegible] |
| LEINSTER | [illegible] | [illegible] | [illegible] | [illegible] | [illegible] | [illegible] | [illegible] | [illegible] | [illegible] | [illegible] | [illegible] | [illegible] | [illegible] | [illegible] | [illegible] | [illegible] | [illegible] | [illegible] | [illegible] | [illegible] | [illegible] | [illegible] | [illegible] |
| CONNAUGHT | [illegible] | [illegible] | [illegible] | [illegible] | [illegible] | [illegible] | [illegible] | [illegible] | [illegible] | [illegible] | [illegible] | [illegible] | [illegible] | [illegible] | [illegible] | [illegible] | [illegible] | [illegible] | [illegible] | [illegible] | [illegible] | [illegible] | [illegible] |
| Totals | [illegible] | [illegible] | [illegible] | [illegible] | [illegible] | [illegible] | [illegible] | [illegible] | [illegible] | [illegible] | [illegible] | [illegible] | [illegible] | [illegible] | [illegible] | [illegible] | [illegible] | [illegible] | [illegible] | [illegible] | [illegible] | [illegible] | [illegible] |

No. 3.—General Summary of previous Tables, in Provinces:—containing, 1. Dispensary Districts formed under § 6 of the Medical Charities Act, 14 & of Dispensaries, Officers, &c.:—2. Financial Statement; showing the 1874, to 29th September, 1875:—and 3. Relief Return; showing the Home, respectively; the Number of Cases in which Tickets for Medical Vaccination performed; Number of Cases of Dangerous Lunatics certified; year ended 30th September, 1875.

| Heads of Particulars in foregoing Tables. | Ulster. | | Munster. | |
|---|---|---|---|---|
| Column 1. | 2. | 3. | 4. | 5. |
| **Statistics of Unions and Districts:** | | | | |
| Population of Unions, in Provinces,—1871, | . . | 1,833,228 | . . | 1,393,485 |
| Area of Unions and Dispensary Districts, in statute acres, | . . | 5,483,206 | . . | 6,067,722 |
| Poor Law Valuation of Unions, in Provinces,—1875, | . . | £4,116,200 | . . | £3,387,860 |
| Number of Unions, | . . | 44 | . . | 50 |
| " Electoral Divisions, | . . | 875 | . . | 1,023 |
| " Dispensary Districts, | . . | 214 | . . | 205 |
| " Dispensaries or Dispensary Stations therein, | . . | 293 | . . | 328 |
| " Medical Officers authorized to be appointed for Dispensary Districts, | . . | 235 | . . | 237 |
| " Apothecaries, | . . | 8 | . . | 20 |
| " Midwives, | . . | 60 | . . | 29 |
| **Expenditure in Year ended 29th September, 1875:—** | £ | | £ | |
| Medicines and Medical Appliances, | 7,046 | . . | 6,906 | . . |
| Rent of Dispensary Buildings, | 2,108 | . . | 3,010 | . . |
| Books, Forms, Stationery, Printing, and Advertising, | 400 | . . | 271 | . . |
| Salaries of Medical Officers, | 24,006 | . . | 24,472 | . . |
| " Apothecaries, | 412 | . . | 934 | . . |
| Vaccination Expenses, | 2,174 | . . | 1,831 | . . |
| Fuel, Attendance, and Incidental Expenses, | 2,004 | . . | 2,604 | . . |
| Total Expenditure in year ended 29th September, 1875, | . . | £39,832 | . . | £40,028 |
| **Relief Returns, and Duties of Medical Officers for year ended 30th September, 1875:—** | | | | |
| Number of Cases attended on Dispensary Tickets, | 116,536 | . . | 150,509 | . . |
| " " on Visiting Tickets, | 63,456 | . . | 54,704 | . . |
| Total New Cases in the year, | . . | 179,992 | . . | 205,213 |
| Number of Cases in which Tickets for Medical Relief were cancelled in the year, | . . | 240 | . . | 87 |
| Number of Cases of Vaccination under Medical Charities Act in the year, | . . | 38,043 | . . | 33,307 |
| Number of Cases of dangerous Lunatics certified in the year, | . . | 272 | . . | 194 |
| Number of Patients attended in Bridewells or Houses of Correction during the year, | . . | 58 | . . | 284 |

**Statistical Statement**; showing the number of Unions, Electoral Divisions, and 15 Vic., c. 68; the total and average Population, Area, and Valuation; Number Expenditure under the Medical Charities Act for the year from 29th September, Number of Cases of Medical Relief afforded at the Dispensary and at the Patients' Relief have been Cancelled by the Dispensary Committee; the Number of Cases of Number of Patients attended at Bridewells or Houses of Correction, &c.; during the

| Leinster. | | Connaught. | | Total for Ireland. | | Average. For Unions. | Average. For Dispensary Districts. | Average. For Medical Officers. |
|---|---|---|---|---|---|---|---|---|
| 6. | 7. | 8. | 9. | 10. | 11. | 12. | 13. | 14. |
| . . | 1,339,451 | . . | 846,213 | . . | 5,412,377 | 33,206 | 7,517 | 6,732 |
| . . | 4,870,984 | . . | 4,392,065 | . . | 20,819,947 | 127,780 | 28,917 | — |
| . . | £4,618,320 | . . | £1,363,220 | . . | £13,485,000 | £82,734 | £18,750 | — |
| . . | 40 | . . | 29 | . . | 163 | — | — | — |
| . . | 944 | . . | 596 | . . | 3,433 | 21 | 5 | 4 |
| . . | 203 | . . | 98 | . . | 720 | 4 | — | — |
| . . | 319 | . . | 144 | . . | 1,084 | 7 | — | — |
| . . | 229 | . . | 113 | . . | 804 | 5 | — | — |
| . . | 12 | . . | 6 | . . | 41 | — | — | — |
| . . | 96 | . . | 18 | . . | 212 | 1 | — | — |
| £ | | £ | | £ | | £ s. | £ s. | £ s. |
| 3,539 | . . | 3,245 | . . | 23,780 | . . | 145 12 | 32 19 | 29 10 |
| 2,688 | . . | 1,000 | . . | 8,811 | . . | 54 1 | 12 5 | — |
| 421 | . . | 160 | . . | 1,252 | . . | 7 14 | 1 15 | — |
| 25,728 | . . | 12,011 | . . | 87,174 | . . | 534 16 | 121 1 | 108 9 |
| 1,124 | . . | 243 | . . | ≈,718 | . . | — | — | 66 3 |
| 1,511 | . . | 2,098 | . . | 7,609 | . . | 46 14 | 10 11 | — |
| 3,792 | . . | 1,097 | . . | 10,157 | . . | 62 6 | 14 2 | — |
| . . | £41,743 | . . | £19,849 | . . | £141,452 | £867 16 | £196 9 | — |
| 168,164 | . . | 60,321 | . . | 495,530 | . . | 3,040 | 688 | 616 |
| 61,844 | . . | 18,658 | . . | 198,662 | . . | 1,219 | 276 | 247 |
| . . | 230,008 | . . | 78,979 | . . | 694,192 | 4,259 | 964 | 863 |
| . . | 117 | . . | 112 | . . | 556 | — | — | — |
| . . | 25,564 | . . | 39,876 | . . | 137,840 | 843 | 191 | 171 |
| . . | 380 | . . | 72 | . . | 904 | — | — | — |
| . . | 54 | . . | 15 | . . | 411 | — | — | — |

No. 4.—VACCINATION:—SUMMARY of the Number of Persons VACCINATED in the Workhouses and Auxiliary Establishments of the several Unions in Ireland, by the Medical Officers of those Institutions; and of the Number VACCINATED in the several Dispensary Districts, by the Medical Officers of Dispensaries under the Medical Charities Act, in the Year ended 30th September, 1875:—abstracted from Returns made by the respective Medical Officers.

| PROVINCES. | No. Vaccinated in *Workhouses* by Medical Officers thereof. | | | No. of Cases Vaccinated by Medical Officers of *Dispensary Districts.* | Total Number returned in Columns 4 and 5. | PROVINCES. |
|---|---|---|---|---|---|---|
| | Successful Cases. | Unsuccessful Cases. | Total. | | | |
| 1 | 2. | 3. | 4. | 5. | 6. | |
| ULSTER, . . . | 411 | 17 | 428 | 38,043 | 38,471 | ULSTER. |
| MUNSTER, . . . | 502 | 25 | 527 | 33,857 | 34,384 | MUNSTER. |
| LEINSTER, . . . | 372 | 25 | 307 | 26,561 | 20,001 | LEINSTER. |
| CONNAUGHT, . . . | 338 | 23 | 301 | 39,876 | 40,237 | CONNAUGHT. |
| Total, . . | 1,023 | 90 | 1,713 | 137,340 | 139,053 | |

No. 5.—NUMBER of CASES of SCARLATINA, SMALLPOX, and FEVER, reported by Medical Officers of Dispensaries in Ireland, as having been attended in the Quarters ended 31st December, 1874, 31st March, 30th June, and 30th September, 1875.

| PROVINCES. | Quarters ended | Scarlatina. | Smallpox. | Fever. |
|---|---|---|---|---|
| ULSTER, . . | December 31st, 1874, . . | 1,035 | 41 | 711 |
| | March 31st, 1875, . . | 1,120 | 27 | 899 |
| | June 30th, 1875, . . | 1,235 | 41 | 907 |
| | September 30th, 1875, . . | 1,153 | 37 | 732 |
| MUNSTER, . . | December 31st, 1874, . . | 221 | 8 | 1,059 |
| | March 31st, 1875, . . | 92 | – | 1,306 |
| | June 30th, 1875, . . | 80 | – | 1,401 |
| | September 30th, 1875, . . | 230 | – | 1,023 |
| LEINSTER, . . | December 31st, 1874, . . | 1,021 | – | 906 |
| | March 31st, 1875, . . | 570 | 5 | 1,112 |
| | June 30th, 1875, . . | 458 | 47 | 953 |
| | September 30th, 1875, . . | 372 | – | 024 |
| CONNAUGHT, . | December 31st, 1874, . . | 241 | 100 | 360 |
| | March 31st, 1875, . . | 312 | 218 | 425 |
| | June 30th, 1875, . . | 220 | 251 | 402 |
| | September 30th, 1875, . . | 03 | 45 | 304 |
| SUMMARY. | | | | |
| IRELAND, . . | December 31st, 1874, . . | 3,118 | 209 | 3,132 |
| | March 31st, 1875, . . | 2,100 | 260 | 3,742 |
| | June 30th, 1875, . . | 2,002 | 339 | 3,723 |
| | September 30th, 1875, . . | 1,848 | 82 | 2,083 |
| | Total, . . . . | 9,068 | 880 | 13,280 |

No. 6.—Index List of Dispensary Districts; with Names of Unions in which they are situate, and References to Pages in which the Districts are to be found in the Appendix.


| Names of Dispensary Districts. | Unions in which situate. | References to: Dispensary Districts' Statistical Table; App. E, No. 1. | References to: Dispensaries' Financial and Relief Table; App. E, No. 2. |
|---|---|---|---|
| | | Page | Page |
| Abbey, | Tuam, | – | 145 |
| Abbeyfeale, | Newcastle, | 112 | 131 |
| Abbeyleix, | Abbeyleix, | – | 140 |
| Abbeyshrule, | Ballymahon, | – | 138 |
| Achill, | Newport, | – | 147 |
| Aclare, | Tobercurry, | – | 148 |
| Adare, | Croom, | – | 130 |
| Aghada, | Midleton, | – | 128 |
| Aghadowey, | Coleraine, | – | 121 |
| Aghalee, | Lurgan, | – | 116 |
| Ahascragh, | Ballinasloe, | 113 | 143 |
| Ahoghill, | Ballymena, | – | 115 |
| Annamoe, | Rathdrum, | – | 143 |
| Annacarriga, | Scariff, | – | 125 |
| Annacotty, | Limerick, | – | 131 |
| Annahilt, | Lisburn, | – | 116 |
| Antrim, | Antrim, | – | 114 |
| Ardagh, | Newcastle, | 112 | 131 |
| Ardara, | Glenties, | – | 118 |
| Ardee, | Ardee, | – | 138 |
| Ardfert, | Tralee, | – | 130 |
| Ardfinnan, | Clogheen, | – | 132 |
| Ardmore, | Youghal, | – | 129 |
| Ardrahan, | Gort, | – | 144 |
| Arklow, | Rathdrum, | – | 143 |
| Armagh, | Armagh, | – | 116 |
| Arran, | Galway, | – | 143 |
| Articlave, | Coleraine, | – | 121 |
| Arvagh, | Cavan, | – | 117 |
| Ashford, | Rathdrum, | 113 | 143 |
| Askeaton, | Rathkeale, | – | 131 |
| Athboy, | Trim, | 113 | 140 |
| Athenry, | Loughrea, | – | 144 |
| Athleague, | Roscommon, | – | 147 |
| Athlone, | Athlone, | – | 141 |
| Athy, | Athy, | – | 136 |
| Aughnacloy, | Clogher, | – | 123 |
| Aughrim, | Carrick-on-Shannon, | – | 145 |
| Aughrim, | Rathdrum, | – | 143 |
| Awenascale, | Dingle, | – | 129 |
| Bagenalstown, | Carlow, | – | 134 |
| Bailieborough, | Bailieborough, | – | 117 |
| Balbriggan, | Balrothery, | – | 134 |
| Balla, | Castlebar, | – | 146 |
| Ballaghaderreen, | Castlerea, | – | 147 |
| Balleen, | Urlingford, | – | 137 |
| Ballickmoyler and Newtown, | Carlow, | – | 134 |
| Ballina, | Ballina, | – | 145 |
| Ballinakill, | Abbeyleix, | – | 140 |
| Ballinalee, | Granard, | – | 138 |
| Ballinameen, | Boyle, | – | 147 |
| Ballinamore, | Bawnboy, | – | 117 |
| Ballinasloe, | Ballinasloe, | – | 143 |
| Ballincollig, | Cork, | – | 126 |
| Ballindine, | Claremorris, | – | 146 |
| Ballineen, | Dunmanway, | – | 127 |
| Ballingarry, | Callan, | – | 136 |
| Ballinrobe, | Ballinrobe, | – | 146 |
| Ballintra, | Ballyshannon, | – | 117 |
| Ballybay, | Castleblayney, | – | [illegible] |
| Ballyboggan, | Edenderry, | – | 137 |
| Ballycarry, | Larne, | – | 115 |
| Ballycastle, | Ballycastle, | – | 115 |
| Ballycastle, | Killala, | – | 146 |
| Ballyclogh, | Mallow, | – | 127 |
| Ballyconnell, | Bawnboy, | – | 117 |
| Ballyduff, | Lismore, | – | 133 |
| Ballyduff, | Listowel, | – | 129 |
| Ballyfarnon, | Boyle, | – | 147 |
| Ballyfeard, | Kinsale, | – | 127 |
| Ballygarvan, | Cork, | – | 126 |
| Ballygawley, | Clogher, | – | 123 |
| Ballyhaise, | Cavan, | – | 117 |
| Ballyhaunis, | Claremorris, | – | 146 |
| Ballyhooly, | Fermoy, | – | 127 |
| Ballybunion, | Listowel, | – | 129 |
| Ballyjamesduff, | Oldcastle, | – | 138 |
| Ballykelly, | Limavady, | – | 121 |
| Ballyleague, | Roscommon, | – | 147 |
| Ballylesson, | Lisburn, | – | 116 |
| Ballylongford, | Listowel, | – | 129 |
| Ballylynan, | Athy, | – | 135 |
| Ballymacarbery, | Clonmel, | – | 132 |
| Ballymagran, | Dungannon, | – | 123 |
| Ballymahon, | Ballymahon, | – | 138 |
| Ballymartle, | Kinsale, | – | 127 |
| Ballymena, | Ballymena, | – | 115 |
| Ballymoney, | Ballymoney, | – | 115 |
| Ballymore, | Ballymahon, | 113 | 138 |
| Ballymote, | Sligo, | – | 148 |
| Ballynacally, | Killadysert, | – | 125 |
| Ballynacargy, | Mullingar, | – | 141 |
| Ballynahinch, | Downpatrick, | – | 119 |
| Ballynoe, | Fermoy, | – | 127 |
| Ballynure, | Larne, | – | 115 |
| Ballyragget, | Castlecomer, | – | 136 |
| Ballyroan, | Abbeyleix, | – | 140 |
| Ballyshannon, | Ballyshannon, | – | 117 |
| Ballyvaghan, | Ballyvaghan, | – | 124 |
| Ballyward, | Banbridge, | – | 119 |
| Baltinglass, | Baltinglass, | – | 142 |
| Banagher, | Parsonstown, | – | 137 |
| Banbridge, | Banbridge, | – | 119 |
| Bandon, | Bandon, | – | 125 |
| Bangor, | Belmullet, | – | 146 |
| Bangor, | Newtownards, | – | 120 |
| Bannow, | Wexford, | – | 142 |
| Bansha, | Tipperary, | – | 133 |
| Bantry, | Bantry, | – | 126 |
| Barronstown, | Dundalk, | – | 139 |
| Belfast, | Belfast, | – | 115 |
| Bellaghy, | Magherafelt, | – | 122 |
| Bellananagh, | Cavan, | – | 117 |
| Bellarena, | Limavady, | – | 121 |
| Belleek, | Ballyshannon, | – | 117 |
| Belturbet, | Cavan, | – | 117 |
| Benburb, | Dungannon, | – | 123 |


[*continued.*

| Names of Dispensary Districts. | Unions in which situate. | References to Dispensary Districts' Statistical Table; App. E, No. 1. | References to Dispensaries' Financial and Relief Table; App. E, No. 2. |
|---|---|---|---|
| | | Page | Page |
| Binghamstown, . | Belmullet, . | - | 146 |
| Blackrock and Stillorgan, . | Rathdown, . | - | 135 |
| Blackwatertown, | Armagh, . . | - | 110 |
| Blanchardstown & Castleknock, | North Dublin, . | - | 134 |
| Blarney, . . | Cork, . . | - | 126 |
| Blessington and Ballymore, . | Naas, . . | - | 136 |
| Boherboy, . . | Kanturk, . . | 112 | 127 |
| Borris, . . | Carlow, . . | - | 134 |
| Borris-in-Ossory, | Donaghmore, . | - | 140 |
| Borrisokane, . | Borrisokane, . | - | 131 |
| Borrisoleigh, . | Thurles, . . | - | 133 |
| Bourney, . . | Roscrea, . . | - | 132 |
| Boyle, . . | Boyle, . . | 113 | 147 |
| Bray and Rathmichael, . . | Rathdown, . | - | 135 |
| Bridewell, . | Athlone, . . | - | 141 |
| Bridgetown, . | Limerick, . . | - | 131 |
| Bridgetown, . | Wexford, . . | - | 142 |
| Broadford, . . | Newcastle, . | 112 | 131 |
| Broadway, . . | Wexford, . . | - | 142 |
| Brookeborough, | Lisnaskea, . | - | 121 |
| Brosna, . . | Tralee, . . | - | 130 |
| Broughshane, . | Ballymena, . | - | 115 |
| Bruff, . . . | Kilmallock, . | - | 130 |
| Bruree, . . | Kilmallock, . | - | 130 |
| Bryansford, . | Kilkeel, . . | - | 110 |
| Bullaun, . . | Loughrea, . | - | 144 |
| Buncrana, . . | Inishowen, . | - | 118 |
| Bunmahon, . | Kilmacthomas, | - | 133 |
| Burt, . . . | Londonderry, . | - | 121 |
| Bushmills, . | Coleraine, . | - | 121 |
| Buttevant, . . | Mallow, . . | - | 127 |
| Caher, . . | Cahersiveen, . | - | 129 |
| Caher, . . | Clogheen, . | - | 132 |
| Caherconlish, . | Limerick, . | - | 131 |
| Caledon, . . | Armagh, . . | - | 110 |
| Callan, . . | Callan, . . | - | 130 |
| Camolin, . . | Gorey, . . | - | 141 |
| Cannaway, . . | Macroom, . . | - | 127 |
| Cappagh, . . | Tipperary, . | - | 133 |
| Cappoquin, . | Lismore, . . | - | 133 |
| Carbury, . . | Edenderry, . | - | 137 |
| Carlingford, . | Dundalk, . . | - | 139 |
| Carlow, . . | Carlow, . . | - | 134 |
| Carndonagh, . | Inishowen, . | - | 118 |
| Carney, . . | Sligo, . . | - | 148 |
| Carrick, . . | Glenties, . . | - | 118 |
| Carrickbyrne, . | New Ross, . | - | 143 |
| Carrickfergus, . | Larne, . . | - | 115 |
| Carrickmacross, | Carrickmacross, | - | 122 |
| Carrick-on-Suir, | Carrick-on-Suir, | - | 131 |
| Carrigaholt, . | Kilrush, . . | 112 | 125 |
| Carrigaline, . | Cork, . . | - | 126 |
| Carrigaline, . | Kinsale, . . | - | 127 |
| Carrigallen, . | Mohill, . . | - | 145 |
| Carrignavar, . | Cork, . . | - | 126 |
| Cashel, . . | Cashel, . . | 112 | 131 |
| Castlebar, . . | Castlebar, . | 113 | 146 |
| Castlebellingham | Ardee, . . | - | 138 |
| Castleblayney, . | Castleblayney, . | - | 122 |
| Castlecomer, . | Castlecomer, . | - | 136 |
| Castlederg and Killeter, . . | Castlederg, . | - | 123 |
| Castledermot, . | Athy, . . | - | 135 |
| Castle Finn, . | Strabane, . . | - | 124 |
| Castlegregory, . | Dingle, . . | - | 129 |
| Castle Island, . | Tralee, . . | - | 130 |
| Castlemaine, . | Tralee, . . | - | 130 |
| Castlemartyr, . | Midleton, . . | - | 128 |
| Castleplunket, . | Castlerea, . . | - | 147 |
| Castlepollard, . | Delvin, . . | - | 141 |
| Castle Quarter, . | Ballymoney, . | - | 115 |
| Castlerea, . . | Castlerea, . | - | 147 |
| Castlereagh, . | Belfast, . . | - | 115 |
| Castleshane, . | Monaghan, . | - | 123 |
| Castletown, . | Abbeyleix, . | - | 140 |
| Castletown, . | Castletown, . | - | 126 |
| Castletown, . | Croom, . . | - | 130 |
| Castletown, . | Navan, . . | - | 139 |
| Castletown Geoghegan, . . | Mullingar, . | - | 141 |
| Cavan, . . | Cavan, . . | - | 117 |
| Celbridge, | Celbridge, . | - | 135 |
| Charleville, . | Kilmallock, . | - | 130 |
| Church Hill, . | Ballyshannon, . | - | 117 |
| Churchhill, . | Letterkenny, . | - | 119 |
| Clane and Timahoe North, . | Naas, . . | - | 136 |
| Clara, . . . | Tullamore, . | - | 137 |
| Claremorris, . | Claremorris, . | - | 146 |
| Clarina, . . | Limerick, . | - | 131 |
| Clashmore, . | Youghal, . . | - | 129 |
| Claudy, . . | Londonderry, . | - | 121 |
| Clifden, . . | Clifden, . . | - | 143 |
| Clogh, . . | Ballymena, . | - | 115 |
| Cloghan, . . | Stranorlar, . | - | 119 |
| Clogheen, . . | Clogheen, . | - | 132 |
| Clogher, . . | Clogher, . . | - | 123 |
| Cloghjordan, . | Borrisokane, . | - | 131 |
| Clonakilty, . | Clonakilty, . | - | 126 |
| Clonaslee, . . | Mountmellick, . | - | 140 |
| Clonavaddy, . | Dungannon, . | - | 123 |
| Clonbrock, . | Mount Bellew, | - | 144 |
| Clondalkin, . | South Dublin, . | - | 135 |
| Clonelly, . . | Irvinestown, . | - | 121 |
| Clones, . . | Clones, . . | - | 122 |
| Clonmany, . . | Inishowen, . | - | 118 |
| Clonmel & St. Mary's, | Clonmel, . . | - | 132 |
| Clonmellon, . | Delvin, . . | - | 141 |
| Clonmoyle, . | Macroom, . | - | 127 |
| Clonroche, . | Enniscorthy, . | - | 141 |
| Clontarf and Howth, . . | North Dublin, | - | 134 |
| Clonygowan, . | Mountmellick, . | - | 140 |
| Cloonbur, . . | Oughterard, . | - | 146 |
| Clough, . . | Downpatrick, . | - | 119 |
| Cloyne, . . | Midleton, . . | - | 128 |
| Coagh, . . | Cookstown, . | - | 123 |
| Coal Island, . | Dungannon, . | - | 123 |
| Coleraine, . . | Coleraine, . | - | 121 |
| Collon, . . | Ardee, . . | - | 138 |
| Collooney, . . | Sligo, . . | - | 148 |
| Comber, . . | Newtownards, . | - | 120 |
| Cong, . . . | Ballinrobe, . | - | 146 |
| Connor, . . | Antrim, . . | - | 114 |
| Cookstown, . | Cookstown, . | - | 123 |
| Coolcappagh, . | Limerick, . | - | 131 |
| Cooleney, . . | Tobercurry, . | - | 148 |
| Coolattin and Clonegall, . | Shillelagh, . | - | 143 |
| Coole, . . | Granard, . . | - | 136 |
| Coolgreany, . | Gorey, . . | - | 141 |

[*continued.*

| Names of Dispensary Districts. | Unions in which situate. | References to: Dispensary Districts' Statistical Table; App. E, No. 1. | References to: Dispensaries' Financial and Relief Table; App. E, No. 2. |
|---|---|---|---|
| | | Page | Page |
| Coolkenno and Hacketstown, | Shillelagh, . | – | 143 |
| Coolmountain, . | Dunmanway, . | – | 127 |
| Coolock and Drumcondra, . | North Dublin, . | – | 134 |
| Coolrain, . . | Mountmellick, . | – | 140 |
| Coom, . . | Killarney, . | – | 129 |
| Cootehill, . . | Cootehill, . . | – | 117 |
| Cork, . . . | Cork, . . | – | 120 |
| Corrofin, . . | Corrofin, . . | – | 124 |
| Courceys, . . | Kinsale, . . | – | 127 |
| Cragaknock, . | Kilrush, . . | – | 125 |
| Creagh, . . | Ballinasloe, . | – | 143 |
| Croagh, . . | Ballycastle, . | – | 115 |
| Croom, . . | Croom, . . | – | 130 |
| Crosgar, . . | Banbridge, . | 112 | 119 |
| Crossabeg, . . | Wexford, . . | – | 142 |
| Crossakeel, . | Oldcastle, . . | – | 139 |
| Crossbane, . | Bailieborough, | – | 117 |
| Crossmaglen, . | Castleblayney, . | – | 123 |
| Crossmolina, . | Ballina, . . | – | 145 |
| Crossroads, . | Dunfanaghy, . | – | 118 |
| Crumlin, . . | Antrim, . . | – | 114 |
| Crushseen, . . | Ennis, . . | – | 125 |
| Cullen, . . | Millstreet, . | – | 126 |
| Cushendall, . | Ballycastle, . | 112 | 115 |
| Darrynane, . | Cahercíveen, . | – | 129 |
| Dawson Grove, . | Cootehill, . . | – | 117 |
| Delgany, . . | Rathdown, . | – | 135 |
| Delvin, . . | Delvin, . . | – | 141 |
| Derrylin, . . | Lisnaskea, . | – | 121 |
| Dervock, . . | Ballymoney, . | – | 125 |
| Dingle, . . | Dingle, . . | – | 129 |
| Dirraw, . . | Ballymoney, . | – | 115 |
| Doagh, . . | Antrim, . . | – | 114 |
| Donaghadee, . | Newtownards, . | – | 120 |
| Donaghmore, . | Newry, . . | – | 120 |
| Donaghmoyne, . | Carrickmacross, | – | 123 |
| Donegal, . . | Donegal, . . | – | 118 |
| Doneraile, . . | Mallow, . . | – | 127 |
| Donnybrook, . | South Dublin, . | – | 135 |
| Doocharry, . | Glenties, . . | – | 118 |
| Douglas, . . | Cork, . . | – | 126 |
| Downpatrick, . | Downpatrick, . | – | 110 |
| Draperstown, . | Magherafelt, . | – | 122 |
| Dripsey, . . | Cork, . . | – | 126 |
| Drogheda, . . | Drogheda, . | – | 139 |
| Dromdaleague, . | Skibbereen, . | – | 128 |
| Dromiskin, . | Dundalk, . . | – | 139 |
| Dromore, . . | Banbridge, . | – | 119 |
| Dromore, . . | Omagh, . . | – | 124 |
| Drum . . | Cootehill, . . | – | 117 |
| Drumahaire, . | Manorhamilton, | – | 146 |
| Drumcondra, . | Ardee, . . | – | 138 |
| Drumkeeran, . | Manorhamilton, | – | 146 |
| Drumlish, . . | Longford, . | – | 138 |
| Drumquin, | Castlederg, . | – | 123 |
| Drumquin . | Omagh, . . | – | 124 |
| Drumshambo, . | Car-on-Shannon | – | 145 |
| Duleek, . . | Drogheda, . | – | 139 |
| Dunboyne, . | Dunshaughlin, | – | 139 |
| Dundalk, . . | Dundalk, . . | – | 139 |
| Dundrum and Glencullen, . | Rathdown, . | – | 135 |
| Dunfanaghy, . | Dunfanaghy, . | – | 118 |
| Dungannon, . | Dungannon, . | – | 123 |
| Dunganstown, . | Rathdrum, . | – | 143 |
| Dungarvan, . | Dungarvan, . | – | 133 |
| Dungiven, . . | Limavady, . | – | 121 |
| Dungloe, . . | Glenties, . . | – | 118 |
| Dunkineely, . | Donegal, . . | – | 118 |
| Dunlavin, . . | Baltinglass, . | – | 142 |
| Dunleer, . . | Ardee, . . | – | 138 |
| Dunmanway, . | Dunmanway, . | – | 127 |
| Dunmore, . . | Glennamaddy, . | – | 144 |
| Dunmore, . | Tuam, . . | – | 145 |
| Dunmurry, . | Lisburn, . . | – | 116 |
| Dunnamanagh, . | Strabane, . . | – | 124 |
| Durrow, . . | Abbeyleix, . | – | 140 |
| Durrus and Kilcrohane, . . | Bantry, . . | – | 126 |
| Dysartmoon, . | New Ross, . | – | 142 |
| Easkey, . . | Dromore, West, | – | 148 |
| Edenderry, . | Edenderry, . | – | 137 |
| Ederney, . . | Irvinestown . | – | 121 |
| Elphin, . . | Strokestown, . | – | 148 |
| Ely, . . . | Enniskillen, . | – | 120 |
| Eglinton, . . | Londonderry, . | – | 121 |
| Emlagh, . . | Caherciveen, . | – | 129 |
| Emly, . . . | Tipperary, . | – | 133 |
| Emo, . . . | Mountmellick, . | – | 140 |
| Ennis, . . | Ennis, . . | – | 125 |
| Enniscorthy, . | Enniscorthy, . | – | 141 |
| Enniskillen, . | Enniskillen, . | 112 | 120 |
| Ennistymon, . | Ennistymon, . | – | 125 |
| Eyrecourt, . . | Portumna, . | – | 145 |
| Fannett, . . | Millford, . . | – | 119 |
| Feakle, . . | Scariff, . . | – | 125 |
| Feenagh, . . | Newcastle, . | 112 | 131 |
| Feeny, . . | Limavady, . | – | 121 |
| Fennagh and Myshall, . . | Carlow, . . | – | 134 |
| Ferbane, . . | Parsonstown, . | – | 137 |
| Fermoy, . . | Fermoy, . . | – | 127 |
| Ferns, . . | Enniscorthy, . | – | 141 |
| Fethard, . . | Cashel, . . | – | 131 |
| Fethard, . . | New Ross, . | – | 142 |
| Finglas and Glasnevin, . | North Dublin, . | – | 134 |
| Finnea, . . | Granard, . . | – | 138 |
| Fintona, . . | Omagh, . . | – | 124 |
| Fivemiletown, . | Clogher, . . | – | 123 |
| Florencecourt, . | Enniskillen, . | – | 120 |
| Fontstown, . | Athy, . . | – | 136 |
| Forkhill, . . | Newry, . . | – | 120 |
| Foxford, . . | Swineford, . | – | 147 |
| Frankford, . . | Parsonstown, . | – | 137 |
| Frenchpark, . | Castlerea, . | – | 147 |
| Freshford, . . | Kilkenny, . | – | 136 |
| Galbally, . . | Mitchelstown, . | – | 128 |
| Galgorm, . . | Ballymena, . | – | 115 |
| Galway, . . | Galway, . . | – | 143 |
| Garrangibbon, . | Carrick-on-Suir, | – | 131 |
| Garristown, . | Dunshaughlin, | – | 139 |
| Garvagh, . . | Coleraine, . | – | 121 |
| Glanbehy, . . | Caherciveen, . | – | 129 |
| Glassan, . . | Athlone, . . | – | 141 |
| Glasslough, . | Monaghan, . | – | 122 |
| Glenarm, . . | Larne, . . | – | 115 |
| Glenavy, . . | Lisburn, . . | – | 116 |
| Glendermot, . | Londonderry, . | – | 121 |
| Glengarriff, . | Bantry, . . | – | 126 |
| Glennamaddy, . | Glennamaddy, . | – | 144 |
| Glenties, . . | Glenties, . . | – | 118 |
| Glenwhirry, . | Ballymena, . | – | 115 |
| Golden, . . | Tipperary, . | – | 133 |
| Goleen, . . | Skull, . . | – | 129 |


[*continued*.

| Names of Dispensary Districts. | Unions in which situate. | References to: Dispensary Districts' Statistical Table; App. E, No. 1. | References to: Dispensaries' Financial and Relief Table; App. E, No. 2. |
|---|---|---|---|
| | | Page | Page |
| Gorey, . . | Gorey, . . | – | 141 |
| Gort, . . | Gort, . . | – | 144 |
| Gortin, . . | Gortin, . . | – | 123 |
| Gowran, . . | Kilkenny, | – | 126 |
| Graigue, . . | Thomastown, . | – | 137 |
| Granard, . . | Granard, . . | – | 138 |
| Grean, . . | Tipperary, . | – | 131 |
| Grey Abbey, . | Newtownards, . | – | 120 |
| Gurteen, . . | Boyle, . . | – | 147 |
| Headford, . . | Tuam, . . | – | 145 |
| Hillsborough, . | Lisburn, . . | – | 116 |
| Hollymount, . | Ballinrobe, . | – | 146 |
| Holmpatrick, . | Balrothery, . | – | 131 |
| Holycross, . | Thurles, . . | – | 133 |
| Holywell, . . | Enniskillen, . | – | 120 |
| Hospital, . . | Kilmallock, . | – | 130 |
| Inchigeelagh, . | Macroom, . | – | 127 |
| Inishannon, . | Bandon, . . | – | 125 |
| Inistioge, . . | Thomastown, . | – | 137 |
| Innfield, . . | Trim, . . | – | 140 |
| Irvinestown, . | Irvinestown, . | – | 121 |
| Islandeady, . | Westport, . | – | 147 |
| Jamestown, . | Car-on-Shannon | – | 145 |
| Johnstown, . | Edenderry, . | – | 137 |
| Johnstown, . | Urlingford, . | – | 137 |
| Kanturk, . . | Kanturk, . . | – | 127 |
| Keadue, . . | Boyle, . . | – | 147 |
| Keady, . . | Armagh, . . | – | 116 |
| Kells, . . . | Kells, . . | – | 139 |
| Kenmare, . . | Kenmare, . | – | 120 |
| Kilbeggan, . | Tullamore, . | – | 137 |
| Kilbrittain, . | Bandon, . . | – | 125 |
| Kilcatherine, . | Castletown, . | – | 126 |
| Kilcock, . . | Celbridge, . | – | 135 |
| Kilcooly, . . | Urlingford, . | – | 137 |
| Kilcullen, . . | Naas, . . | – | 136 |
| Kildare, . . | Naas, . . | – | 136 |
| Kildarry, . . | Londonderry, . | – | 121 |
| Kildorrery, . | Mitchelstown, . | – | 128 |
| Kilfinane, . . | Kilmallock, . | – | 130 |
| Kilgarvan, . . | Kenmare, . | – | 120 |
| Kilgobban, . | Tralee, . . | – | 130 |
| Kilkee, . . | Kilrush, . . | – | 125 |
| Kilkeel, . . | Kilkeel, . . | – | 119 |
| Kilkelly, . . | Swineford, . | – | 147 |
| Kilkenny, . . | Kilkenny, . | – | 137 |
| Kilkishen, . . | Tulla, . . | – | 125 |
| Killaan, . . | Ballinasloe, . | – | 143 |
| Killala, . . | Killala, . . | – | 146 |
| Killann, . . | Enniscorthy, . | – | 141 |
| Killanniv, . . | Ennis, . . | – | 125 |
| Killarney, . . | Killarney, . | – | 129 |
| Killashee, . . | Longford, . | – | 138 |
| Killea, . . | Londonderry, . | – | 121 |
| Killeagh, . . | Youghal, . . | – | 129 |
| Killeen, . . | Dunshaughlin, | 113 | 139 |
| Killenagh & Wells | Gorey, . . | – | 141 |
| Killenaule, . | Cashel, . . | – | 131 |
| Killererin, . | Mount Bellew, | – | 144 |
| Killeshandra, . | Cavan, . . | – | 117 |
| Killiney, . . | Rathdown, . | – | 136 |
| Killorglin, . . | Killarney, . | – | 129 |
| Killough, . . | Downpatrick, . | 112 | 119 |
| Killoughy, . . | Tullamore, . | – | 137 |
| Killucan, . . | Mullingar, . | – | 141 |
| Killybegs, . . | Glenties, . . | – | 118 |
| Killygordon, . | Stranorlar, . | – | 119 |
| Killyleagh, . | Downpatrick, . | – | 119 |
| Killyon, . . | Parsonstown, . | – | 137 |
| Kilmacthomas, . | Kilmacthomas, | – | 133 |
| Kilmacrenan and Milford, . . | Milford, . . | – | 119 |
| Kilmakevoge, . | Waterford, . | – | 133 |
| Kilmallock, . | Kilmallock, . | – | 130 |
| Kilmeaden, . | Waterford, . | – | 133 |
| Kilmihil, . . | Kilrush, . . | – | 125 |
| Kilmoganny, . | Callan, . . | – | 136 |
| Kilmood, . . | Newtownards, . | – | 120 |
| Kilmore, . . | Monaghan, . | – | 123 |
| Kilnaleck, . . | Cavan, . . | – | 117 |
| Kilpatrick, . | Cashel, . . | – | 131 |
| Kilrea, . . | Ballymoney, . | – | 115 |
| Kilrush, . . | Kilrush, . . | – | 125 |
| Kilsallaghan, . | Balrothery, . | 113 | 134 |
| Kilshannig, . | Mallow, . . | – | 127 |
| Kilsheelan, . | Clonmel, . . | – | 132 |
| Kilskeer, . . | Kells, . . | – | 139 |
| Kiltamagh, . | Swineford, . | – | 147 |
| Kiltegan, . . | Baltinglass, . | – | 142 |
| Kiltinan, . . | Clonmel, . . | – | 132 |
| Kiltoom, . . | Athlone, . . | – | 141 |
| Kiltormer, . | Ballinasloe, . | – | 143 |
| Kilworth, . . | Fermoy, . . | – | 127 |
| Kingscourt, . | Bailieborough, | – | 117 |
| Kingstown, . | Rathdown, . | 113 | 135 |
| Kinlough, . . | Ballyshannon, . | – | 117 |
| Kinnitty, . . | Parsonstown, . | – | 137 |
| Kinsale, . . | Kinsale, . . | – | 127 |
| Kinvarra, . . | Gort, . . | – | 144 |
| Knockbracken, . | Lisburn, . . | – | 116 |
| Knocktopher, . | Thomastown, . | – | 137 |
| Labasheeda, . | Kilradysart, . | – | 125 |
| Laby, . . | Donegal, . . | – | 118 |
| Larne, . . | Larne, . . | – | 115 |
| Laurencetown, . | Ballinasloe, . | – | 143 |
| Leighlinbridge, | Carlow, . . | 113 | 134 |
| Leitrim, . . | Car-on-Shannon | – | 145 |
| Letterkenny, . | Letterkenny, . | – | 119 |
| Lettermore, . | Oughterard, . | – | 145 |
| Limavady, . | Limavady, . | 112 | 121 |
| Limerick, City of, | Limerick, . | – | 131 |
| Lisbellaw, . . | Enniskillen, . | – | 120 |
| Lisburn, . . | Lisburn, . . | – | 116 |
| Lismore, . . | Lismore, . . | – | 133 |
| Lisnaskea, . . | Lisnaskea, . | 112 | 121 |
| Listowel, . . | Listowel, . | – | 120 |
| Littleton, . . | Thurles, . . | – | 133 |
| Londonderry, City of, . . | Londonderry, . | – | 121 |
| Longford, . . | Longford, . | – | 138 |
| Loughbrickland, | Banbridge, . | – | 119 |
| Loughgall, . . | Armagh, . . | – | 116 |
| Loughrea, . . | Loughrea, . | – | 144 |
| Louisburgh, . | Westport, . | – | 147 |
| Louth, . . | Dundalk, . . | 113 | 139 |
| Lowpark, . . | Swineford, . | – | 147 |
| Lucan, . . | Celbridge, . | – | 135 |
| Lurgan, . . | Lurgan, . . | – | 118 |
| Lurganboy, . | Manorhamilton, | – | 145 |
| Lusk, . . . | Balrothery, . | – | 134 |
| Macroom, . . | Macroom, . | – | 127 |
| Maghera, . . | Magherafelt, . | – | 122 |
| Magherafelt, . | Magherafelt, . | – | 122 |


[continued.

| Names of Dispensary Districts. | Unions in which situate. | References to Dispensary Districts' Statistical Table; App. E, No. 1. | References to Dispensaries' Financial and Relief Table; App. E, No. 2. |
|---|---|---|---|
| | | Page | Page |
| Maguiresbridge, | Lisnaskea, . | – | 121 |
| Malahide, . . | Balrothery, . | – | 134 |
| Malin, . . | Inishowen, . | – | 118 |
| Mallow, . . | Mallow, . . | – | 127 |
| Manorcunningham, . . | Letterkenny, . | – | 119 |
| Manorhamilton, | Manorhamilton, | – | 146 |
| Markethill, . | Armagh, . . | – | 116 |
| Marlfield, . . | Clonmel, . . | – | 132 |
| Maryborough, . | Mountmellick, . | – | 140 |
| Maynooth, . . | Celbridge, . | – | 135 |
| Meigh, . . | Newry, . | – | 120 |
| Midleton, . . | Midleton, . | – | 128 |
| Milford, . . | Kanturk, . . | | 127 |
| Millstreet, . . | Millstreet, . | – | 128 |
| Milltown, . . | Killarney, . | – | 129 |
| Milltown, . . | Mullingar, . | – | 141 |
| Miltown Malbay, | Ennistymon, . | – | 125 |
| Mitchelstown, . | Mitchelstown, . | – | 128 |
| Moate, . . | Athlone, . . | – | 141 |
| Mohill, . . | Mohill, . . | – | 145 |
| Moira, . . | Lurgan, . . | – | 116 |
| Molahiffe, . . | Killarney, . | – | 129 |
| Monaghan, . | Monaghan, . | – | 123 |
| Monasterboice, | Drogheda, . | – | 139 |
| Monasterevan, . | Athy, . . | – | 135 |
| Moneymore, . | Magherafelt, . | – | 122 |
| Mount Bellew, . | Mount Bellew, | – | 144 |
| Mountcharles, . | Donegal, . . | – | 118 |
| Mountmellick, . | Mountmellick, . | – | 141 |
| Mountnorris, . | Newry, . . | – | 120 |
| Mountrath, . | Mountmellick, . | – | 141 |
| Mountshannon, | Scariff, . . | – | 125 |
| Moville, . . | Inishowen, . | – | 118 |
| Moycullen, . | Galway, . . | – | 143 |
| Moynalty, . . | Kells, . . | – | 139 |
| Moyne, . . | Thurles, . . | – | 133 |
| Mullaghglass, . | Newry, . . | – | 120 |
| Mullinahone, . | Callan, . . | – | 136 |
| Mullingar, . . | Mullingar, . | – | 141 |
| Multyfarnham, . | Mullingar, . | – | 141 |
| Murragh, . . | Bandon, . . | – | 126 |
| Murroe, . . | Limerick, . . | – | 131 |
| Naas & Curragh, | Naas, . . | – | 136 |
| Navan, . . | Navan, . . | – | 139 |
| Nenagh, . . | Nenagh, . . | – | 132 |
| Newbridge, . | Rathdrum, . | – | 143 |
| Newbridge, . | Naas, . . | – | 136 |
| Newcastle, . | Newcastle, . | – | 131 |
| Newcastle, . . | Rathdrum, . | 112 | 143 |
| Newmarket, . | Ennis, . . | – | 125 |
| Newmarket, . | Kanturk, . . | 112 | 127 |
| Newport, . . | Nenagh, . . | – | 132 |
| Newport, . . | Newport, . . | – | 147 |
| New Ross, . . | New Ross, . | – | 142 |
| Newry, . . | Newry, . . | 112 | 120 |
| Newtownards, . | Newtownards, . | – | 120 |
| Newtownbarry, . | Enniscorthy, . | – | 141 |
| Newtownbutler, | Clones, . . | – | 123 |
| Newtowngore, . | Bawnboy, . | – | 117 |
| Newtownhamilton, . . . | Castleblayney, | – | 122 |
| Newtown Stewart | Strabane, . | – | 124 |
| Nobber, . . | Kells, . . | – | 139 |
| North City, . | North Dublin, . | 113 | 134 |

| Names of Dispensary Districts. | Unions in which situate. | References to Dispensary Districts' Statistical Table; App. E, No. 1. | References to Dispensaries' Financial and Relief Table; App. E, No. 2. |
|---|---|---|---|
| | | Page | Page |
| Oldcastle, . . | Oldcastle, . | – | 139 |
| Old Ross, . . | New Ross, . | – | 142 |
| Omagh, . . | Omagh, . . | – | 124 |
| Oranmore, . . | Galway, . . | – | 143 |
| Oughterard, . | Oughterard, . | – | 143 |
| Oulart, . . | Enniscorthy, . | – | 141 |
| Painestown, . | Navan, . . | – | 139 |
| Pallaskenry, . | Rathkeale, . | – | 131 |
| Palmerstown, . | South Dublin, | – | 135 |
| Parsonstown, . | Parsonstown, . | – | 137 |
| Pettigoe, . . | Donegal, . . | – | 118 |
| Piltown, . . | Carrick-on-Suir, | – | 131 |
| Philipstown, . | Tullamore, . | – | 137 |
| Plumb Bridge, . | Gortin, . . | – | 123 |
| Points Pass, . | Newry, . . | – | 120 |
| Pomeroy, . . | Cookstown, . | – | 123 |
| Portadown, . | Lurgan, . . | – | 116 |
| Portaferry, . | Downpatrick, . | – | 119 |
| Portglenone, . | Ballymena, . | | 115 |
| Portlaw, . . | Carrick-on-Suir, | – | 131 |
| Portroe, . . | Nenagh, . . | – | 132 |
| Portumna, . . | Portumna, . | – | 145 |
| Powerscourt, . | Rathdown, . | – | 135 |
| Queenstown, . | Cork, . . | – | 126 |
| Quin, . . . | Tulla, . . | – | 126 |
| Raferagh, . . | Carrickmacross, | – | 122 |
| Rahan, . . | Mallow, . . | – | 127 |
| Randalstown, . | Antrim, . . | – | 114 |
| Raphoe, . . | Strabane, . . | – | 124 |
| Rathangan, . | Edenderry, . | – | 137 |
| Rathcoole, . . | Celbridge, . | – | 135 |
| Rathcormack, . | Fermoy, . . | – | 127 |
| Rathdowney, . | Donaghmore, . | 113 | 140 |
| Rathdrum, . . | Rathdrum, . | – | 143 |
| Rathfarnham, . | South Dublin, . | – | 135 |
| Rathfriland, . | Newry, . . | – | 120 |
| Rathgormuck, . | Carrick-on-Suir, | – | 131 |
| Rathkeale, . . | Rathkeale, . | – | 131 |
| Rathmelton, . | Milford, . . | 112 | 119 |
| Rathmines, . | South Dublin, | – | 135 |
| Rathmore, . . | Naas, . . | – | 136 |
| Rathmullan, . | Milford, . . | – | 119 |
| Rathvilly, . . | Baltinglass, . | – | 142 |
| Ratoath, . . | Dunshaughlin, | – | 139 |
| Ravensdale, . | Dundalk, . | – | 139 |
| Rhode, . . | Edenderry, . | – | 137 |
| Rich Hill, . . | Armagh, . . | – | 116 |
| Ringville, . . | Dungarvan, . | – | 133 |
| Rinvyle, . . | Clifden, . . | – | 143 |
| Riverstown, . | Parsonstown, . | – | 137 |
| Riverstown, . | Sligo, . . | – | 148 |
| Roadford, . . | Ennistymon, . | – | 125 |
| Robertstown and Kilmeague, . | Naas, . . | – | 136 |
| Roosky, . . | Strokestown, . | – | 148 |
| Roscommon, . | Roscommon, . | – | 147 |
| Roscrea, . . | Roscrea, . . | – | 132 |
| Rosguill, . . | Milford, . . | – | 119 |
| Rosscarbery, . | Clonakilty, . | – | 126 |
| Roslea, . . | Clones, . . | – | 122 |
| Rostrevor, . . | Kilkeel, . . | – | 119 |
| Roundstone, . | Clifden, . . | – | 143 |
| Rowan, . . | Mohill, . . | – | 145 |
| Rynn, . . | Mohill, . . | – | 145 |
| Saintfield, . . | Lisburn, . . | – | 116 |


[continued.

| Names of Dispensary Districts. | Unions in which situate. | References to Dispensary Districts' Statistical Table; App. E, No. 1. | References to Dispensaries' Financial and Relief Table; App. E, No. 2. |
|---|---|---|---|
| | | Page | Page |
| St. Mary's, | Drogheda, | - | 139 |
| St. Mullin's, | New Ross, | - | 142 |
| Scotstown, | Monaghan, | - | 123 |
| Scrabby, | Granard, | - | 138 |
| Seskinan, | Dungarvan, | - | 133 |
| Shanagolden, | Glin, | - | 130 |
| Shercock, | Bailieborough, | - | 117 |
| Shinrone, | Roscrea, | 112 | 132 |
| Silvermines, | Nenagh, | - | 132 |
| Six Mile Cross, | Omagh, | - | 124 |
| Skibbereen, | Skibbereen, | - | 128 |
| Skreen, | Dromore West, | - | 145 |
| Skull, | Skull, | - | 129 |
| Slievereagh, | Macroom, | - | 127 |
| Sligo, | Sligo, | - | 145 |
| Sneem, | Kenmare, | - | 129 |
| South City, | South Dublin, | - | 135 |
| Spiddal, | Galway, | - | 143 |
| Stamullen, | Drogheda, | - | 139 |
| Stewartstown, | Cookstown, | - | 123 |
| Strabane, | Strabane, | - | 124 |
| Stradbally, | Athy, | - | 136 |
| Stradone, | Cavan, | - | 117 |
| Strangford, | Downpatrick, | - | 119 |
| Stranorlar, | Stranorlar, | - | 119 |
| Street, | Granard, | - | 138 |
| Strokestown, | Strokestown, | - | 148 |
| Summerhill, | Trim, | - | 140 |
| Swanlinbar, | Bawnboy, | - | 117 |
| Swineford, | Swineford, | - | 147 |
| Swords, | Balrothery, | - | 134 |
| Taghmon and Glynn, | Wexford, | - | 142 |
| Tallaght, | South Dublin, | - | 135 |
| Tallow, | Lismore, | - | 133 |
| Tanderagee, | Banbridge, | - | 119 |
| Tarbert, | Glin, | - | 130 |
| Tartaraghan, | Lurgan, | - | 116 |
| Templemartin, | Bandon, | - | 126 |
| Templemichael, | Youghal, | - | 129 |
| Templemore, | Thurles, | - | 133 |
| Templepatrick, | Antrim, | - | 114 |
| Templeudigan, | New Ross, | - | 142 |
| Tempo, | Enniskillen, | - | 120 |
| Termon, | Bailieborough, | - | 117 |
| Termonfeckin, | Drogheda, | - | 139 |
| Terryglass, | Borrisokane, | - | 131 |
| Thomastown, | Thomastown, | - | 137 |
| Thurles, | Thurles, | - | 133 |
| Timoleague, | Clonakilty, | - | 126 |
| Tinahely, | Shillelagh, | - | 145 |
| Tipperary, | Tipperary, | - | 133 |
| Tiscoffin, | Kilkenny, | - | 137 |
| Tobercurry, | Tobercurry, | - | 148 |
| Toome, | Ballymena, | - | 115 |
| Toomevara, | Nenagh, | - | 132 |
| Tralee, | Tralee, | - | 136 |
| Tramore, | Waterford, | - | 133 |
| Trim, | Trim, | - | 140 |
| Tuam, | Tuam, | - | 146 |
| Tulla, | Tulla, | - | 125 |
| Tullagh, | Skibbereen | - | 128 |
| Tullamain, | Cashel, | - | 131 |
| Tullamore, | Tullamore, | - | 137 |
| Tullaroan, | Kilkenny, | - | 137 |
| Tullow, | Carlow, | - | 134 |
| Tullyvin, | Cootehill, | - | 117 |
| Tuosist, | Kenmare, | - | 129 |
| Turloughmore, | Galway, | - | 143 |
| Tynan, | Armagh, | - | 116 |
| Tyrrellspass, | Mullingar, | - | 141 |
| Ullid, | Waterford, | 112 | 133 |
| Union Hall, | Skibbereen, | - | 128 |
| Urlingford, | Urlingford, | - | 137 |
| Valencia, | Cahersiveen, | - | 129 |
| Ventry, | Dingle, | - | 129 |
| Virginia, | Oldcastle, | - | 139 |
| Walshtownmore, East, | Midleton, | - | 128 |
| Waringstown, | Lurgan, | - | 116 |
| Warrenpoint, | Newry, | - | 120 |
| Waterford, | Waterford, | - | 133 |
| Westport, | Westport, | - | 147 |
| Wexford, | Wexford, | - | 142 |
| Whitechurch, | Cork, | - | 126 |
| Whitechurch, | Dungarvan, | - | 133 |
| Williamstown, | Glennamaddy, | - | 144 |
| Woodford, | Loughrea, | - | 144 |
| Woodstown, | Waterford, | - | 133 |
| Youghal, | Youghal, | - | 129 |

# DIAGRAM

SHOWING THE FLUCTUATIONS FROM WEEK TO WEEK IN THE NUMBER OF WORKHOUSE INMATES IN IRELAND,

During the 53 Weeks, ending 12th February, 1876 and during the corresponding Weeks of the SIX previous Years.

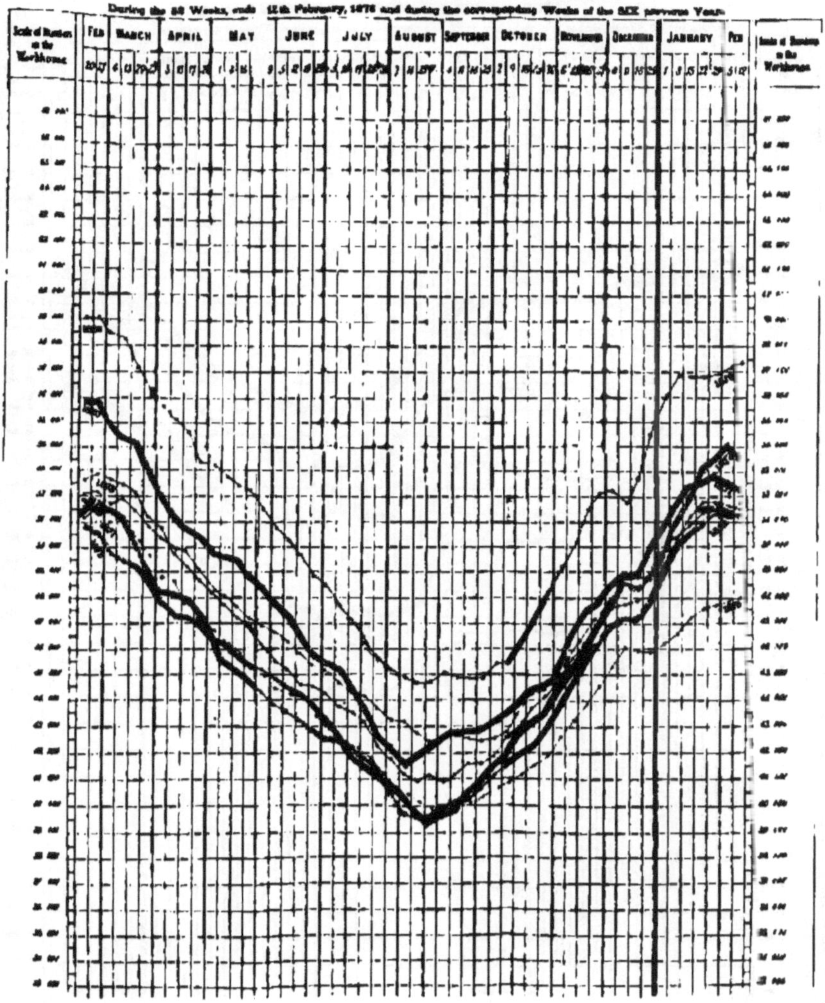

# DIAGRAM

SHOWING THE FLUCTUATIONS FROM WEEK TO WEEK IN THE NUMBER OF PERSONS IN THE RECEIPT OF OUT DOOR RELIEF IN IRELAND,

During the 52 Weeks, ended 14th February, 1876 and during the corresponding Weeks of the SIX previous Years

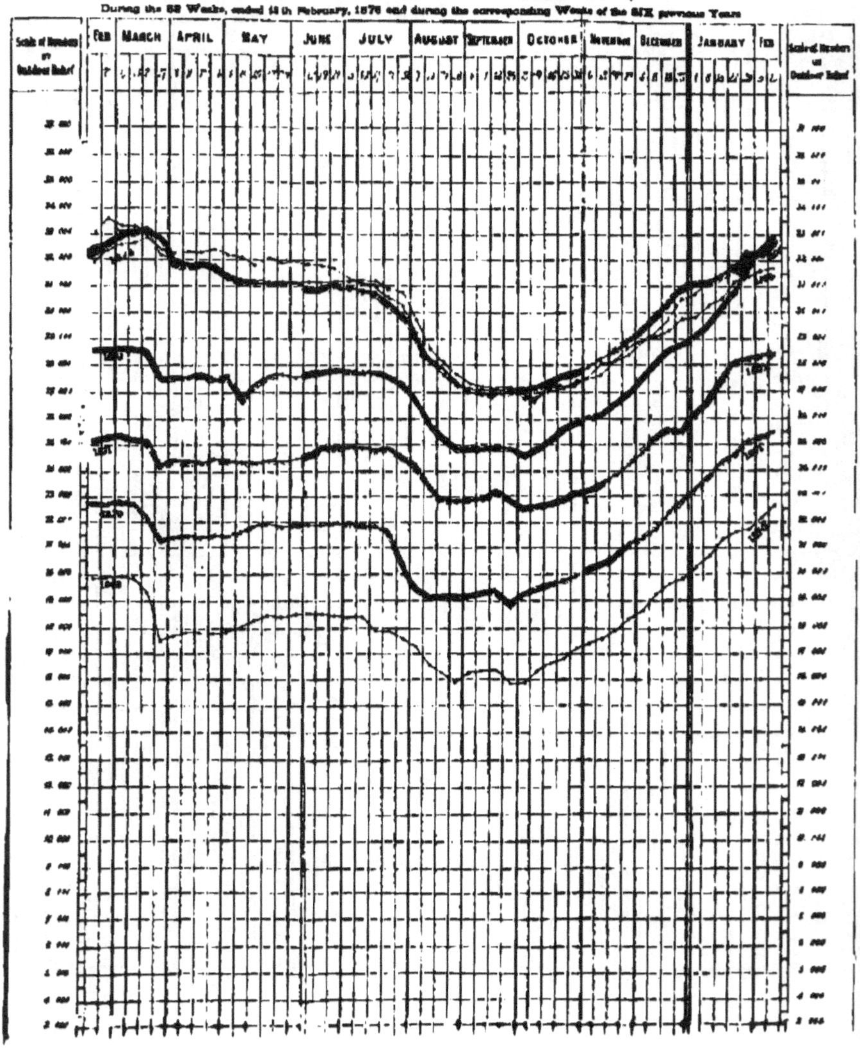

www.ingramcontent.com/pod-product-compliance
Lightning Source LLC
Chambersburg PA
CBHW030301170426
43202CB00009B/826
* 9 7 8 3 7 4 1 1 0 5 2 0 3 *